The War Within

The War Within

Diaries from the Siege of Leningrad

Alexis Peri

III

Harvard University Press

Cambridge, Massachusetts

London, England

2017

First Printing

Library of Congress Cataloging-in-Publication Data

Names: Peri, Alexis, author.
Title: The war within : diaries from the Siege of Leningrad / Alexis Peri.
Description: Cambridge, Massachusetts : Harvard University Press, 2017. |
Includes bibliographical references and index.
Identifiers: LCCN 2016018187 | ISBN 9780674971554 (cloth)
Subjects: LCSH: Saint Petersburg (Russia)—History—Siege, 1941–1944—
Personal narratives, Russian. | World War, 1939–1945—Russia (Federation)—
Saint Petersburg—Personal narratives, Russian. | Russians—Diaries.
Classification: LCC D764.3.L4 P46 2017 | DDC 940.54/217210922—dc23
LC record available at https://lccn.loc.gov/2016018187

For my parents, my greatest teachers

Some day thousands of diaries will lie on the historian's table, and then we shall see how much there was that was remarkable in the unremarkable biographies of simple Russian people.

—*Nikolai Tikhonov*

Contents

Conclusion: After the Ring Broke   235

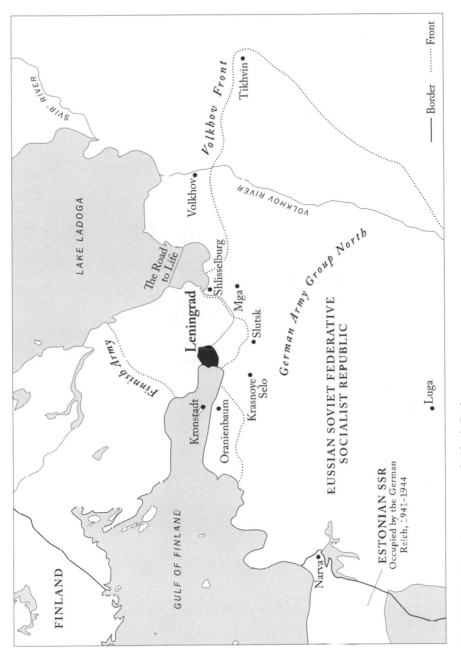

Encircled Leningrad, 1941–1944. © Alexis Peri

FINLAND

SVIR' RIVER

LAKE LADOGA

Volkhov Front

Tikhvin

Volkhov

VOLKHOV RIVER

The Road
to Life

Shlisselburg

Mga

Slutsk

Leningrad

German Army Group North

Finnish Army

Kronstadt

Oranienbaum

Krasnoye
Selo

GULF OF FINLAND

RUSSIAN SOVIET FEDERATIVE
SOCIALIST REPUBLIC

Luga

ESTONIAN SSR
Occupied by the German
Reich, 1941–1944

Narva

—— Border ······· Front

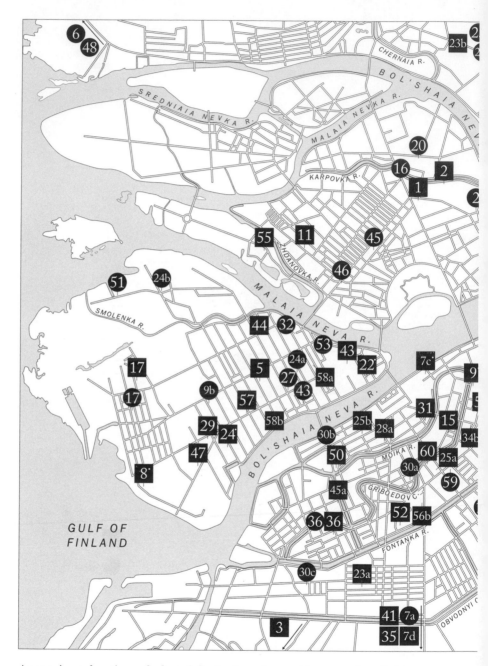

Approximate locations of selected diarists' wartime residences and workplaces, based on a 1940 survey of Leningrad published by Lenizdat. © Alexis Peri

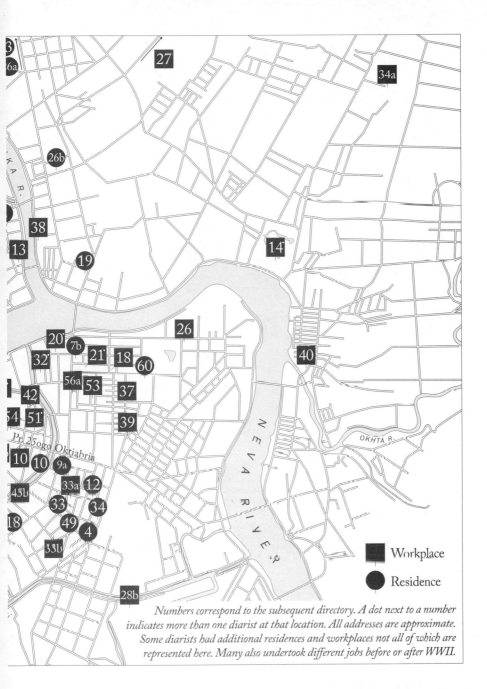

Numbers correspond to the subsequent directory. A dot next to a number indicates more than one diarist at that location. All addresses are approximate. Some diarists had additional residences and workplaces not all of which are represented here. Many also undertook different jobs before or after WWII.

■ Workplace

● Residence

Directory of Diarists

This list is keyed to the map on the previous page.

# on map (R) residence or (W) workplace Street *(Imperial Name)*, Building, Apartment	Last Name, First Name *Occupation,* **Workplace**
1 (W) Kirovskii *(Kamennoostrovskii)* pr., d. 27	**Enman,** Natal'ia Aleksandrovna *Senior Academic Employee,* **Kirov Museum**
2 (R) Ul. Skorokhodova, d. 23, kv. 29 **2 (W)** Ul. Tolstogo, d. 4	**Erokhana** (née Klishevich), Nina Nikolaevna *Student; Medic,* **Erisman Hospital**
3 (W) Pr. Stachek, d. 47	**Gal'ko,** Leonid Pavlovich *Party Representative,* **Kirov Factory**
4 (R) Ligovskii pr., d. 76, kv. 6	**Gorshkov,** Nikolai Pavlovich *Former Bookkeeper,* **Leningrad Institute of Light Industry**
5 (W) 13aia liniia and Musogorskaia ul.	**Kedrov,** Aleksandr Tikhonovich *Deputy Director,* **Factory 224,** *Sverdlovsk District*
6 (R) Dubkovskoe shosse, d. 61	**Kolbantseva,** Rogneda Viktorovna
7a (R) Mezhdunarodnyi *(Moskovskii)* pr., d. 120, kv. 3 **7b (R)** Maiakovskaia *(Nadezhynskaia)* ul. **7c (W)** Nab. 9ogo Ianvaria *(Dvortsovaia nab.),* d. 36 **7d (W)** Mezhdunarodnyi pr., d. 116	**Konopleva,** Mariia Sergeevna *Archivist and Librarian,* **Russian Museum** *and The Hermitage* (c); *Secretary,* **Medical Clinic 22** (d)
7c (W) Nab. 9ogo Ianvaria *(Dvortsovaia nab.),* d. 36	**Kalinin,** Vladimir Vasil'evch ***The Hermitage***
8 (W) Kozhevennaia liniia, d. 40	**Kozlovskii,** Aleksei Kornil'evich *Director,* **North Cable Factory (Sevkabel')**
8 (W) Kozhevennaia liniia, d. 40	**Komsomol Organization,** *Sevkabel'*

9a (R)	Sverdlovsk Hospital, Fontanka, d. 52	**Makarov,** Vladimir Kuz'mich
9b (R)	22aia liniia	*Preservationist and Historian of Art and*
9 (W)	Ploshchad' Iskusstv	*Architecture,* **Russian Museum**
9 (W)	Ploshchad' Iskusstv	**Lebedev,** Georgii Efremovich
		Artist and Art Scholar, **Russian Museum**
10 (R)	Ploshchad' Ostrovskogo and	**Levina,** Esfir' Gustavovna
	Architekt Rossi ul.	*Architect*
10 (W)	Architectural Union, Ploshchad'	
	Ostrovskogo, pr. 25ogo Oktiabria	
	(Nevskii pr.)	
11 (W)	Ul. Krasnogo Kursanta, d. 25/27	**Likhacheva,** Anna Ivanovna
		Medical Doctor, **Red Banner Factory Clinic**
12 (R)	Kuznechnyi per. near the Market	**Liubovskaia,** Aleksandra Pavlovna
		Translator and Librarian
13 (W)	Petrogradskaia nab. 32	**Frumberg,** Aleksei Mikhailovich
		Party Representative, **Voskov Factory**
14 (W)	Timofeevskaia ul., d. 24	**Mantul,** Vladimir Grigor'evich
		Grinder and Polisher, **Stalin Factory**
14 (W)	Timofeevskaia ul., d. 24	**Gel'fer,** Gesel' Aizikovich
		Engineer, Electrician, and Machinist in Workshop
		3, **Stalin Factory**
15 (W)	Nab. Reki Moiki, d. 48	**Rudnev,** Aleksei Georgievich
		Philologist and Teacher, **Herzen State Pedagogical**
		Institute
	Artists' Dormitory, Kirovskii pr. and	**Matiushina,** Ol'ga Konstantinovna
16 (R)	Malyi pr.	*Artist and Writer*
17 (R)	Gavanskaia ul., d. 37, kv. 14	**Mironova,** Aleksandra Nikolaevna
17 (W)	Ostroumogo ul., d. 19	*Teacher,* **School 10;** *Inspector,* **District Department**
		of National Education (RONO)
18 (R)	Zagorodnyi pr., d. 26	**Mukhina,** Elena Vladimirovna
18 (W)	Chernyshevksii pr., d. 20	*Student,* **School 30**
19 (R)	Ul. Akademika Lebedeva, d. 10, kv. 4	**Ostroumova-Lebedeva,** Anna Petrovna
		Artist
20 (R)	Pesochnaia ul. by Erisman Hospital	**Inber,** Vera Mikhailovna
20 (W)	Union of Soviet Writers, Leningrad	*Writer and Poet*
	Branch, Ul. Voinova *(Shpalernaia*	
	ul.), d. 18/19	
20 (W)	Union of Soviet Writers, Leningrad	**Ostrovsksia,** Sof'ia Kazimirovna
	Branch, Ul. Voinova *(Shpalernaia*	*Writer and Editor*
	ul.), d. 18/19	
21 (W)	Ul. Saltykova Shchedrina	**Peterson,** Valia
	(Kirochnaia ul.), d. 3	*Student,* **School 239**
21 (W)	Ul. Saltykova Shchedrina	**Polzikova-Rubets,** Kseniia Vladimirovna
	(Kirochnaia ul.), d. 3	*Teacher,* **School 239**

# on map (R) residence or (W) workplace Street *(Imperial Name)*, Building, Apartment	Last Name, First Name *Occupation, Workplace*
22 (W) Universitetskaia nab., d. 7	**Rabinovich,** Mikhail Borisovich *Teacher, Leningrad State University*
22 (W) Universitetskaia nab., d. 7	**Zveinek,** Asia *Student, Leningrad State University*
23 (R) Ul. Kol'tsova, d. 11, kv. 1 23a (W) Krasnoarmeiskaia ul., d. 36 23b (W) Bolshaia Ozernaia ul., d. 50	**Grizova-Rudykovskaia** (née Rudykovskaia), Tat'iana Leonidovna *Student, School 105* (a); *Student, School 114* (b)

24a (R)   Pr. Proletarskoi Pobedy *(Bol'shoi
                   pr.),* d. 61, kv. 8
24b (R)   Pereulok Dekabrista Kakhovskogo,
                   d. 3, kv. 18
24 (W)   25aia liniia, d. 8
	Savinkov, Ivan Alekseevich
	Engineer and Brigade Leader, Molotov Factory

24 (W) 25aia liniia, d. 8	**Malysheva,** Vasilisa Petrovna *Newspaper Editor, Molotov Factory*
24 (W) 25aia liniia, d. 8	**Osipova,** Natal'ia Petrovna *Statistician in Workshop 4, Molotov Factory*
25a (W) Ul. 3ogo Iiulia *(Sadovaia ul.),* d. 38 25b (W) Ul. Mira and Kotovskogo	**Rusakov,** Sergei Aleksandrovich *Journalist and Correspondent, Telegraph Agency of the Soviet Union (TASS)* (a); *Editor, Molodaia gvardiia* (b)
26a (R) Vyborgskoe shosse, d. 30 26b (R) Baburin per., d. 6, kv. 148 26 (W) Tavricheskaia ul., d. 39	**Sokolova,** Elizaveta Aleksandrovna *Acting Director, Istpart*
27 (R) 8aia liniia, near d. 25 27 (W) Sosnovka Area	**Zelenskaia,** Irina Dmitrievna *Statistician and Manager, Electrical Station 7 and Lenenergo*
28a (W) Ul. Gertsena *(Bolshaia Morskaia ul.),* d. 35 28b (W) Obvodnyi Kanal, d. 32	**Borovikova,** Aleksandra Nikiforovna *Factory Manager, Lengorpromstroi* (a) *and Sawmill Factory on Obvodnyi Kanal* (b)
29 (W) Pr. Proletarskoi Pobedy, d. 67	**Ots,** Liudmila *Student, School 11*

30a (R)   Kaznacheiskaia ul. near Sennaia
                   ploshchad'
30b (R)   Orphanage 28, Galernaia ul.,
                   d. 19
30c (R)   Orphanage 17, Derptskii per., d. 11
	Chepurko (née Malkova), Margarita Sergeevna
	Student

31 (W) Ul. Gertsena, d. 45	**Evlakhov,** Orest Aleksandrovich *Composer and Professor, Leningrad Conservatory; Secretary, Leningrad Branch of the Union of Soviet Composers*
32 (R) 3aia liniia, d. 42, kv. 7 32 (W) Solianoi per., d. 9	**Chernovskii,** Aleksei Alekseevich *Historian, Museum of the History and Development of Leningrad*

32 (W)	Solianoi per., d. 9	**Tikhomirova,** Marina Aleksandrovna *Historian of Material Culture and Tour Guide, **Museum** **of the History and Development of Leningrad***
33 (R) 33a (W) 33b (W)	Bol'shaia Moskovskaia ul., d. 14 Bol'shaia Moskovskaia ul., d. 10 Sotsialisticheskaia ul., d. 7	**Molchanov,** Anatolii Vladimirovich *Student, **School 300** (a);* *Student, **School 321** (b)*
34 (R) 34a (W) 34b (W)	Ligovskaia ul., d. 71 Ul. Kurakina, d. 1/3 Anichkov Palace, pr. 25ogo Oktiabria, d. 39	**Sedel'nikova,** Zinaida Sergeevna *Medical Student, **Second Leningrad Medical** **Institute** (a); Medic, **Hospital 95** (b)*
35 (W)	Mezhdunarodnyi pr., d. 111	**Propaganda and Agitation Department** (collectively-authored diary), ***Moscow*** ***District Raikom***
36 (R) 36 (W)	Ul. 3ogo Iiulia, d. 80	**Gorbunova,** Nina Georgievna *Director, **Orphanage 58***
37 (W)	Sapernyi per.	**Ianushevich,** Zoia Vasil'evna *Student, **Vavilov All-Union Institute of Plant** **Industry***
38 (W)	Nab. Fokina, d. 13/15	**Iushekhonov, Aleksei Gavrilovich** *Worker, **Diesel Engine Factory***
39 (W)	Ligovskaia ul., d. 7	**Ivleva,** Valentina Mikhailovna *Teacher, **School 36***
40 (W)	Krasnogvardeiskii District	**Sinitsina,** Zinaida Pavlovna *Party Representative, **Factory 370***
41 (W)	Mezhdunarodnyi pr., d. 111/113	**Kapitonova,** Vera Mikhailovna ***Propaganda and Agitation Department,*** ***Moscow District Raikom***
42 (W)	Italianskaia ul., d. 13	**Ketov,** Aleksandr Dmitrievich *Artist and Set Designer, **Theater of Musical** **Comedy***
43 (R) 43 (W)	7aia liniia, d. 2 Universitetskaia nab., d. 1	**Kniazev,** Georgii Alekseevich *Historian and Archivist, **Academy of Sciences,** **Leningrad Branch***
44 (W)	5aia liniia, d. 70	**Kok,** Gerorgii Mikhailovich *Head of Planning Department, **Kozitskii** **Factory for Radio Technology***
45 (R) 45a (W) 45b (W)	Bol'shaia Pushkarskaia ul. Kirov *(Mariinskii)* Theater, Teatral'naia ploshchad' Department of Pedagogy, Petrograd Choreography School	**Kostrovitskaia,** Vera Sergeevna *Ballerina and Choreographer, **Kirov (Mariinskii** ***Theater)***
46 (R)	Zverinskaia ul., d. 2, kv. 21	**Tikhonov,** Nikolai Semenovich *Writer and Correspondent, **Union of Soviet** **Writers, Leningrad Branch***
47 (W)	Kosaia liniia, d. 15	**Korneeva,** Glafira Nikolaevna *Director, **School 3**; Inspector, **RONO***

# on map (R) residence or (W) workplace Street *(Imperial Name)*, Building, Apartment	Last Name, First Name *Occupation, Workplace*
48 (R)	Voskov Factory, Dubovskoe shosse, d. 61	**Kolbantseva,** Rogneda Viktorovna *Student*
49 (R)	Ul. Dostoevskogo, d. 1	**Liubovskaia,** Aleksandra Pavlovna *Translator and Librarian*
50 (W)	Ploshchad' Truda, d. 5	**Larionov,** Leonid Vasil'evich ***Naval Museum of Leningrad***
51 (R) **51 (W)**	Morskoi pr., d. 37, kv. 9 Italianskaia ul., d. 27	**Lepkovich,** Arkadii A. ***Leningrad Radio***
51 (W)	Italianskaia ul., d. 27	**Ginzburg,** Lidiia Iakolaevna *Writer and Editor, **Leningrad Radio***
52 (W)	Nab. Reki Fontanki, d. 117	**Lesin,** Boris Apollonovich *Writer and Editor, **Oktiabr'skaia Magistral'** and **Stalinets***
53 (R) **53 (W)**	Tuchkov per., d. 5, kv. 7 Ul. Vosstaniia, d. 41	**Lukin,** Vladimir Andreevich, and **Nekliudova,** Tamara Petrovna ***Kamernyi Theater***
54 (W)	Mikhailovskaia ul., d. 2	**Matus,** Kseniia Markianovna *Musician, **Leningrad Philharmonic***
55 (W)	Petrovskii pr., d. 1	**Zlotnikova,** Berta Abramovna *Technical Control Department, **Northern Press Factory***
56a (W) **56b (W)**	Italianskaia ul., d. 19 Moskovskii pr., d. 212	**Nikitin,** Fedor Mikhailovich *Actor, **Kommisarzhevskaia Theater** (a); Agitator, **House of the Red Army** (b)*
57 (W)	Pr. Proletarskoi Pobedy, d. 55	**Zabolotskaia,** Lidiia Korlovna *Inspector, **RONO (Sverdlovsk District)***
58a (W) **58b (W)**	3aia liniia, d. 20 9aia liniia, d. 8/10	**Buianov,** Aleksandr Matveevich *Assistant to Military Procurator; Political Instructor, **Vasil'evskii Island Raikom***
59 (R)	Ul. 3ogo Iulia, d. 34, kv. 2	**Riabinkin,** Iurii (Iura) Ivanovich *Student*
60 (R) **60 (W)**	Ul. Saltykova Shchedrina Ul. Plekhanova *(Kazanskaia ul.)*	**Uskova,** Natal'ia Borisovna *Philologist; Grenade Manufacturer, **Factory 278***

Abbreviations and Acronyms

Istpart	Institute of History of the All-Union Communist Party (Bolsheviks)
Komsomol	Young Communist League
Lengorispolkom	Executive Committee of the Leningrad City Soviet
Lengorkom	Leningrad City Committee of the All-Union Communist Party
Lenobkom	Leningrad Regional Committee of the All-Union Communist Party
Lenoblispolkom	Executive Committee of the Leningrad Regional Soviet
LP	*Leningradskaia Pravda* (local newspaper)
MPVO	Local Anti-Aircraft Defense
NKVD	People's Commissariat of Internal Affairs
raikom (RK)	district committee (of a party, trade union, or other organization)
RAN	Russian Academy of Sciences
RONO	District Department of National Education
Sovinformbiuro	Soviet Information Bureau
Sovnarkom	Council of People's Commissars
VKP(b)	All-Union Communist Party (Bolsheviks)
VSLF	Military Soviet of the Leningrad Front
VTEK	Medical-Labor Expert Commission

The War Within

Introduction

Year Zero

"WE THE SOVIET PEOPLE have a sacred date, 25 October 1917, which all of us experienced as a new era of humanity's rebirth. That is how it was until 22 June 1941. On that day, our terrible tragedy began. Now it is clear that our October era will not remake the world for long. History has taken several steps backward. The epoch created by the October Revolution is reaching its limit."[1] Georgii Kniazev penned these lines in his diary on 29 November 1941. This was three months after the Leningrad blockade—one of the most devastating sieges in history—began. In that short time, Kniazev claimed, an epochal shift had taken place, one that eclipsed the 1917 Bolshevik Revolution as the new "year zero." It was already evident to him that World War II had rerouted history and was remaking his world anew.

When the Bolsheviks seized power in 1917, they promised to usher in a new era. They pledged to construct a new civilization by reorganizing society around socialist principles. The new socioeconomic base they planned to establish would give rise to a fundamentally different type of people. These New Soviet People promised to be superior to their predecessors in every way—physically, morally, and intellectually. Armed with an elevated political consciousness and a penetrating vision of the future, they would conquer first the natural world and then the limitations

1

of human nature. The Bolsheviks did not regard the establishment of socialism and the subsequent perfection of humankind as lofty ideals but as certainties guaranteed by the science of Marxism-Leninism.

But for Kniazev, war had laid waste to that certainty, that life, that era. Soviet leaders continued to inspire him, but the world they created was gone. For three months, Kniazev had watched as the blockade and bombardment of Leningrad plunged his city into crisis, reducing its streets to rubble. By the time he wrote this diary entry in November 1941, food rations had plummeted to an all-time low. Starvation had begun to assault Leningraders, body and mind. And from this devastation, a new world indeed was emerging, one that in many ways was the antithesis of the Bolshevik ideal. These horrific conditions birthed new beings, the *blokadniki*, or people of the blockade. Reflecting on these changes to the city and its inhabitants, Kniazev confided to the future reader of his diary, "reading these lines, you will share with me all of my profound anxiety for man, humanity, and humanism."[2]

As a historian at the Academy of Sciences, Georgii Kniazev was a keen observer of historical transition. From his office window on Leningrad's University Embankment, he commanded a view of the Neva River along with several bridges and thoroughfares. He penned a massive, eight-hundred-page diary based in part on insights gleaned from monitoring the landscape below. Kniazev took this on as a professional duty. He assumed that others were too busy fighting for their lives to write and that if he did not do so, future historians would have only retrospective accounts to study. "And what will be written later, in the form of memoirs, will be a far cry from what we are living through now," he predicted.[3]

Unbeknownst to Kniazev, over a hundred *blokadniki*—of various ages and backgrounds—were keeping diaries. Some of them passed below his window on a regular basis. One was a fellow historian at the Museum of the History and Development of Leningrad, Aleksei Chernovskii. Chernovskii traversed the University Embankment each day as he walked to work. Like Kniazev, he lived on Vasil'evskii Island, the largest of the city's many islands. Home to a university, numerous academies, and neatly numbered streets (called "lines"), Vasil'evskii Island epitomized the rational, modern metropolis envisioned by the city's founder, Peter the Great. After Chernovskii reached the University Embankment where Kniazev worked, he typically turned down the Ninth Line to head home. Here, on any given day, Chernovskii might have brushed past Aleksandr Buianov, a party instructor and housing inspector, coming out of his office at number 10.[4] The two diarists' paths might have merged as they wound down Bolshoi Prospekt to the Fourth Line and past the Andreevskii Market, where several diarists—including thirteen-year-old Dima Afanas'ev—traded family heirlooms for food. At the Third and Fourth Lines, Buianov and Chernovskii would have parted ways. Before heading home, Buianov typically stopped to inspect a new clinic he was helping to establish on the Fourth Line.[5] Chernovskii would have made his way to number 42 on the Third Line and trudged up four flights of icy stairs to his apartment, where he hoped to find his wife, Tonia, preparing something for supper.

Vasil'evskii Island was home to many diarists. A quick tram ride from Chernovskii's home took one past the apartments of the school director Glafira Korneeva, the engineer Mikhail Krakov, the art historian Vladimir Makarov, and the journalist Arkadii Lepkovich, to name a few. And Vasil'evskii Island was not unique. Diarists hailed from most of the city's fifteen districts, and their paths intersected as they went about their daily lives. They unknowingly frequented the same bakeries, washed in the same bathhouses, and worked in the same factories. As they moved about the city, they carried their diaries with them. They wrote from breadlines, shelters, and deathbeds. They wrote when it was painful and exhausting to do so. They also diverted precious resources—money, time, and energy— away from the hunt for food and kept writing through months of relentless starvation and intense bombardment.

Until recently, the prevalence of diary writing in besieged Leningrad was unknown.[6] Interestingly, members of Leningrad's communist party organization had intended just the opposite to occur. Like Kniazev, they hoped to prepare the history of the blockade by encouraging Leningraders to keep journals. Many of the 125 unpublished diaries used in this study come from their efforts. However, just after the war ended, the authority to narrate the blockade experience was turned over to professional writers and state actors, who crafted a very different story from the ones articulated in the diaries.

Why did so many Leningraders choose to keep diaries under such horrific conditions? What questions haunted their minds as death approached? Did the siege experience alter their attitudes toward Soviet society? Why didn't these diaries become the foundation of the regime's official history of the blockade, as originally planned?

The War Within investigates these questions. It reveals how starvation and isolation tore into every aspect of everyday life and into every recess of the mind, compelling many individuals to take up writing in order to make sense of their suffering.[7] As they endeavored to supply their ordeal with meaning, the diarists were forced to reckon with core concepts, practices, and narratives that shaped life in the Soviet Union. This critical examination would have made them unsuitable as the documentary basis for the regime's celebratory narratives of the siege in the postwar era.

The Battle for Leningrad

The Leningrad blockade was one of the most horrific events of World War II. The city was the centerpiece of a 1,127-day battle and an 872-day siege. That siege, which lasted from September 1941 to January 1944, was one of the lengthiest and deadliest of the modern era. All told, the battle for Leningrad took between 1.6 and 2 million Soviet lives, including roughly 800,000 civilians or 40 percent of the city's prewar population.[8] This staggering death toll is about equal to the total number of American military who died in all wars between 1776 and 1975. Under siege, the historian John Barber explains, "Leningrad suffered the greatest demographic catastrophe ever experienced by one city in the history of mankind."[9] Most civilians died of starvation, but tens of thousands perished from enemy fire and disease.[10]

The story of the Wehrmacht's surprise invasion of the USSR, its rapid advance across Soviet territory in the summer of 1941, and its encirclement of Leningrad that autumn already has been well documented. In August 1941, Hitler's Army Group North and his Finnish allies began to encircle Leningrad. They rapidly extended their territorial holdings first in the west and south and eventually in the north. By 29 August 1941, they had severed the last railway line that connected Leningrad to the rest of the USSR. By early September, Leningrad was completely cut off, save for a heavily patrolled water passage over Lake Ladoga. City leaders managed to evacuate nearly 500,000 residents before Leningrad was encircled, but over two million people remained inside.[11]

On 4 September, while fighting the Red Army outside of the city, Hitler's troops began to shell and bombard Leningrad day and night, for up to eighteen hours at a time. As a major industrial center, Leningrad was an important military target. But its symbolic significance was equally critical. As the birthplace of the Bolshevik revolution, the city of Lenin was an emblem of the world communist conspiracy so despised by the Führer. Through relentless air raids, Hitler pledged to "erase St. Petersburg from the face of the earth."[12] Within two months, his troops had launched 612 aerial attacks on Leningrad. And before the siege was lifted in 1944, 148,478 artillery shells, 102,500 incendiary bombs, and 4,638 highly explosive bombs were dropped on the city.[13] These assaults reduced much of Leningrad's infrastructure, housing stock, and industry to ruins. For months, the *blokadniki* were left without motorized transport, running water, or sufficient electricity to heat homes or power factories.

Leningrad was one of several cities German troops besieged. Although considered a military anachronism, siegecraft enjoyed a revival during World War II. This is especially true of a particular form, the blockade, which aims to sever encircled populations from supply lines and trading partners.[14] Compared to London and Berlin, both besieged by air, there was no regular contact or mobility between Leningrad and its environs. The *blokadniki* could not escape to the countryside but instead were cut off from the USSR for most of the war. They described their encircled city using two central metaphors, "the ring" and "the island." Accordingly, the USSR was the "mainland" *(bol'shuia zemlia)* from which they were far adrift.[15]

Leningraders were not only separated from their fellow countrymen; they were isolated from the enemy. Unlike besieged Stalingrad or Sevastopol', Leningrad was never invaded. In summer 1941, Leningraders dug antitank trenches, built barricades, and braced themselves for an invasion that never came. Until 1944, they inhabited a space that was neither front nor rear, neither occupied nor free. The enemy that surrounded them remained impersonal, represented by planes, bombs, and leaflets. Most *blokadniki* first glimpsed German soldiers only in 1944, when they were paraded through the city as prisoners. Frontline correspondents Aleksandr Werth and Vsevolod Vishnevskii even claimed that Leningrad children did not know that Germans were people, having only seen them depicted as beasts and monsters on propaganda posters.[16] While this claim may be exaggerated, it could never have been made about children in Stalingrad or Sevastopol', where the enemy was clear and present. Moreover, there were times when Leningrad's besiegers were inaudible. During the winter of 1941–42, when hunger was at its height, air raids were largely suspended. As the skies above Leningrad grew quiet, the external enemy seemed even more distant.

Leningraders' crushing sense of remoteness was surpassed only by the anguish of starvation. The Luftwaffe destroyed the city's meager food reserves, which local authorities foolishly had concentrated in the Badaevskii Warehouses. They were obliterated between 8 and 10 September 1941. Subsequent food barges dispatched across Lake Ladoga fell under heavy fire; only 10 percent of shipments actually arrived.[17] And unlike residents of other Soviet cities, Leningraders could not access regional farm produce; nor could they plant "victory gardens" until after six months of famine. With just seventeen days of food to sustain the population, the Military Soviet of the Leningrad Front (VSLF) was forced to cut rations five times. Between September and November 1941, they slashed norms by 80 percent. On 20 November, rations hit an all-time low. Two-thirds of the population received little more than 125 grams (4.4 ounces) of bread a day—a fraction of the calories needed to sustain life.[18] In truth, residents received even less. In order to stretch the city's flour supply, VSLF and the Executive Committee of the Leningrad City Soviet (Lengorispolkom) ordered bakeries to add malt, sawdust, hemp, and cellulose to the bread. Fillers constituted up to 50 percent of a loaf.[19]

During that hungry winter of 1941–42, temperatures plummeted. The city's water pipes froze. Lacking the water needed to make bread, bakeries handed out small lumps of flour or nothing at all. *Blokadniki* scoured the city for anything edible, consuming everything from glue, leather, and bark to human flesh. In such frigid conditions, their emaciated bodies could not keep warm. It also was too cold for the enemy to fly. Hitler shifted his attention from bombing and shelling Leningrad to starving the city into submission. He resolved to let the city devour itself. And indeed, Leningraders' bodies literally began to feed on themselves.[20]

Under these conditions, the war became for the diarists an internal battle against physical deterioration and mental collapse. A few months earlier, during the summer and fall of 1941, many diarists diligently reported on news from the front, pinning their hopes on a military breakthrough. But by winter, they paid scant attention to the besieging troops stationed just three miles away. Instead, they turned their attention inward to the battles raging inside their bodies, minds, and community. Even when the rations increased and heavy bombardment resumed in mid-1942, the diarists continued to fixate on inner conflicts and questions—the war within.

Disorientation and Discovery

Inside the ring, the *blokadniki* were confronted with the transformation of virtually every aspect of daily life, the defamiliarization of all that was known, the depersonalization of all that was intimate. With few contacts and little information from outside, they became estranged from Soviet society. The blockade destroyed the routines and rhythms of everyday life; it destabilized attitudes, overturned assumptions, and even assaulted conceptual categories fundamental to human understanding. These include notions of space and time as well as binaries like self and other, male and female, young and old, alive and dead, human and inhuman, ordinary and extraordinary. During 1941 and 1942, the networks of meaning that anchored Leningraders within their communities and within themselves unraveled. In her landmark study of torture, Elaine Scarry revealed how physical and psychological torment can "unmake the assumptive worlds" of its victims. Pain not only preys on the body; it violates expectations, reverses norms, and dislodges long-held beliefs.[21] In the wake of such an ordeal, Leningraders had to remake their worlds anew. And many turned to diary writing to do so. Ultimately, the blockade emerges from their accounts not just as a destructive force but also as a constructive one.[22]

This story of the siege as an internal crisis of profound questioning and intellectual tumult hardly seems surprising in retrospect. However, for decades it has been obscured by more coherent and triumphant narratives

that tend to cast the blockade as an epic battle between two opposing
forces: a ruthless military foe and a beleaguered but determined civilian
population bent on military victory. During the war, members of the Soviet press and political leadership worked to incorporate the siege into
the master narrative of socialism's triumph over human, material, and
ideological foes. They urged Leningraders to see themselves as citizen-
soldiers in this ongoing battle and to place military concerns before personal ones. Andrei Zhdanov, the city's party secretary, put it this way: "In
Leningrad, there is no divide between the front and the rear. Everyone
lives by one idea, one spirit—do everything to destroy the enemy."[23]
Echoing Zhdanov, postwar commemorations of the siege first in the USSR
and later the Russian Federation stressed that hatred of the enemy, combined with patriotism and social solidarity, empowered Leningraders
to victory.[24] This narrative of the blockade has been quite durable.
Soviet and post-Soviet depictions of the blockade are very similar and
mostly differ on the point of ideology. The Russian Federation has replaced Soviet emphases on socialism and the party with patriotism and
nationalism.

The state-sanctioned narrative gained traction in the postwar period
in part because some Leningraders adopted it as their own. This has made
it impossible, Lisa Kirschenbaum has argued, to disentangle the myth of
the blockade from the accounts of survivors, many of whom have found
solace in official commemorations and commendations. This is evident
among some diarists as well. When the technical translator Aleksandra
Liubovskaia reread her journal in 1975, she identified hard work, social
solidarity, and "unshakable faith in victory" as the overriding features of
her siege experience. However, these themes are virtually absent from her
account.[25] Heroism, camaraderie, and patriotism certainly crop up in the
diaries but not as central themes, especially when compared to those of
inner turmoil and creative tumult.

To be sure, the diaries are *depictions* of the siege just as much as officially sponsored accounts or events are. I am not claiming that the diaries
are more authentic or accurate. My aim is to show how they tell a different
story, one that the *blokadniki* took great pains to record. They suggest
that, far from strengthening Leningraders' sense of patriotism or resolve,
the siege created a violent sea change that unleashed personal and intel-

lectual crises. Especially in 1941 and 1942, when most signs indicated that the city would fall, many diarists came to internalize the blockade, feeling "besieged" by their own uncertainty and despair.[26] As the literary scholar and siege survivor Lidiia Ginzburg explained, the metaphor of the ring not only referred to the line of German troops around the city but "was the siege symbol of an introverted mind."[27] Of course, the diarists directed some energy toward the besiegers; most journals contain outbursts of anger or vows for vengeance. However, at least on the page, the diarists were more consumed with breaking the elliptical patterns of thought that immobilized them than with breaking the German lines.

Although research on siegecraft has not received much consideration from scholars of the Leningrad blockade, it helps to explain why sieges may be internalized in ways that pitched battles generally are not. In basic terms, a siege is a brutal, drawn-out offensive aimed at breaking the will of the encircled society by any means available.[28] For this reason, it has been called "the oldest form of total warfare."[29] When troops lay siege to a city, they effectively force the community inside to adapt politically, socially, and culturally—to reconfigure its very way of life—in order to survive. The besieged must interrogate their prewar lives, customs, and attitudes in light of the exigencies of war. Rocco Coronato has likened a siege to a "hermeneutic interlude," a "freezing pause wherein the besieger and the besieged [a]re made to reflect upon themselves."[30] During this prolonged encounter, questions about identity, society, politics, and morality inevitably come to the fore. In Leningrad, as Ales' Adamovich and Daniil Granin observed in their landmark publication *A Book of the Blockade*, "diarists often displayed not only an ability to record facts and experiences but also a desire to comprehend both man and history in a new way and, in general, the whole world."[31]

Many of the diarists' insights had universal reach. They voiced fundamental questions about the human condition. In this respect, their journals strongly resonate with accounts from the Holocaust and from other episodes of life in extremis. At the same time, the Leningrad diarists grappled with these universal concerns by drawing on terms, concepts, and situations particular to the Soviet context. As they worked to "remake their worlds," they weighed their wartime experiences against ideas, practices, and discursive elements that dominated official speeches and press

publications.[32] They questioned—sometimes deliberately, sometimes
inadvertently—the concept of the New Soviet Person, Marxist-Leninist
theories of history, Soviet models and ideals of family, and socialist policies regarding the distribution of food, medicine, and labor.

The physical and existential isolation wrought by the blockade created
a critical distance between Leningraders and the mainland. This afforded
the diarists a certain independence of thought as well as a unique vantage
point from which to reflect on Soviet society. This is not to say, however,
that the diarists were anti-Soviet. Many were supporters and members of
the party who kept diaries at the bidding of local party officials. Yet as the
diarists tried to accommodate the siege using concepts, terms, and patterns of prewar life, they scrutinized and sometimes scorned aspects of
Soviet ideology and policy. In the end, some diarists upheld and others
criticized Bolshevik tenets and practices, but all did so on the basis of insights, which stemmed from their wartime experiences. They evaluated
their circumstances by thinking *with* but not solely *within* Soviet ideological concepts. Moreover, the insights and decisions they articulated
seem as motivated by personal and practical considerations as by political
ones. The ways in which the diarists interrogated both official messages
and their own personal convictions demonstrate how their prewar assumptive worlds were tested by the blockade.

In this way, the diaries speak both to extreme conditions of war and
to everyday life in the Soviet Union as it appeared from inside the ring.
After all, a siege can both attack and insulate a community, intensifying
preexisting patterns of life there. In the case of Leningrad, the blockade
created a precarious mixture of familiar and foreign elements. On the
one hand, bombardment and starvation left Leningrad and its residents
virtually unrecognizable. On the other hand, the city remained under
Soviet control for all 872 days. The same institutions and ideological
principles held force over Leningraders and shaped their experiences of
hunger and loss. The blend of continuities and discontinuities, circularity
and rupture, inside the ring led the diarists to think anew about their
prewar lives. As they came to terms with the tragic and the extraordinary,
they also reconsidered the ordinary and mundane.

The siege journals not only expand our understanding of the blockade
experience but also expand our view of diary writing in the Soviet Union.

In the prewar Stalinist period, the diary occupied a privileged place in the regime's mission to transform its people into model citizens. Pioneering research by Jochen Hellbeck, Igal Halfin, Oleg Kharkhordin, and others has presented autobiographical accounts as "laboratories of the self," where individuals worked to perfect themselves by confessing any un-Soviet impulses and internalizing Soviet values.[33] What happens to life writing when that life is in peril? Despite the exigencies of war, the siege diarists demonstrated similar impulses to monitor their development and to understand themselves in historical terms. However, their circumstances and motivations were different. For the *blokadniki,* diary writing became tied to survival. They were driven less by a desire to fashion themselves into Soviet subjects and more by a desire to preserve traces of themselves in the face of annihilation.[34] The diarists did construct a "self" on the page, but not one consistent with articulated Soviet ideals. It was unstable, fragmented, and often unknown, even to them. My aim is not to propose a new model of Soviet subjectivity, especially at a time when self-concepts were so in flux. Rather, I hope to demonstrate how the siege journals exhibit a wide range of expressed self-concepts, which suggests that Soviet individuals conceptualized themselves in a variety of ways, ways that were as contingent on their particular historical moment as on Soviet ideology.

The Diaries

Just as there was no typical blockade experience, there is no typical siege diary. Each journal is unique. Many warrant individual studies in their own right. Despite their distinctiveness, *The War Within* highlights the major inquiries that united the diarists regardless of their age, background, profession, or relationship to Soviet power. For this reason, it is arranged by areas of investigation and not by biography. Of the 125 unpublished diaries that inform in this study, sixty-two were written by men and boys, sixty-one by women and girls, and two by groups. The authors include thirteen students, twenty-one workers in heavy industry, nineteen artists and intellectuals, thirteen midlevel professionals (such as nurses, doctors, teachers, and managers), sixteen party workers, and seven professional writers who later revised and published their diaries.

I also use about twenty-five published diaries and occasionally refer to diary-like accounts written during the siege, such as Lidiia Ginzburg's *Notes of a Blockade Person* and Ol'ga Berggol't's *Daytime Stars,* to show how they compare to unpublished accounts penned by amateur writers.

The journals vary widely in style, structure, and substance. Some are personal, others impersonal in tone; some were written for private, others for public purposes. Some are verbose, others notational. Two are pictorial.[35] A few diarists addressed a specific reader—a family member, friend, future Soviet citizen, or future version of themselves. In other accounts, a reader is implied vaguely. Most of the diaries are structured by dated entries, but some contain loose sequential fragments or are organized into thematic subsections, such as breakfast, lunch, and dinner.[36] In addition, they often incorporate elements from novels, letters, maps, calendars, medical case studies, and ethnographies. The flexible nature of the diary form made it readily adaptable to this wide range of approaches and needs. Felicity A. Nussbaum and Irina Paperno have suggested that the diary is a mode defined less by strict formal features than by tensions. Paperno has called it "a generic matrix" that can accommodate rupture and continuity. The diary "creates and tolerates crisis in perpetuity," Nussbaum explains, crises not unlike the 872-day blockade.[37] Structured by constant stops and starts, beginnings and endings, the diary captures both the fragmentary and continuous nature of experience. It preserves the shifts, reversals, and inconsistencies in Leningraders' stated beliefs and in their narrative styles over the course of the siege.

The *blokadniki* kept their diaries at a great price. It was difficult to pro-cure notebooks, paper, and ink, which froze in the bitter cold. Writing was time-consuming and emotionally taxing. Vladimir Mantul, who worked at the Stalin Factory, had a love-hate relationship with his journal. He vacillated between writing to distract himself from the stresses of work and hunger and working to avoid "getting lost in the wild, hurly-burly of [his] diary."[38] Despite these difficulties, Leningraders wrote for several reasons, which varied by author and for the same author over time. They used the diary as a repository of thought, a confessional space, a site of self-examination, a medium for communicating with far-flung relatives, a historical chronicle, and a coping mechanism.[39] For the engineer and electrician Gesel' Gel'fer, writing provided a much-needed emotional release. Gel'fer worried that "to an outsider" his notes might appear "childish" and "bitter": "But what can be done? I wrote and I write not for some person, not for history, and not for someone to criticize. I feel lighter when I express all of my meager thoughts. [. . .] Ideas crowd my mind, and the only outlet I have found for them is in the diary."[40] Gel'fer wrote to preserve his mental stability, but others wrote as a way to affirm and even prolong their existence, at least on the page.[41] The teenager Iura Riabinkin, for instance, dreaded reaching the end of his notebook and started writing in tiny letters: "it seems that the diary itself is determining the length of time I will be keeping it."[42]

Another crucial reason why many Leningraders kept journals was that the party asked them to do so. As early as November 1941, members of the Kirov District's party committee *(raikom)* began encouraging Leningraders to chronicle their experiences for posterity. On 9 December 1941, the Kirov *raikom,* together with that district's propaganda and agitation division, established a commission to solicit materials, especially diaries that documented their district during the siege. The October District and several others followed suit.[43] The work flagged during the brutal winter of 1941–42 but gathered steam in spring 1942. Other organizations including the Institute of History of the All-Union Communist Party (Istpart), the Historical Institute of the Leningrad branch of the Academy of Sciences, and the Museum of the History and Development of Leningrad began securing diaries and other materials that would provide a foundation for future historiographies of the blockade. Some of their staff began journaling themselves.[44] The efforts to encourage diary writing remained unsystematic until 1943. On 3 April 1943, after Soviet forces had broken through the ring and the blockade's end was nigh, the joint bureaus of the Leningrad City Committee of the All-Union Communist Party (Lengorkom) and the Leningrad Regional Committee of the All-Union Communist Party (Lenobkom) established a central commission "For the Collection of Materials and for the Preparation of a Chronicle on 'Leningrad and the Leningrad Region during the Patriotic War against the German-Fascist Invaders.'" The committee put Istpart in charge of the campaign and called on the city's *raikoms* to gather materials from their districts.[45]

The diarists whose journals made up this official collection, however, had begun to write years earlier and without formal instructions from local officials. In their initial meeting in autumn 1941, delegates from the Kirov District—the first to launch a diary-writing campaign—were unable to agree on what guidelines, if any, they should provide to diarists. They debated whether the journals should be collectively or individually authored and whether they should focus on events or experiences.[46] Isakov, a delegate for the district soviet, argued that the diaries should highlight news from the front. But others, including the district's party secretary, V. S. Efremov, argued that diarists should focus on personal matters as long as they were "socially useful."[47] If they were subjective, would they still be historically valuable? One committee member proposed that officials review the diaries periodically to ensure that they were accurate as well as to gauge the level of morale in the city. They might double as chronicles and tools of surveillance. Efremov warned against this: "if Comrade Vasil'eva is going to look at my diary every day, maybe I won't write everything in it," he remarked.[48] I did find two diaries that were reviewed by superiors and covered in red-pencil marginalia, but this was a rare occurence.[49] The *raikom* delegates' conversation then evolved into a broader discussion of what a diary *is*—a notoriously difficult task.[50] Must it be written daily or just when something noteworthy happened? Might it include retrospective entries? Must the entries be dated? After wrestling with these questions, the Kirov *raikom* made only general recommendations that the diarists should write regularly and focus on their everyday lives *(byt)* and experiences.[51]

For this reason, the diaries deposited into the Istpart collection are as diverse in structure, approach, and style as those from other sources. Moreover, the journals from Istpart constitute only a portion of the diaries used in this study, which come from eight archives and from private sources. I was surprised to find that diaries collected by the party revolve around a similar constellation of concerns and are just as critical of local leaders and policies as are journals from other collections.

Despite the many advantages of diaries, they have limitations as historical sources. They are *articulations* of experience, mediated by the process of writing and by self-censorship. They cannot be considered direct points of entry into Leningraders' inner thoughts. Some diarists crossed out sections of their accounts, used pseudonyms, or admitted to keeping secrets from their journals.[52] In addition, the *blokadniki* had limited access to information about affairs in the city and at the front, so their accounts contain factual errors. "When I was writing a diary, I still did not know anything," the engineer Aleksandra Borovikova admitted.[53] However, as the historian Luise White has noted, the factual unreliability of such personal accounts is what makes them so valuable: "they offer historians a way to see the world the way that storytellers did, [. . .] with all the messy categories and meandering epistemologies" they used to understand their predicament.[54]

Although I have endeavored to gather a diverse sample, the diarists do not represent Leningraders as a whole. Journaling was more widespread during the siege than previously supposed, but it still was an unusual act taken up by a subset of the population. These accounts represent just over one hundred voices out of two million possible ones. They do not capture all aspects of the blockade experience, nor do they capture all aspects of the diarists themselves. They are incomplete, fragmented, often contradictory texts, which evoke but do not encapsulate the siege in its entirety.

I do not attempt to tell the whole story of the siege through the diaries. I read them not for empirical data about the blockade but to get a sense of their authors' reported experiences and interpretive strategies. I am interested in where they put their attention and how they narrated their lives amid a crisis of meaning and belief. I treat the journals as both practices and products. The diaries represent practices in that they function as "sense-making" texts, where the authors worked through ideas that may have been fleeting, incomplete, or later revised.[55] But they also are carefully crafted textual products. I attend to the devices, tropes, and modal elements through which they were constructed. All diaries can be located on this process-product continuum and may reside closer to one pole or the other at various points in their development.[56] The versatility of the diary mode, combined with the unique conditions of the blockade, yielded narratives that are rich and varied.

The Ring and the Island

This book focuses on the years 1941 and 1942 and is organized to follow the patterns of thought that structure most journals. In both individual entries and in the accounts as a whole, the diarists tended first to focus on their bodies—which signaled their transformation most powerfully—and then to broaden their horizons from personal concerns to social and political ones. *The War Within* is divided into two parts, each anchored by a major metaphor of the siege: the ring and the island. The former conjures images of military encirclement, circularity, and disorientation, while the latter conveys isolation and exotic otherness. Part 1, "Inside the Ring," focuses on three critical dimensions of identity: body, self, and family. As these intimate aspects of the diarists' lives were transformed, the diarists became unhinged from attitudes and experiences that had defined their prewar existence. The diary practice provided a critical tool with which they aimed to break the "self-siege" that held them captive. As the blockade survivor Lidiia Ginzburg put it, "to write about the circle is to break the circle."[57]

Part 2, "Exploring the Island," highlights social and cultural insights that the diarists gleaned about their city, made strange by bombardment, isolation, and starvation. As one diarist explained, "we are living the primitive life of savages on an uninhabited island cut off from the rest of the world."[58] In fact, the diarists repeatedly compared themselves to one figure, a fellow diarist also trapped on an island. "To some extent, all of us are Robinson Crusoe," the schoolteacher Aleksandr Vinokurov proclaimed. "We live like Robinsons," Sof'ia Ostrovskaia echoed, "no people, no newspaper, no radio. I am the [only] connection to the outside world."[59] Or, as Lidiia Osipova put it during the harsh month of December 1941, "Robinsonia *[robinzon'ia]* is beginning."[60] Crusoe had been a popular figure in the USSR for decades, in part because he exemplified qualities of the New Soviet Person. Dauntless, independent, and resourceful, Crusoe was a skilled farmer, hunter, inventor, and scholar who catalogued the flora and fauna around him. By using all his faculties, he managed to build a brand-new civilization, a feat to which the Bolsheviks also aspired.[61] Siege diarists like the artist Tat'iana Glebova considered Crusoe a model for how to allocate one's resources and withstand the most extreme scarcity.[62]

Defoe's novel inspired the diarists, but it also unnerved them. They wondered if they would thrive and eventually be rescued like Crusoe. "Time goes by very slowly in that there is no light and the radio does not work, I sit like Robinson Crusoe with Friday on an island," the radio worker Arkadii Lepkovich noted. The novel's tidy ending magnified for Lepkovich the dire, unfinished state of his own story, making it "an unfortunate comparison, a possibly worse [one]": "Well, Robinson returned to life, but I don't know what will happen next."[63] Crusoe was shipwrecked onto a lush island full of exotic fruits and animals, whereas Leningraders were trapped in urban ruins. "Even Robinson on a deserted island had more opportunities in terms of food than we do in the city," Gesel' Gel'fer observed.[64] *Blokadniki* had to contend with state policies, corrupt officials, starving relatives, and thieving neighbors to survive. "I think Robinson Crusoe was a lucky person," the diarist Elena Skriabina reflected. "He knew with certainty that he was on an uninhabited island and had to rely only on himself. But I am among people."[65]

However, as a community in captivity, Leningraders had opportunities for social observation that Crusoe did not. As part of the struggle to eke out an existence, diarists surveyed the geographical and social terrain, documenting the community, customs, and culture developing there. Some diarists embraced this ethnographic work as a solemn duty. "It is difficult but interesting to live at this moment in time," the tenth-grader Berta Zlotnikova admitted. "I want only one thing: for my legs to become steely so that all day long, every hour, I could be a witness to and participant in the course of history."[66]

Part I

Inside the Ring

Chapter One

The Ring Takes Shape

W AR ERUPTED during one of the most festive times of the year for Leningraders, the summer solstice. On 20–21 June 1941, residents of the northern metropolis enjoyed almost twenty-four hours of sunlight. In the early morning hours of 22 June, 3.2 million German troops crossed over into Soviet territory in what was the largest invasion in the history of warfare. It was a Sunday. A brass band played on the radio.[1] Most Leningraders were on holiday, many relaxing at nearby dachas. "Hello freedom!" sixteen-year-old Elena Mukhina declared, welcoming vacation.[2] She and other members of the city's youth were starting their summer adventures. University students, still in the throes of exams, were eager for theirs.

Natal'ia Uskova, a philology student, found it impossible to study on such a glorious day. "On the twenty-second of June, around twelve o'clock," she wrote, "I was sitting behind my writing desk (on Kirochnaia Street) preparing to take my exam on dialectical materialism early. I wanted to extend my vacation and go to my parents in Kiev, my favorite city, where I spent my barefoot childhood. [My] train ticket was already bought, and through the philosophical wisdom I was reading I could see fragrant acacia, Kievan chestnuts. [. . .] I am dreaming about all of this, anticipating it in between quotes by K. Marx, Hegel, Kant, between class

theories. I need to hurry, hurry and be rid of these philosophical maxims."
Uskova's daydream suddenly was interrupted when she heard "some sort
of strange noise coming from the stairwell." She went into the hall to in-
vestigate: "I open the door and see emotional faces, eyes. . . . 'The war
has begun, the Germans bombed Kiev,' someone's voice sounds. That
terrible word descended like a tornado, like a landslide, 'War.' First thought:
'This does not happen, it is a misunderstanding, it's just a border incident,
which will be resolved.' That's what I thought that morning, and the
morning was so sunny, with such a clear, blue sky. Today, a week later, I
no longer think that. This is war. What it will bring our people, country,
each of us? We know nothing."[3] Within weeks, Uskova lost contact with
her parents, and it was several years before she returned to the city of her
childhood. By September, Kiev was under occupation and Leningrad
under siege. Uskova's husband, Vladimir, left for the front. Without him,
she struggled to endure the intense bombardment and extreme starvation
that followed. As her sense of normalcy broke down, so too did her diary.
It became peppered with cross-outs, misspellings, and grammatical
mistakes, as the philology student struggled to come to terms with life
inside the ring.

Uskova reconstructed this moment eight days after it occurred. While
this delay may seem surprising, it is typical. Most diarists started to keep
journals only after the reality of war had set in. By the time Uskova began
hers, she was already nostalgic for the lost summer of 1941. Moreover, she
took care to explain that she heard about the war from her neighbors
because her radio was off. Most Leningraders, she knew, learned of the
invasion when Minister of Foreign Affairs Viacheslav Molotov announced
it over the airwaves. His address shattered the holiday mood inside the
city and plunged the entire country into a state of frenzied activity.

Comparatively few diarists recorded those early summer months before the blockade began, but those who did described feeling overcome
with shock, outrage, and a patriotic determination to defend their country.
Aleksei Evdokilov, a foreman at the Red Banner Factory, lashed out at
German troops in his diary, threatening, "You lying reptiles, you do not
scare us. We will fight with triple strength."[4] Sixteen-year-old Iura Riabinkin
framed the war as an ideological battle: "Two opposing systems, socialism
and fascism, have clashed! The welfare of all mankind hangs on the outcome of this great historical battle." "Victory will be ours, comrades," the

schoolgirl Elena Mukhina echoed in between her summaries of the daily news, "We will do anything to save humanity from tyranny."[5] Diary entries from this early phase of the war tend to replicate the discourse and affirm the explanations offered in the Soviet press. However, it did not take long for the diarists to seek alternative frameworks and terms with which to articulate their plight.

Inspired by Molotov's radio announcement, 100,000 Leningraders immediately enlisted in the army and in a people's militia that would defend the city, house by house if necessary.[6] By October 1941, 298,700 Leningraders had joined the army and 128,800 the militia. Leningrad was the first city to create such local militia units, a practice eventually emulated across the country. Another 17,000 Leningraders formed combat units through their factories and prepared to defend the city.[7] Nearly all joined the war effort in some capacity, compelled both by their own enthusiasm and by a series of mandates passed by the city's party and executive committees. Those not in the army or militia were conscripted into preparing fortifications for the city and its environs. They dug anti-tank ditches, laid mines and barbed wire, and constructed pillboxes and barricades at a feverish pace. Most of these 500,000 workers were women, including teenagers and expectant mothers. Natal'ia Uskova was among them. The language specialist found such labor trying but edifying. It gave her new insight into some of Russian's colorful idioms: "I found out that 'to sleep like a murdered person [*spat' kak ubityi*]' is not just an imaginative turn of phrase."[8] Other women, like the teacher Aleksandra Mironova and the architect Esfir' Levina, boasted in their diaries about the carpentry, camouflaging, and wood-clearing skills they were acquiring.[9] In addition to building fortifications, women and children served as medical assistants and sentries for the Local Anti-Aircraft Defense, or MPVO, where they watched for bombs and shells, guided residents to shelters, tried to extinguish explosives, and rescued people from the debris. By the end of September, 270,000 Leningraders had been organized into 3,500 antiaircraft crews.[10]

Indeed, hundreds of thousands of children remained in the city after the encirclement of Leningrad was complete and bombardment of it began. Children were a top priority for evacuation, but because of the Germans' rapid advance and Soviet officials' delayed and often disorganized efforts, only 500,000 Leningraders (less than 25 percent of the population) were evacuated before the city's railroad lines were severed in August 1941. These evacuees included cultural and political elites, workers whose factories were to be reestablished in the rear, archivists fleeing with the city's cultural treasures, and 243,833 children. Unlike the industrial convoys bound for Siberia, children were sent only to nearby farms and often into the path of the Wehrmacht.[11] The teachers Nina Gorbunova and Aleksandra Mironova shepherded children out of the city only to return with them weeks later. In their diaries, they described how parents tearfully clutched their returning children, grateful to have them back safe and sound.[12] Parents did not realize that now their children were in greater danger. As Richard Bidlack and Nikita Lomagin have observed, "almost two out of every five Leningrad civilians who were not evacuated would perish in the city from hunger and cold in the first winter and spring of the siege."[13] Major evacuations did not resume until April 1942.

Despite this partial evacuation, Leningrad's population actually increased. Refugees fleeing Hitler's armies poured into the city. One of them was thirteen-year-old Dima Afanas'ev, a native of Gatchina.[14] Afanas'ev proudly described in his diary how he spent the first day of the war "on duty," patrolling his neighborhood, gas mask in hand, and alerting his neighbors that war had begun.[15] Afanas'ev also helped to build fortifications, but he was scolded for doing more playing than working.[16]

Komsomolki (members of the Communist Youth League) Maia Bubnova and Elena Mukhina volunteered as medics and MPVO sentries.[17] Like Afanas'ev, they were thrilled to participate in the war effort. The exhilarated tone of their diaries became tinged with trepidation, however, as German forces approached and became audible. Before the bombers reached the city, the diarists listened to the distant explosions and waited for the metronome, broadcast on Leningrad radio, to quicken and then air-raid sirens to erupt. The metronome was used initially as a warning device; it sped up as enemy aircraft approached. Natal'ia Uskova listened to the ominous ticking as if to a time bomb and imagined the terror of aerial bombardment. "Night. The metronome peacefully taps out seconds. It keeps us on alert and anxious all the time. Any second it could stop, and the siren ~~could~~ will sound, and the announcer's voice will proclaim 'Attention! Attention! Air raid, Air raid.' Somewhere over there in the sky, which you do not see, hovers death, the cruelest, basest [death]."[18] Uskova shifted from the conditional to the future tense, as the horrors of bombardment became a certainty in her mind. Six weeks later, on 4 September 1941, German bombers began their aerial assault on Leningrad. That first month of attacks proved to be the most intense, resulting in 7,188 casualties.[19] On 19 September, one of the worst days, the besiegers dropped 528 highly explosive and 2,187 incendiary bombs as well as firing long-range artillery shells at Leningrad.[20] But bombs and shells accounted for roughly 2 percent of civilian deaths.[21] The more devastating consequence of the air strikes was that they obliterated the city's food reserves and thus unleashed a famine that took almost a million lives.

Aerial warfare struck the first blows to everyday life in Leningrad and defined the first phase of the blockade for the diarists. The attacks shattered the confident air of the diarists' initial entries. On the street, interspersed with explosions, one could hear "true human pain: 'we are not prepared for war . . . we have nothing to fight with . . . no planes, no equipment . . . Where is this 'war with few losses on foreign territory?' . . . Or were we betrayed?' These conversations are frightening," the actor Fedor Nikitin observed.[22] Irina Zelenskaia, an economist who worked at Electrical Station 7, described this constant uncertainty as living "on a volcano."[23] Echoing this sentiment, Aleksandra Liubovskaia proclaimed that the populace was perched "atop an unexploded bomb." This was more than a metaphor. The city soon became strewn with undetonated shells, including one that lay menacingly in the courtyard of Liubovskaia's apartment building.[24]

In a few weeks' time, homes, workplaces, and schools were in ruins. Along with the physical geography of the city, bombardment devastated the diarists' mental landscapes, destabilizing patterns of behavior and thought. Support and informational networks began to unravel; language began to diverge from official discourse; even abstract dimensions of experience, like time and space, were disrupted. As these conceptual markers—like the geographical landmarks of the city itself—were transformed, the diarists became alienated from their prewar lives. Disorientation and fear became the primary motors driving their narratives.

Work—the rhythms, routines, and identities it produces—was one of the first aspects of everyday life to be disrupted. The war created two extreme possibilities of being either under- or overworked. In the weeks following the invasion, many factories, museums, and institutes were evacuated to the rear, along with much of their staff and equipment. Those who stayed behind in Leningrad experienced a loss of community and a diminished sense of purpose. With less work to go around, many lost their jobs altogether.[25] In this "city full of unemployed people," Ol'ga Matiushina explained, they had to reinvent themselves. After the archivist Mariia Konopleva helped pack up artifacts from the Russian Museum and the Hermitage, she found work in a medical clinic. As soon as Natal'ia Uskova passed her doctoral exam in philology, she took a job making grenades.[26] Such shifts in the nature and meaning of work altered not only Leningraders' routines but also their bodies, social circles, and identities.

At the other end of the spectrum were laborers who were overworked, beset by enormous production quotas. On the day after the invasion, Lengorkom extended the shifts of workers in defense industries by three hours.[27] Between June and October, they labored feverishly, churning out munitions for eleven hours a day. To make up for losses incurred by conscription and evacuation, Lengorkom authorized the recruitment of teenagers as young as fourteen into the industrial labor force. Both adults and teens frequently moved into workplace barracks, so they could labor around the clock. They were permitted to go home once a week to see their families. Between 1941 and 1943, the engineer Mikhail Krakov left the factory to visit his apartment just twice.[28]

After several months, production slowed. German troops destroyed electrical lines and power plants, rendering most of the city's industrial sector inoperable. Without sufficient electricity and staff to power factories, work hours and quotas fell.[29] Shop-floor activity ground to a halt around November 1941. Employees spent most of the workday repairing damage, building fires to keep warm, and eating at the canteen. Most left work after lunch.

In light of these changes, workers became defined less by their labor or income and more by their ration category. Food replaced money as the main currency. "Bread," as Natal'ia Uskova put it, "reigns supreme. Bread rules, bread can do anything, it dictates and chooses."[30] Work identities became overlaid with ration categories because they were assigned primarily by labor contribution. Although there was some consideration of biological need—some special provisions were made for children and

pregnant women—occupation was the chief determinant of ration category because it indicated both caloric expenditure and contribution to
the war effort. Officially, there were five types of civilian rations, based
on the labor and class categories used in the prewar period. Those who
received the most were laborers in "hot" industries related to the war
economy, followed by specialists in engineering and technical fields,
service workers (which included workers in light industries and white-
collar employees), nonworking adults, and children under twelve.[31] However, the bread ration for the last three groups was identical or nearly so
during the hungriest period, October 1941 through March 1942.[32] For this
reason, diarists tended to consolidate the five groups and to speak just
about three: Category I included "workers" in heavy industry, Category II
"service employees," and Category III nonworking "dependents." None
of these categories provided sufficient food for long-term survival.

Students, who received the smallest rations, found their lives upended
much as workers did. Most Leningrad schools were either requisitioned
by the military for hospitals or bombed during air raids. German directives specified that schools, like factories, be targeted specifically. By the
end of the war, the USSR had lost roughly 40 percent of its schools and
Leningrad about 90 percent.[33] Students were consolidated into a handful
of primary and secondary institutions, and lessons often had to be held
in shelters. According to the eighth graders Maia Bubnova and Elena
Mukhina and the seventh grader Valia Peterson, a typical day was structured not by lessons but by interruptions of them.[34] "It is not studying at
all," Mukhina exclaimed, "but the devil knows what."[35] In Anatolii
Molchanov's school notebook, where he was supposed to track daily as-
signments, he tracked air raids instead.[36] One school director, Glafira
Korneeva, disparaged the very idea of keeping a diary because it would
only record all that was *not* taught: "For example: '8/XI—we read *The
Cherry Orchard.* 9/XI—did not finish the lesson—air raid. 10/XI—no
lesson—air raid,' and so on."[37] Yet students continued to attend classes
for the same reason their parents went to work. "I go to school, and they
ask me: 'how can you still?' And what else will I do? At least at school
they give out soup," Valia Peterson explained. For this reason, the geography teacher Aleksandr Vinokurov noted, "to a large degree, school will
henceforth be a care-giving and not an academic institution."[38] Like

workers, many students left after lunch or stopped attending altogether. By late November 1941, air raids, subzero conditions, and a dearth of resources and personnel forced most schools to close.[39]

Along with schools and workplaces, clubs, theaters, restaurants, and even streets began to empty in the autumn of 1941. Without electricity or gasoline, motorized transport disappeared. Forced to travel everywhere on foot, Leningraders stayed closer to home. Their worlds began to shrink. As Lidiia Ginzburg put it in her retrospective *Notes of a Blockade Person,* "the accepted unit of the city became the house, just as previously it had been the street."[40] Leningraders restricted their movements to a ring much smaller than the one that surrounded the city. The historian and diarist Georgii Kniazev called this inner ring his "small radius."[41] It encompassed the area between his apartment, place of work, and local bakery.

Home was at the center of this circle. But it soon ceased to be a refuge of comfort and security. All told, the aerial assault of Leningrad completely destroyed a total of 840 industrial buildings and 3.3 million square meters of living space; another 3,090 factories and 2.2 million square meters of housing were damaged to the point of being uninhabitable.[42] On two occasions, the painter Ol'ga Matiushina claimed she had trouble recognizing her home, it was so buried under dust and debris.[43] "With a heavy heart," the actor Fedor Nikitin entered his apartment after a bomb struck the textile factory across the street. The walls had crumbled. Glass crunched under his feet. On the floor were possessions belonging to other, now homeless, Leningraders—"iron bolts, hooks, a child's slipper, a piece of wood, with a lace curtain nailed to it."[44] Shells literally tore the intimacy of the home asunder, violently exposing it to the outside world. Elena Skriabina, who later became a professor of Russian literature at the University of Iowa, described one demolished apartment that had "etched itself" into her memory: "In the corner, an icon; on the floor, toys scattered everywhere as if the children had just finished playing. Further down was a room half buried under debris, but against the wall, a bed with fluffy pillows and a lamp . . . household items, surviving by chance, open to the eyes of the passerby—silent witnesses to the fact that someone or something alien tore mercilessly into the private life of people and barbarously defaced it."[45]

Displaced or anxious Leningraders, forgetting their emotional attachments to their homes, searched for apartments they hoped were more
structurally sound or less likely to be hit. As Ginzburg recalled, "each
house was now a defense and a threat," and its walls and stairways were
"regarded analytically" for their protective capacity.[46] Homes, like schools
and like Leningraders themselves, were repurposed and revalued based
on wartime utility. On average, the diarists moved three times during the
first year of the siege, often into relatives' homes. Skriabina dubbed these
forced reunions "the barbarian invasions" *(velikoe pereselenie narodov).*[47]

By late October, Leningraders confronted new assailants—hunger and
cold. At this point, some diarists relocated again, often to first-floor apartments. This made it easier for them to haul water, firewood, or their own
bodies back and forth. Moreover, they perpetuated the assault on the landscape themselves by ripping apart 9,000 wooden buildings as well as
fences and furniture for firewood. As "sheds and fences disappeared,"
Ol'ga Matiushina observed, "the city became an enormous country village.
It [wa]s possible to walk freely between buildings, not entering the street."[48]
In the absence of these physical barriers, conceptual boundaries of public
and private, inside and outside, near and far, urban and rural, shifted.
Frost gathered inside apartment stairwells and corridors. To conserve
strength and warmth, many Leningraders confined themselves to their
rooms; going "outside" began as soon as they emerged from under the
bedclothes. Ice collected in doorframes and made doors difficult to close,
so many left them open, doubtful that others would leave their beds to
intrude on them.

Bombing and shelling began to rupture Leningraders' sense of time as
well as space. Along with architectural landmarks, temporal reference
points were obliterated. Street clocks, the poet Vera Inber observed, were
"the first victims" of bombardment and simultaneously "displayed different times: 2:30, 11:55, 5:15."[49] Other traces of time's passage, the prattle
of trams, whistle of locomotives, and billowing of smokestacks, also faded.
The metronome was reminiscent of a clock but one that ticked interminably
without a sense of forward progress. In the absence of reliable timekeepers,
the diary became a key safeguard against temporal disorientation. Mariia
Konopleva kept a journal primarily to keep track of the day and date.[50]
As autumn gave way to winter, the northern metropolis became enshrouded

in darkness. Day and night melded together. This fact, combined with the primitive conditions of the city, gave the impression that time seemed to be at a standstill or moving in reverse.

Life inside the ring became a tedious waiting game. "It is as if you were sitting in a train station and expecting something—you yourself do not know what—a train that you cannot stand to wait for any longer. That is the kind of feeling I have," the mechanical engineer Aleksandra Borovikova explained. "It would be better to die immediately than to die gradually."[51] It became increasingly difficult for diarists like the eighteen-year-old student Nina Klishevich to envision a future or a world outside the ring: "When will this torture end? I no longer believe that there will be an end. That is, it is not that I don't believe it; it is that I cannot imagine it; I don't feel it. It seems to me that now this life will always be without end."[52] Within several weeks of the siege's beginning, therefore, diarists began to express a sense of dislocation, spatially and temporally, which only intensified as the length and severity of their confinement expanded. "A ring," the Russian proverb teaches, "has no end" (u kol'tsa net kontsa).

Leningraders were hampered by the constriction of both informational and physical space. When the war broke out, the Soviet Union, like most other combatant nations, strictly limited the circulation of information as part of heightened security measures. For Leningraders, already unmoored from the mainland, this deepened the sense of isolation. The day after the invasion, city authorities began confiscating guidebooks, maps, and private radios. Construction crews painted over street signs, camouflaged city landmarks, and disconnected private phones.[53] Leningraders needed official permits to photograph, sketch, or survey the cityscape. In the final weeks of tram service, drivers refrained from calling out stops and sometimes took alternate routes. "The conductors themselves do not know where their tram is going," Nina Klishevich remarked.[54]

City officials further restricted the circulation of information and bodies within Leningrad through other measures like imposing a curfew and confiscating bicycles. The Leningrad branch of the People's Commissariat of Internal Affairs (NKVD), or secret police, tried to limit contact between the city and the front by confiscating mail sent and by keeping hospitalized soldiers and civilians in separate wards.[55] Other ways of disseminating potentially harmful ideas, such as reading enemy leaflets, listening to foreign broadcasts, or spreading rumors, were punishable by death.[56] These restrictions, while hardly surprisingly in the context of war, relegated Leningraders to even greater seclusion. With so few reliable contacts and sources of information, they soon had little basis for distinguishing rumor from reality.

The Soviet Information Bureau (Sovinformbiuro), established on 24 June 1941 by the Council of People's Commissars (Sovnarkom) and the Central Committee of the Communist Party, had sole authority to release information about the war, either over the airwaves or in print. Its reports, however, were sparse and selective. Leningrad radio, due to the siege situation, was disconnected from 75 percent of the national broadcasts recorded in Moscow.[57] In addition to (and sometimes in lieu of) providing substantive news, print and sound media offered stories, music, and human-interest pieces designed to comfort and inspire.[58] Initially, this tactic met with great success among the diarists. During the first months of the war, they avidly read newspapers and listened to the radio, desperate for clues about how the war would unfold. "You hardly breathe and the heart beats so that sometimes you can hardly hear the broadcast," Irina Zelenskaia explained in July 1941.[59] The incredible detail of journal entries from that period indicates that many diarists took notes on the news summaries, adopting official rhetoric and explanatory categories in the process. Diarists who later cultivated unique writing styles and unorthodox views initially penned entries that were highly reminiscent of official discourse. By fall 1941, however, the language and content of their journals began to diverge from that of radio and newspaper reports.

Official media had the opposite effects of consoling and unsettling the diarists. On the one hand, the constancy of the radio and of the main city newspaper, *Leningradskaia Pravda (LP)*, which, incredibly, was published every day of the siege except one, gave the diarists a much-needed sense of normalcy.[60] The content was reduced, and the print runs were tiny; the few copies made were posted in public areas. Still, just the sight of printed articles and announcements about theatrical performances and lectures cheered Aleksandra Liubovskaia.[61] They reminded her that life endured in the city. Radio's comforting presence is especially evident in how the diarists celebrated when broadcasting resumed after a hiatus in December and January 1942. When the medical student Zinaida

Sedel'nikova's receiver erupted in sound, she declared, "once again today I have become connected to the world!"[62] Thirteen-year-old Dima Afanas'ev shared her exuberance: "Today the radio suddenly started to talk unexpectedly. At first we did not even understand what was going on, and when we understood, there was no end to our happiness . . . [. . .] Deep silence is the most frightening of all. Mama said that sometimes (especially at night) she thinks that we are the last people on earth and that we will live out our last hour in this empty, frozen city."[63]

On the other hand, while the constancy of broadcasts and newspapers consoled the diarists, their lack of substance unsettled them.[64] "Why is Moscow silent?" Irina Zelenskaia demanded in summer 1941: "Today the radio broadcast was ten minutes late and then instead of the usual news summaries, it played 'correspondence from the front.' [. . .] Disturbing thoughts crept into mind: Moscow is quiet—why? Where is the summary created such that it can be so delayed? So, with a cold, empty, sinking feeling, the torture continued until seven o'clock when, finally, they broadcast the morning news report. Still the same. [. . .] How difficult it is sometimes to be in the dark. Because of this, one fishes greedily for every kind of rumor and story. You filter them through the most critical prism, and as a result you end up once again with nothing, everything is idle chatter."[65] Irina Zelenskaia, Elizaveta Sokolova, and other diarists in the party worried that such silences signaled a growing "estrangement between the powers that be and the masses."[66] Indeed, the city's party secretary, Andrei Zhdanov, received reports that the party was not providing a powerful enough voice to temper panic in the city. Conscription, evacuation, and death reduced Leningrad's party membership by half and the Komsomol by 90 percent.[67]

The diarists described the news summaries as "stingy" or "meager," like their rations. Georgii Kniazev, a diarist who devoted considerable energy to summarizing news reports, grew tremendously frustrated: "Short lines of the summary: 'Over the course of 14 August our troops carried out fierce battles against the enemy on all fronts from the Arctic Ocean to the Black Sea.' What do these stingy lines mean? An offensive? Whose? Ours? The Germans'? Mutually?" "I have lost any orientation on current events." If we flash forward momentarily to the winter of 1942, we can see that the analogy between nutritional and informational sustenance became more pronounced over time. "Yet another day of war," Kniazev remarked. "I know nothing of what is going on in the outside world. The crumbs of information that are reported in newspapers and by radio actually do nothing to clarify what is happening in the world. 'We occupied point L., we surrendered point B., the spoils of war were such and such . . .' They don't actually say anything."[68] Despite his frustration, Kniazev did not brush these crumbs aside. Quite the opposite: he worked to disambiguate cryptic stock phrases like "fighting continues on all fronts" and "nothing of substance has occurred." "From practice," the school inspector Glafira Korneeva observed, "it has become clear that they are hiding things with short, stereotypical announcements . . . 'Several planes have managed to break through . . . the military targets were not hit . . . there were deaths and casualties . . .'"[69]

Many diarists, including children, came to interpret the Sovinformbiuro's omissions as indications of defeat. "Why do they always only write about the directions [of front movements]," thirteen-year-old Dima Afanas'ev demanded in August 1941, "and do not write which cities have been surrendered or taken back? Or is this a military secret?"[70] Even after several months, his incredulity about these vagaries did not subside: "'Offensive battle.' But where—that is completely unclear. For a long time now, no names are given in the summaries. After all, if our [troops] are attacking, shouldn't they [say] which villages they are traversing? Incomprehensible."[71] "They reported that a battle of 4,000 tanks is taking place," echoed Ivan Savinkov, a Molotov Factory worker, "but they announced nothing about the results of that battle—that means we lost. I don't like these summaries—they are far too short and make nothing known. How can it be that you don't know where the Germans are?"[72]

Good news could be just as alarming. The diarists caught on quickly that the press concealed massive losses by highlighting individual acts of valor.[73] These stories aroused their suspicion, not patriotism. Aleksandr Buianov, who served as an instructor for the party committee of Vasil'evskii Island, grew weary of hearing about "individual heroic operations—this has become so typical and it does not create any astonishment at all."[74] Once Dima Afanas'ev figured out the formula, he began reading reports of individual achievement as indications of collective defeat: "Why are they always honoring pilots above everything else?" he asked in July 1941. "Clearly, we are fighting more poorly on the ground than in the air."[75]

The most upsetting omissions pertained to conditions inside Leningrad. The newspaper focused on the front and the city's efforts to serve it rather than on severe hardships of civilian life. Slogans like "all for the front" and "we live only to work and think only about victory" cast Leningraders as citizen-soldiers.[76] Several diarists, including the party members Aleksandr Buianov and Irina Zelenskaia, objected to this "heroic defender" rhetoric because it deemphasized their suffering.[77] In response to Aleksandr Fadeev's nationally syndicated article "What I Saw in Leningrad," Buianov remarked, "there were a million things that were not reflected upon, which can be seen on the streets of Leningrad in the dark nights and frosty winter days," especially "dozens of bodies on the streets."[78] Similarly, upon reading one of the correspondent Il'ia Ehrenburg's articles, Irina Zelenskaia complained, "Like every other newspaper article, it rings out on too high of a note. [. . .] Something from that article reached me, forced me to take a good look around and with merciless clarity to verify that all of us, even residents of the front-city, live by our own interests, our own routines and habits, our self-preservation, etc., and very little by the military front."[79] The high-mindedness that Ehrenburg ascribed to the *blokadniki,* "that is what we lack—purposefulness," Zelenskaia claimed.[80]

Starvation, full blown by November 1941, also was taboo in the press. The regime never denied it, but it continually downplayed the seriousness of the situation in order to boost morale and prevent questions about its management of the food supply. *LP* broached hunger through veiled language about shortages or the need to economize resources. It blamed thieves for pilfering food but never was transparent about the sheer lack of supply, the primary problem. Moreover, it printed information about rations on the bottom right-hand corner of the last page of selected issues, and the norms it listed—especially for items other than bread—often were inaccurate.[81] By contrast, the newspaper abounded with stories, centrally positioned, about hunger elsewhere in German-occupied Europe. This included an article on how Germany's rat population was starving.[82] Only when the worst period of hunger subsided did *LP* acknowledge it directly and explicitly.

In fact, the watchwords of the siege experience that appear in all diaries were conspicuously absent from *LP* until 1943. They include *blokada* (blockade); *osada* (siege), *blokadnik* (person of the blockade), and *distrofik* (person with *distrofiia*, or one dying from starvation). Instead of the term "blockade," which conjures up images of confinement and deprivation, the newspaper editors preferred "battle" or "defense" of Leningrad or to describe the city as a "fortress." "Blockade" and "siege" do appear in editorials starting in November 1941, but they were not featured in an official headline or Sovinformbiuro report until 20 January 1943, when the piercing of the siege was announced.[83] In other words, *LP* explicitly acknowledged the blockade as such only when it was clear that it soon would be lifted. By contrast, the diarists developed their own rich vocabulary to describe their suspended, isolated state. "The ring" was the one term *both* newspapers and diarists used regularly. In addition, "Leningraders have several terms for the life and territory outside of the ring of the blockade," Aleksandr Grishkevich noted, "'the other side *[ta storona]*,' 'beyond the ring *[za kol'tsom]*,' 'on the other shore *[na tom beregu]*,' 'on the mainland *[na bol'shoi zemle]*.'" Grishkevich, who worked in the Lengorkom's printing department, kept track of these and other linguistic developments.[84]

As the world of the ring diverged from the mainland, so too did the diarists' language from that of the Sovinformbiuro and *LP*. Small talk came to reflect the centrality of food and death in defining the blockade experience. "Instead of good morning," Zinaida Sedel'nikova greeted her roommates by calling out "are you alive?"[85] A common good-bye was to wish a fellow Leningrader not to end up "caught in a trench." By this Leningraders did not mean trenches at the front but the new mass graves created in the city.[86] Or, instead of starting conversation by commenting on the weather, Leningraders inquired, "what kind of [ration] card do you have?" and "where do you eat?"[87]

Through the diarists' efforts to decode news reports, we can glimpse the practices of interrogation and the devotion to documentation that propelled their diary narratives. The diarists turned toward other sources of information—from social observation and rumors to historical scholarship and medical analysis—as they came to terms with the crisis pervading their lives. In this way, their journals can be read as alternative

news sources, albeit highly subjective ones concerned with war on an experiential level. This is how Mariia Konopleva presented her diary when
she gave it to the city library in 1943. She explained that it documented
blockade life "during the period when there were neither newspapers nor
radios and the post and telephone did not work."[88] In fact, the newspaper
was published nearly every day, and the radio fell silent for only a few
weeks. But Konopleva remembered them as absent. Perhaps she felt that
they were too peripheral, sparse, or unreliable to capture the siege
experience.

Between June and October 1941, everyday life in Leningrad was upended
by the chaos of mobilization, evacuation, and bombardment. The routines and patterns that constituted the diarists' daily lives, professional
and domestic, were forcibly restructured. So too were informational networks, language, spatial concepts of urban and rural, inside and outside,
and temporal demarcations between past, present, and future. When
bombardment and isolation were compounded by starvation, this conceptual disorientation intensified and came to encompass the body, the
sense of self, the family, social hierarchies, and ideological principles.

Through diary writing, these Leningraders endeavored to work
through the crises, rumors, and announcements that they encountered
daily. For them, the struggle to survive was in large part a struggle to understand, to analyze, to bring some semblance of order to the devastation around them. "I want, with definite clarity, to memorize Leningrad
at this time, to know, remember, and to pull through," Esfir' Levina declared in her very first entry. Or, as Irina Zelenskaia put it, "curiosity about
tomorrow is one of the stimuli sustaining me to live."[89] The instinct to
fight for life was matched by an equally strong impulse to imbue that life
with meaning.

The diarists analyzed the world of the siege from rooftops, bomb shelters, and breadlines as well as from their own attitudes and bodies. Every
moment, every face presented an opportunity for inquiry. Many started
these investigations by examining themselves in mirrors. It is with the
mirror that the next chapter begins.

Chapter Two

Becoming New People

O N 14 December 1941, Aleksandra Borovikova sat writing late into the night. This was unusual for her. Borovikova was a reluctant diarist who frequently resolved to quit journaling. But on this occasion, she poured her concerns onto the page, hoping to unburden her mind enough to fall asleep. Earlier that day, Borovikova had studied herself in the mirror and was still haunted by what she saw: "I look like all those other devils, I have become just bones and wrinkled skin."[1] A few months before, the thirty-six-year-old mechanical engineer had been an energetic foreman and active party member. But the mirror displayed no traces of her youth or vitality. "Compared to what you were during the first days of the war, you have become unrecognizable, Sasha," Borovikova later reiterated to herself.[2] The diarists were not only trapped inside the city; they were imprisoned in unfamiliar bodies produced by starvation.

Leningraders were hungry even before the blockade began. The city was on rationing during the USSR's winter war with Finland (1939–40) and again in July 1941 after Germany invaded. Between July and November 1941, rations were slashed five times to norms much smaller than those given to civilians in other Soviet cities.[3] By December 1941—when Borovikova recorded her entry about looking in the mirror—Leningrad

officials received the first reports of cannibalism. During the winter and
spring of 1941–42, the torment of hunger eclipsed that of bombardment.
Instead of studying the skies for German planes, Leningraders began to
study themselves. Mirror scenes, like the one penned by Borovikova, were
a common way they confronted the scars of deprivation on their bodies.[4]

The diarists often presented their encounters with the mirror as chance
occurrences. The party worker Aleksandr Buianov, for instance, was
doing laundry when he felt an urge to glance in the mirror. What he saw
sent him into a "fit of madness."[5] While dressing for work, the health inspector Leonid Gal'ko discovered his legs were too swollen to fit inside his
boots. Suddenly curious about the rest of his body, Gal'ko peered into
the mirror and discovered a huge growth protruding from his face. "With
great effort," he turned away from his reflection, crammed his feet into
his boots, and went to work.[6] The mirror elicited a multitude of reactions
including surprise, horror, and disgust or more often a combination of
these. Buianov panicked. After seeing his reflection, he stopped writing
diary entries and instead penned farewell letters to his wife and daughter.
Filled with self-loathing, the chemist Elena Kochina spat at herself in the
mirror.[7] Others, however, could not help but smile at the incongruity of
their wartime and prewar reflections. Before seventeen-year-old Elena
Mukhina was evacuated in May 1942, she took a final look in the mirror.
It struck her as "quite funny" that she, "a young woman who has everything ahead of her," could look into a mirror and see an "old man" staring
back.[8] Her unique physical appearance, along with markers of sex and
age, had been erased.

Of course, mirrors are classic symbols of illumination and distortion.
The diarists were unsure whether the image they glimpsed was an accurate likeness or an illusion. How could their appearance have become so
foreign? How could the human body have become so unrecognizable?
Leningrad doctors struggled with mirrors in a similar way. They used
pocket mirrors to see if their patients were still breathing. "If it did not
turn cloudy when held up to the face of a dying person, then doubt was
resolved," the doctor and siege survivor Svetlana Magaeva explained.
However, doctors too found mirrors unreliable. Leningraders' starved
bodies reduced their homeostatic functioning so drastically that breathing
could be difficult to detect. The pocket-mirror test was administered un-

successfully to Magaeva at age ten as she lay dying in a children's hospital. She was led halfway to the mortuary before the attending physician had second thoughts and gave her an injection of glucose, which revived her.[9] That experience of being pronounced dead prematurely captures the difficulty of understanding the siege body, to which conventional medical assumptions and practices seemed to no longer apply.

The mirror not only displayed surface-level changes to personal appearance; it alerted the diarists to more fundamental changes in their anatomy and physiology. Body parts and systems operated in new, unpredictable ways. Legs and stomachs acquired lives of their own. Reflexes, once automatic, now had to be willed. Changes in sense perception radically altered Leningraders' grasp on reality. Most studies of the siege emphasize how hunger dehumanized the besieged community, leaving them physically deficient, impaired, and disfigured.[10] The diaries suggest, however, that the siege left them not disfigured but transfigured. They tell a story of corporeal differentiation, not just of degeneration. The 872 days that Leningraders spent in conditions inimical to human life gave rise to a new mode of being in and apprehending the world. It transformed them into qualitatively different beings, into *blokadniki*.

Formidable physical and perceptual changes led the diarists to conceptualize themselves and the world around them anew. The siege precipitated, if not the destruction, then the deconstruction of many received concepts about the body—biological, ontological, and ideological. The diarists developed new understandings of corporeality that were in conversation and often in conflict with Soviet ideology.[11] They did not always couch their observations in political terms, but in coming to terms with their own transformations, they probed core assumptions about human nature that were predominant in Soviet society. Chief among these was the notion of physical perfectibility incarnated by the New Soviet Person.

As both a physical and metaphorical entity, the body has been central to how many cultures envision the individual, the societal, and the political. In numerous polities, ranging from democratic to authoritarian, the body serves as an allegory for state sovereignty, societal unity, and individual identity. Revolutionary societies typically use corporeal imagery to depict the decrepitude of the old regime and the rebirth of society under the new order.[12] The USSR was no exception. Soviet scientists

and ideologues championed the plasticity of human physiology and consciousness. They sought to perfect both by immersing individuals in a
socialist environment. Through a variety of policies ranging from labor
to education to incarceration, Soviet authorities aimed to cultivate New
Soviet People. Paragons of physical health and proletarian consciousness,
they would embody the values of a revolution intent on remaking the
natural world. The New Soviet People would learn to overcome the limitations of their bodies and bring order to their unconscious impulses.
And, as Jochen Hellbeck has pointed out, in the 1930s, diary writing was
a key tool through which Soviet citizens practiced controlling their "psy-
chic and bodily processes" with the ultimate goal of self-mastery.[13]

Although the body was a constant feature of Soviet ideology, the principles and policies regarding it changed over time. In the 1920s, Soviet
theorists and scientists emphasized the importance of external, material
conditions in remolding people. By the mid-1930s, however, they stressed
the power of human consciousness and will over the natural world.[14] This
line of thinking granted individuals a more active role in remaking their
world and themselves. It also helped to justify Stalin's labor policies
during the First (1928–32) and Second (1933–37) Five-Year Plans, which
relied on the personal initiative of workers to meet soaring production
quotas. The new emphasis on individual responsibility and willpower
was enshrined in the 1937 criminal code, in which infractions were no
longer blamed on an adverse environment or upbringing.[15] In health care,
illness evolved from an indication of environmental hazards to a reflection
of personal weakness. The regime expected that, with proper consciousness and determination, individuals could overcome mental and physical ailments.[16] Stigma against persons with disabilities remained
strong, therefore, even when World War II created millions of wounded,
disfigured veterans.[17]

In wartime Leningrad, local leaders and journalists tried to integrate
residents into this narrative of overcoming and eventually mastering the
body. Starting in the spring of 1942, the wartime press proclaimed that
Leningraders—having endured the horrific winter of 1941–42—*were* New
Soviet People. A glance through *LP* reveals that this was an oft-repeated
claim. "They are new people," the correspondent Nikolai Tikhonov declared, "born in the fire of war. Their hardening is incomparable."

Taking one boy as an example, Tikhonov declared that Leningraders "will not be broken by cold, hunger, or bombs—nothing." They personified strength and discipline. In 1942, he published a collection of stories for readers on the mainland that celebrated these resolute, battle-hardened Leningraders, entitled *Features of the Soviet Person*.[18] Aleksandr Fadeev, the future head of the Soviet Writers' Union, voiced this same sentiment after observing a classroom discussion between students and teachers on "the question of the 'new person'": "It was impossible to listen without emotion to how my interlocutors, from the older and the younger generations, spoke about the new person, not suspecting that they themselves are living new people, whose every step in the Great Patriotic War illuminates great thoughts and actions."[19] Similarly, internationally distributed publications announced, "The citizens of Leningrad had become a selected people. [. . .] The very appearance of the people had changed. They seemed taller, their faces were calm and determined, their purpose evident in every motion."[20] Such declarations suggested that Leningraders were not impaired by the blockade but possessed even greater physical and mental prowess than before.

The diarists described their physical transformations in different, less heroic terms. They upheld claims that they had been remade by the war. But they described their bodies as skeletal, not steely, and as qualitatively different from either their prewar bodies or those of other Soviet citizens. The siege body was frail, unruly, and unpredictable. Instead of mastering their bodies, the diarists bore witness to the physical demands that overpowered them. Starting with surface changes visible in a mirror and extending to gender, age, sense perception, and anatomy, the diarists studied their new bodies in hopes of turning them from adversaries into allies in the struggle for survival. Ultimately, they crafted narratives of a new siege body that, perhaps inadvertently but effectively, overwrote that of the New Soviet Person.

Overcoming Age and Gender?

Whether the diarists gazed at themselves in the mirror or at those around them, they had difficulty identifying the siege body according to conventional notions of age and gender. As the librarian and translator Aleksandra

Liubovskaia walked along the city's snow-covered streets, she peered at the faces she encountered. Each one was "yellowish, dark, and [with] dim faces, lifeless eyes," heavily muffled, and either so sunken or so swollen that "it was hard to understand if it belongs to a man or a woman or a child."[21] The streets were crowded with children's sleds—now the main form of transportation—that pulled or were pulled by indistinguishable beings. Commenting on one such sled, the poet Vera Inber noted, "The shape of the human form was clear enough, but you could not tell whether it was of a man or a woman. It had become merely a body belonging to earth."[22] "Everybody looks the same," Elena Kochina echoed. "Leningraders have lost their sex and age."[23]

Soviet socialism had long advocated the eradication of gender- and aged-based inequalities, which, it claimed, were produced by the exploitive and patriarchal conditions of capitalism.[24] Ironically, the violence of starvation did equalize Leningraders bodies, in a way, by erasing conventional signs of sexual difference. Because their emaciated bodies conserved resources to maintain basic homeostatic functioning—which one diarist described as "the strange economy of the organism in these difficult times"—sex organs atrophied, and hormonal levels declined.[25] Men became impotent; the count and mobility of their sperm decreased. Women became sterile. They stopped menstruating, and their breasts hardened and ceased to lactate. Most Leningraders lost the inclination to have sex. The few women who did conceive between 1941 and 1943 rarely carried their babies to term. Similarly, adolescence slowed dramatically in boys and girls. Numerous aspects of development, from height and weight gain to sexual maturation, became delayed in youths.[26]

It grew harder for the diarists to delineate, based on physical evidence, between male and female or masculine and feminine. And yet the city's population had become overwhelmingly female. Most able-bodied men under fifty-five were drafted, and the men who remained in the city initially died at much higher rates than women. This was because men tend to carry smaller stores of fat (3–5 percent) than women (8–10 percent).[27] Women constituted more than 70 percent of the city's industrial labor force and made up the bulk of the civilian defense—a pattern replicated across the USSR. Moreover, the domestic duties of finding and preparing food, tending the sick, and fetching water became the primary activities of survival. In light of this demographic disparity and the centrality of women's labor, Cynthia Simmons and Nina Perlina have argued that the blockade should be understood as a fundamentally female experience.[28] Although the gendered aspects of the blockade seem very pronounced in retrospect, they appear to have been less salient for the diarists, at least on the page. They occasionally designated household duties as "feminine" or noted gender disparities in the mortality rate. However, they mostly broached gender as an increasingly hazy dimension of experience and identity. They attended less to gender's steadfast importance than to its apparent disappearance.

New norms of dress and behavior helped to destabilize gender conventions. During the record cold winter of 1941–42, Leningraders wrapped their bodies in whatever garments they could find. Women dressed in men's trousers, boots, overcoats, and naval uniforms, which, Georgii Kniazev noted, "suit[ed] them extremely well." He called these women "dry-land sailors." Meanwhile, men like him donned women's fur coats, scarves, and kerchiefs.[29] These strategies of dress obscured outward markers of occupation as well as gender. For instance, the architect Esfir' Levina recalled one afternoon in the spring of 1942 when she glimpsed "ladies" don the trappings of working-class men, including "sealskin coats, enormous felt boots," shovels, and axes, while men wore "women's kerchiefs, blankets, and drapes on their shoulders."[30] These "ladies" were among the workers conscripted to remove ice and human waste from the city that spring. While working on one such brigade, the philologist Natal'ia Uskova also noticed how the heavy labor and ambiguous dress obscured the gender of the (mostly female) workers. "What a picture we must have made under the bright March sun," Uskova exclaimed: "Mercilessly, it clearly illuminated all our blockade flaws, at a glance. It's funny and scary at the same time. Some sort of formless scarecrows. Neither gender nor age can be determined. People are wearing all sorts of things; all that matters is that they are warm. I am in Volodia's [her husband's] winter coat, which reaches my heels, belted up, like a coachman, I have a hat on my head, and over it a black scarf [pulled] down to my brows, like a nun. Other 'snow maidens' are no better than I. And we all look alike, like ghosts."[31] Along with age and gender, humanness itself seemed to have faded from their bodies.

Fading sexual difference also manifested itself linguistically. In light of female diarists' epicene appearance, they tended to favor more gender-neutral terms like *blokadnik* (man or person of the blockade) rather than *blokadnitsa* (woman of the blockade). And when they referred to persons afflicted with symptoms of starvation, termed "nutritional dystrophy," they generally used the term *distrofik* (man or person with dystrophy) rather than *distrofichka* (woman with dystrophy). In well-known accounts of the blockade, the philologists Ol'ga Freidenberg and Lidiia Ginzburg chose to posit themselves as ambiguous narrative subjects. Freidenberg titled her recollections of the blockade *The Siege of a Human Being,* while Lidiia Ginzburg's autobiographical *Notes of a Blockade Person* features a genderless protagonist, "N."[32]

The apparent loss of gender and age resonated with aspects of Soviet ideology, and party writers noted vague resemblances between these female *blokadniki*—whose labors and bodies now more closely resembled those of men—and the New Soviet Woman. Indeed, most of the prized attributes of the ideal Soviet person were considered masculine.[33] In *LP* and in other published writings, Nikolai Tikhonov, Aleksandr Fadeev, and Vera Inber selectively acknowledged the decline of gender-based distinctions under siege in terms of labor. They celebrated it as a sign of the empowerment and equality of women.[34] In published excerpts from Fadeev's diary, he proclaimed, "Women of Leningrad! Will words ever be able to express the grandeur of your labors. [. . .] You wear the workers' overalls, the militiaman's uniform, the uniform of the antiaircraft defense, the railway man, the army surgeon, and telegraphist!"[35] Fadeev focused on the transformation of Mariia Konstantinovna, the wife of fellow correspondent Nikolai Tikhonov. He noted how her delicate painter's hands had become leathery and her arms sinewy from life under siege. Clad in heavy overalls, "she looked like a lanky young workman. [. . .] She was a different woman, a woman of besieged Leningrad."[36] This piece shifts the focus from the violence of starvation to the power of labor to overcome obstacles. It suggests that the blockade had strengthened and enhanced Leningraders rather than dispossessing them of gender and age.

The emphasis on labor masked the anguish of starvation and of losing one's femininity. In general, wartime poets and correspondents proclaimed that Leningrad women had become physical and industrial equals to men without losing their sexual characteristics or neglecting domestic duties. During the late 1930s and 1940s, the historian Anna Krylova has argued, Soviet gender roles were sufficiently flexible to allow for the "merger of woman and soldier," so that women could be both feminine and ruthless defenders of the motherland.[37] Almost daily, *LP* featured women who "took up male specialties" at the front or in factories, proving that "there is no such thing as 'male' work," while remaining steadfast mothers and wives.[38] Vera Inber underscored this in her wartime poem "The Nurturing Feminine Hand," which celebrated Leningrad women for laboring "with unwomanly strength," while assiduously attending to their children. And in her 1945 poem "Female Victor," Inber had the following praise for Leningrad women: "you remembered that, aside from the professions of men / You are first and foremost a woman."[39] Such works acknowledged the destabilization of gender within limits. They presented female Leningraders' physical transformations as signs of growing equality, not androgyny. Leningrad press and propaganda, however, never acknowledged, let alone celebrated, the reciprocal phenomenon: the apparent feminization of men. By contrast, the diaries capture the pain of losing one's sexual virility and identity for both men and women. Male diarists did remark that their activities and clothes were increasingly feminine, but they tended not to refer to their bodies as feminized. Instead they associated their frail, gaunt physiques with another category, age.

Age was another fundamental aspect of human nature overturned by the siege. While the ideal Soviet person was typically young and virile, the *blokadniki* looked just the opposite. Hunger had aged them. Starvation shrinks the body, darkens skin, makes bones brittle, and taxes bodily systems. In light of such symptoms, the theater director Aleksandr Dymov presented age as operating independently from the passage of time: "Old age is the fatigue of well-worn components that are involved in the working of the human body, an exhaustion of man's inner resources. Your blood no longer keeps you warm, your legs refuse to obey you, your back grows stiff, your brain grows feeble, and your memory fades."[40] Even though time seemed to slow inside the ring, the human life cycle seemed to accelerate. With great sadness, Aleksandra Liubovskaia noted how she and her daughter Natasha, more than twenty years her junior, now appeared to be the same age; both were "wrinkled and gray haired."[41]

The cruelest aspect of aging this way, according to thirty-four-year-old artist Nikolai Byl'ev, was that the mind was still "lively" enough to comprehend the injustice of it. "To know that you are young," he explained, "and yet to see yourself in a condition of decrepitude and apathy is a terrible thing." Byl'ev discovered he had become elderly when he tried to perform simple tasks like tossing a fallen ember into the stove. "You realize: this [task] is a trivial business. But you feel: this is impossibly difficult. Through an effort of will, you overcome your own stiffness, you lift yourself slightly from the stool, and leaning on it slowly, squat down on your disobedient, completely weak legs and, crouching on the floor, get the firebrand. If I am destined to survive, then sometime afterward I will be able to describe what old age is. I will say: I know all about it. I myself was an old man once."[42] Byl'ev hoped to survive the war, regain his youthful physique, and then someday reflect back on his elderly years. Whether the mind would recover from this ordeal was another matter.

Although most adult *blokadniki* looked older, the diarists struggled to determine the age of children because hunger arrested their physical development. On the one hand, Leningrad children acquired the arthritic gait and stooped posture associated with agedness. They hunched over and leaned on canes for support. These "little old people," as Vasilisa Malysheva described them, also developed another feature that flouted conventional notions of age and gender.[43] Both boys and girls grew significant amounts of facial hair. This shocked the evacuation staff that welcomed them as they returned to the mainland in spring 1942. "We called them little elderly people," one Leningrad evacuation worker recalled.[44] On the other hand, because of their shrunken frames and delayed physical and sexual maturation, some medical professionals, like the diarist and doctor Ol'ga Peto, regularly underestimated the ages of their young patients, assuming they were younger than they were.[45] Age became a point of confusion once it was unhinged from the passage of time.

How, then, should age be measured? By outward appearance, years of life, or state of mind? The diarists wrestled with these questions on both theoretical and personal levels. "When do you end your youth?" Esfir' Levina asked as she celebrated her first birthday under siege. "It was [in] another time that age seemed to correspond with life."[46] Aleksandr Dymov concluded that age ought to be measured by physical markers—such as weariness and frailty—and not by years: "We are, all of us, old people now. Regardless of our age. The pace of old age now governs our bodies and our feelings . . ."[47] New rules and principles governed Leningraders' bodies. In the diarists' entries from winter 1941–42, they repeatedly commented on the instability of age and gender, which in turn raised more fundamental questions about the human body and the prospects of comprehending and controlling it.

The Evolution of Sense Perception

Not only did Leningraders' bodies look and feel different; they exhibited new physiological, anatomical, and sensory characteristics. The diarists paid particular attention to their senses because the senses connect humans to the outside world and mediate their apprehension of reality.[48] Sense perception impacted everything the diarists did, from finding resources and hearing air-raid warnings to writing in their journals. Moreover, by orienting Leningraders in their environment, the senses informed nearly all of their behaviors and beliefs.[49] After all, the sensory system is, at its core, a system of interpretation. And the perceptual and physiological changes incurred by starvation subsequently provided the foundation for the diarists' reinterpretations of numerous aspects of their lives.

The primary way most people apprehend the world is visually, so much so that in many languages "I see" can mean "I understand." Not surprisingly, when the blockade began, diarists quickly turned to visual metaphors to convey deep uncertainty about their fate. They both upheld the dominance of visual apprehension and called its efficacy into question. The diarists described Leningrad, then under heavy bombardment, as an opaque, illegible landscape, engulfed in smoke, fog, or darkness. The lack of electricity only exacerbated their disorientation. When bombardment gave way to starvation in November 1941, references to visual impairment remained strong. The diarists now couched their bewilderment in somatic terms as a "dystrophic fog" or "dystrophic blackout" that clouded the mind.[50]

Blindness was not just a powerful metaphor; it was a physical reality. When Leningrad doctors began researching visual impairment in spring 1942, they discovered that poor eyesight had become common among *blokadniki.*[51] Emaciation, vitamin A deficiency, and hypertension—all widespread in the city—could trigger neuroretinitis, an inflammation of the retina and optic nerve, or the production of mucopolysaccarides, which make the body vulnerable to infection and night blindness. City optometrists recorded more incidences of damaged blood vessels in the eye and of degenerated optic nerves than in the prewar period.[52] In addition, starvation often induced dramatic swelling of the body (edema), including the area around the eyes, which could compromise vision.[53] Several diarists, including the artist Anna Ostroumova-Lebedeva and the writer Sof'ia Ostrovskaia, described losing their eyesight. In February 1942, Ostrovskaia revealed how blindness and uncertainty about the future seemed to blend together and reinforce each other: "Things are very bad with [my vision]. Almost all the time I live in a deep dusk—and I write and work that way. At night my eyes tear up constantly. It is very unpleasant for me and very alarming. I find it curious and frightening to think about the future. What kinds of prospects are there for my city? When will they finally break through and remove the blockade? When will people stop dying from emaciation? When will people return to basic conditions of the so-called cultured life of the city?"[54] For Ostrovskaia, blindness signified both physical degeneration and an altered perception of reality, making the blockade difficult to accommodate, physiologically and conceptually.

While the physical and environmental conditions forcibly altered some diarists' eyesight, several also chose to adjust their field of vision and so modify their perception of the outside world. Ostrovskaia admitted that a measure of sightlessness could be adaptive. It could help her focus on survival and block out distressing aspects of her predicament. In September 1941, when German troops dropped as many as 6,000 shells a day on Leningrad, Ostrovskaia tried to shut her eyes: "I did not see any sort of explosions in the city. I do not want to see. I am protecting myself. A case of prolepsis of the eyes."[55] Whether physiological or metaphorical, Ostrovskaia welcomed prolepsis as a safeguard against a disturbing reality. Irina Zelenskaia, a manager at an electrical plant, also practiced selective vision. She chose to focus on small daily tasks in order not to become overwhelmed by the monumental undertaking of survival. This strategy became integral to how she navigated the ring: "We live in a state of half consciousness, absorbed with small concerns, and only at moments of such clear, torturous vision does all the craziness and cruelty of our existence become exposed. This opens a door to truth, which you instantly slam shut and press against with all your might, so that it flings open less often. Otherwise, it is unbearable."[56] Blindness meant more than impaired vision. It offered an alternative way for the diarists to envision the world of the blockade, through a shielded version of reality.

A strong example of this appears in a rare openly autobiographical moment in Lidiia Ginzburg's retrospective notes about the blockade. Ginzburg described how, during the first months of the siege, she chose not to wear her glasses in order to distance herself from the devastation around her. Then, when her spectacles broke in spring 1942, she wrote, "the world was wiped out, extinguished, as were many aspects of my former life." At first this disoriented her. But Ginzburg soon grew so accustomed to her new vision of the city that, even after the war had ended, she explained, "I didn't want my visual integrity back at all. I had a madman's fear that all this would be coming to an end. After all, that would mean the end of the life I was now leading, a strange, simple existence, stripped to the bare minimum with its agony and intense relief. A complex, difficult process of restoring normal or apparently normal life was going to begin, with all its tedious desires."[57] Ginzburg felt at home in this world dimmed by her broken glasses. The restoration of her sight meant the restoration of a prior reality that now seemed alien to her. Leningraders attempted to expand or restrict their visual horizons. Such were the optics of survival.

One diarist who experimented extensively with forms and meanings of blindness was Ol'ga Matiushina. As a professional painter, Matiushina was interested in parsing the relationship between impaired vision and creative visualization. She was of two minds on this issue and wrote two texts illustrating each viewpoint. In the diary she kept between 1941 and 1942, Matiushina thematized sightlessness as a boon to her creative self-expression. However, in the autobiographical novella she wrote concurrently, Matiushina presented blindness as an impediment to expression. In an unusual move, Matiushina wrote her diary in the third person and attributed her experiences to a fictional heroine she called Evgeniia Mikhailovna. Still, she labeled and presented the work as a diary. By contrast, her novella, *A Song about Life,* presents many of the same events and conversations but through a first-person narrator.

Both texts use blindness to capture the reconfiguration of Matiushina's body, identity, and perspective under siege. But they do this very differently. According to the diary, the fictionalized heroine, Evgeniia Mikhailovna, is partially blind at the start of the war. The diary gives no explanation of how she lost her sight, although age and illness are the implied culprits. In the first entry, the diary's narrator recalls vaguely, "Blindness came. It tore at and destroyed all that was dear to her," especially her urge to capture nature's beauty in painting.[58] *A Song about Life,* however, suggests a causal link between them. Speaking as "I," Matiushina claimed she became blind *because of* the war. This injury, highly dramatized in its description, provides the foundational trauma for the novella. It was a picturesque summer day. Matiushina was sitting in her garden, watching a pretty young girl stroll down the street. Suddenly, the tranquil afternoon was interrupted by the wail of air-raid sirens, followed by a multitude of explosions. Matiushina momentarily lost consciousness but then quickly recovered and ran after the girl, fearing for her safety. She returned home defeated and with her head throbbing. The "blunt physical pain fused with the horrible experience." "In the morning I could not understand—my eyes saw almost nothing . . . I was frightened. 'What is happening to me?' 'I am not blind, am I?' " Three days later, a doctor confirmed Matiushina's suspicions.[59]

The novella blames the blockade for Matiushina's visual disorientation, while the diary suggests that the siege merely preyed on her existing vulnerabilities. These two different presentations of blindness set the diary and novella on different trajectories. According to the novella, Matiushina struggled. *A Song about Life* shows her painstakingly relearning the motor skills needed to walk and write. Frustrated, Matiushina questioned whether a life enshrouded in darkness was worth living: "What will I do blind? Is it possible to live like this? Not to see the sun! For me, not to see the sun! [. . .] 'Such darkness will be the whole world for me now,' I thought. No, it is impossible to bear this. I don't want to give in!"[60] By contrast, in the diary, her invented heroine mastered these tasks quickly and drew inspiration from blindness. Evgeniia Mikhailovna took on dangerous activities like standing guard on watch duty, assisting the local fire brigade and anti-air-raid corps.[61] Blindness stirred her to sacrifice for the common cause.

One moment—which appears in both the diary and novella—illustrated these different conceptualizations of blindness particularly well. It occurred when Natal'ia Vladimirovna (Nal'ia), Evgeniia Mikhailovna's/Ol'ga Matiushina's best friend, gave her a bunch of peonies. As an artist, Evgeniia/Ol'ga was inspired to re-create the bouquet on paper, but she had to develop a new way of seeing and comprehending in order to do so. According to the diary, she succeeded in drawing them. The journal's presentation of this moment abounds with references to sight and luminance, which in turn are inflected with the language of patriotism and victory:

> Red-white, vibrantly delicate, they [the peonies] looked at her and Evgeniia Mikhailovna could not tear herself away from them. [. . .] She could not tear her eyes from them. No matter what else she did or what she thought about, she returned to the flowers and gazed at them for a long time. [. . .] And as she looked to her inner strength, she began to draw. How she drew, she did not know herself. Only she wanted to draw them in such a way that they would be signs of the coming victory of her country, her beloved city. And the flowers were radiant. They shone, trying to help the poor-sighted person to transmit their beauty.
>
> "Look Nal'ia, I drew your flowers almost with my eyes closed. These are flowers of our victory, these are of the defeat of fascist darkness." And Natal'ia Vladimirovna looked at the flowers and the artist: "How grand! You have conquered blindness!" So too will our country conquer the hateful dark clouds of fascism.[62]

Evgeniia Mikhailovna's triumph over blindness foreshadowed almost certain victory over "German darkness." The heroine's political vision was sharp and her willpower tremendous. In fact, she resembled a New Soviet Person who had triumphed over personal and physical obstacles. Matiushina seemingly endowed Evgeniia Mikhailovna with qualities she herself hoped to acquire.

In *A Song about Life,* however, Matiushina emphasized her failure to master herself and her subject. The peonies did not exchange kind glances or words with Matiushina as they did with her alter ego. Rather, drawing them was "torturous" and took two days to complete. It was a modest victory and one that was highly personal, not infused with political significance. In the end, when Nal'ia exclaimed, "You conquered blindness!" Matiushina did not return her enthusiasm. Instead, she vowed this would be her last drawing and reluctantly resolved to become a writer instead.[63] Moreover, she continued to regard blindness as a hindrance. In several postwar statements, Matiushina confessed her dislike for writing and even apologized for her decision to take it up, saying, "the blind cannot and should not write."[64] In her diary and novella, therefore, Matiushina used the theme of blindness to experiment with new ways of envisioning herself—personally, professionally, and physically—in concert and in contradistinction to official models. Between her two works, she both lamented her diminished eyesight and observed that a limited or selective view could be advantageous as a protective shield, as a source of creativity, or as an impulse to sacrifice.

By assaulting vision, the siege altered the hierarchy of the senses, elevating the importance of audition, taste, and smell. Before Matiushina lost her sight, she admitted that her hearing "was very weakly developed," but the blockade forced her "to replace vision with hearing." Sound became the primary mediator of her reality: "At first, in the city noise, I was not able to detect the sound of a gradually approaching car, to catch from what side it was approaching. Slowly I began to distinguish various sounds. Now only my hearing holds meaning for me. Having grown accustomed to feeling life deeply, I wanted to know everything about it as before. I could not read. I had no radio. I walked to the neighbors' or to Kirovskii Prospekt to listen to broadcasts. From questions, random conversations, I tried to learn about life as it had been created by war."[65] Matiushina was determined to make this sensory shift in order to survive and to document the blockade. Because she could no longer study physical appearances or facial expressions, she relied on dialogue, intuition, and imagination "to unlock the psychology of a person." "To be an artist with bad vision is impossible," she observed, "but for a writer sound means a lot." Thanks to these audio cues, she wrote, "once again I learned to see life."[66] Even the title of Matiushina's novella, *A Song about Life,* signals a shift toward audition.

There appears to be less scientific research supporting the idea that starvation damages hearing than there is for vision. Still, this was a subject of inquiry during the siege. Between late 1942 and early 1943, Leningrad's Ear, Nose, and Throat Research Institute mounted eight studies, which tentatively suggested that bombardment and malnutrition impaired Leningraders' audition, often by damaging the vestibule of the ear.[67] The diaries, however, provide more diverse indications as to how the experience of audition seemed to change. Some diarists suffered from hearing impairment, while others claimed that their audition improved out of necessity. The historian Georgii Kniazev and the physician Anna Likhacheva were among those who complained of severe hearing loss. Kniazev became partially deaf from booming explosions and flying shrapnel, and he often hallucinated air-raid sirens. "I still cannot make out whether what I hear is a noise inside my ears or the drone of propellers," he confessed.[68] Likhacheva attributed her diminished hearing to malnourishment, which made her ears ring. "This most frightening noise in my ears grows stronger with physical exertion. It torments me and disturbs my thinking." Likhacheva considered this one of the most debilitating symptoms of starvation.[69]

Other diarists, however, stressed how the blockade ultimately forced the *blokadniki* to cultivate more acute methods of hearing. They documented numerous situations in which survival depended on how well they could hear news broadcasts, air-raid sirens, or the differences between friendly and enemy fire. As with vision, the diarists' meditations on audition were not just physiological but also psychological and political in nature. Some linked their inability to hear to political obstacles, namely, Soviet censorship of the press and post. They referred to the brief and vague Sovinformbiuro reports as "deaf-mute" *(glukhonemye)* because they inhibited understanding.[70] Mariia Konopleva presented the besieged city as a deceptive auditory environment. Cautionary notes appear throughout her journal, especially in her entries from spring and summer 1942, when her hearing began to decline. This was probably due to a combination of prolonged malnutrition and resumed bombardment. Konopleva, however, attributed it to sonic deception. She underscored how official sirens could be erroneous, sounding after the fact or not at all. Radio broadcasts were deliberately misleading or silent about subjects like food shortages and the mounting death toll. Leningraders, she noted, also manipulated the soundscape by spreading false rumors or even playing fake air-raid sirens in order to scatter breadlines and thus improve their position in line. Others deliberately circulated false rumors.[71]

Konopleva's journal reveals both her anxiety and her aptitude for deciphering the sounds of the siege. She, like many diarists, worked to strengthen her powers of audition in order to hear in more meaningful ways. They learned how to interpret official speeches and reports, to anticipate the trajectory of falling shells, and to distinguish between explosions from Soviet antiaircraft guns and from enemy gunfire. The poet Vera Inber claimed that *blokadniki* could deconstruct air raids as one could a concert of Tchaikovsky or Glinka.[72] Konopleva likened the sounds of aerial warfare to a conversation intelligible only to the *blokadniki* with expanded powers of audition. The military and political soundscape of the besieged city necessitated these new "regimes of listening."[73]

Depending on the threat, sometimes the best way to navigate this sonic environment was to embrace some measure of deafness. Irina Zelenskaia, for instance, advocated not just shutting one's eyes but "holding one's ears" to block out the terrifying sounds of artillery fire.[74] Aleksandra Liubovskaia, a professional translator, was legally deaf when the war began. This left her vulnerable to bombardment and to starvation because she had fewer opportunities to work and qualify for larger food rations. Liubovskaia also worried that being deaf limited what she could observe and write about the blockade, so she relied on her children to supply her with information. She sometimes referred to her journal as "our diary."[75] But if deafness made Liubovskaia vulnerable to environmental dangers, it helped her avoid some sociopolitical ones. In the confessional space of the diary, she relayed how she was stopped by a police officer during a raid because she had not gone to a shelter, as she was legally required to do. When confronted, she wrote, "I responded that I was deaf and didn't know what he wanted from me. (It is true that deep down I started to guess what was going on)." Similarly, at work Liubovskaia avoided reprimands for ignoring sirens, for damage done to the library, and for other difficulties. "I diplomatically pretended that I did not know anything about the bombs, and having learned a lesson from the rudeness of several co-workers, I avoided asking questions," she noted on another occasion.[76] In these descriptions of her sensory limitations, Liubovskaia revealed her sensitivity to the political environment. The blockade prompted both new ways of hearing and new incentives for choosing not to hear.

Compared to vision and audition, taste and smell played a smaller role in mediating reality. However, taste and smell were essential because they informed the diarists' attitudes toward food. An obsession with food lies at the heart of every siege diary. Whether monitoring one's food reserves, describing meals, or fantasizing, diarists revealed that eating—as both a social and a physiological experience—was transformed dramatically by the blockade. It touched off a "cooking mania"; even those who previously had little interest in cooking became preoccupied with discovering new ways to prepare food.[77] This required imagination and some measure of self-deception. Successful cooking consisted of transforming seemingly inedible items until they resembled food. The journals abound with "culinary experiments" and recipes for newly discovered edibles like *duranda* (cakes—usually fed to cattle—formed from processing oil from linseed, hemp, or sunflowers); meat jellies concocted from boiling leather belts; soups made from glue, grasses, nettles and dandelions; and pancakes formed from coffee grounds or crushed noodles. Aleksandra Liubovskaia regularly recorded her family's wartime recipes, including a homemade peanut butter her son made from oil paint.[78] Similarly, during January 1942, while the Stalin Factory was inoperative, the engineer Gesel' Gel'fer spent his time obtaining "new specialized skills and learn[ing] new 'substitutes' this [includes] the manufacture of jelly from carpenter's glue." "I have found a new source of protein!" he declared proudly.[79]

This obsession with food prompted many diarists to reflect on the bodily systems that regulated taste and smell. In the absence of wartime scientific experiments on smell and taste, the diaries provide insight into how these senses might have evolved or at least been experienced. Smell and taste are difficult to measure systematically because they are the most malleable, ephemeral, and intimate of the senses. By definition, taste is subjective, not shared.[80] As with vision and audition, there was disagreement in the corpus of diaries as to whether these senses improved or diminished under siege. The doctor Anna Likhacheva studied the evolution of taste among the Leningraders she treated at the Red Banner Factory clinic. She worried that malnutrition had so altered the physiology of their tongues that they were no longer able to discern flavors. In her diary, she hypothesized that the body needed a variety of tastes, not just a number of calories, to quell the sensation of hunger. "In a typical canteen nowadays, they give out noodles or some kind of kasha, pouring over it a broth made of the same stuff, lavishly thinned with water. Here, one's stomach feels full for a very short period of time." The problem, however, was that the entire meal was "dry," "under-salted and flavorless," and did not allay the body's appetite for saltiness or sweetness. "After all of this, there remains a somehow bitter taste in your mouth and dryness of the tongue. This condition persists for two hours after the meal. There is too little saliva, and the sense of taste is noticeably weakened; it is difficult to distinguish between sour and salty [items] and sugar—there is too little sweetness" in the diet of the *blokadniki*."[81] If the taste buds remained understimulated, Likhacheva worried that Leningraders might not recover their full ability to taste.

Other *blokadniki* suggested that their sense of taste had become keener. Intense hunger compelled them to develop an exceptional ability to discern seemingly undetectable tastes and smells. "Our olfactory senses," Elena Kochina observed, "have become quite acute. Now we've learned what sugar, grain, peas, and other 'odorless' goods smell like."[82] Moreover, Lidiia Ginzburg recalled in her *Notes of a Blockade Person,* even in the blandest foods, *blokadniki* "discovered a multitude of novel taste sensations, but nothing recalled so many as bread, which had been hitherto unexplored territory."[83] It was with regard to taste and smell that the diarists drew the strongest contrasts between themselves and their compatriots on the mainland. Unique powers of detection and a deep appreciation for tastes and smells set the *blokadniki* apart and marked them as a community privy to a richer sensory world.

For instance, when the philologist-turned-factory-worker Natal'ia Uskova miraculously came across unexpected sources of food, she pitied her implied reader, who, not being a *blokadnik,* would be unable to taste as fully as she could: "Our future progeny, You will never understand the taste of potatoes. [. . .] Those who didn't experience this feeling will never understand it, and if I stay alive, I don't know whether I myself will be able to conjure up these sensations from memory or if food will once again recede to the background."[84] Uskova expanded on this theme a month later when she described how her husband, a soldier at the Leningrad front, managed to procure a chicken for her. Her reader, she knew, could never understand her rapture because he or she inhabited a different sensory and emotional world: "He who hasn't lived through these sweet moments will remain gruff and will think that he understands the essence of the tale [about the chicken]. We often feel bad, hungry, cold, and sharp-tongued, and for that we understand happiness all the more acutely and fully in a way that is inaccessible to a well-fed citizen. The well-fed [person] eats, gobbles, pigs out, stuffs his face—in a word, he performs the act of putting food into himself. We revel [in eating]; it resembles a liturgy. How strange life is, what joy it can give, suddenly, generously, in the most difficult moment, when it seems that life is becoming unbearable."[85] Here, the sensory acuity that hunger had forced on the *blokadniki* drove a wedge between the island and the mainland. The hungry and the full not only had different diets and rituals of eating; they inhabited different perceptual realms.

This newfound sensory acuity, however, could be dangerous. Natal'ia Uskova and Sof'ia Ostrovskaia observed how an enhanced sense of smell rendered Leningraders vulnerable to the power of memory. "Smell, song, music are great for associations," Uskova observed. When she smelled an old perfume, it conjured up "a whole sliver of life, young, sunny, filled with love. A whole flow of tender memories, of [her] thoughtless, crazy youth" flooded her mind. Intrigued, Uskova searched psychology textbooks for more information about such "associations."[86] Ostrovskaia, by contrast, was pained by her potent sense memories, concerned they might weaken her ability to withstand the hardships of the blockade. Ostrovskaia described one incident when she became overpowered by her sense of smell, overstimulated to the point of hallucination:

> For some reason I opened a bottle of French perfume (Ambre Molinard Paris), took a whiff of it, and suddenly, so sharply and terrifyingly, I started yearning, recalling, understanding, feeling, so precisely, all the frightening and deathly obtuseness and the pettiness of my current life, its senselessness, circularity, sense of doom, and horror.

The tender and already foreign scent of expensive fragrance made me see myself as an animal in a cage, as a wounded bird. I wanted to yell: someone save me . . . I am perishing! . . . Then I recomposed myself and smiled. The olfactory mirages and hallucinations disappeared. My mood reassumed its usual, soldier-like form. One must not recollect. One must not think. One must not read or write poetry. One must not listen to music. Under no circumstances should one touch bottles of foreign perfume, of which I have several.

> I have many tasks to do today
> I must kill my memory completely,
> I must turn my soul to stone
> I must learn to live again.
> Or else . . .[87]

As the fragrance transported Ostrovskaia to another, happier time, it reminded her of her present state of captivity. The siege had reduced her to "an animal in a cage," and the luxury of this foreign perfume exacerbated the primitiveness of her current condition. In order to survive, Ostrovskaia resolved to become like a "stone," to dull her senses and quiet her memory. Yet at the end of this pronouncement, she contradicted herself by recalling a verse from Anna Akhmatova's "Requiem," which at the time was known only to a few of the poet's close friends. The presence of this verse defies Ostrovskaia's resolution not to recite poetry. It suggests that Ostrovskaia was deeply conflicted about how to handle these unpredictable shifts in sense perception and doubted whether she could regain control over her body by becoming numb, blind, deaf, or otherwise impervious.

In sum, the diarists watched with curiosity and concern how their bodies acquired altered powers of vision, audition, olfaction, and taste. Some described their faculties as diminished, others as enhanced. Some of the changes seemed conducive and others maladaptive to survival. What is consistent among diarists is the recognition that these physiological and perceptual changes made them distinct from their prewar selves and from people living outside the ring.

The Unruly Body

As the diarists struggled to navigate their new sensory world, their most combative encounters centered on the sense of touch and their lack of tactility, dexterity, and coordination. This was a phenomenon that Leningrad scientists investigated as well. During the spring of 1942, they noted that vitamin B1 (thiamine) deficiency could slow reflexes and weaken muscles in the legs, fingers, and toes, making it very difficult to control and move one's body.[88] The diarists echoed that they experienced slower reaction times and consistent numbness in their extremities. Writers like Vera Inber and Lidiia Ginzburg particularly bemoaned their trembling, maladroit hands, as each one degenerated into a "paw," a "stump," and finally a clumsy "club-like *(palkoovbraznyi)* implement."[89] Motor reflexes, to say nothing of refined movements, now had to be willed consciously.

The battle to control the body raised questions about the mind-body connection. Ginzburg reflected that starvation had rendered the *blokadnik* "a graphic embodiment of philosophical dualism."[90] This Cartesian dilemma was at the forefront of Ol'ga Matiushina's mind as she struggled to stand, walk, or even move her head: "It was impossible to withstand this dualistic feeling," she declared. "Death is better!"[91] The body, Aleksandra Liubovskaia despaired, refused to obey her commands. "My arms and legs poorly obey the orders of my brain. My arm movements are imprecise. My steps are not rhythmic, poorly measured. Because of the cold, after a bit of walking, my limbs refuse to obey."[92] Awkward yet defiant, Liubovskaia's legs sapped her physical and mental stamina. They joined forces with the cold, the darkness, and other hostile elements of the environment. Without control over her body, Liubovskaia could not go to work and collect her rations. She could not survive. She dreaded her regular trips to the local housing bureau or the grueling five kilometers to the factory where she worked, calling it "a loathsome and exhausting journey," a "death march," and "a great migration."[93] Liubovskaia likened her inability to walk to existing "without legs," a powerful statement of transfiguration.[94] Ivan Savinkov regularly trekked the distance from his apartment to the Molotov Factory until he was no longer able to make his legs move. Pain and weariness combined to make each step "awkward" at best. At worst, he felt that he had lost ownership over his own body:

"You get the impression that your legs are not yours but belong to another," he observed in February 1942.[95] Each step alerted him to a growing disconnect between his external body and his "self," which apparently resided somewhere else.

During the winter of 1941–42, the shop floor under Savinkov's charge fell into disorder, but without the command of his arms and legs, there was little he could do. "My skin has begun to atrophy, my hands resemble the hands of a seventy-year-old man."[96] And after suffering a terrible bout of scurvy in March 1942, Savinkov literally had to learn to walk again. His diary chronicles each stage of this fight to reassert himself over his body—from the terrifying experience of "lying helpless, unable [to] move," to his agonizing first steps. It also helped him to formulate a recovery strategy. In his journal, Savinkov calculated that he must take more than 10,000 steps a day, even though he could manage no more than twenty before collapsing in exhaustion.[97] Savinkov was reduced to crawling. But some diarists could not even crawl. In one of Uskova's final entries, scrawled upside down in a frantic hand, she exclaimed, "I am chained to the bed!"[98] She was being held hostage not just by enemy troops but also by her own body.

The body part that was the most aggressive and most successful in resisting the diarists' attempts at self-mastery was the stomach. The legs were leaden and clumsy, but the stomach was willful and defiant. To describe their stomachs, the diarists frequently made recourse to personification—a move that underscored the splitting of body and mind, which they experienced. The diarists breathed life into their stomachs at the same time that they bemoaned their own loss of vitality and humanity.

As the military enemy faded from view during the winter of 1941–42, the internal enemy of the stomach loomed large. Zinaida Sedel'nikova explained that the "stomach war" (*zheludochnaia voina*) was a battle she fought and lost on a daily basis. For the medical student, this experience was a great revelation about the nature of human anatomy. "I never thought that a hungry stomach could dictate behavior so powerfully," she exclaimed. "I cannot force myself to study the latest chapter of microbiology and am delaying my exam." Sedel'nikova wielded an arsenal of weapons to overcome her stomach's demands, including willpower, imagination, and physical force; but "once again you lose the 'stomach war.' You draw your legs into your stomach, you press a fist into your stomach," but in the end "it demands its own."[99] In this struggle of mind over matter, the latter was usually victorious. Similarly, Ol'ga Matiushina tried to placate her stomach by using various tricks. Like many Leningraders, she divided her bread ration into three portions to create the impression that she ate three meals a day or soaked her bread in water to make it more filling. "But the stomach is poorly convinced by this persuasion," she admitted. "The body demands attention, and the will ought to obey its requests."[100] By depicting the stomach in this way, the diarists suggested that they were not just fighting the impulse to eat but were at war with themselves.

In a few cases, this stomach war was politically charged. A handful of diarists likened the stomach to a political actor—a dictator, a Soviet bureaucrat, or a rival to Soviet power. They would have encountered similarly unyielding Soviet officials in the tense political atmosphere of blockaded Leningrad. It is notable that they tended not to Germanize the stomach but rather characterized it as an internal or domestic enemy. The image of a dictator-stomach appears in Irina Zelenskaia's diary as early as September 1941, by which time "everything [wa]s defined by rations" and "events [we]re experienced only through the stomach."[101] Leningraders "only listen to the little voice of their stomachs," she declared, heedless of any other authority or objective. The party's call for Leningraders to sacrifice themselves, Zelenskaia noted, was overpowered by the stomach's demands to be fed at any cost. The dictatorship of the proletariat was being undermined by what she called "the dictatorship of the stomach."[102] A newly minted party member, Zelenskaia tried to rouse the crowd, but she was drowned out by "the voice of the stomach." "Every day I wreck my voice trying to convince, explain, and reproach." But Leningraders had forgotten the Nazi invasion, "the direct cause of this impoverishment": "When I remind people that we are in a besieged city, they answer me: 'Don't agitate! We should be full!' For me, this wall of obtuseness is the worst of all."[103] Despite Zelenskaia's disdain for what she deemed to be the weakness of the masses, she herself struggled to withstand the demands of her own stomach: "[it] is starting to remind you of itself vigorously."[104]

Ivan Savinkov took this imagery a step further. He described hunger as a ruthless dictator that "made everyone slaves to the stomach itself,

obeying it so that every thought, care, conversation, connection, etc. is
about hunger."[105] His demanding stomach threatened his freedom to think
and act in pursuit of desires other than eating. For Savinkov and others
like Aleksandr Dymov, the chief danger of the dictatorship of the stomach
was thought control. While Savinkov portrayed the stomach as an auto-
crat, Dymov envisioned it as a petty, myopic Soviet functionary, who
forced the *blokadnik* to obey out of a blind determination to follow the
rules. "All thoughts and emotions are subject to its editorial control,"
Dymov wrote, "not only mine. I am constantly aware of this crude inter-
ference of my stomach into my intellectual and emotional sphere."
Dymov, a theatrical director, staged this confrontation of his stomach as
political drama. And he cast his stomach in the role of a Soviet editor,
whom he implored to stop editing his thoughts while he read:

> You take up another book. "Your neighbor, my dear, provides food
> for all kinds of rumors . . ." You must not read any further. "Food!"
> The much-respected editor of my sense organs (my stomach) swiftly
> directs them along the lines of edible associations, although the word
> "food" is clearly used metaphorically in the book. "Grief gnaws at my
> heart," it says on page 35. That is also a metaphor. But my unsophis-
> ticated editor could care less. What is important to him is to evoke
> the act of gnawing fat pieces of roasted meat. [. . .] These are cases of
> the associative influence of the superstructure on the base.
>   "Much respected citizen editor! Comrade Stomach! [. . .] You
> want me to look at everything around with your eyes. You insist on
> that. And in the majority of cases, you succeed. But that's not normal,
> I protest. [. . .] I want to read books and appreciate their content just
> as I did in the past and not in your interpretation and not from your
> narrow, prejudiced viewpoint. I refuse to think of nothing but
> gorging. [. . .] You understand, I want to be a human being. Don't
> stand in the way."[106]

This stomach-censor threatened not only the diarist's freedom of thought
but also his very humanity. Dymov's entry represents a kind of literary
act of rebellion, especially his assertion that food had replaced class conditions as the "base" on which the "superstructure" of Leningrad society
rested. When Adamovich and Granin published excerpts from Dymov's
diary in their seminal work *A Book of the Blockade,* they noted that critics
had labeled this entry too intricate to be authentic—that is, to be conceived

by a mind operating on so little food. It is indeed unusually elaborate compared to other diaries, but it is far from the only mention of a stomach-dictator and a stomach war, which crop up in a number of accounts.

At the core of these battles with the body—whether against tyrannical stomachs or uncooperative legs—was pain. The physical torment of hunger demanded that the diarists, once again, consider whether sensory acuity was advantageous or maladaptive under siege. While the diarists avoided pain, they also avoided becoming too physically and emotionally numb. After all, apathy was one of the most recognizable symptoms of imminent death. Natal'ia Uskova called this "the indifference of the doomed."[107] Zelenskaia, Kochina, and Likhacheva were among the diarists who insisted apathy was a core cause of their sons' or husbands' demise. Therefore, they tried to walk a fine line between remaining aloof to the pain of others without becoming apathetic toward their own fate. "We are strong only in our reserve and our numbness," Irina Zelenskaia declared in May 1942, "only in indifference to our fate and that of other people." This isolation brought her "a soaring calmness in the presence of shelling, deaths, and when face-to-face with perilous dangers."[108] Sofia Ostrovskaia vowed to become "a tin soldier." "I shackle myself in armor, I have a cold, tin shell on me: through touching me, people can get hurt. However, I am no longer hurt by the human touch [of others]."[109] Not unlike the New Soviet Person, Ostrovskaia proclaimed, "I disciplined myself. I mechanized myself." The best way to survive the ring was to draw an even tighter ring around oneself. However, at times she regretted that this hardened approach had left her devoid of human emotion. For instance, when she watched her mother's death agony, the diarist demanded, "where is my heart?"[110]

Even pain could be adaptive in certain situations. Zinaida Sedel'nikova, for instance, came to cherish a paroxysm of pain precisely because it proved she was still alive. In December 1941, after another exhausting shift at Hospital 95, the medical student hiked all the way to the Vyborg District to take an examination at the Second Leningrad Medical Institute. When she finally arrived, Sedel'nikova discovered the institute was closed. She trekked back to the student dormitory, dragging her body along "as though carrying a heavy load": "It kept pressing down, down on me, and I moved my legs with great difficulty." Suddenly everything went black. The next thing Sedel'nikova knew, she was lying in a lorry.

Seated across from her was the soldier who had picked up her lifeless body off the street. Sedel'nikova was only vaguely aware of how she made it back to her dorm room. As she "dropped down onto the edge of the bed," she began to examine herself for vital signs: was she still alive, or was the numbness she felt the torpidity of death? The blockade had reconfigured her body so dramatically that it had thrown her very existence into question. As she lay there, feeling neither alive nor dead, Sedel'nikova began to mourn the loss of her own life.

> Everything around me has lost meaning. It was as if I was steadily gazing at myself, listening attentively, as though I wanted to understand what it means to be alive. Were these symptoms of life reliable? [It was] as if I was standing outside myself and studying all the details of what had occurred but not grasping what was wrong with me . . . and how it could have happened that I was already dead [menia uzhe net]? . . . Immeasurable pity for myself filled my chest, a lump reached my throat, ready to burst into sobs . . .
>   I froze, as though a corkscrew suddenly had pierced my heart. There flashed [a thought]: 'well, now a second death has come for me, only this one is not muted but painful.' [. . .] Suddenly the screw fell out, and in its place a new pain took root . . . faint exhalation became intense inhalation . . . life returned to me. [. . .] I sensed the hellish cold and a painful spasm of my hungry stomach. I am alive![111]

The whole scene—from the moment when she forced her legs to walk to the moment when she checked to see if she was conscious—captures how corporeality evolved under siege. Mystified by these foreign bodily sensations, the medical student had to check her vital signs in order to become "convinced of life." In this task, pain became her ally. Pangs of hunger and cold shocked her back to life and jolted the diarist toward new discoveries about her body. Death convinced her that life, even a painful one, was better than an anesthetized existence in unchartered oblivion.

During the blockade, especially during the winter and spring of 1941–42, the diarists experienced a whole new way of being in and apprehending the world around them. This was because their bodies seemed to operate according to new sensory and physiological principles. They saw, heard, smelled, tasted, felt, and interpreted the world differently than they had before the war. Numerous aspects of their corporeality, from age and gender to sense perception and the functioning of specific appendages and organs, became so altered as to render them new beings.

There is no question that bombardment and starvation brutally assaulted Leningraders' bodies. But the diaries tell a story not just of physical impairment but also of physical alterity that, at times, seemed advantageous in the fight for life. It might appear strange, even offensive, to make such a claim. Still, to dismiss the moments when the diarists marveled at and experimented with their new bodies would be to mischaracterize their narratives. For them, this physical metamorphosis was both tragic and illuminating. And as they struggled first to recognize and then to regain control of their bodies, they interrogated notions of gender, age, sense perception, pain, and the mind-body connection. Their accounts suggest that a new experience of embodiment, in fact a new body, developed under siege.

A powerful articulation of physical alterity appears in the diary of Sof'ia Ostrovskaia. In an entry from February 1942, she joyously announced that running water had been restored to her apartment. In the midst of her celebration, Ostrovskaia reproached her European readers, who, she was sure, would not understand her joy or her ability to have survived without running water for so long. The reason for their confusion, she proclaimed, was that these besieged people were altogether different from Europeans. They were armed with unique powers of resistance, and they operated with six senses, not five: "You, all manner of Europeans, can you really understand this fully, you who have not known the hunger and collapse of 1919–20, you who do not apprehend with your petty bourgeois five senses what the Russian citizen endures having entered for the second time 1919 in 1942? Yes, yes, dearest Europe, you do not know that among us there is developing—or perhaps already has developed—a sixth sense."[112] Leningraders, here cast as Russians, had honed their sixth sense during two sieges of their city first in 1919 and then in 1941.[113] They were not advanced people, distinguished by heightened powers of rationality and mastery as the Soviet regime proclaimed. In fact, they were ancient. They had inherited this unique sensibility, she claimed, from their legendary ancestors, the Scythians: "We are very poor, very dirty, and very ignorant. We are clumsy. We are rude and cruel. But we are Scythians; we are Scythians, bearers of a new sixth sense. Just think about that, dear Europeans! Are you not frightened of us? [. . .] You are older than us, you are much, oh so much, smarter. In us, however, still lives an ancient human being, one wise in instinct and *living* then by his sixth sense."[114] Ostrovskaia presented the *blokadniki* as unique beings, transfigured by sieges, both in 1919 and in 1941. They were not merely dehumanized shadows of their prewar selves, nor were they models of New Soviet People. From this foundation of altered sense perception, the diarists looked to other concepts from dictator-stomachs to the Scythians in order to characterize their new bodies. The world of the siege reconstituted the body, and the siege body in turn reconstituted the world that diarists perceived around them.[115]

These changes in body consciousness quickly raised questions about self-consciousness. What happened when they put pen to paper and tried to describe the enigmatic figure that the mirror reflected back? This challenge of presenting the besieged self is the subject of the next chapter.

Chapter Three

The Elusive I

O N 14 APRIL 1942, the architect Esfir' Levina returned home after spending two weeks in a clinic being treated for influenza. Levina had regained her physical strength, but her mental health seemed to have deteriorated during her hospital stay. In the clinic, Levina watched other patients "losing their character" as they slipped into death. Consumed by grief and hunger, they not only forgot the basic details of their lives; they lost all sense of themselves. Haunted by these experiences, Levina wrote longingly of a day when "*distrofiia* is no longer the fashion," "the country is on the rise," and the *blokadnik* "sets out on a journey in search of himself, and through various circumstances he finds pieces of his 'I': his sex, age, honor, morality, attachments, and habits. He reassembles himself, and the result is something entirely new (a reforging by war)." This, Levina explained, was the best-case scenario: the *blokadnik* would successfully recover "pieces" of his self even though the act of reconstructing them might render him an "entirely new" person. The worst-case scenario, she feared, was that his "individual traits might not be found" at all. Someday, when the siege was over, Leningraders would have to reassemble the pieces of their "I," and this formidable task could "lead either to tragedy or to a complete regeneration" of the self.[1]

Members of Leningrad's medical community shared Levina's concern about the effects of extreme isolation, bombardment, and starvation on selfhood. One of wartime Leningrad's leading scientists, Mikhail Vasil'evich Chernorutskii, sketched a clinical picture of the *blokadnik* consistent with Levina's observations. He explained that starvation "left its stamp" on a person by "wiping out the individual qualities of personality" and creating either "a major or minor degradation of the self *[lichnost']*."[2] Chernorutskii's remarks highlight the mutually constitutive relationship between body and self-concept, a connection that has been analyzed in a variety of disciplines. The literary scholar John Eakin and the neurologist Antonio Damasio, for instance, have argued that the body and the autobiographical impulse depend on and regulate each other. Narrative and biological processes together create "stability in the human individual through the creation of a sense of identity."[3] Conversely, "when the 'I' is ruined, one's world is destroyed irreparably," the diarist Georgii Kniazev observed.[4] The story of the self is contingent on the story of the body—its neural sequences, homeostatic systems, physiological functions—and vice versa.

Did the practice of life writing help the diarists' reconcile and reassemble the "I," as Levina had hoped? Many siege diarists alluded to the destabilization of the self under siege and struggled to reconstruct themselves textually. In this chapter, I focus on the efforts of two diarists who penned especially vivid and uniquely literary articulations of this phenomenon: sixteen-year-old Elena Mukhina and Ol'ga Matiushina, a professional painter who was fifty-five at the time of Germany's invasion.

The concepts of self and subjectivity have been extensively debated by scholars. The notion that the self exists as a knowable, unified, or stable entity is highly disputed. "I" is hardly ever a straightforward evocation of a definitive or fixed self-concept because the ways that we discuss and represent ourselves shift depending on our historical moment, our immediate circumstances, and our audience.[5] By using the term "self" in reference to the diaries, I do not purport to have access to the authors' inner selves, nor do I make any ontological claims about the nature of the self as such. A diary, like a mirror, does not grant admittance to the inner self but reflects a particular image. The siege journals offer only textual remnants of Leningraders' self-reflections. My argument and analysis are based on these narrative *representations* of self.

Despite vast differences in the backgrounds, abilities, and life stages of Mukhina and Matiushina, they used similar strategies to convey a growing alienation from the self during the siege. Two self-distancing techniques stand out. First, they made extensive use of devices associated with fiction in order to capture the ordeal of self-transformation through a broader literary repertoire. Second, they refrained from consistently saying "I" and instead endeavored to write their life stories from an outside perspective. Using both techniques, Mukhina eventually converted her journal into a novella about herself, whereas Matiushina penned virtually her whole diary from the perspective of her fictionalized heroine, Evgeniia Mikhailovna. As a result of these two moves, their journals read simultaneously as document and fiction.[6] They bring together the documentary authority associated with diaries and the creative freedom of the novel in order to showcase multidimensional and conflicted aspects of the self under siege. Mukhina and Matiushina depicted the self with both intimacy and detachment, maintaining an uneasy balance between saying and avoiding "I." And, as a form, the diary was sufficiently flexible to allow their multiple self-presentations to coexist on the page.

Why did Mukhina and Matiushina incorporate elements of fiction and third-person narration into their wartime accounts? There is no evidence from their earlier writings that Mukhina and Matiushina hid their "I" as a matter of routine. This decision appears to have been brought on primarily (although maybe not exclusively) by the blockade. Their inconsistent approach to the "I" reflects a larger uncertainty about how to represent a self under duress. Matiushina's physical strength and vision were waning before the war, but the invasion deeply unsettled her sense of purpose and identity. She began to parse the self in the pages of her diary as early as June 1941. Over time, blindness and starvation exacerbated her uncertainty about who she was and what role she should occupy in society. By contrast, sixteen-year-old Mukhina's inquiry into the self began a few months into the siege, after she was overcome by hunger and isolation.

By making recourse to fictionalization and third-person narration, the diarists may have hoped to bring some measure of control or coherence to self and story.[7] Ultimately, however, their accounts underscore the difficulty of doing so. By frequently switching between narrative persons and staging confrontations between them, Mukhina and Matiushina presented a self that was disjointed and unstable. In their accounts, "the self," to borrow a phrase from the traumatologist Jeffrey Kauffman, "is understood to be *that which fragments* in traumatic loss."[8] Mukhina's and Matiushina's wartime writings vividly dramatize how self-concepts could crack and splinter under the blockade's assault.

One might argue that Mukhina and Matiushina had other motivations for incorporating fiction and avoiding "I." Perhaps they were trying to fashion new Sovietized selves that were more collectivist in nature. Jochen Hellbeck has argued that, in the 1930s, Soviet diarists often avoided "I" in an attempt to eliminate their individualistic tendencies and "align" themselves with the collective.[9] Once trapped inside the ring, however, Mukhina and Matiushina did not seem intent on purging their individual traits but rather on trying to maintain some semblance of self in the face of war. They avoided "I" but did not cleanly substitute it for "we." Another possibility is that Mukhina and Matiushina eschewed "I" to shield themselves from reprisals for what they had written. That is, they may have tried to dissociate themselves from their texts and their contents. This too seems unlikely. Both journals bear their authors' signatures, a sign of approval and ownership. In addition, both accounts contain numerous criticisms of the regime, some of which are articulated in the *first* person. While many diarists disguised their critical attitudes by attributing them to others, they usually did not take this additional step of consistently writing about the self as an "other." Fear alone does not explain this move.

The Diary of Elena Mukhina

When Germany invaded, Elena Vladimirovna Mukhina (1924–91) had just completed the eighth grade level at School 30. Because her biological mother, Mariia Mukhina, was chronically ill, Mukhina lived with her aunt and adoptive mother, Elena Bernatskaia, and a family friend, the grandmotherly Azaliia Konstantinovna "Aka" Krums-Strauss. All three women died in the first year of the siege, a staggering loss for the young

diarist. Researchers at the Historical Institute of the St. Petersburg branch
of the Academy of Sciences have uncovered much about Mukhina's biography, including the facts that she managed to be evacuated in summer
1942 and later pursued careers in industry and in the arts.[10] From an early
age, Mukhina aspired to become either a zoologist or a writer. In her diary,
she sketched animals and drafted various compositions. Despite her
youth, uneven spelling, and occasionally poor marks on assigned essays,
Mukhina's diary is highly literary. It blends conventional dated entries
with creative works including poems, short stories, and a novella.

During the first months of the blockade, Mukhina described feeling
"tortured" by a deep sense of uncertainty. Frustrated by the lack of information about the city and front, she repeated over and over, "I understand nothing."[11] She became even more disoriented as she began to lose
the people closest to her. In July 1941, her biological mother died.[12] That
summer and fall, she lost friends to evacuation and many classmates to
the restructuring and eventual closure of city schools. Without her regular school routine and personal contacts to ground her, Mukhina's sense
of purpose began to falter. Then, in the winter of 1942, Aka and Bernatskaia died within months of each other. The entry Mukhina wrote after
her adoptive mother's death on 7 February 1942 resounds with grief. "How
hard it is to be alone. After all, I am only seventeen. I am completely inexperienced in life. Who will advise me now? Who will teach me how to
live now? I am surrounded by strangers, and everyone is indifferent to
me. They all have their own concerns. God, how will I live alone? No, I
can't even imagine it."[13] After she became an orphan, Mukhina rarely attended school, and except for a few days in March 1942 when a friend's
family took her in, she lived alone. Her world increasingly became one of
the mind—a space that could be more confining than that of the blockaded city.

During the solitary months, Mukhina yearned for companionship and
guidance, afraid she could not survive without them. Diary writing became her primary form of sociability, and her journal grew more conver-
sational in tone. Mukhina wrote heart-wrenching letters to her departed
mother, distant relatives, and the city of Leningrad in its pages. She en-
tertained her journal with jokes and appealed to it for advice. "How hard
it is to be alone. No one to tell my thoughts, concerns, and sorrows. In

this regard, however, my diary helps me a lot."[14] "My dear, invaluable friend, my diary," she continued on another occasion, "I have only you, you are my only guide. I have only you in which to preserve my sad story." Later, as she tried to decide whether to be evacuated, Mukhina lamented, "dear diary, what a pity that you can't give me advice."[15]

Alongside these entreaties, Mukhina wrote poetry and creative prose. She penned several "story-fantasies" *(rasskazy-fantazii),* as she called them, in which she invented new personas and circumstances for herself. She crafted them about her ideal home and her future professional life, but most of her story-fantasies focus on escaping from Leningrad. Mukhina composed the first such story in October 1941, two months into the blockade.[16] Upon studying a postcard that her (then deceased) biological mother had sent from Piatigorsk three years before, Mukhina recalled a time during the winter of 1940 when she and her mother dreamt of a holiday on the Volga. Suddenly, the reader finds Mukhina and her mother lunching in a comfortable railway car, while a speeding locomotive, the Red Star Express, carries them toward freedom:

> I remember how my mother and I had resolved to travel somewhere in the summer. And this will still happen. Mama and I still will enter a comfy carriage [. . .] and soon that happy moment will come when the train will depart, leave the glass dome of the station *[vogzal (sic)],* and break free. And we will speed off into the distance, far, far away, we will sit at a little table and eat something tasty and know that ahead await us great amusements, delicious things, unfamiliar places, and nature with its blue sky, greenery, and flowers. Ahead of us, every pleasure awaits, each one better than the last. And we will talk, looking at how Leningrad floats away into the distance behind us. That city where we endured so much, suffered so much, where we sat hungry in a cold room and listened attentively to the thunder of the *zenitki* [antiaircraft guns] and the hum of enemy planes. And we will brush aside these recollections as if they were a nightmarish dream. We will redirect our gaze ahead, somewhere in the distance, to where the Red Star Express is rushing us.

In this entry, which emulates a travel narrative, Mukhina endeavored to write herself out of the ring. The text moves smoothly between diaristic, memoiristic, and fictional modes, with only shifts in tense to signal each transition. First she moved from past to future tense and then brought her fantasy even closer to reality by switching to the present tense: "Mama and I are looking out the window and, goodness, how happy we are. Memories repeatedly fly to my mind, and I recall them and delight in the fact that one can only recollect this now, that all of this has already past, that it will never return. [. . .] Everything glitters and comes together on this first day of celebration."[17] Through the Red Star Express, Mukhina tried to push the siege into the past and usher in a better future.

The story-fantasy draws numerous parallels between the shifting physical and mental landscapes of Mukhina's world. The train carried her through space and time, to the end of the war. Gazing out the window, she glimpsed hills and fields scarred from battle, trenches, bomb craters, and bodies. Mukhina and her mother stared at these signs of destruction, but already they had forgotten the siege. This may be the most fantastical feature of this story-fantasy. "Mama and I will stare unthinkingly at the empty, grass-covered hillsides, but already we will see nothing there that reminds us of the war we experienced. Although recent, everything that occurred is in the past, those historic days when a breakthrough was achieved and the Germans stopped advancing, when the Germans fell back and started to retreat, when the Germans fled, when we entered Berlin, when the last volley was fired from the guns, when the last shell exploded, when the last rifle was discharged. Those days [. . .] already have floated behind us, melting away and covering themselves in the haze of distant and gray-colored Leningrad."[18] The tale expresses conflicting impulses to escape and engage Leningrad, to forget and remember. In the first part of the story, Mukhina delighted that war had become a mere memory, whereas in the latter part, she and her mother were unable to remember it. By setting these past, present, and futuristic configurations of herself in dialogue—the Mukhina who was pained by "how much the city has suffered," the Mukhina who witnessed the war's end, and the Mukhina who rode past obliviously—the diarist simultaneously inhabited different temporalities and epistemological positions. Moreover, she forced them to confront each other on the page.[19] Blending elements of short story, diary, and memoir together, Mukhina transgressed the limitations of genre as well as of time and space in order to create a new reality for herself.

Mukhina gave this story to Bernatskaia to read, and her adoptive mother enthusiastically encouraged her to develop it further. But Mukhina confided to her diary, "I do not want to write any more of it," and resolved to study more instead.[20] Yet she did evoke the Red Star Express when her thoughts turned to escape. "What do I want?" she asked herself. "Only one thing: that the days fly by one after the other like telegraph poles past the window of an express train. If only these hard winter days would fly by faster, faster, faster. If only spring, its warmth and greenery, would hurry up. Events, come and unfold before us like frames on a screen. Hands of the clock, spin faster, faster, faster."[21] Literary scholars typically stress the "immediacy of the diary idiom" as one of the features that distinguish it from autobiography. Compared to the autobiographer, who is at greater liberty to direct the narrative away from the present, the diarist is "shortsighted," Roger Cardinal has claimed.[22] But through devices like the train, Mukhina worked to overcome this shortsightedness, to obtain a new perspective and usher in a brighter future.

Mukhina returned to the Red Star Express again in April 1942 after Bernatskaia's death and while she was trying to evacuate. In this iteration of the fantasy, many details are the same—the expansive sky, exhilarating ride, cozy train compartment, and abundant food. But now the train was more than a metaphor; it represented the possibility of a real escape. The story begins with Mukhina riding on Tram 9 traveling to the Finland Railway Station, where she would board an evacuation train. While glancing at the buildings, landmarks, and faces receding into the background, Mukhina proclaimed, "Good-bye, Leningrad. Look at how people on the tram platform look at us. They are probably thinking how jealous they are of us or saying, 'good riddance, there will be more bread for us!'" Mukhina's use of "we" in this story identifies her with a new collective, not the *blokadniki* but the evacuees. Mukhina bound her "I" to this new collective so tightly that the *blokadniki* now appeared strange to her. Through the tram window, Mukhina spotted a young girl in the crowd. Young, wraith-like, and clad in white, the girl resembled Mukhina during the winter of 1941–42. The girl was so preoccupied with securing her next meal that she did not even notice the departing tram. "How many times I [. . .] like she," Mukhina reflected, "walked down this very street, carrying a doctor's certificate [for extra food]. The only differences were

that it was winter, then everything was covered with snow and now it is
spring, May, ahead you can see flowering trees . . ."²³ The wintry under-
tones of the female figure in this scene clash with the signs of spring that
Mukhina was able to detect from aboard the tram. As a passenger,
Mukhina glimpsed the beautiful sky and the budding flowers lining the
path ahead of her, while the *blokadniki* remained fixated on food, blind
to these small indications of renewal and rebirth.

This imagined evacuation sharpened Mukhina's vision of her ideal
future and of what she would leave behind—her former struggles, attitudes,
and mind-set. Alighting from the tram, Mukhina boarded the train that
finally carried her out of the ring and beyond the patterns of thought that
consumed the *blokadniki:* "The train moves faster and faster. How grand.
I open my suitcase, cut off a big slice of bread, look out the window, and
eat. I am full. In the train station before our departure, they fed us well:
a bowl of soup with noodles. The soup is thick, thick, and pea kasha, a
whole tin of it. I still have some kasha left. They also gave us 800 grams
of blood sausage and a kilo of bread—that is until we reach Ladoga. And
there they will give us hot food. That is how wonderfully I have imagined
leaving Leningrad. But in fact I am still sitting here with my feet under a
warm blanket. [. . .] My stomach is not very full. Honestly, I would eat
anything right now, anything at all. But I have nothing."²⁴ This evacuation
fantasy is populated by multiple self-constructions. They inhabit the
tram, the platform, the train, and a cold Leningrad apartment. Even before Mukhina abruptly burst the fantasy with the final image of her hungry
and huddled under a blanket, she inadvertently revealed her status as a
besieged person through her detailed descriptions of food. Despite her
efforts to write new circumstances for herself, she was still caught up in
the struggle for food, warmth, and freedom.

Mukhina fantasized about escaping hunger as well as Leningrad. Like
her vignettes about the Red Star Express, her stories about food are fan-
ciful but also convey a profound sense of self-fragmentation. In November
1941, Mukhina received a wondrous birthday gift of fifty grams of chocolate. Although she planned to ration the sweets, she could not stop herself from immediately eating them. To convey her "shame," Mukhina cast
herself in the role of a bloodthirsty monster devouring her helpless victims, the chocolates. "The poor things," she explained, tragically "met

their end in my unscrupulous mouth." "It seems I could have left those miserable victims in peace, but instead they were doomed to be eaten, so it would not have hurt to let them live a day or so longer. But no, I could not wait. [. . .] I could not be stopped until I devoured every edible thing within my grasp." As she condemned and dehumanized herself, she humanized the chocolates: "My bar, beautiful bar of real English chocolate, where are you? Why did I eat you? You looked so enticing that I should have only feasted my eyes on you, but [instead] I gobbled you up. What a pig I am."[25] This story about a starving girl's desperate desire for food reverberates ironically with the siege situation. Just as Leningraders' emaciated bodies attacked and fed on themselves, Mukhina launched this moral assault on herself for lacking willpower. The victim cast herself as the aggressor. By partitioning Mukhina into subject and object, villain and victim, the story dramatizes another aspect of the internal struggle that the blockade unleashed within the *blokadniki*.

In April 1942, Mukhina stopped writing story-fantasies and began reworking her diary into a novella. She played with the expectations of her reader by writing her first entry in this new mode and only later announcing, "I decided to now write my diary in a new form, from the third person in the manner of a novella. Such a diary can be read as a book."[26] This decision came at a particularly trying time—"the hardest days of my life"—when the young orphan was struggling for companionship, bigger rations, and permission to evacuate. "From now on, life will be hard on me," she reflected. "I am so unhappy, so desperately unhappy. No one cares about me. I have been left all alone in the world."[27] To chronicle these difficult days, Mukhina used a detached third-person voice. This move split the self and fostered dialogue between various aspects of it. At the same time, Mukhina preserved the dated-entry structure of the diary, so that her text reads both as novella and diary—a diary about someone else.

The novella marks the apex of Mukhina's self-distancing and self-study. It stands out from her earlier entries in its tone, pacing, and content. The novella is structured around a plot propelled by events and activities. Most sentences begin with action-focused phrases like "Lena went" or "Lena visited." By contrast, her earlier entries were penned in a stream-of-consciousness style and driven by emotional developments more than by events or actions. The intense interiority and the air of raw, unfiltered emotion in her early entries are absent from the novella.

Why did Mukhina disappear her "I"? Given that she did so at a very traumatic point in the siege, Mukhina may have hoped to distance herself from her pain or become her own companion and counselor. The literary scholar Robert Folkenflik has proposed that authors present the self as an other in order to shield, elevate, historicize, or ridicule themselves.[28] Other scholars suggest that writers employ such self-distancing in order to gain more narrative flexibility as storytellers. By alternating between narrative persons, they can circumvent the limitations that any one literary mode imposes on self-presentation.[29] Moreover, they can make freer use of stock scenes and of characters that "condense a whole group of relationships" rather than draw only from real life.[30]

Mukhina's novella lends support to both these psychological and literary explanations. This can be seen in her entry for 2 May 1942. It presents Lena sitting on a park bench trying to read but distracted by a group of children playing nearby. The sight of their joy prompts Lena to reflect on her own tragic childhood: "Lena thought, well they are little children now, and when they reach her age, they will be happier than she was and in general they will have their youth! Light and happy. They will not have to go through all that she has experienced. Their parents will not die, yes, they will be happier."[31] The element of invention, while certainly present in Mukhina's previous entries, is quite pronounced in this scene. This incident may have been real, but it has a stock quality and the symbolism is very transparent: the children represent Lena's lost youth. Childhood, especially one free from responsibility, suffering, and loss, passed Lena by. Shadowed in melancholy tones of winter, Lena sits alone while the children play in warm sunshine. As she watches them, she grasps a book in her hand, which suggests she still clings to text as a way to connect with the world outside herself. However, despite her efforts, she can neither read nor interact with the children—a double failure to overcome her solitude. This scene presents Mukhina in several guises: the lonely orphan, the carefree child she wished to have remained, and the knowing narrator. It allows her to inhabit multiple life stages, emotional states, and epistemological perspectives.

The novella also is self-effacing, literally and metaphorically. Its narrator watches Lena with a critical eye, pointing out her mistakes and naïveté.[32] On 1 May 1942, Mukhina's narrator peers critically into Lena's prewar life, reproaching her for not sufficiently appreciating simple pleasures like sharing a meal with her mother and Aka. In contrast to the scene in the park, the narrator suggests Lena *did* have a carefree youth but took it for granted:

> At the time, Lena did not value it. [. . .] It seemed to her that there was nothing special about having her Aka and mama. [. . .] And it is only now that she has lost Aka and mama that she really values all of her past life. [. . .] Yes, fate has taught her a much-deserved lesson, although perhaps too severely. Now, contemplating all of this, Lena said to herself, "Let this be a lesson to you, you will value every crumb, you will know the value of everything, and it will be easier for you to live in this world. 'There is no bad without good,' the wise Russian proverb says." Of course, after this "school of life," the future [begins]. It will become easier for Lena to live. And not only for her. Postwar life will be easy, happy, and productive for all Soviet citizens, who have lived through this horrible time.[33]

The narrator points out Lena's past mistakes but also tries to lift her spirits in a variety of ways. It paraphrases Stalin's adage that "life has become easier" and notes that Lena's suffering is not unique and that she might find solace in the collective struggle. The narrator also draws on folk wisdom and more general notions about the virtues of sacrifice and suffering. This suggests that a combination of moral, cultural, and ideological influences helped Mukhina find comfort and determination to keep fighting for her life. Mukhina had long hoped for someone to give her advice; eventually she invented this narrative persona to fill that need. Her narrator speaks in an authoritative, parental tone, and its foresight and perspective place it outside the ring. Mukhina's storyteller does not resemble a *blokadnik* but rather an older and wiser version of herself.

A final example of how Mukhina showcased the multidimensional and conflicted aspects of her self consists of two mirror scenes in her last few entries. She wrote the first scene about Lena ("she") in the style of her novella, but in the second, she used "I." In the first scene, written on 2 May

1942, Lena noted that Leningraders were beginning to pay more attention to their outward appearance, and she worried about how she might appear to others, especially men. Glancing into the mirror, Lena "noted with satisfaction" that "her face was no longer as frightening as it had seemed before," even though "her body had really grown thin, just bones, and nothing remained of her ample breasts."[34] Heartened by these improvements, Lena resolved to take greater pains with her hygiene and clothing.[35]

A few weeks later, Mukhina inspected herself in the glass once more. But this time she barely recognized her reflection, let alone any improvements. She returned to the first person to pen this, her final entry:

> Already my brain is unable to respond to anything, I live as if in a half dream. I am becoming weaker by the day, and my last reserves of strength are declining with each hour. [. . .] To be honest, it is quite ridiculous [smeshno]: after all, I am not some kind of invalid, neither an old man nor an old woman. [. . .] Meanwhile, I take a look at myself, at what I have started to resemble. An indifferent, melancholy expression, I look like a Level III Invalid. I can scarcely shuffle along, and it is difficult for me to go up three steps. And I am not making all of this up or exaggerating. I really do not recognize myself. [. . .] Earlier, perhaps a month ago, during the day I had sharp pangs of hunger, and I developed the energy to find something to eat. For an extra bit of bread, something else to eat, I would have gone to the ends of the earth, but now I almost do not feel hunger, I generally don't feel anything at all.[36]

In this final entry, Mukhina returned to the "I" but for the purpose of showing its elusiveness. She was unable to recognize that figment of her self, which had transformed to a "ridiculous" degree. Mukhina was so disconnected from this figure that she felt suspended between states of consciousness—in a "half dream," asleep and awake, alive and dead, and unable to "feel anything at all."

The two-week gap between the first and second mirror scenes may account for the despondent tone of the second one. Mukhina ("I") alluded to a shift, stating that she no longer had the strength to search for food. Her health may have deteriorated substantially between these entries. It is also possible that the contrast between these scenes stems from their different narrative modes. The novella highlights how Lena appeared to outsiders—the narrator, the reader, or other Leningraders. The diary illuminates her inner emotional state. And Mukhina and Lena had different outlooks on siege, survival, and self.

This difference in perspective becomes especially apparent at the very end of this final entry, when Mukhina concluded both diary and novella. She provided very different endings to each one. After noting how alienated she felt from her reflection in the mirror, Mukhina ("I") went on to remind herself that evacuation was imminent and the blockade would soon be over for her. There is a sense of resolution to Mukhina's story. Then the diarist returned to Lena's story but without providing it any closure. The last image the reader has of Lena features her busily attending to the evening meal, "boiling some soup from nettles and meat."[37] Lena remains inside the ring and immersed in the present. In a way, the two endings bring Mukhina's story-fantasy to fruition. Mukhina was evacuated and left behind Lena—that girl in white—standing on the train platform and planning her next meal. To the very last lines, therefore, this journal illuminates the problem of self-representation under siege. After evacuating in June 1942, Mukhina did not continue her diary, even though she had blank pages left in her notebook.[38] The project of parsing the self became less pressing outside the ring.

The Diary of Ol'ga Matiushina

Ol'ga Konstantinovna Matiushina (1885–1975) was fifty-five when the war began. She was the widow of the artist Mikhail Vasil'evich Matiushin and a well-connected member of the Soviet intelligentsia. In the years before the 1917 revolution, Matiushina studied at St. Petersburg's Psycho-Neurological Institute, and she joined the Bolshevik movement and worked for the party's underground press. Tsarist police arrested her twice for these activities. Matiushina then began a career as a painter, and in the 1930s, she worked on the Agricultural Exhibition in Moscow. She returned to Leningrad shortly before the German invasion and penned her remembrances of the writers Gorky and Mayakovsky. In spite of this work, Matiushina often cast herself as an amateur author, claiming she learned to write during the war and as a result of becoming blind.[39] The manuscript of her diary, which friends and relatives recopied into a clearer hand, covers the first year of the blockade and was given to Istpart in November 1943. It was certified by the author's signature and promise of authenticity. After the war, Matiushina was decorated with the Order of the Red Banner. She went on to write several books on a variety of topics.

Matiushina labeled her manuscript a diary, but it is an unconventional one. The text is structured both by dated and undated sections. It also contains several short stories. A few entries are out of chronological order, and it is unclear if they were mislaid or added retrospectively.[40] The diary conveys an even stronger sense of fictionalization than Mukhina's. It is possible that Matiushina considered her account a literary work more than a diary. Indeed, she produced two major pieces based on the diary manuscript. In 1943, she published a collection of revised excerpts from the diary under the title "Notes" in the journal *Star (Zvezda).* In 1946, she published *A Song about Life,* which she called "an autobiographical novella." Unlike the diary manuscript or "Notes," *A Song about Life* covers the full period of the siege, 1941–44.

In the diary manuscript, "Notes," and novella, Matiushina retold the same set of experiences, each time from a different perspective and narrative position. Together, these texts showcase Matiushina's reluctance to say "I" and claim her experiences as her own. Except for a few uses of "I," the diary manuscript is written in the third person about a fictionalized heroine, Evgeniia Mikhailovna. Matiushina never revealed that Evgeniia Mikhailovna was a literary creation; she "hid and dispersed the narrative 'I'" to an even greater extent than Mukhina did.[41] As a result, Matiushina's diary manuscript reads as a chronicle of someone else, perhaps a friend or neighbor. Matiushina not only masked her own identity but also used pseudonyms for other people mentioned in the manuscript, including that of her close friend the artist Mariia Vladimirovna Ender (1897–1942), called Natal'ia (Nal'ia).[42]

Matiushina's 1943 "Notes" also revolve around Evgeniia Mikhailovna, and in terms of content, they are based on the diary manuscript. As the more ambivalent title suggests, the "Notes" are structured more loosely; the textual installments appear in chronological order but stripped of their dated headings. Even though Evgeniia Mikhailovna is the protagonist of "Notes," Matiushina used a first-person narrator in them, as though letting Evgeniia Mikhailovna speak for herself. However, Matiushina still signed her own name (not her alter ego's) to the text as its author, thus creating the impression that in "Notes" the author was relaying the personal testimony of another individual.

In the novella *A Song about Life,* however, Matiushina showed none of this hesitancy to claim the described experiences as her own. The novella, also written during the war, between 1942 and 1945, is explicitly autobiographical and written in the first person. Many of the experiences that Matiushina attributed to an other in her diary manuscript and "Notes" she presented as her own in this novella.[43]

Both Mukhina and Matiushina incorporated a detached, third-person style of storytelling into their diaries. But their narrators differ in revealing ways. While Mukhina crafted an authoritative and omniscient narrator, Matiushina favored a third-person limited narrator who, although intimately acquainted with Evgeniia Mikhailovna's innermost thoughts, could not see beyond the confines of the ring. Matiushina's narrator was a besieged Leningrader who shared Evgeniia Mikhailovna's anxieties, concerns, and confusion. Their voices often blend through the use of free indirect discourse. Narrator and protagonist also share a more equal relationship. The narrator always addresses Evgeniia Mikhailovna respectfully using her full name and patronymic. By contrast, Mukhina's parent-like narrator makes imaginary flights outside the siege and speaks with certainty and foresight. It also refers to the heroine tenderly and sometimes a bit condescendingly as "Lena" and "Alenushka."

Like Mukhina, Matiushina drew on elements of fiction—including dramatic tension, extensive dialogue, and an array of devices and tropes— to articulate yet distance herself from her own experiences. Matiushina interspersed short stories or "fairytales," as she called them, between diary entries. Unlike Mukhina's "story-fantasies," Matiushina's stories do not feature herself ("I") or Evgeniia Mikhailovna ("she"). Instead, they are inspired by episodes in the newspaper or incidents Matiushina herself witnessed. As Matiushina's narrator explains, "the fairytales grew on their own," and "they began to intertwine themselves with reality."[44]

Matiushina's diary also is far less intimate than Mukhina's in that she omitted from her diary some of the traumatic experiences and anxieties that she later discussed in *A Song about Life.*[45] Instead, many of the entries in the manuscript of Matiushina's diary record the conversations and experiences of other Leningraders. There are large sections conveying the sounds of the street or the breadline, where overheard remarks are reproduced but not attributed to any particular speaker. "Evgeniia Mikhailovna loved to overhear conversations. Sometimes she noted them down exactly, in shorthand," Matiushina's narrator explains.[46] The chorus of voices in Matiushina's diary includes that of the party. Its slogans and the voices of its leaders are featured more strongly in this diary than in any other I have studied, but they make fewer appearances in the novella. By contrast, *A Song about Life* focuses on Matiushina's personal struggles, arguments with friends, and shame at becoming blind and dependent on others. In this way, her accounts flout the usual conventions of self-construction associated with diaries on the one hand and memoirs and autobiographies on the other. Typically, the literary scholar Alain Girard has explained, "the 'I' of the memoir-writer is proud and glorious; the diarist's 'I' is a suffering being."[47] However, the autobiographical "I" of Matiushina's novella suffers more openly and intimately than the "I" of her diary. The journal is much more inclusive of the community, its voices and perspectives.

It is difficult to keep track of all the similarities and differences in Matiushina's accounts. This task is even more challenging because of inconsistencies within texts. For instance, Matiushina did not (or could not) avoid "I" entirely in her diary manuscript. There are moments when she slipped into the first person.[48] These fluctuations might have occurred accidentally, but they were preserved deliberately. Matiushina made stylistic edits to her diary before depositing it into Istpart's archive. She must have been aware of these shifts in narrative voice but let them stand. Likewise, her "Notes" and her novella attribute the same set of experiences to different figures. Matiushina could have provided some explanation as to why there was such a discrepancy between these two accounts, which were published only a few years apart from each other, but she did not. Her writings, therefore, invite a conflicted and ambiguous reading of self.

Matiushina's complex presentation of self is apparent in the very first diary entries, which recount the news of the German invasion. Given the deterioration of her eyesight, Matiushina already was concerned about losing her professional identity as a painter. The trauma of the invasion then immediately put pressure on Matiushina's sense of self. Her apparent uncertainty about saying "I" seems closely connected to her stated uncertainty about that "I's" purpose. Matiushina penned two entries about the invasion, one about Evgeniia Mikhailovna ("she") and the other about an "I." The first entry, dated 23 June 1941, emerges as a conversation between different narrative personas and aspects of the self.

> Yesterday, Hitler's troops burst into our country. Every person of the Soviet country, having learned about this frightening betrayal, has posed the question to himself, "How will I help the motherland?" This question also arose before Evgeniia Mikhailovna. "To the ranks! Together with everyone, wherever I can put my strength," she answered. "But after all, you are almost blind, you cannot even read a newspaper!" "True, all that is true. But at such a time, can one really sit at home? But your heart will stop from the slightest exertion, this is true . . . what will I do? I will write. About what? About the usual things—impossible at such a moment. [. . .] I will try to note down the feelings, thoughts, and words of what I have gone through.[49]

Thus, the slippage between "I" and "she" begins in the very first entry. Initially, Matiushina used quotation marks to indicate that there were two speakers. But when the marks disappear, the identity of the speaking subject becomes blurred. The text claims that both "I" and "she" had already "gone through" a great deal by this point. This may refer not only to the shock of the invasion but also to the onset of blindness and a bout of tuberculosis—all of which destabilized the protagonist's sense of purpose and worth. When the "I" chose a new purpose and resolved to keep a written record of the war, it was immediately beset by self-doubt. The self-effacement then intensifies. Could someone so physically weak and with such poor vision really make a suitable "chronicler" of the war? Matiushina's diary raises questions about this from the outset, even though it is not clear who exactly posed them. Her journal begins on this foundation of uncertainty about the writer and the viability of chronicling the siege.

The very next entry in the diary manuscript adds ambiguity to the narrative voice and presentation of self. It retells the same moment but through a first-person perspective. There is no mention of Evgeniia Mikhailovna. This entry is dated 22 June 1941, one day before the previous entry. It bears traces of retrospective construction. Now speaking as "I," Matiushina portrayed herself as being more confused and indecisive than Evgeniia Mikhailovna had been. Again she heard Molotov's radio address announcing the invasion, but this time she confessed, "I am listening and don't understand anything; I think they are broadcasting a story from the past. I look around. Long faces. Everyone is perplexed." Once it became clear to her that Germany had invaded, Matiushina grew even more skeptical about how she might contribute to the war effort: "How will I help the motherland? Never before have I been so tormented by blindness. It is very hard to be an invalid at such a time. What am I to do? There is nothing I can do."[50] What appeared as a conversation in the first entry takes the form of an emotional monologue in the second, as Matiushina herself voiced the doubts that previously she had attributed to an other.

Whether written as a dispute between aspects of self or as a private reflection, the diary manuscript's two opening entries highlight how Matiushina's self-constructions were manifold and conflicted from the beginning of the war. Her "I" becomes even more ambivalent when these entries are read alongside their equivalents in "Notes" and *A Song about Life*. In "Notes," Evgeniia Mikhailovna's reaction to the invasion is written as a conversation between her and Nal'ia. It becomes an exchange between two women, not two aspects of the self.[51] This moment of self-doubt takes yet another form in *A Song about Life*, that of an inner monologue. This version lingers the longest over Matiushina's disbelief about the invasion and her bewilderment over how to help: "We stood silently, it was difficult to talk. We did not know, could not find, the words. [. . .] . . . what now? I am an artist, but now one cannot draw nature, flowers. What must I do? . . . I must enter the ranks. Most likely, some kind of artists' brigades will be formed, but for what [purpose]? what for? . . . my mind is all a tangle."[52] The novella's iteration of this moment allows room for much more intimacy and incoherence, which one traditionally associates with a diary. The frequent use of ellipses underscores this. Therefore, when read together, the diary manuscript, "Notes," and novella showcase the discrepancies between "I" and "she."

The two opening entries of Matiushina's diary manuscript suggest two narrative trajectories. One provides a detached vantage point of an other,

and the second offers a first-person account in an intimate, confessional
tone. Judging from the remainder of the diary, it is clear that Matiushina
chose the first. She rarely wavered from Evgeniia Mikhailovna's point of
view except when she inserted short works of fiction. As a diarist, therefore, Matiushina was much more consistent than Mukhina. However, she
alluded to self-estrangement in other ways. Evgeniia Mikhailovna's self
concept began to fragment during the very first months of the war as she
lost neighbors and relations to mobilization and evacuation. "War changed
her life with frightening rapidity," the diary's narrator explains. "Evgeniia Mikhailovna did not even have time to think during the first days, and
she herself forgot about literary work."[53] Nal'ia became her major companion
and eventually her caregiver. Unable to work, Evgeniia Mikhailovna received the smallest, Category III ration. Her physical strength declined
rapidly. But the most potent symbol of Evgeniia Mikhailovna's estrangement from her self is the complete loss of her eyesight. Blindness compounded her sense of lost purpose and social disconnection. The assault
on Evgeniia Mikhailovna's body, however, is described from a distance
through a third-person narrative.

There are a few moments, however, when this impersonal diary
becomes quite intimate. This occurs when Matiushina brought the "I"
back into the text and reunited narrator and protagonist. For instance,
she crafted long conversations between Evgeniia Mikhailovna and Nal'ia
in which the protagonist describes her suffering directly and candidly.
Another device Matiushina used was the letter. One of the more poignant
articulations of Evgeniia Mikhailovna's transformation emerges in a letter
she crafted in February 1942 for women in Britain and America. Such letters actually were exchanged as part of a campaign to cultivate international friendship between the Allies. This letter is infused with a sense
of emotional urgency, as Evgeniia Mikhailovna "somehow needed to tell
them about the unavoidable internal restructuring created by the war."
In her opening lines, she hints at the awkwardness of divulging her personal experiences to total strangers: "Women of England and America! I
don't know any of you, but I really wanted to write to you [. . .] to sketch
out a little piece of our world." Evgeniia Mikhailovna goes on to describe
the terrifying air raids, her anxious shifts on air-raid duty, her physical
weakness, and her emotional despair. "Melancholy crawled into my soul,"

she confesses. "I felt small and terribly alone. And our city, surrounded by the enemy, seemed to me to be the same way." Evgeniia Mikhailovna seems aware that this tone is a departure for her and perhaps inappropriate for an official letter exchange. Handing the letter to her friend, she asks, "Nal'ia, is it too intimate?" "On the contrary," Nal'ia replies, "this is something wonderful. We feel like one person, you convey the feelings of us all." In this way, the diary hints at the detached quality of its own narrative. After all, this heartfelt letter ostensibly is aimed at a different audience, the reader of the letter, not of the diary. At the same time, Nal'ia highlights a virtue of this impersonal approach. The protagonist serves as an everywoman of the siege who can articulate the experiences of others. Evgeniia Mikhailovna certainly did this for Matiushina. In the end, Evgeniia Mikhailovna does not send the letter.[54] It simply remains a device that momentarily returns an intimate "I" to the diary.

The traumas of invasion, isolation, lost purpose, and physical transformation disrupted Mukhina's and Matiushina's lives and their acts of self-narration. Trapped in the besieged city, bereft of their regular routines, occupations, and companions, Matiushina and Mukhina struggled to come to terms with the war's assault on the self. They adopted vantage points, crafted personas, and invented scenarios that provided new perspectives on themselves and their circumstances. Using techniques of self-distancing, Matiushina and Mukhina displayed their selves from various, often conflicting angles and manipulated the boundaries between aspects of the self and between self and other.[55] In the process, they blurred the lines between self and other, reality and fantasy, document and fiction.

Diary writing has often been understood as an avenue to self-knowledge and, by extension, self-mastery. This was the case in the Stalin era, when diary writing was considered a tool for helping individuals internalize revolutionary values and transform themselves.[56] Outside the Soviet context, literary scholars have suggested that diary writing frequently is an exercise in self-actualization. Narration offers a writer the opportunity to bring some measure of clarity or control over fragments of their life experiences.[57] Mukhina and Matiushina may have intended to write for this purpose, but in the end, their accounts highlight the destabilization and unpredictability of the self rather than lend coherence to it. They showcase the mazes of the self.

The diarists' experiments in self-representation illustrate how the siege rendered the most familiar aspects of Leningraders' lives unrecognizable. Family constituted a third, critical realm of intimacy made strange by the blockade. Like the body and the self, kinship profoundly shapes identity—the sense of who one is and where one belongs. But even the fundamental bonds between parents and children faltered under siege.

Chapter Four

Family Life and Strife

On 22 November 1941—two days after rations dropped to their lowest point of the siege—Irina Zelenskaia was making rounds and checking on her coworkers at Electrical Station 7. As a manager and party representative, Zelenskaia approached her fellow employees with the intention of keeping them positive and productive. What she discovered, however, was that "many people [we]re starting to permanently give in, physically and morally." Her first chat that morning was with a young machinist, Shura Fokina. Fokina ate relatively well because she earned a Category I (workers') ration and because she did not have any relatives with whom to share food. However, Fokina lacked the moral support of a family, which left her feeble and depressed: "I am completely without strength. I can't work. It is better to quit work and stay at home in bed," she told Zelenskaia. "She is lonely," Zelenskaia surmised, "living in the barracks. She eats twice a day, but she completely lacks a sense of internal energy." Next, Zelenskaia strolled to the joinery, where she discovered that all but three of the staff were missing. Two workers, Frolov and Romanov, were particularly ill. "They have to feed dependents," she explained. "They both have teenaged children. Here, the situation is even more serious because they have to give their [ration] cards to their families. On a dependent's ration, one can live for only two to three days out of every ten, no more." Zelenskaia described the mood in the joinery as one of "utter dejection." Finally, she turned her attention to a fourth worker, Churkin. "They are jealous of Churkin," she observed. "He is stronger. His family was evacuated. He lives in the barracks, he eats a bit better and spends his workers' ration on himself alone." Churkin was physically stronger than Frolov or Romanov and emotionally stronger than Fokina.[1]

Family—its forms, functions, and meanings—evolved dramatically during the blockade. Households trapped together inside the ring were transformed to such a degree that some Leningraders began to question the practical and moral merits of family, an institution so often assumed to be necessary and natural. The most fundamental of all social and economic units, the family provides a network for pooling resources, a model of social interaction, and a touchstone of identity. But as the familiar spaces and faces of home were made strange by bombardment and starvation, many diarists felt their familial affections and obligations shift. In the midst of their own family struggles, the diarists studied other households for clues about the state of Leningrad society more generally. And they contemplated whether rising rates of abandonment, betrayal, and crime between kith and kin indicated a larger social and moral collapse in the city.

Could the family withstand the blockade's assault? The answer to this question depended, as Zelenskaia indicated, on how families were configured. The three types of family most commonly identified and studied by the diarists were nuclear families trapped together inside the ring; non-biological collectives that developed to replace them; and biological families that were dispersed, with some members living inside, some outside of Leningrad. Each household signaled different understandings of kith and kin, and each raised distinct moral and practical dilemmas regarding survival. Alarmingly, the diaries suggest that Leningraders who remained with their families inside Leningrad fared worse—in terms of both material and emotional well-being—than those who were separated from them. Such "intact" families faced the painful task of distributing resources, which placed an enormous strain on their relationships. Leningraders in this situation often turned to their diaries to air grievances, levy accusations, confess misdeeds, and fantasize about abandoning their families. In a few cases, Leningraders did leave and join new collectives. By contrast, diarists whose kin lived outside the city tended to view the family as a stronghold of moral and emotional support. True, their ties were strained by distance but not by the obligation to share food. Such diarists used their journals to reach out to loved ones and strengthen the bonds between them through correspondence, reminiscence, and imagination. These separated families were bound together by text, not by material interdependency.

The diaries speak to how meanings and functions of family evolved inside the ring. However, they do not prove how Leningraders actually behaved, be it altruistically or self-servingly. The accounts abound with perceptions, fantasies, and suspicions, which might be inaccurate or exaggerated. For instance, many diarists—especially young people—indicated through offhand references that parents and others made tremendous sacrifices for them, but they were much more preoccupied, at least in the confessional space of the diary, by what they perceived as strife and selfishness within the family. Thus, the diaries do not attest to how families actually fared. Rather, they enable us to glimpse the war that raged within Leningraders as they wrestled with ethical considerations, socialist values of collectivism and sacrifice, and the imperative of survival.

Even if these accounts are more impressionistic than factual, they challenge the conventional wisdom about blockade families that has dominated Soviet and post-Soviet discourse. Official propaganda memoirs and commemorative events from the postwar Soviet and post-Soviet periods tend to present the family as a bastion of loyalty and sacrifice, as one of the few institutions that endured the ordeal of war. By contrast, the journals tend to present it as a site of anguish. The diarists questioned the nuclear family model at precisely the same time official publications and policies championed it.

Soviet leaders began to endorse the nuclear family around the mid-1930s. Amid budget shortfalls, a declining birthrate, and rising rates of child abandonment and delinquency, new decrees enforced parental responsibility, prohibited abortion, made divorce difficult, and created a foster-care system so that children without parents might still benefit from a home environment.[2] This was a stark reversal of the state's stance in the late 1910s and early 1920s that the traditional family was a bourgeois institution, which needed to be replaced by a collective family with proletarian values. It was better to raise children in state-run schools and orphanages, the thinking went, than in individual family homes.[3] In the years before the war, however, policy makers moved in a new direction, which they justified ideologically by citing the apparent achievement of socialism in 1934. By this time, the regime claimed, the nuclear family, like all major institutions, had become fully Sovietized and therefore was an appropriate setting for raising children to develop a socialist consciousness.[4]

After Germany invaded the USSR, the Soviet regime elevated its celebration of the nuclear family to new heights. It now relied on the family both to maintain a stable, sizable population and to elicit moral outrage against Hitler's armies. *LP,* like most Soviet newspapers, depicted mothers, wives, and children as the chief targets of Nazi aggression and stressed the connection between a soldier's duty to defend his mother and his motherland. As one headline explained, "Leningraders! Bravely stand at your posts! You are defending your motherland, your city, your family." Posters reminded workers and soldiers that "Your mother needs you," "Protect 'our children, our hearths,'" and "Death to the child killers."[5] Devotion to motherland and family became deeply intertwined. The first time Stalin addressed the Soviet public about the war, he referred to the populace, rather uncharacteristically, as "brothers and sisters."[6] This rhetorical emphasis on family only intensified over the course of the war. In 1943, Sovnarkom urged families to take in orphaned children; adoption, once considered a necessary evil, was now an act of patriotism.[7] Finally, in 1944, a new family law code enshrined pronatalist values into law. It labeled abortion as infanticide, awarded money and medals to women who had five or more children, and taxed adults who were childless.[8]

Leningrad's wartime radio and print media assured the *blokadniki* that familial bonds were not only surviving but thriving inside the ring. The experiences of shared suffering and collective resistance had transformed the populace into one great family, into "blockade brethren," as the poet Ol'ga Berggol'ts put it.[9] "When a newcomer talks to Leningraders," the war correspondent Aleksandr Fadeev echoed in 1942, "[he gets] this feeling of belonging to a single house, to a single united family, which makes him think about big and important things, about the war and its meaning, about our country, its past, present and future."[10] Writing for an international audience, Boris Skomorovskii and E. G. Morris argued that familial love was the engine that powered Leningraders' resistance to the German onslaught. "During the siege, for the first time in all of history, it was exactly as if all the inhabitants of the tremendous city suddenly became members of one small family. They combined closely with a deep intent to protect their children and the feeble among them, and there was not a member of the family who was not proud to sacrifice his own share for the common good."[11]

Since World War II, personal and scholarly accounts have reinforced this narrative of familial resilience.[12] Oral histories with those who were children during the siege generally show a deep appreciation for their parents' devotion and self-denial, whereas children's wartime diaries, like those of adults, remark on such sacrifice sparingly. It seems likely that survivors became more mindful of those who helped them once the war was over, once they were no longer caught up in the fight for life. The diaries do not disprove these positive portrayals of the blockade family. They do mention episodes of extreme sacrifice. However, they underscore that feelings of sympathy, selflessness, or solidarity did not always undergird such actions. They also voice an attitude, seemingly widespread, that the nuclear family could be a regrettable burden and even an impediment to survival. Moreover, it is telling that the few diarists who portrayed their own loved ones in an altruistic light still depicted *other* besieged families as rife with animosity and suspicion. Such accounts attest to a shared concern that the institution of family was in crisis. My aim is not to contradict such positive portrayals of the blockade family but to trace the practical, moral, and political tensions that afflicted Leningrad families. The family ultimately survived the blockade, but this was far from obvious to those who were monitoring it during the siege.

Families inside the Ring

Domestic stability was one of the first casualties of war. Months before the city was encircled, Leningrad households were upended by conscription, mobilization, and evacuation. The intense bombardment that

began in September 1941 devastated their homes. However, it did not destroy family bonds as swiftly. During those turbulent first months, some
diarists described feeling closer to and more protective of their families
than ever before.[13] But hunger changed everything. The competition for
resources pitted husbands against wives, children against parents, and
Leningraders against themselves. Diarists were torn between dueling
impulses to save themselves and to save their loved ones. Many grafted
their material struggles onto family relationships, blaming relatives for
their hardships or characterizing them as liabilities or rivals. Some diarists, like the artist Tat'iana Glebova, suggested that solitude within the
family could be more powerful and painful than isolation from the Soviet
Union: "Robinson Crusoe on a desert island was less lonely than I am,
abandoned by everyone. And no one in my own family truly loves me.
[. . .] Thanks to abandonment and loneliness, I no longer find myself
spiritually dependent on those I loved."[14] The family became another
realm in which the blockade was internalized and manifested itself in
inner as well as interpersonal conflicts over the ethical and practical dimensions of survival.

Family troubles were so ubiquitous that the diarists encountered them
in the course of their daily routines. Irina Zelenskaia, for instance, learned
a great deal about familial strife while sitting in the cafeteria of Lenenergo (the firm that managed the local electrical grid). Her ears pricked
up when she heard one coworker, Il'chenko, talk about his family. "He
has nothing to feed his long-awaiting child. Father and mother give him
everything they can from their rations and go hungry themselves. All of
their reserves are used up. He himself lives from soup to soup once daily."[15]
Like many parents, Il'chenko and his wife faced an impossible dilemma:
how much food should they give to their child, and how much should they
eat in order to stay alive and keep providing for him? Il'chenko needed
to stay healthy enough to keep attending work and to maintain his Category I ration status, but each bite he took meant one less mouthful for his
son. Leningraders with such family obligations were marked by their
telltale anxious expressions and by the pails in which they carried their
cafeteria rations home. The state issued rations according to certain criteria, but families redistributed them according to other, personal considerations. Aleksandra Liubovskaia dubbed this the "family soviet"

(semeinyi sovet).[16] Most parents, like Il'chenko, labored under the hopeful but cruel illusion that they might save their families if they just discovered the best way to share food. This opened the door to agonizing decisions, painful self-doubt, and new household dynamics.

By reallocating food, the diarists effectively redistributed authority and dependency in the family. This in turn transformed the dynamics between spouses and between parents and children. With age and gender norms heavily in flux, new factors began to determine one's status within the family. The first was one's earning power—that is, the size of one's rations. A second factor, which was often but not always related to the first, was able-bodiedness. Those who were strong enough to assume major household duties or care for their ailing relatives obtained new authority. Often these were children. Thirteen-year-old Dima Afanas'ev and sixteen-year-old Iura Riabinkin, for instance, waited for up to twelve hours at a time in line to collect the family rations while their mothers worked. Parents, like Il'chenko, who gave most of their rations to their children subsequently became ill and had to rely on them for food and care. Nine-year-old Tat'iana Rudykovskaia nursed her father and grandmother after they became gravely ill, and she helped run the household for her working mother. Over time, Rudykovskaia ceased writing about school, games, or friends and instead inventoried the family's food reserves, budgeted her mother's salary, and monitored prices on the black market.[17]

Far from going unnoticed, this phenomenon was widely acknowledged by Soviet authorities. During and after the blockade, children garnered official praise for tackling adult-sized responsibilities at home, in factories, and in the war effort. When the war began, children helped to build fortifications and neutralize explosives as part of the local air defense. They also assisted in hospitals, read to and performed for wounded soldiers, and gathered warm clothes for the front. In recognition of their contributions, they received similar honors as adults: 36,000 schoolchildren were decorated, and of these, 15,000 were awarded the highest honor, "For the Defense of Leningrad."[18] The poet Iurii Voronov put it this way: "In 1943 / they gave us medals / and only in '45 / passports."[19]

Such commendations mask how these responsibilities stemmed from and contributed to the destabilization of the family. This was certainly true for Rudykovskaia. She came to resent her father and grandmother, who increasingly resembled "small children" the closer they drew to death.[20] Young *blokadniki* who bore the burden of family dependents became a familiar sight to Irina Zelenskaia. In May 1943, she began to work for the Department for the Settlement of Military Families, which arranged benefits and employment for the families of military servicemen in the Sverdlovsk District. This new job marked a turning point for her professionally as well as textually. She stopped writing entries about herself and instead profiled local children who were supporting their families virtually on their own. She met seven-year-old boys who nursed their sick parents while shouldering the household chores and a thirteen-year-old girl who, having lost both her parents, consulted the diarist about apartment rents and budgeting.[21] "The children are the ones who touch me to the depths of my soul. They are alone, but carrying out the fight for life like adults, at a time when not every adult is up to it." Zelenskaia was particularly taken with another thirteen-year-old, who came in to request her father's pension. The way she presented the girl's story underscores the evolving roles of parent and child: "As it turns out, her mother is one of these people who have gone wild, in whom hunger and deprivation have stifled even maternal instincts. She abandoned her daughter, lives separately, and not only does not help her but takes away her last [crumb]. The girl is now alone but has not quit school and is an excellent student; her teacher gives her the very best recommendations. She does her own sewing, laundry, looks tidy, speaks with cheerfulness, smiles, and only at the end, turning from the door, blushed and embarrassed, asked, 'Don't tell mama when she comes that I [asked for] the books separately because she would be so offended.' "[22] Zelenskaia presented the girl and her mother as opposites. While the mother emerges as thoughtless, emotionally unstable, and incapable of caring for the family, the girl appears composed, organized, and embarrassed at having to take the responsibility for the family's finances away from her mother.

Even adult children remarked on the emotional strain that these new dynamics produced. Because of her relatively good health, the writer Sof'ia Ostrovskaia, became the chief caregiver for her "two children: mother and brother."[23] Rather than bring them closer together, their dependency left the diarist feeling alone and overwhelmed: "I feel very clearly that all the responsibility for my mother's and brother's lives rests with me alone, that no one can help me, that I will not receive any kind of help from anywhere even if I bang my head against the wall, even if I scream at the top of my voice! No one will help me. I am completely alone."[24] Through competing displays of maternal sacrifice, she and her mother tried to make each other's health the top priority. The diarist would try to share her rations, and her mother would resist out of "a kind of illogical but benevolent motherly love," claiming she was full. The diarist resorted to scolding her mother "in a pedagogical tone."[25] Like Rudykovskaia, Ostrovskaia grew resentful of her "children." When they died, she admitted feeling considerable relief.

The journal of Aleksandra Liubovskaia describes this same phenomenon but from the perspective of a mother who had lost her authoritative role. Compared to those of other diarists, Liubovskaia's family remained close throughout the blockade. But even they buckled under the strain. When arguments erupted between her son, Igor', and daughter, Natasha, Liubovskaia hesitated to intervene because her Category II (service workers') ration had made her feel subordinate. Her children received Category I (workers') rations. Still, determined to reestablish her authority, she resolved, "I will restore my strength and ability to work so that once again the leadership role in the family will return to me. Even though my children are more able-bodied than I am now, they are young, and they do not have life experience. They have not passed through that severe school, which I had to go through. Up to this point, their lives have flowed smoothly without concern."[26] Her children may have been better providers, but they lacked the maturity and strength of character necessary to guide the family through such trying times.

Liubovskaia disapproved of the shifting parent-child dynamic she witnessed in other families as well. In February 1942, she wrote at length about an acquaintance, Mariia Aleksandrovna, who had lost her ration card and relied on her sisters and children for survival. Her children, however, blamed their mother for losing her card and only grudgingly gave her food.[27] With an eye to larger social developments, Liubovskaia presented this case as part of a citywide decline in familial loyalty and duty. "Now relations in the family are very abnormal, even hostile. The children all reproach their mother for eating more than her share at this very difficult time, winter. Now they are taking their ration cards from her, and they each eat their own food parcel. Perhaps she was not exemplary, but nevertheless she is their mother, and to leave her at such a moment, ill and without a ration card, is cruel."[28] In Liubovskaia's remarks, we glimpse her understanding of the commitments, responsibilities, and roles that each family member ought—but was failing—to fulfill. Later, Liubovskaia crossed out every mention of Mariia Aleksandrovna's family, including the one just quoted. Perhaps she was concerned that her comments seemed like gossip, not social observation.

The redistribution of food, authority, and dependency in besieged households sparked tensions over how to divide food fairly. In nearly every entry that sixteen-year-old Iura Riabinkin penned between October 1941 and his death in March 1942, he described how the meals he shared with his mother and sister turned into shouting matches. His mother and eight-year-old sister, Ira, he claimed, "tortured" him during meals.[29] "At meals, Ira eats slowly on purpose, not just to derive pleasure from eating but also to enjoy the feeling that she is still eating while the rest of us, who have already finished eating, sit there watching her with hungry eyes. Mother is always the first to finish her share, and then she takes a bit from each of us. When the bread is divided up, Ira bursts into tears if my little piece outweighs hers by as much as half a gram."[30] The conflict was about competing entitlement claims. Riabinkin's mother, as the breadwinner who fed her children from her Category I ration, felt entitled to take from her children's shares. Riabinkin insisted he deserved more than his sister because of his age and service to the family: it was his job to wait in line to redeem the family's ration coupons while his mother was at work. But this responsibility also carried risks; if he brought home an underweight portion of bread, for instance, he was blamed for pilfering or for not checking the ration. Ira, by contrast, had no such responsibilities but also was considered an innocent by her mother. Because of these competing claims, all three were dissatisfied with how the food was divided. "When mother doles something out, Ira and I watch her like hawks to make sure that she does it accurately. It's a bit embarrassing to write such things down," he admitted.[31] Any inequities, Riabinkin assumed, were deliberate and reflected an unspoken alliance between Ira and his mother.[32] Much more than sibling rivalry, Riabinkin came to see his sister's well-being as an obstacle to his own and by November 1941 begged his mother to give him Ira's ration card even though he knew this would seal her fate.[33]

Together, official and familial practices of food distribution produced the shameful status of dependency. The state used the title "dependent" to describe Leningraders who did not work and thus received the smallest (Category III) rations. Without help from others, these rations were a death sentence. But dependency was a fluid concept. During the worst period of starvation, the bread ration for service workers (Category II) and dependents (Category III) became identical, which forced families to shift their distribution practices once more. In the prewar period, the dependency of children on adults might have seemed quite natural. But under siege, even dependents like Riabinkin saw this reliance as burdensome and humiliating. He and others berated themselves as "parasites" for living at their loved ones' expense. Parasite was an ideologically inflected term used in Soviet society to describe anyone who unfairly benefited from the labors of others—shirkers, speculators, thieves, and so on. "Mother is so rude to me nowadays," Riabinkin continued. "Sometimes she hits me, and she curses me at every turn. But I am not angry with her for that. I can see that I am a parasite, hanging around her and Ira's necks. Yes, death, death is up ahead. And there is no hope at all, only the fear that I will force my own mother and sister to perish with me."[34]

The dependency of adults was regarded differently than that of children. Diarists tended to see their children as victims, and they were more willing to sacrifice for them than for adult relatives, especially spouses, whom they blamed for their difficulties. Marriage, the journals suggest, was the most vulnerable familial relationship. There are almost no mentions of new love affairs or marriages in the diaries. The closest I found was the brief romance between the musician Kseniia Matus and her lover, Vova. They became engaged early on in the war, but Vova's insatiable appetite ruined her affection for him. Matus was shocked at her rapid change of heart. "I was ready to sacrifice myself at any minute for him. And now? Where did my feelings go? Where has everything gone wrong? Has he really become so foreign to me? I myself do not know."[35] There were, however, sardonic references to how romance had been impacted by the siege. The tour guide Marina Tikhomerova, who was a great chronicler of wartime folk verses *(chastushki),* recorded several examples.

One, a love song, ended with the couplet, "The reason why I love you / Is that you bring rations."[36] Procuring and sharing food were the ultimate signs of devotion. It was the decline of such selflessness between lovers that the diarists lamented in their accounts.

According to the diarists, couples that stayed together began to loathe their dependency on each other. As early as July 1941, Elena Kochina noted how the war drove a wedge between her and her husband, Dima. With each entry, enmity mounts. "We sleep together," she wrote, "there's only one bed in the room. But even through padded coats, it's unpleasant for us to feel each other's touch."[37] Despite this emotional distance, they were bound together by material interdependency: "Dima and I have become like one organism. If one of us is sick or feels bad or is in a bad mood, the other instantly feels it painfully. And at the same time, we've never been removed from each other as we are now. Each of us struggles silently with his own sufferings. There is no way we can help each other."[38] In addition to the burden of sharing food, the physical and emotional deterioration of one spouse afflicted the other. Hunger and duress produced violent mood swings, irritability, and erratic behavior that could ruin sympathy and affection. Although Kochina regularly contemplated leaving Dima, she remained with him, and she continued to pour her animosity on the page, using her diary to release these unvoiced thoughts.

The radio worker Arkadii Lepkovich documented the extreme vulnerability of marriages inside the ring from the husband's perspective. Before December 1941, Lepkovich described his wife, Vera, with tenderness and affection. He repeatedly thanked her for helping him endure hunger, cold, and illness: "From the bottom of my heart, I am very grateful to her in general for her attitude toward me. Thank you, Verochka," he wrote on one occasion.[39] At the same time, Lepkovich began to worry that their friends might undermine their union. He suspected that the troubled marriage of one couple, Lena and Grisha, might drive Vera away. His misgivings grew stronger during the winter. By February, not only did Lepkovich assume that Lena "was trying to starve Grisha to death." He suspected that Lena "was teaching Verochka not to look after me, as if I was going to die anyway, saying it is better to protect yourself. But so far Verochka has done such a good job. Thanks to her, I have not seen any changes. Rather, I have felt her help and concern." Mindful of the vulnerability of marriage, he continued, "She is good to me, and I am happy to have such a wife, such a friend. I don't know what will happen in the future, but we shall see."[40]

Just ten days after Lepkovich trumpeted his wife's loyalty the now-bedridden diarist began to lose faith in their union. Starvation, he proclaimed, would ruin their relationship as it did *all* relationships: "Hunger, what it has done to people and to their relationships, it is frightening to think about and imagine such a life. My personal life and the lives of people I know are examples of this. Up until now, my relationship with Verochka could not have been better. I felt her concern for me, and I paid her back with concern for her. Never shall I forget the love and care that Vera showed me during surgery (my illness) and during the war—this is truly pure, crystalline love for a person, a husband. But what has it become now? For her, I am a hated burden." Like Riabinkin, Lepkovich's self-loathing led him to presume that Vera too begrudged his dependency on her. He became convinced that Vera would succumb to Lena's suggestions and hasten his demise: "Vera—not even Verochka but some devil in a skirt—where did her love disappear to and what has happened to her I cannot understand. One thing is clear to me. It is their [Vera and Lena's] conversation that [Vera] should not to kill herself for the one condemned to die. And so Verochka began to divide even the bread and hide it in order to strengthen herself at the expense of my already poor health. All this is true, but I think I might be exaggerating due to severe nervous exhaustion."[41] Lepkovich knew hunger could induce paranoia, but this did not allay his sense of betrayal. In entries for March, April, and May 1942, the diarist described himself as a victim of persecution and a burden to everyone, from his wife to friends to the police. "[Everyone] cannot seem to wait for my death, I don't know why, and Lena and Grisha are planning to separate, and I am the reason for this."[42] Like Riabinkin, Lepkovich used his diary both to confess and to record injustices he suffered.

As a model for social intimacy, the family was at the center of Leningraders' doubts about the fate of society more generally. Aleksandra Liubovskaia and Gegorii Kniazev drew the floor plans of their communal apartments in their journals and annotated the diagrams with notes about every neighbor and how they fared. From this, they tried to generalize about deaths, divorces, and social disruptions in the city as a whole.[43] For Lepkovich, his estrangement from Vera represented both a personal tragedy and evidence of a general breakdown of social relations in the city. After six months of "fight[ing] for [his] life not only against strangers but even against [his] formerly beloved wife," he embarked on a larger investigation of the family under siege: "The question is whether hunger, having torn through the city and country, has made relations between people completely different than in normal, satiated *[sytnaia]* life." Extrapolating from his own deteriorating marriage, Lepkovich argued that prosocial, cooperative behaviors were declining across the city. Hunger not only ruined camaraderie between strangers but also made strangers of intimate friends and relatives: "Even relations between mother and child, husband and wife, and vice versa have been made completely inhuman, I would say. A mother wishes death for her child, and a husband for his wife, and vice versa. One does not need to go far [to find] examples. The whole city has become this way because the battle for life has brought despair to every living individual. [. . .] People have become so coarse that those who survive this time are not who they used to be." At the time he wrote this, in May 1942, Lepkovich noted that food rations had increased, and order in the city had improved. He estimated that life in Leningrad was "85 percent normal." What had not yet recovered was the family.[44] The final blow came some months later when Vera, unable to find her coat, angrily accused her husband of "eating it"—that is, selling it for food.[45] Wounded by this accusation, Lepkovich resolved to evacuate without her. And with the apparent end of their marriage, he ended his diary. In the absence of this record, it is unclear whether Lepkovich's health, marriage, or faith in humanity ever recovered.

Family Crime

Resentments over interdependency sometimes escalated into full-scale accusations about theft and other crimes. Stealing had become common between strangers in Leningrad, but the diarists gave special attention to crime within families. Perhaps this was because the sense of personal betrayal was greater between relations or because it was easier for Leningraders to steal from home. Many *blokadniki* kept their food reserves in their apartments or had relatives redeem their rations for them. These practices bred mistrust. The chemist Elena Kochina, for instance, constantly suspected and occasionally caught her husband stealing food from their toddler. So she began carrying the family's food reserves around with her, feeling they were safer in public than at home.[46]

Theft within the family reflected the diarists' mounting concerns about the larger debasement of human nature. Esfir' Levina observed, "relatives and neighbors tended to blame each other for thefts. [. . .] Under the influence of hunger even the most honest person becomes an animal *[zvereet]*."[47] The seventh grader Valia Peterson, for instance, penned a litany of allegations against her stepfather, Aleksandr Petrovich. Unable to confront him in person, she used her diary to accuse him of stealing her rations and eating her Irish setter, Sylvie. "I hated him terribly. Hunger uncovered his filthy soul, and I have gotten to know him," she wrote, intimating that his darkest self was his true self. When he died some months later, Peterson celebrated: "At first I did not believe it. Then my face became distorted into a horrible smile. I was happy. Yes, happy at his death. Oh, if someone had seen the expression on my face at that moment, he would have told me that I am capable of cruel hatred. He dies and I laugh! I was ready to jump for joy, but I was too weak, did not have enough strength. Hunger had done its work." Although she could no longer run and jump like the seventh grader she was, Peterson's joy was not dampened: "Look at that, what I wanted came true!" she exclaimed.[48]

The diarists often levied allegations of theft, but they rarely admitted fault themselves. An exception to this is the diary of the schoolboy Iura Riabinkin, who admitted that he regularly stole from his mother's and sister's rations after he retrieved them from food stores. Shocked at his own depravity, he declared, "How self-centered I am! I am becoming callous. What has happened to me? I secretly stole butter and cabbage from the hidden reserves for this ration period, I watched greedily how mother divided a sweet into pieces for Ira and me, and I picked a quarrel over every little fragment of food, each tiny crumb. What has happened to me?"[49] Despite numerous vows to reform, he was unable to resist the temptation to pilfer from the family reserves. Starvation thrust Riabinkin into a quandary. He stole food to stay alive, but the deception was irreparably destroying his character. "Well, this is really it . . . I have lost my integrity, lost my belief in it, I have reached the end of the road," he declared in December 1941:

> Two days ago I was sent out to get sweets. It was bad enough that in-
> stead of sweets I bought sweetened cocoa (counting on Ira not
> wanting to eat it and so increasing my share), but also that I helped
> myself to half of the total amount—a miserable 600 grams that is sup-
> posed to last us for the whole ten days—and invented a story about
> how three packets of cocoa had been snatched from my hands. I acted
> out the whole comedy at home with tears in my eyes, and I gave
> Mother my word of honor as a Pioneer that I have not taken a single
> packet of cocoa for myself . . . and later on, watching with a hardened
> heart mother's tears and distress at being deprived of something
> sweet, I ate the cocoa surreptitiously.
>   [. . .] I have slid down into that abyss called depravity, where the
> voice of conscience is totally silent, where there is dishonesty and dis-
> grace. I am an unworthy son to my mother and an unworthy brother
> to my sister. I am an egoist, a person who, in a moment of adversity,
> forgets all about his nearest and dearest. [. . .] I am a ruined person.
> Life is over for me. The prospect that lies ahead of me is not life.

Here, Riabinkin drew on both personal and political measures of integrity, calling himself a bad son and a bad Pioneer because he broke his word. He lied, cheated, and put himself ahead of others. Hunger had blinded him to all other motivations, leaving him "a ruined person." Having already witnessed the death of his conscience, Riabinkin gave up hope of redeeming himself and instead focused on recording his misdeeds, so that his sister and mother might understand him someday: "I would like two things to happen immediately: for myself to die here and now, and for mother to read through this diary. May she curse me as a filthy, unfeeling, and hypocritical creature, let her renounce me . . . I have sunk too low, too low . . ."[50]

In Riabinkin's final entry, penned three days later, he recounted how his family finally was relieved of him. His mother and sister boarded a convoy and were evacuated from Leningrad. In an interview that Adamovich and Granin conducted with Riabinkin's sister Irina (Ira) Ivanovna Riabinkina many years later, she explained that her brother was too weak to walk and they too weak to carry him. They had to leave him behind. Antonia Mikhailovna Riabinkina, the diarist's mother, died on 26 January 1942 en route to Vologda, and Ira lived in an orphanage before returning to Leningrad in 1945.[51] When Iura Riabinkin's diary was published, first in *Change (Smena)* in 1970 and then in Granin and Adamovich's 1984 *A Book of the Blockade,* his wish came true. Countless readers, including his sister, realized how profoundly he struggled between family devotion and self-preservation.

Few diarists discussed theft within their families as candidly as Riabinkin. Ol'ga Matiushina preferred to explore the phenomenon through short works of fiction, which allowed her to address it without implicating herself or her loved ones. Matiushina penned seven stories about seven families, ideal types distilled from the families she heard about or knew inside the ring. The tales are abstractly drawn, undated, and separated from the diary entries by breaks on the page. They do not feign a sense of "the real" by referring to exact times, locations, or last names. However, she also likened them to "a frightening fairy tale about reality."[52] Of the seven tales, six are about parents and children, brothers and sisters, or aunts and nephews who jeopardized each other's survival. Most are either thieves or victims of theft. One story depicts a six-year-old child who, fooled by the maternal warmth of a stranger, hands over the family ration cards to her "for safe keeping." Another tale presents the opposite situation: a mother loses the family's bread rations to a thief and descends into despair, knowing she has doomed her child to die.[53] The remaining stories depict *blokadniki* who kept themselves alive by stealing from relatives. There is the tale of Igor' Aleksandrovich, a young man who takes food from his dead sister and then is immediately beaten and robbed in the street.[54] The central thrust of all of these vignettes is that the siege brutally pitted survival instincts against familial commitments and social codes of behavior.

What of theft not within but between families? Diarists also grappled with the ethical dilemma of whether to eat food procured illegally by relatives. Even if it strengthened them physically, the act of sharing stolen food could weaken trust within the family. The architect Esfir' Levina described how her brother Lenia's stealing and graft put the household at odds. After Lenia initially lied about how he had obtained some sugar, he admitted to accepting bribes and stealing ration cards. He rationalized his behavior, claiming he took the cards from a man who was probably going to die anyway. Should Lenia be held accountable for his actions? "Is he sick or a criminal?" Levina wondered. The family deliberated. The diarist affirmed, "He is a criminal, of course, an engineer, a trust director, and a party member. Mama is making a weak effort to 'soften the picture' with fear of death by starvation." But her children retorted, "According to your theory, you can just run down and rob a comrade?" At the same time, Levina confessed her own desire to "go home and take all of the emergency provisions" from the family reserves. "I catch myself in such extreme egoism," she admitted.[55] "People have been crystallized by the war," Levina concluded. "Good and bad are presented very clearly. If we survive, we will know a lot: the value of bread, fire, and human compassion"—three of the scarcest commodities in Leningrad.[56] In this way, the diaries of parents, children, and siblings suggest, the blockade lifted the veil on human nature by eliminating niceties and obligations between loved ones, let alone between strangers.

Another crime that occurred inside families was the illegal use of a dead relative's ration card. Leningraders often welcomed death in the family because it not only ended the suffering of the dying but made more food available to the living. Levina explained that *blokadniki* "passed away at the right time" if they died at the beginning of the month, leaving their families extra ration coupons to use.[57] Arkadii Lepkovich also taught his readers about this coveted "inheritance" by recounting a conversation he had with his seven-year-old niece, Musia: "Uncle Arkadii, my mom died," she exclaimed "in a fit of joyful excitement." " 'Why are you happy?' 'Because I still have the [ration] cards. They reverted to us.' "[58] Because the law required families to hand over the deceased's ration card in order to obtain a death certificate, many kept their departed relatives at home until that month's coupons had been used. Such attachment to the dead, the party worker Aleksandr Grishkevich asserted, "was not love, but first 300, then 400 grams of bread a day."[59] Even after the rations of the dead were used, their corpses lingered in apartments, stairwells, and balconies. Few *blokadniki* had the strength or the means (bread) to give them a proper burial.

Some families lived off dead relatives literally. In both the Soviet and post-Soviet eras, cannibalism during the blockade has remained a widely acknowledged yet taboo subject. The Leningrad press regularly evoked cannibalism to demonize the Germans.[60] The slogan "Death to the Fascist cannibals!" emblazoned posters and newspapers. In the diaries, however, the cannibal epithet was directed squarely at the *blokadniki*. The Russian language distinguishes between *trupoedtsvo* (eating flesh from an already dead human body) and *liudoedstvo* (killing and eating a human being), and both took place in Leningrad.

Rumors of cannibalism likely exceeded the number of actual incidents. Even so, the historians Richard Bidlack and Nikita Lomagin have found that 1,500 Leningraders were arrested for it during the siege. The city police and NKVD were sufficiently alarmed by the escalation of cannibalism that they created special divisions of police and of psychiatrists to handle it.[61] Recent documents published by Bidlack and Lomagin also suggest that city leaders perceived a link between cannibalism and the family. In a secret memorandum to Leningrad's Second Party Secretary Aleksei Kuznetsov, the city's military procurator explained that cannibalism often was perpetrated to save the lives of children. This might explain why two-thirds of those who were prosecuted were women. Another classified report from Leningrad's NKVD chief, Petr Kubatkin, to his boss in the Kremlin, Lavrentii Beriia, detailed nine cases of cannibalism, both *trupoedtsvo* and *liudoedstvo*. Of the nine, four were committed within families.[62] Similarly, the diarists focused on cannibalism between relations much more than between strangers. This does not necessarily mean that cannibalism occurred more frequently within the family. Diarists and officials alike may have fixated on these stories because they indexed their worst fears about social collapse inside the ring.

Cannibalism represented an extreme display of either familial betrayal or familial devotion. The diarists recorded stories about parents both eating their children and feeding their children the flesh of the dead. Aleksandr Grishkevich, for instance, listed the names and addresses of his colleagues who "humanely" fed their children human flesh. He later handed his diary over to Istpart, effectively informing on them.[63] Aleksandra Mironova, whose job it was to rescue abandoned children from their homes, wrote about the Kaganov children, whose mother fed them human flesh in a desperate attempt to save them. The diarist admitted she was scared to interact with these "ghastly, dirty" children and that "the doorman did not want to go with [her] to this apartment." It was difficult for Mironova to coax the children into accompanying her to an orphanage because "the[y] did not want to leave their uncooked meat."[64] These anecdotes, however disturbing, indicate that parental sacrifice indeed endured under siege.

More often, however, the diarists relayed stories of parents and children eating each other. "They are talking about cases of cannibalism," Esfir' Levina reported. "A woman eats a child, children eat their mother."[65] Irina Zelenskaia presented this as a widespread phenomenon, remarking, "There are many cases of cannibalism, missing children, even eating one's children. The police are inundated with such reports."[66] Zelenskaia personally encountered this impulse when she visited an ill coworker, Kuptsova, in the hospital. Delirious, Kuptsova threatened to eat her daughter, Liusa, to "bite her somewhere." "I will drink the fresh blood and get well." As Kuptsova spoke, Liusa was within earshot, "sitting on a chair, lifeless, like a doll. Only there were teardrops in her swollen eyes."[67]

The painter-turned-writer Ol'ga Matiushina tackled this theme in one of her tales about the besieged family. It tells the story of Andrei Ivanovich, a man so tormented by hunger that he contemplates murdering his son, Tolia. As Andrei Ivanovich watches Tolia play, he surmises that the boy is growing weaker and will not survive the siege anyway. "They say that human flesh is delicious . . . if it is boiled . . . it probably makes a tasty soup. But what am I talking about? . . . He turned away from the children. Their voices were irritating . . . Nevertheless Tolia, the youngest, is sickly; he won't survive. Already he looked indifferently at the boy. He thought how easy it would be to finish him. An iron against the head would be enough—that is it. The boy noticed his father's intent glance. Smiling, he looked at him with big, blue eyes, and raised his light blond brow." Andrei Ivanovich, appalled by his own thoughts, tries to confide in his wife: "I am afraid for myself . . . I could . . . you yourself know how hungry I am." This scenario, Matiushina implied, was not unique. Directly below it, she relayed how artillery shells struck the typographical center responsible for printing ration cards, which delayed the printing for February 1942. "The first days of February were borderline for the hungry. In those days, many succumbed, resorting to cannibalism." She also added, "Several people used their last bit of strength to restrain themselves. Many have risen above themselves, to the level of heroism." Her story of Andrei Ivanovich, however, casts a shadow over this hopeful claim.[68]

These images of eating, murdering, or sacrificing one's children, which call to mind the dramas of antiquity, magnify the profound human tragedy taking place under siege. Whether relaying actual incidents, rumors, or fantasies, the diarists often referred to cannibalism in a family context. This revealed their worst fears about the decline of the family and about the baseness of human nature as revealed by the siege. Cannibalism symbolized the most extreme forms of dependency and animosity that threatened households inside the ring.

Accidental Families

With the nuclear family in turmoil, new collectives, bound by circumstance or mutual advantage, developed in its wake. These alliances took many forms, but most still had to contend with the problem of dividing food. One collective that did not was the children's home. Although the rations were far from adequate in these orphanages, all children received the same rations without consideration of entitlements or responsibilities.[69] This meant fewer disputes over how food was allocated. The orphanage inspector Glafira Korneeva noted that the promise of food attracted both children and staff to the orphanage, where all assumed that they "would be more full." "At that time, we were already half crazy with hunger, so that you can forgive us for this horrible thought," she added apologetically.[70]

The notion that adults and children might find orphanages preferable resonates ironically with Soviet policies of the late 1910s and early 1920s, when the regime sought to abolish the nuclear family, which it considered a repository of bourgeois individualism and female oppression. At that time, the young Soviet state advocated that children be raised collectively in state-run homes and schools, which could better instill socialist values. The diaries suggest that, in a way, this vision came true during the siege when thousands of children became wards of the state. By that point, however, the preference for state-run homes over family ones had far less ideological backing.

The blockade left thousands of children homeless or abandoned. This was a familiar problem. Since the revolutionary and civil war periods, the regime struggled with the persistent presence of homeless and abandoned children. This situation worsened in the 1930s, when the combination of famine, collectivization, political repression, and forced relocation created "a genuine plague" of children living on the streets. Their numbers reached into the hundreds of thousands. In response, the regime ordered a 150 percent increase in the number of children's homes and passed new laws to catch runaways and enforce compulsory education in order to discourage childhood neglect and juvenile delinquency.[71] World War II erupted before this plan was fully realized. Even after the incomplete evacuation of children in fall 1941, at least 400,000 children remained in Leningrad. The city had only seventeen children's homes, which became overcrowded with youths whose parents had died or had demanding military or labor duties that prevented them from looking after their children. Promising that "there will be no orphans among us" on 13 February 1942, Lengorispolkom planned sixty-two new orphanages and temporary reception centers for children. Two additional decrees established commissions to find parentless children and arrange residence for them in an orphanage, collective farm, labor colony, or foster family.[72]

Unlike in the 1910s and early 1920s, Leningrad's wartime orphanages were not glorified as suitable long-term replacements for the nuclear family. Rather, they were seen as necessary responses to the Germans' assault on house and home. Catriona Kelly has argued that the regime adopted an uncharacteristically sympathetic attitude to orphans during the war, seeing them as innocent victims of Nazi crimes.[73] Heartfelt stories of Leningrad foster parents encouraged adoption to augment, not replace, biological families. By the end of World War II, the regime resumed its "hard-line" attitude, associating orphans with youth rebellion and delinquency. Although it continued to rely on adoption throughout the 1940s, it did not provide material assistance to adoptive parents.[74]

The diaries of wartime orphanage workers illuminate the breakdown of nuclear families inside the ring as well as the prominence of "accidental families," which formed inside children's homes. I focus on two accounts: the diaries of Aleksandra Mironova and Nina Gorbunova. They describe different periods and aspects of the relocation process. Mironova's diary covers the children's transition out of the family apartment and into a state-run home, while Gorbunova's examines the later transition out of the orphanage and back into the home of their biological family.

Aleksandra Nikolaevna Mironova was a history teacher by profession. But after her school closed in the fall of 1941, she took a job in an orphanage where twenty of her former pupils now lived. There, Mironova became the head of a new kind of family of her adopted children. She took one little girl, Lelia Bogdanova, under her wing and let the girl live with her when "[Lelia's] mama did not return from the factory."[75] Then from January to March 1942, Mironova began working for the Sverdlovsk District's Commission for the Protection of Children, where her task was to find abandoned children and bring them to temporary detention centers or orphanages.[76] Her diary documents the children's experiences, not her own. In 1945, she gave her diary to Istpart, despite its candor regarding cannibalism and ineffective officials and policies.[77] In 1968, an edited version was published that redacted nearly all of the following quotations.[78]

Mironova's diary takes the reader inside war-torn homes on Leningrad's Vasil'evskii Island. Each day, following leads from the local school, housing administration, and party organization, Mironova searched for children who intentionally or unintentionally had been abandoned by their parents or who had run away from home. Some, like the Golubev children, had been living alone for some time and attracted the authorities' attention because of a household accident.[79] Others found Mironova and implored her to take them. Galia Nikolaeva, for instance, came to the detention center because her parents could no longer feed her.[80] Eleven-year-old Vitia Krasnobaev begged Mironova to take him to a children's home, pleading, "I don't want to go to Smolensk Cemetery anymore. I am afraid that they will send me there."[81]

Many of Mironova's foundlings were living alongside their parents' remains. She discovered Verochka and Ania in their apartment scrounging for food, while the two-day-old corpse of their mother sat on a nearby chair. But a more "astonishing" sign of that family's demise was the behavior of the girls' uncle, who dropped by the apartment a few days earlier to take an oak dresser but left the children behind. The girls were too emaciated to walk. Mironova dragged them to the children's home on a sled.[82] Six days later, she found eleven-year-old Shura Sokolova lying in a pile of dirty laundry underneath a mattress. Her father was at the front, and her mother was dead. The corpse still lay in the kitchen. Shura explained that a kindly stranger *(tetka)* had taken the family's ration cards. "I was not able to find the lady's address," Shura added naively.

Mironova's diary suggests that there was a citywide epidemic of child abandonment: "How many have begun to abandon their children. It is horrible that the mothers themselves leave their children. The house manager for number 23 left a child without registration [so he could not renew his ration card]. In February, nine individuals ranging from age one and a half to three years old cannot explain [what happened], but they wait for mama and believe she is alive."[83] Of the twenty or so incidents that Mironova reported, she recorded only one where she emphasized any enduring affection between mother and child. When she lifted nine-year-old Iura Stepanov from the bed where he lay next to his mother's body, he cried, unwilling to abandon her: "'Mama, what did they do to you, mama, what are you doing to me? I do not want to go to the children's home.' It took a lot of strength and words to talk the boy into it," Mironova admitted.[84]

Mironova devotedly chronicled these families under siege, but she only mentioned her biological children once. In an entry from February 1942, the diarist indicated why she was so committed to rescuing the city's children: she had been unable to save her own: "Kostia died. Ania and Vasia died. My dear ones. What will become of the children? How much grief! I ought to live and save more children. They will replace Kostia, Vasia, Ania and everyone."[85] This reticence about one's own family, exhibited by Mironova, Zelenskaia, Matiushina, and others, is another reason why the diaries are so rich in observations and reflections about the families of others and about kinship more generally.

Mironova saved many children by bringing them to orphanages, but these were not the edens that many children imagined. Facilities were overcrowded, poorly equipped, and understaffed. The children were dirty and poorly clothed, and infectious disease ran rampant. These conditions prompted Sovnarkom to mandate regular inspections of children's homes in 1943.[86] Glafira Korneeva reported that the children simply lay on their bunks, unable to sit up and too exhausted to cry or whine. Other children spoke passionately about food and traded stories about stealing from neighbors or hunting down dogs and cats to eat. They spoke dispassionately, however, about their parents' deaths or abandonment of them. When Korneeva asked one boy about his family, he answered that his warmest memory was eating the compote and jam his father took from a store on Vasil'evskii Island. The boy's father, mother, and sister were all dead now; however, according to Korneeva, "he did not feel these losses, but his recollections about the compote were radiant. [. . .] It is obvious that people have little self-control and powerfully acute animalistic characteristics."[87] Echoing this sentiment, Mironova noted that the children often were vicious with each other. "They all sit at the stove, dirty and mean. No one wants to go to sleep, the beds are not made," she observed. "In the cafeteria," she remarked, "they behaved in a disgraceful manner, snatching bread from the teachers' trays. The children look like starving baby animals. Ten to fifteen die each day in the orphanage."[88] Gradually, as she and other diarists indicated, most children came to be at home in the orphanage and bonded with the staff and other youths.

Around the time Mironova's diary ends, the journal of the orphanage director Nina Grigor'evna Gorbunova begins. Like Mironova, Gorbunova hardly recorded a word about her own family situation but wrote at length about the children in her charge. There are clear differences between Mironova's and Gorbunova's perspectives on the family, differences that may stem from the distinct moments in which they wrote. Mironova's diary covers the first blockade winter and spring. It highlights children's troubled relations with their parents and their rocky transition to life in an orphanage. Gorbunova's journal, which covers January 1942–May 1943, describes relatively happy relations between the orphans. This might be because the children had adjusted to their new home, because food rations had increased, or because of the diarist's personal outlook on the situation.

The children in Gorbunova's care came from a variety of circumstances. Some had lost parents, some were abandoned, and some lived at the orphanage while their parents were at the front or working long shifts in Leningrad factories and hospitals. Such parents visited their children and eventually came to retrieve them. Gorbunova described these reunions between parents and children in great detail. Her notes suggest that, as the biological family declined, this collective family grew stronger. Despite the children's difficult transition to the orphanage, they grew so used to it that, she claimed, they refused to leave. They agreed to be evacuated with the orphanage but generally resisted going home with their parents. Gorbunova quoted one group of girls exclaiming, "Yes, we really, really love our children's home. It is our family [rodnoi] home!"[89] "The children really love their children's home," the director remarked in December 1942. "They refer to it simply as 'our home.'"[90] The diarist continued,

> Today there was an incident. Mothers who are returning from work for good must come and take their children from the orphanage. So Shurik's mother was returning and wanting to take her child. Shurik was very upset, he did not want to leave. Then Shurik's mama arrived and said she could not take him because they were sending her back to work and asked that I call him so that she could say good-bye. Shurik came out and asked, "Mama, you came for me?" "No, my son, I am going away again, but don't you miss me, I am coming again soon," the mother said. "No mama, I will not be sad." Having said good-bye to his mother, Shurik ran to his group and shouted loudly to his caregiver, "Ol'ga Ivanovna, I am staying at home with you, and mama has again left for work! How happy I am!!!"[91]

Gorbunova described these awkward reunions in a bittersweet tone without commenting on them directly. On the one hand, the estrangement between parent and child must have been painful to witness. On the other hand, she may have been proud that her staff had created such an appealing home for the children. This might be one reason why the diarist focused on the children's refusals of their parents so extensively. Ten-year-old Vasia Dmitriev, for instance, trusted that the orphanage staff could feed him better than his parents could. When his mother came for him, he hesitated to leave. Vasia told Gorbunova, "I am going to mama, but I don't know how we will live. Will there be enough to live on through our cards? Well, I will live and learn. If it is bad, then I will ask to move back into the children's home," he resolved. Similarly, when Larochka Iliushchenko's aunt came for her, she refused to go, claiming her aunt had withheld food from her.[92] Whether or not this was true, the accusation speaks to the child's skepticism that her family could provide sufficient quantities of food and distribute it fairly.

Perhaps these family members had become emotionally distant because of disputes over food or because of the considerable time they were forced to live apart. Parents sometimes appealed to orphanage workers, who were closer to their children, for advice on how to raise their kids. Gorbunova recalled how fifteen-year-old Nadia Sorokina's mother returned her daughter to the orphanage after a row. The mother accused Nadia of stealing food and selling off her belongings. In a desperate plea, the mother burst into Gorbunova's office and demanded, "Help me raise my daughter into an honest person!" The mother requested not only practical help but also insight into the ethics of her daughter's behavior, asking Gorbunova, "Can such things be forgiven?" In the end, as Nadia herself put it, she was "dumped" back in the children's home. Gorbunova was sympathetic toward the mother but critical of her decision: "I got the impression that Nadia's mother loves her daughter, but not unconditionally *[ne slepo]*. She asked for help with correcting and guiding Nadia. She [Nadia] will keep visiting us, and I, along with the caregivers, will mind her particularly strictly."[93] In this way, Gorbunova seemed to agree that the orphanage was better equipped to raise Nadia than the child's own mother, who had limited time, resources, and parenting skills.

Some parents and children became so estranged that they did not even recognize each other. In January 1942, a soldier came to visit his seven-year-old daughter. The girl was so emaciated and ill with scurvy that her father was unable to identify her. The little girl sobbed as her father refused her: "Not recognizing his own child, [he] said, 'No, this is not my child. [. . .] Can it really be you, Valia? This is what you have become? No, no, this is not my daughter!'" He demanded proof, testing the child by showing her a family photograph and asking her to identify everyone by name. In the end, Gorbunova remarked, "The father was satisfied, but I was watching how he was not himself, how he had to hold himself together a bit. He sat down with the child, became himself again and was silent . . . the silence lasted about five minutes. Then he stood up, warmly kissed her, and left. When he arrived at my office, his strength left him, and he started to cry. I did not say anything to him. His tears were ca-thartic."[94] Conversely, there were episodes when children mistook certain adults for their parents. Gorbunova especially observed this on holidays like Red Army Day or International Women's Day, when various groups visited the orphanage or when the children visited military hospitals.[95] During a youth recital at a hospital on the Fifteenth Line of Vasil'evskii Island, four-year-old Slavik Andrienko was about to recite his poem when suddenly he yelled, "Papa!" and ran to a soldier in the audience. In the popular press, soldiers often were presented as father figures to Soviet children. Slavik was certain he had found his father and stayed by the man's side for the entire day.[96] Slavik's desperate attempt to find surro-gate parents illustrates both how families deteriorated and how the de-sire for familial affection and support remained strong.

At the same time that the state was trying to strengthen the nuclear family, collective families grew stronger and sometimes were preferred by both children and parents because they removed the burdensome task of reallocating food. The diaries testify to a growing emotional distance be-tween parents and children, who at times had trouble recognizing each other, let alone their duties and loyalties to each other.

Families Divided by the Ring

For diarists whose families were outside the city, the painful task of di-viding food was of little concern. Family held different meaning for them. It provided a touchstone of identity, a form of companionship, and a reason to live. The prospect of one day reuniting with loved ones propelled these *blokadniki* to fight for survival, and their marital and familial bonds seemed to grow stronger as a result. Such family ties were maintained not through physical contact but through text, memory, and imagination. Proximity created emotional distance and tension within the family, whereas geographical distance, bolstered by memory and fantasy, fostered a sense of emotional closeness.

Diarists who had family both in and outside the ring revealed the dis-tinct pressures and meanings associated with each type of household configuration. The engineer Gesel' Gel'fer, for example, continually grew in affection for his wife, Gitele, and daughter, Mulia, who had evacuated to Gor'kii, while he had a turbulent relationship with Tania, a relation with whom he lived in Leningrad. The fact that he never indicated how exactly he was related to Tania seems revealing. Gitele was his "bright beacon," the force that kept Gel'fer on the path to survival.[97] "Now I dream only about leaving," he wrote, "to return to my beloved and loving Gitele, to look at her and Mulia, and to rest a little. Then, it seems to me, I could die peacefully." He envisioned their reunion as a joyous occasion, a far cry from the awkward ones Gorbunova relayed. By contrast, Gel'fer's relationship with Tania was hampered by the "torturous" and "terrible burden" of sharing food. To help alleviate the challenge of dividing dinner rations, Gel'fer and Tania agreed to sleep in separate locations for January 1942. During that time, the diarist lamented his acts of self-denial, repeating, "She was, is, and will remain an egoist. My acquaintances at work scold me for this self-sacrifice. But what can I do! It pains me to see Tania's suffering, and after all, of all people around me, she is my closest and dearest relative. Moreover, none of my near and dear ones are left here. Those who are closest to my heart, Gitele and Mulia, are far from me."[98] Although Gel'fer was slow to acknowledge it, many of his entries illustrate that Tania shared a good deal of food with him. Each felt obligated to help the other. After Tania got a job in a medial station in February 1942, a position that gave her greater (and illegal) access to food, Gel'fer's resentment softened: "My dark thoughts about her egoism have receded into the background. My self-sacrifices bore and are bearing fruit, and it is left for me to repent my initial [diary] notes."[99] Still, his affections fluctuated with the food situation, especially after the clinic closed and Tania's contributions dwindled.

Gel'fer's tenderness for his far-flung family, however, never waned. Even when Gitele demanded more assistance from him, Gel'fer never expressed chagrin. In fact, sharing resources with "Gitka" and Mulia brought him deep emotional comfort that outweighed any material losses. When he was unable to send them money, the diarist berated himself for being "swinish" or declared, "I am committing a crime against Gitka."[100] Gel'fer felt obliged to share resources with relations both inside and outside the ring, but these acts aroused very different emotions in him. The bitterness

and suspicion he expressed about sharing with Tania had no corollary
when it came to Gitele and Mulia.

Gel'fer penned his most joyous entries when he was able to help Gitele
and Mulia, and his most despondent ones when no words or parcels
passed between them. "They write to me, and I really count on them [the
letters], but now their letters are lying somewhere, aging and losing their
sharpness. I really want to know now how they are living, did they receive my money, and what is their food situation."[101] Uncertain about
why Gitele did not write, about whether he would ever see her again, he
wrote, "shackles all of my thoughts and aspirations."[102] "I live on a powder
keg and feel such uncertainty that it annihilates my desire to do anything,"
he professed. Although his work and status as a reservist kept him in Leningrad, Gel'fer began to contemplate leaving anyway: "I could answer
that I live only for them, and if they were not there, then I would not be
worth living at all."[103] A month later, while on a business trip, Gel'fer fled
to his family in Gor'kii and never returned. His diary was handed over
by someone else—perhaps Tania—to Istpart in 1945.

Gel'fer was not alone. Other diarists, like Mikhail Krakov, were equally
eager to share their precious resources with kin who were far away and
whom they viewed as fellow victims, not competitors, in the fight for
life. Krakov both cherished and dreaded the letters from his wife. When
he read that she was hungry or his daughter had no winter boots, he became
overwhelmed with worry: "Now the state of my spiritual consciousness
has been severely disrupted by what an infinitely difficult situation they
are in!" he exclaimed.[104] For such diarists, correspondence was a veritable
lifeline to kith and kin. At the same time, the post was censored and mail
delivery unreliable. Although diarists still mailed letters, just as often they
used their journals to craft imaginary or potential correspondence. They
addressed diary entries to their kin or recopied posted letters into their
notebooks.[105]

Aleksandra Zagorskaia, for instance, tried to hold her family together
through writing and reminiscing in the pages of her journal. For her, active correspondence signified her family's vitality; silence meant death.
Zagorskaia was a chairperson for the Red Case-Maker artel. She remained
behind in Leningrad, while her son, Pavel (Pavlik), and husband, Mikhail
(Misha), went to the front. She wrote to them almost every day and copied

many of their letters into her journal. She also used her regular entries to speak with them directly and inquire about their well-being. The diary, a surrogate for interaction, became the core of her emotional existence. Zagorskaia lived for communicating with them, and the absence of news devastated her.[106] Between March and May 1942, Zagorskaia's letters were returned to her because her son and husband could not be located. "Got a letter from Misha," she wrote on 4 March 1942, "which was sent on 25 November [1941] from Mulovki. The letter traveled for three months and had lost all meaning. Now I don't know how Misha is—is he alive or not?"[107] The more her letters went unanswered, the more her diary became an analysis of these silences. It was not until 20 May 1942 that Zagorskaia received word that her husband had been dead for five months.[108] Then, a month later, she received an arresting note. Attached to one of her returned letters was a notice that the addressee, Mikhail, was in a military hospital. "What does this mean?" she implored her diary. "I was in complete bewilderment. Happiness filled my soul. But I don't know what to believe—the notice that Mikhail was killed or the letter with the enclosed notice that Mikhail is in the hospital." With this note, Mikhail and her hopes were resurrected. The next post, however, brought confirmation that he was dead.[109]

No news arrived from her son, Pavel, for six more months. Zagorskaia assumed the worst. Finally, in November 1942, she received word that he was wounded in February and convalescing in Leningrad. Despite a thorough search, she found no trace of him. The thought that he might be alive and close by tormented her. She never received final confirmation of Pavel's death, and this left her vacillating between hope and despair. In one entry, she insisted that "obviously" Pavel had died, but in the next, she pictured him alive and stronger than ever. "Today is Pavel's twentieth birthday," she observed, "if he is alive, then how he has grown up, having been hardened in battle. He has become a grown man. But how is he [really]? I still know nothing after a year and four months!"[110] The text switches between past, conditional, and present tenses as the diarist's confidence wavered.

The account of the art historian and preservationist Vladimir Kuz'mich Makarov provides a remarkable example of this mélange between diary and letter and of the role both genres played in preserving relationships.

Makarov wrote most of his diary while a hospital patient in 1942. He passed the time by reading and corresponding with his daughter, Vera, and his soon-to-be wife, Zinaida Pavlovna Annenkova.[111] Makarov mentioned Annenkova in his diary as early as October 1942, but only in passing. She was an acquaintance then, a kind medic who visited him and other patients in the hospital.[112] Their relationship became intimate in the winter of 1942. Shortly thereafter, Annenkova departed for the front, where she remained until the end of the war.[113] From this point forward, Makarov's correspondence with Annenkova became his lifeline. Letters nurtured the emotional connection between these individuals whose direct personal interactions had been rather limited.

Makarov's diary is so full of correspondence that it often reads like a coauthored text. The letters in turn resemble diary entries in content and form. Many were written in installments and subdivided into dated (sometimes hourly) sections.[114] Moreover, Makarov and Annenkova elaborated on previous conversations by numbering their letters and continuing previous exchanges by citing the letter number.[115] In this way, even without Annenkova, Makarov spoke with her constantly and lived with her daily. The letters became constitutive of their life together.

Makarov also composed some letters in his diary that he never posted. Just the act of writing connected him to his beloved.[116] In both sets of letters, sent and unsent, Makarov repeatedly emphasized how close they were, how they actually felt each other's pain and laughter.[117] As Makarov read Annenkova's letters or wrote his own, he claimed he could hear her voice and asked if she could hear him.[118] "With what pleasure, with what relish and delicacy, I read your lines 'Konti, you are a treasure' . . . I hear this . . . it is not written but said, uttered. I saw your smile at this, your smile, how terribly sweetly your lips and head move, helping me to understand, to feel the whole meaning of this form of address . . ."[119] Each day that Makarov did not receive a letter filled him with foreboding. There was a time in early 1945 when Makarov was unable to send any letters because Annenkova was moving between clinics and had no stable address. The inability to contact her seemed to threaten his survival: "If she does not return, then I will not live. This is worse than living as a cripple. Life, frightful and dear life, spare and protect her for us. We still have not drunk the full glass of 'our happiness.' "[120] Makarov's vitality hinged on this connection to another, even to someone whom he knew mostly through writing.

In May 1945, Germany surrendered. But Makarov was more elated by the latest letter from Annenkova than by the news of victory.[121] In fact, rather than bring comfort, the war's end brought him anxiety. When would Annenkova return home? With this prospect in mind, the diarist became somewhat dissatisfied with their epistolary relationship and felt his loneliness more acutely. "In life, I love only her and 'ours.' I am waiting."[122] Makarov penned numerous (many unsent) letters and entries beckoning her to hurry home, a home that they had not yet shared but that he was preparing in his mind. *"I am waiting for you. I am waiting every minute."*[123] The more he waited, the more her return subsumed his life's meaning. "After you will not be, outside of you is not real . . . I remember when 'before you' I often asked myself in horror, 'will it really be this way?' This is what my life is . . . but now that you entered it you became my life, I am afraid of only one thing, the thought of the inevitable ending of everything, even the most lively and wonderful [experiences] did not come before that time. [. . .] I am waiting for you. Write. Look after yourself. I am your Konti."[124] When Annenkova did return to the city, Makarov ended his diary. The practice was no longer needed to sustain their relationship.

Makarov and Annenkova drew tremendous comfort from reminiscing about prewar experiences and inventing new ones. The brevity of their acquaintance and the age difference between them, however, yielded only a few common memories for them to discuss. Makarov was nineteen years old when Annenkova was about two. In light of this, he advanced their relationship by imagining their past lives and future home together. He was intrigued by the thought that their paths accidentally crossed many times in the past, and he looked for potential points of intersection on the cityscape.[125] He imagined strolling with her, trying to anticipate her observations and reactions. On the first warm spring day in 1945, he wrote, "I passed through the Summer Garden, our favorite broad pathway along the Mars Field . . . the beauty in the garden is 'Somov-like.' 'Konti, how nice,' you would say, placing your face under the almost hot rays [of sun]. [. . .] There, every little path reminds me of our walks. Let's go there this summer. I will wait for you."[126] Equally important were the moments when he imagined her waiting at home for him. "Sometimes I, lingering by the door of our building, ring the bell . . . and I wait and summon from my memory the sound of your steps behind the door and your voice, forever beloved . . . 'Who is it?' or 'Konti is it you?' My love, my fate, I wait for you."[127] Through this combination of imagined and real remembrances, Makarov summoned Annenkova to him and created common experiences to bind them together. These letters and entries were a pledge of his determination to survive.

Imagination and reminiscence also constituted the core of Esfir' Levina's diary practice—that is, one of two versions of that practice. There are published and unpublished editions of her diary. Both center on the theme of family but different types of families. In the archival version, Levina openly discussed her household's efforts to pool their resources and share food inside the ring. However, the 1947 edition published by Istpart focuses on a far-flung loved one who functioned as a beacon of strength and support for her. Aside from a few entries that match down to the exact phrases, Levina's two diaries are completely different. While the published version begins in December 1941, the manuscript does not begin until January 1942. Moreover, the manuscript is laid out in chronological, dated entries, whereas the published diary is structured as a series of dated "letters to a friend."[128] The published version, like Makarov's diary, highlights the resemblances between the diaristic and epistolary modes.

Levina's "letters to a friend" are tender and romantic in tone, but the addressee's identity is kept secret. Limited biographical information is available about Levina, so it is hard to ascertain whether her friend actually existed. The text suggests it was a male soldier with whom she had a long, intimate relationship in Leningrad. Levina worried about his safety and occasionally tried to guess on what front he was fighting.[129] She also reminisced with him about their life before the war. She referred to their private jokes, previous correspondence, and mutual friends. Because she never mentioned her vibrant household in this epistolary diary, Levina's "friend" provided her with a reprieve from what she presented as a rather solitary life. At one point, she paused to reflect on why she bothered to relay her daily activities to him so painstakingly: "Which one of us needs such letters more? I think it is me. My discussions with you provide me with constant ways to control myself."[130]

Like Makarov, Levina frequently imagined strolling with her friend. As a professional architect, she interpreted the landscape as they went, commenting on the historical or aesthetic significance of certain structures. "Do you want to go out with me along the streets of Leningrad?" she asked in one entry. "We will choose 'windows' as the theme for today's stroll. We will see shop windows covered with antishatter boards."[131] Levina led these walks with gusto. But there also were moments when her friend guided her. During one walk, Levina lost consciousness, faint with hunger and fatigue. However, in her mind and on the page, she kept strolling, propped up by her friend: "I walked slowly and felt that you were walking next to me. I wanted to lean on your arm and say that I am very tired, that sometimes it is hard for me to write composed letters. Then I came to. I was alone on a deserted street."[132] Regardless of whether the letters were sent or unsent, real or invented, they articulate a particular need and conceptualization of social support that many diarists developed under siege. The presence of Levina's beloved outside the city pushed her narrative forward and drove her to keep fighting for life. Once physically separated from their relatives, these diarists nurtured their emotional connections to them and sometimes made material sacrifices as well. Whether they communicated with relatives directly through letters or indirectly through journaling, imagining, and remembering, distant kith and kin inspired them to struggle on and survive. Their journals in turn highlight the diary's similarities to the letter, especially its potential as a socially interactive genre, not just an introspective one.

After the blockade, many families remained scattered. The number of children in Soviet orphanages peaked in 1946–47.[133] The reunions that children, parents, and spouses imagined often were delayed or never occurred at all. Children in orphanages were among the first evacuees to return, and many arrived to find their parents and homes gone. Evacuated workers were ordered to remain in the rear with their factories and institutes until late 1945. Once they were allowed to return, they had to prove they still had living space in the city. This was challenging even for longtime residents because much of the housing stock had been destroyed or taken over by others.[134] For many Leningraders, home was no more. Unfortunately, the diaries do not document how most of these families and marriages fared after the war. Most end before or with the lifting of the siege.

The blockade transformed the forms and functions of familial belonging. *Blokadniki* often adopted new residences, new domestic roles, and new attitudes toward familial responsibility, trust, and loyalty. There was no single concept, configuration, or meaning of family under siege. Depending on the arrangement of space and resources, the family could be a center of sacrifice or of strife, an asset or a liability. The number of family members as well as their ages, ration categories, and physical proximity to one another strongly influenced how families fared. The diaries point to three main familial arrangements. Each one signaled different understandings of kith and kin. Each one led the diarists to different conclusions about the family's staying power under siege.

Under most circumstances, the act of eating together nourishes bodies as well as relationships. The blockade, however, placed these outcomes in conflict. The extreme scarcity of resources and the fraught task of dividing them equitably strained the bonds of trust, affection, and loyalty among family members inside the ring. The diarists were torn between competing motivations and struggled to make choices within a cruelly narrow range of options, none of which appeared morally tenable or practically sustainable. Parents, children, and spouses contemplated theft, abandonment, and cannibalism; a few acted on these impulses. More typically, the diarists continued to pool resources with their relations. A sense of familial duty inheres in their descriptions of how they begrudgingly shared food or felt the sting of a loved one's betrayal. At the same time that blockade strained family ties inside the city, it seemed to strengthen intimacy—imagined, remembered, and anticipated—between distant spouses, parents, and children. For those *blokadniki*, family represented stability and companionship, not competition for resources. Depending on their individual circumstances, the diarists used their journals to nurture familial bonds, on the one hand, or to air grievances, suspicions, or confessions, on the other. In both cases, journaling provided a much-needed emotional release. It was in the diary—a domain tolerant of ambivalent emotions and a space of intimacy—that the plight of these families received naked, painful expression.

Taking the family as a model of social intimacy, the diarists wondered what familial strife revealed about social ethics, relationships, and human nature more generally. They pondered whether hunger had distorted or exposed true human character and worried that Leningraders might never recover impulses toward altruism and sacrifice. Part 2 of *The War Within* examines these and other social concerns. It traces how the diarists analyzed the besieged society taking root on this desolate island through the lenses of ethnography, medicine, social hierarchy, and history. For them, the blockade was not just a horrific trial to endure; it also became a fascinating object of study.

Diarist Dima Afanas'ev, (*left*), age eleven, and his brother Iurii, age nine, ca. 1939.

"Gatchina burns." December 1941 drawing from the diary of Dima Afanas'ev
depicting his native Gatchina under bombardment.

"Adolf Hitler." 1941 drawing from the diary of Dima Afanas'ev.

Diarist Aleksandra Liubovskaia.

Diarist Kseniia Matus with the oboe she played in the Leningrad debut of
D. D. Shostakovich's Seventh Symphony.

"Manuscripts Department." Drawing from the diary of N. I. Sinitsyna satirically dramatizing the rat infestation at the Central Branch of the Leningrad Public Library.

"Destroy the German Monster!" Poster on Nevskii Prospekt, winter 1941–42, by Nikolai Chandogin.

Leningraders gathering water from the frozen Neva River in 1942,
by Nikolai Chandogin.

A sled carrying a corpse on a Leningrad street, 1942–43, by V. Mel'nikov.

Leningrad in winter 1942, by Efim Uchitel'.

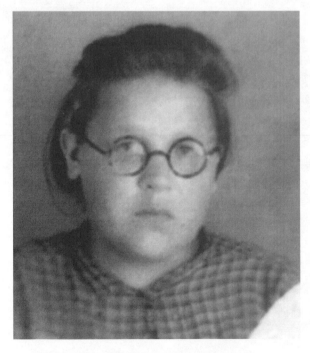

Diarist Elena Mukhina as a teenager, ca. 1940.

A healthy man and a *distrofik*, December 1942, by Nikolai Chandogin.

First page of the diary of Nina Mervol'f, listing the deaths of her family members.

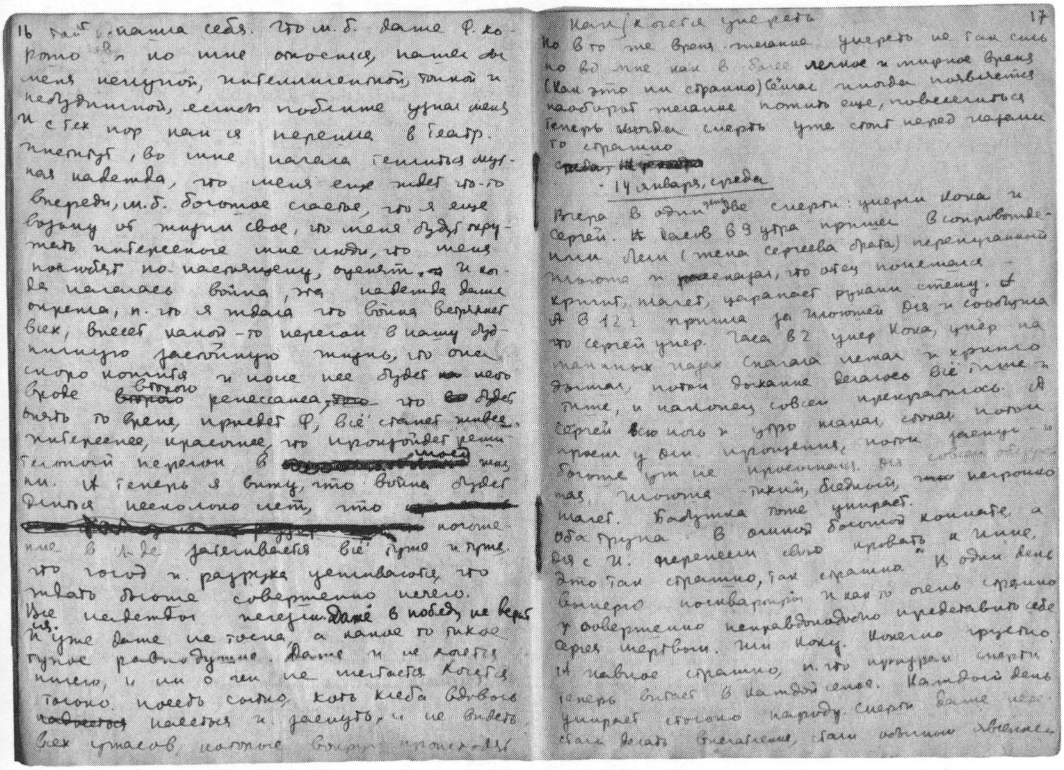

Pages from the diary of Nina Mervol'f, January 1942.

Leningraders queue for bread, ca. 1941–43, by M. A. Trakhman.

Leningrad clinic treating children for starvation, 1943, by Nikolai Chandogin.

в значительной мере зависит от обилия кариозных зубов и качества ухода за полостью рта. У детей, еще не имеющих зубов, воспалительных явлений со стороны слизистой полости рта, как правило, не бывало. Выраженных проявлений ксероза и ксерофтальмии у дистрофиков почти никогда не было.

Отеки

Отеки — почти постоянный симптом в клинической картине алиментарной дистрофии у детей. Степень их выраженности весьма

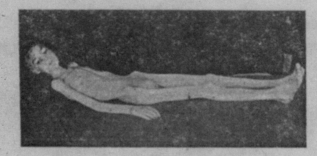

Рис. 27ᶦ Отек лица у ребенка с дистрофией.

различна — от небольшой одутловатости и пастозности до резко выраженной отечности всего тела со скоплением жидкости в се-

Рис. 28. Отек мошонки.

розных полостях. Отеки раньше всего выявляются на лице (рис. 27); одутловатость последнего при почти полном исчезновении подкожного жира придает лицу ребенка характерное, несколько

246

Page from M. V. Chernorutskii and V. G. Garshin's 1947 study *Nutritional Dystrophy in Blockaded Leningrad (Alimentarnaia distrofiia v blokirovannom Leningrade)* (Leningrad: Medgiz, 1947).

"Prophetic Prediction: Napoleon and Others—our past, our future," by V. Gal'ba,
Leningradskaia Pravda, 28 September 1941, 4.

A truck on the corner of Nevskii Prospekt and Sadovaia Street gathers corpses after an artillery attack, 8 August 1943, by Nikolai Chandogin.

"Broken Ring." This 1966 monument by Konstantin Simun commemorates the breaking of the siege.

Part II

Exploring the Island

Chapter Five

The Hierarchy of Lives

IN ADDITION to documenting their own lives, the diarists devoted tremendous time, energy, and ink to describing the peculiar society taking shape on the island. Most diarists, regardless of age or background, demonstrated strong ethnographic impulses. They jotted down observations at work, in line, and on the tram. The historian Georgii Kniazev, for example, logged snatches of conversation "for the language specialist" and literary panoramas of the cityscape "for the stage producer."[1] Young Dima Afanas'ev and Elena Mukhina monitored their classmates' conversations and schoolyard games.[2] Similarly, Esfir' Levina recorded "scenes from everyday life" *(zhanrovye kartinki),* such as these snapshots from February 1942:

1. A woman entered a courtyard in a fur coat and hat, squatted down in the middle of the courtyard, and busied herself with a particularly personal activity. It was a clear day, but she did not look for a secluded spot.
2. A funeral procession was passing by the Finland [Railway] Station: a horse pulled the cart, and there was a wreath on the coffin. The splendid corpse was not delivered to the place of

burial because the horse died. The coffin lay on the snow until
evening, then disappeared—obviously for fuel.

3. The night after the engineer Nina Minina defended her thesis, she
   sewed beads onto a ball gown for her neighbor, a bakery worker,
   who paid her with four large potatoes.

4. A man walked along the street, leaned on a post, and said, "How
   tired I am." The next day he [still] lay at the post—dogs had snapped
   off his nose. The moral: there are still some dogs alive in the city that
   haven't been eaten—eat them quickly, or they will eat you.

5. Yesterday Polina Borisovna Pal' buried her two brothers. The
   public's reaction: "she buried them, she must be rich."[3]

These five unusual sketches capture how dramatically prewar social conventions and hierarchies had fluctuated. Behaviors and associations that
would have been considered peculiar in the prewar era had become
normal: a well-dressed woman defecates in broad daylight, a coffin represents fuel. Accomplished academics perform menial tasks for their new
superiors, food-service workers, while animals reassert their dominance
over humans. Through these snapshots, Levina captured a city transformed by the siege.

The diarists dedicated themselves to social observation, sometimes
with scholarly seriousness and sometimes as a form of entertainment. A favorite pastime of both Esfir' Levina and Nina Klishevich was to categorize
passersby based on the objects they carried.[4] While aboard a newly running
tram in autumn 1942, Levina noted, "cleaning: scraps, shovels, and sleds;
gardens: shovels, stolen buckets, watering cans; fuel: axes and saws. We
know where to and from where a person is going."[5] If people carried a
shovel or a knapsack, they were headed to the gardens; if an axe, they were
heading to a damaged building; if splinters of wood, they were coming
from a ruined building. Klishevich also excelled at this guessing game,
and she used it to identify the new social types that inhabited the island:

Here are several Leningrad types:

1. A young guy of about twenty is walking along the street. On his
   right shoulder he is carrying boards and sand, and in his left

hand he holds a book in front of his face, which he is reading as he walks. Dressed entirely in old and shabby [clothes].

2. A woman in felt boots and a tight dirty skirt, her stomach swollen from [eating] grass. On the left shoulder she had several boards, [. . .] and in her hand she had a jar with sweet water, five rubles a glass. Somewhere in the middle between the jar and the log hung a gas mask from which a hydrogenation tube and a bottle of soy milk stuck out. In the other hand—a net bag with bread and a kasha pot with vegetarian cabbage soup inside. On top of these items were some sprats. Also, sticking out of the net bag many splinters of wood to heat the pot-bellied stove *[bur-zuihka]* . . . and on her face a smile because she managed not to spill anything. She marched along in a lively way.

3. A well-dressed woman, hair curled, manicured, heavily made up, in extremely high heels—a blockade wife *[blokadnaia zhena]*.[6]

Klishevich did not specify what social types these people represented, forcing the reader to play her game of categorizing people based on the clues provided. The first individual resembles a bookish *intelligent* who threw himself into practical tasks—such as cooking and carpentry—with the zeal he once had for scholarship. Esfir' Levina and Lidiia Ginzburg noticed this phenomenon among their colleagues at the Architects' and Writers' Unions, respectively.[7] The second type, overloaded with merchandise, might be a peddler or a hated speculator carrying wares to sell. Klishevich's third figure, a "blockade wife," refers to a woman who exchanged sexual favors for food.

All of these types were born of the food crisis inside the city. Food was the central axis around which blockade life revolved. It recast norms, determined hierarchies, and colored all social interactions, both intimate and mundane. "Wherever two or three people happen to meet, at work, on watch duty, or in line, the conversation is only about food. What are they giving out based on ration cards, which norms, what one can get, etc.—this is everyone's cardinal, vital question," Anna Likhacheva observed.[8] Instead of "complaining about the weather," Klishevich echoed, Leningraders initiated small talk through other queries: " 'What kind of card do you have?' 'What kind of ration are you on?' 'Where do you eat?' 'Got enough bread?' "[9]

Likhacheva and Klishevich witnessed such routine exchanges all across the city, especially while standing in food lines, eating in cafeterias, or bathing to stave off illness. Although extreme hunger and cold kept many diarists at home conserving energy and warmth, they routinely interacted with the public in lines, canteens, and bathhouses *(banias)* because these places were integral to survival. And from such settings, the diarists tried to draw broader conclusions about the social order taking shape on the island.

Lines, canteens, and bathhouses powerfully shaped how the diarists envisioned their society and perceived the social distinctions institution-alized by the ration system.[10] Officially, there were five ration categories, but because of overlap, diarists tended to consolidate them into three. Category I, or "workers'," rations went to people doing heavy labor; much smaller Category II, or "service workers'," rations went to all other fully employed Leningraders; Category III, or "dependents'," rations went to youths, students, invalids, and pensioners. The classifications were ver-sions of categories that the Bolshevik state had used since it initiated ra-tioning in 1918. They were determined largely by labor contribution but also were bound up with ideologically infused notions of class and status.

None of the categories provided enough food for long-term survival. Still, they indicated the relative privileging of some groups over others. The diarists watched how these distinctions operated in lines, cafeterias, and bathhouses, and based on specific features and configurations of these settings, they attempted to map the hierarchy of blockade society. But this hierarchy looked different from the perspective of someone standing in a linearly shaped queue as opposed to in a large dining hall or among a dispersed crowd of bathers. The diarists' impressions were highly spatialized and variable across settings. What remained consistent was the diarists' fixation on the disparities they perceived between their own portions, behaviors, and bodies and those of other groups. Using these criteria, they identified elites, inferiors, class enemies, and new so-cial types inhabiting the island. All of the diarists I studied, regardless of personal background, political outlook, or ration category, suspected they were disadvantaged by the food distribution system. They blamed this on either flawed principles or execution of the ration system. Further-more, nearly all of them attributed their suffering to local culprits and conditions. Of course, they knew the German besiegers had created the food shortages, but in their journals, they focused more on how food was allocated than on the military situation. They searched for explanations in the peculiar society developing around them.

The diarists critiqued the ration system in accordance with how they read lines, canteens, and bathhouses and with their personal understandings of various socialist principles. In the process of formulating these critiques, the diarists mapped the social geography of the blockade. They also offered their own assessments of who was worthy or unworthy, deserving or undeserving, of more food. The diarists based these claims of entitlement on a variety of factors beyond occupation, such as actual productivity, work ethic, decorum, morale, and political commitment—qualities I refer to as Soviet values. Through their daily rituals of interaction and consumption, the diarists formulated their own notions of legitimacy and deservedness. Their entitlement claims were bound up with broader, at times vague, understandings of class or status—two concepts often conflated in Soviet society.[11] Most diarists did not object to inequality per se; they did not advocate that all Leningraders—soldiers and civilians, children and adults—receive exactly the same portions.[12] However, nearly all questioned the legitimacy of the particular order of stratification they gleaned in Leningrad.

Rationing and inequality were fixtures of Soviet life. Class hierarchy had been a cornerstone of Soviet ideology since 1917, but so was the promise of social justice. The Bolsheviks rose to power with a pledge to solve the food crisis created by the tsarist state and World War I. However, severe shortages made it impossible to feed everyone adequately and equally. As the Civil War ensued, the Bolsheviks discontinued the doctrine of "equal shares" practiced by the imperial and provisional governments in favor of one based on "social differentiation." In cities like Petrograd (the city's name was changed to Leningrad in 1924) and Moscow, food came to be distributed according to two criteria: one's class status and one's labor. Additional provisions were made for people with special nutritional needs, like expectant and breastfeeding mothers.[13] This practice of resource distribution was undergirded by Lenin's "doctrine of necessary inequality," which preached that inequity was temporarily necessary during the transitional phase of socialism for ideological and practical reasons. True equality would arise later under communism.[14] Protests and strikes erupted, but "by the end of the Civil War," the historian Mauricio Borrero explained, rationing "evolved from a right shared by all citizens to a privilege granted to groups whose labor and preservation the Bolshevik government considered crucial to the survival of its revolution."[15]

Various iterations of "necessary inequality" were preached to the Soviet people during War Communism, the New Economic Policy that followed, and then Stalin's First Five-Year Plan. Resources were distributed differently in each era, as the schemas used to rank-order social groups and types of labor shifted when political and economic priorities evolved. The doctrine often was applied flexibly to reward certain groups and disadvantage others. Moreover, within each era, resources were distributed inconsistently as individuals, especially well-connected ones, successfully petitioned for better ration status. Still, the state continued to evoke the principle that it distributed or granted access to foodstuffs on the basis of two criteria: labor contribution and class credentials.

In light of the variable way that principles of distribution were translated into practice, it is not surprising that during the 1920s and 1930s there were persistent complaints about how the state allocated resources. Public outcry intensified during World War II, when both scarcity and expectations of sacrifice were at a premium. The siege survivor Lidiia Ginzburg summed up the combination of these familiar practices of distribution with the new, extreme circumstances of war as "old (bureaucratic) form and new content (people dying of hunger)."[16] The key question for the diarists was how the necessary inequalities created by extreme wartime scarcity should be weighed against socialist principles and practices that, having fluctuated greatly in the past, were themselves in dispute. The diarists endeavored to tackle this question based on their impressions of the line, canteen, and *bania,* where disparities were unmistakable, status was displayed, and entitlements were in effect.

The Psychology of a Line

In the winter and spring of 1941–42, Leningraders awoke before dawn to stand in line at food stores and bakeries. By that time, they were required to use certain shops located in their region of the city. This had not been the case at first. Initially, Leningraders could redeem ration coupons at any shop, but this policy led to chaos and panicky runs on stores rumored to be well stocked. The ballerina Vera Kostrovitskaia speculated that city leaders deliberately cultivated this confusion to mask chronic shortages: "city authorities did not attach each person to one particular store, knowing that, no matter what, they were in no condition to give out full norms to the entire population."[17] By December 1941, Leningraders were required to reregister their ration cards frequently and to use them in certain nearby stores.[18]

Undeterred by bombs, shells, or fatigue, the *blokadniki* waited for as many as ten hours without knowing what goods, if any, the shops had to distribute and whether they had the right coupons to obtain them. Leningraders also endured long lines to be admitted to canteens and bathhouses. Irina Zelenskaia, a manager at Electrical Station 7, likened one crowd waiting to enter a canteen to "a procession of half corpses so frightening that one cannot put it into words."[19] Indeed, *blokadniki* frequently died in line. Their gaunt remains silently reminded the others of how essential it was to reach the front. "An old woman, waiting for bread, slowly slides to the ground," Kostrovitskaia wrote of a November 1941 queue, "but no one cares—either she is already dead or she will be trampled to death. They watch out of the corners of their eyes to see if perhaps her ration card has fallen to the ground, [or] perhaps it is still tightly clutched in her stiffening hand." Such indifference to all but the prized ration card "is the only way to respond to death."[20] Lines were so pervasive that they extended into death. Fedor Nikitin, Nikolai Punin, and Mariia Konopleva observed how piles of corpses seemed to queue at mortuaries and cemeteries, waiting for burial.[21]

The diarists regarded wartime lines as both peculiar and representative bodies. On the one hand, they likened the queue to a "many-headed monster" or a "long tapeworm" that acquired a life of its own.[22] On the other hand, they approached the line as a kind of microcosm from which they tried to generalize about society as a whole. They scanned the crowd for clues about the state of public health and compared the numbers of men and women in line to estimate demographic shifts.[23] The constancy, magnitude, and interminability of blockade queues added to the notion that they represented society in miniature. After all, they were among the largest assemblies of living bodies inside the city.

The diarists were particularly eager to uncover what they called "the psychology of the line."[24] Conversation was one point of entry into Leningraders' thoughts and moods. The diarists recorded common topics of discussion or relayed exchanges they overheard. Most were about what foodstuffs were being dispensed and in what quantities, about sick and departed relatives, about light-fingered food-service workers, and about events at the front.[25] The architect Esfir' Levina compiled this set of exchanges from January 1942 between line waiters and "speculators" trying to sell them high-priced goods: "I am returning to the bakery, I am standing in line. A group of women count their dead, some fellow suggests, 'and you will follow them if you are going to wait [in line]. Buy from me 300 grams for 90 rubles—it's really cheap.' The policeman talks about [Lengorispolkom Chairman] Popkov's speech."[26]

During that first winter, some diarists claimed they could glean little substantive information from these mundane discussions. They found the tenor and frequency of chatter more revealing. Irina Zelenskaia, for instance, noted the contrast between the muted tones that Leningraders used to recount deaths in the family and the affectionate way they described food.[27] Others claimed that silence was more telling than conversation. In Lidiia Ginzburg's retrospective *Notes of a Blockade Person*, she analyzed "eerily quiet" wintertime lines. "Gripped by one all-consuming passion, they hardly uttered a word: with manic impatience, they stared ahead over the next man's shoulder at the bread."[28] *Blokadniki* felt compelled to wait even when they knew that they had little hope of reaching the front before supplies ran out. The sixth-grader Dima Afanas'ev, for instance, admitted that he preferred standing long hours in line than staying home because it gave the illusion of activity. Besides, he noted, it was just as cold indoors as it was on the street.[29] "It was psychologically impossible" to resist queuing, Ginzburg echoed.[30] From this perspective, the psychology of the line centered on the private agony of individuals doomed to wait irrationally, endlessly, and silently.

Other diaries, however, characterized queue psychology by the compulsive desire to size up other line waiters in order to gauge one's relative chance of survival. The linear arrangement of the line encouraged this. These diarists categorized waiting *blokadniki* into status groups based not on considerations of gender, class, or education but on location.[31] There were two groups: the people in front of and the people behind the diarist. "The psychology of a line," Esfir' Levina explained, "[is that] everyone is envious of the one in front and desires 'all sorts of misfortunes' to befall them so that they will leave the line."[32] As Levina suggested, Leningraders generally "compared upwardly" to those who stood in front of them—an act that often ignited resentment and jealousy. Social psychologists suggest that line waiters typically compare downward, pitying the people behind them or at the end of a line. However, they have found that individuals in crisis, like the *blokadniki,* fixate on those who are ahead and thus relatively privileged.[33]

Leningraders at the front of the line emerge from the journals as a kind of chosen people. "The [line] manager, like the 'gatekeeper of paradise *[vratar' raia]*,' counted off the 'faithful souls,' letting them inside ten at a time. I stood and gazed mindlessly at this 'procedure,'" the chemist Elena Kochina observed.[34] Conversely, line waiters were "a little scornful of those behind them," Levina noted.[35] Having lower status, the people behind were supposed to obey those standing in front and heed their calls to move back, keep quiet, stop shoving, and so on. Those in back also deferred to the superior knowledge of those in front, who had a better view of the proceedings. Although this pecking order was temporary and reshuffled with each new queue, the diarists fixated on assessing and improving their position every time.

The long stretches of waiting magnified social antagonism as well as inequality. How could one beat the line? "Only those who are lucky or who have the strength to push the more feeble people aside and snatch 200 grams of grain from the seller get something," Vera Kostrovitskaia explained.[36] Georgii Kniazev likened a chain of assembled women to "a small circle of Dante's hell. [. . .] Each person acts [like] a wolf and is ready to cut each other's throats. [. . .] These are not women but some kind of furies, witches inside of women, in a feminine form." He hastened to add that "even ruder and crueler are the men who are especially needy and weak."[37] The musician Kseniia Matus called the blockade line "a raging ocean that will crush you and trample you to death, and no one offers you so much as a helping hand."[38] For sixteen-year-old Iura Riabinkin, a queue was "a crush of people" with whom he had to "fight hand-to-hand combat" to keep his place.[39] In terms of survival, the daily fight to improve one's position became a more pressing battle than the one taking place at the military front.

Matus, Levina, and others waged this battle by cutting or cheating. Food stores often used lists or numbered tickets to maintain order in line. This system was easily manipulated. "At home," Levina confessed, "I prepare hundreds of numbers and give them out on the street before the store opens, keeping for myself a place in the first hundred. Every hour—there is a check, rivals appear; they also arrived with numbers, and arguments take place over whose numbers are real."[40] The librarian Mariia Konopleva voiced her rage about other tricks used to remove people from line, such as spreading rumors about food deliveries at other stores or sounding fake air-raid sirens.[41]

The diarists also witnessed how Leningraders vied for position in more congenial ways, devising systems for saving places or dividing the wait into smaller shifts. Some tried to forge temporary alliances through emotional appeals. They shared stories about their sick or starving loved ones to win the sympathy and the place of the person in front of them. Although sob stories may have worked in prewar lines, Levina noted that *blokadniki* were unaffected by them: "In general, the public is self-restrained—nothing moves you. When one says that her husband is dying and her children lie there swollen, another answers that her husband has already died and, of her three kids, two have died." Such indifference to the plight of others became so common that Levina wondered if it was an inherent trait of the Russian character laid bare by the duress of war: "Where does this self-restraint come from—from Russian endurance, discipline, or hope?"[42] Leningraders remained so focused on the goal of obtaining food that they rarely took collective action or intervened in others' disputes. When Elena Kochina's bread was snatched out of her hands, she fought the thief to get it back, while bystanders simply dodged blows and kept their eyes fixed on the bread counter.[43]

Kochina became so accustomed to strife in line that, when a stranger allowed her to cut in, she described it as a kind of marvel—an exception that proved the general rule of wartime queue behavior. Incidents of altruism and cooperation frequently appear in memoirs and interviews of *blokadniki* but rarely in diaries.[44] The diarists did document moments of cooperation when individual and shared interests aligned. Together, Leningraders ganged up on line jumpers or, when the pipes froze in January 1942, passed buckets of water from the Neva River to the bakeries so they could make bread.[45] But such moments are overshadowed and outnumbered by recorded incidents of competition. Perhaps the diarists studied here simply did not witness many incidents of cooperation, or perhaps moments of partnership came into sharper focus after Leningraders were no longer competing for survival. The diaries neither prove nor disprove the existence of social solidarity. But, as accounts of subjective experience, they repeatedly emphasize "swearing, shoving, and cutting," not camaraderie, in line.[46] It is notable, however, that none of the diarists studied here reported witnessing riots or uprisings in line. Even though Leningrad's NKVD documented several attacks on lines and shops, queues do not appear to have been the major sites of protest that they were in Moscow in October 1941.[47] Perhaps it was exhaustion or the watchful eye of the police that prevented such outbreaks. Or perhaps the atomization and antagonism that the diarists experienced in line created the appearance of order in the city.

In sum, the diaries present the line as a condensed version of the social order, where thousands of social dramas and struggles were performed daily and where the entangled processes of social comparison and self-evaluation were manifest. The line was only a temporary hierarchy, but this did not prevent the diarists from using it to generalize about city demographics, collective psychology, and the prevalence of social strife. Because they viewed the collective from their particular location in line, their maps contain both insights and blind spots. After all, many political and cultural elites did not have to wait because they shopped at "closed" stores or ate at "closed" canteens. These privileges, far more extreme, were outside the purview of most diarists.[48] Moreover, once the *blokadniki* reached the front of the queue of a bakery or shop, portion size—based on ration category—became the chief determinant of status.

Status on Display: The Cafeteria

Like lines, canteens were a mainstay of Soviet life. Communal dining was established as a practical way to feed people and as a method for liberating women from domestic work and infusing a collectivist ethos in the population. During the siege, most canteens were linked to institutions like schools, trade unions, factories, or hospitals. One had to be associated with the organization to use its cafeteria. Affiliates usually had to pay with ration coupons for the watery soup and small portion of kasha they typically received. This changed only when the available food per capita markedly increased.[49] Eventually, the city expanded the network of municipal canteens open to the public, but this occurred after the brutal winter of 1941–42.[50] Moreover, as the staggering death toll attests, canteen access was necessary but not sufficient for survival.

Once the diarists braved the line and entered a cafeteria, they were presented with new opportunities for social comparison. The politics of location were different here. In the linearly shaped queue, society appeared bifurcated. In the canteen, social groupings were numerous and intermixed. Fortunates and unfortunates could sit together and observe each other at length. The diarists glimpsed an array of social types in the canteen, depending on where and with whom they sat. In line, status was based on proximity to the front. In the cafeteria, the diarists categorized Leningraders on the basis of how much food they received and how they behaved while eating. Indeed, the diarists' impressions of the social order were highly spatialized.

What kind of social data did the diarists extract from the canteen? During the first siege winter, social interactions were muted in cafeterias as they were in lines. Leningraders refrained from talking so that they could focus on eating, chewing slowly to make the experience last longer.[51] Conversations were sparse, sometimes composed of mere glances. "They eat their neighbor's plate with their eyes, 'are you going to eat that bit later?' and 'how do you allocate your bread?' 'I have come to believe that one should eat 200 grams in the morning,'" Esfir' Levina observed.[52] Many preferred to savor their food in silence and solitude.

Along with small talk, other courtesies disappeared. Leningraders dropped certain table manners and picked up new habits like licking their plates clean. In the Architects' Union, Levina noted, women tried to sit separately, so that men did not see them do these things. "They do not have enough willpower to leave [their plates] alone."[53] The hungriest *blokadniki* were the least able to control themselves at table. Lidiia Ginzburg created two composite types of Leningraders on the brink of death, "A" and "B," on the basis of her observations in the Writer's Union canteen. At the smallest "trifle," " 'A' fell into despair" and disrupted other diners, while "B" could not resist licking the empty bowls of his fellow patrons.[54] Hunger could breed callousness, emotional instability, or rudeness. Leningraders who had lost all sense of decorum, the actor Fedor Nikitin remarked, resembled ravenous animals to be pitied and perhaps a bit despised. By contrast, the radio worker Arkadii Lepkovich took pride in Leningraders' coarse manners as a sign of their warrior status: "such a people is frightening and ruthless to the enemy."[55] Although norms of comportment were in flux, the diarists still used them to classify the *blokadniki* sitting nearby as fortunate and unfortunate, normal and deviant, deserving and undeserving. Thus, the partitioning of goods gave rise to an "underlying partitioning of society" into types and status groups.[56]

Manners were much more than niceties. They could indicate status, evidence that one ate more, or worthiness, that one deserved to eat more. Conduct and behavior, along with class, were important determinants of social standing in Soviet society. Self-control and consumption practices were especially prized as hallmarks of *kul'turnost'* (culturedness).[57] Perhaps to reinstate such values, when the food situation improved in late 1942, prewar etiquette returned to many canteens, sometimes forcibly.[58] Levina observed how heads of the Architects' Union tried to resocialize the staff by teaching them: " 'Blow your nose into a handkerchief, and do not wipe your fingers on the tablecloth, do not lick the plate with your tongue.' In normal times, such remarks would be deemed offensive but now are being obeyed. They are teaching people to live as one teaches invalids how to walk."[59]

In the canteen, the diarists certainly studied the unfortunates below them on the social ladder. However, they expended the most energy (and text) on elites. They compared upwardly in the canteen, as they did in line, to those who received larger portions or whose bodies or decorum indicated a more robust diet. They range from "new elites" who gained power because of the famine, like food-service workers, and more "traditional elites" like workers and party members, who had long enjoyed material and ideological privileges. The diarists wielded the rhetoric of class struggle and Soviet values to repudiate these groups' elite status and to justify their own claims of entitlement. I found only one instance when a diarist positioned herself as an elite, and then it was done in jest. This was when the librarian Aleksandra Liubovskaia joked that she and her children were "playing gentry" when they ate well.[60] The vast majority— regardless of ration category or other privileges—presented themselves as victims of the bureaucratic distribution of hunger.

New Elites

Perhaps the most despised new elites, empowered by the famine, were food-service personnel, including cooks, servers, and bookkeepers. In lines and canteens, they occupied coveted space "behind the counter." In both settings, the diarists scrutinized food workers' actions and bodies, and they accused them of undermeasuring portions, playing favorites, stealing food, and generally feeding themselves at the expense of the population. After waiting in line from seven a.m. to nine p.m. for bread, the musician Kseniia Matus slandered the bakery workers: "What a merry life! Bastards! How far is it still possible to drive such miserable, helpless people? If they were to be left just one day without eating, if they were to endure but one hundredth of the lot we've endured—."[61] Her text broke off before she completed the threat. Matus cast the bakery workers as out-siders ("them") because, in her eyes, they did not undergo the profound suffering that united the *blokadniki* ("us"). Irina Zelenskaia called lunch at the power station where she worked "a joke" and accused the manage-ment of shortchanging Leningraders. "We never get full portion at the canteen. For our own 250 people, 200 soups are given out, not every day, 80–100 second courses" for 250 people, and "because of that, there is always a terrible fight."[62] Thus, in identifying other status groups, the diarists presented themselves as true *blokadniki,* suffering undeservedly. Zelenskaia's suspicions became acute in spring 1942, when the regime increased norms but gave Leningraders less than the promised portions. Zelenskaia, however, did not realize (at least on paper) that the norms were misleading. Instead, she blamed the shortfall on those who transported, cooked, and served food: "On the way to the consumer, an awful lot [of food] sticks to the hands of the cafeteria, the storehouse, and other workers despite all kinds of workers' inspections. If it were not for that, everything would be good."[63]

Like Matus and Zelenskaia, most diarists were certain that there were enormous disparities between what they and food-service workers ate. They presented these disparities as fact. The actual scale of the discrepancy, although difficult to ascertain, seems more modest. Richard Bidlack and Nikita Lomagin have suggested that workers in the food industry had a 10–20 percent lower rate of starvation than the general public did, but the rate varied by institution. At certain bakeries and candy factories, 90 percent of workers survived. Food theft was a reality. The NKVD arrested 17,000 Leningraders for theft between June 1941 and September 1942.[64]

Even diarists who benefited from their connections to food-service personnel still blamed them for their hunger.[65] These personal exemptions and oversights underscore both the severity of the food crisis and the particularity of the diarists' visions of it. The engineer Ivan Savinkov managed a shop floor at the Molotov Factory. He held a Category I card, obtained doctors' prescriptions for additional food, and occasionally got extras from the factory's cafeteria director, a friend.[66] Even so, Savinkov suffered from numerous hunger-related illnesses and was bedridden for several months. Rather than focus his rage on German bombardment of food trucks and barges, Savinkov lashed out at those who handled the few deliveries that made it inside the city. "It is an interestingly organized affair," he remarked. "Any server has a full staff that carries food out of the cafeteria. The guards work together because they also want to eat— this is the first small party of swindlers. The second is much larger: this is the acting assistant, the head cooks, and the supply keepers. Here, a much bigger game takes place, consisting of compiling a list of spoilage, loss, evaporation. [. . .] Terrible self-provisioning is taking place."[67] Savinkov identified two rings of conspiracy, one operated by the kitchen staff and the other by delivery and warehouse personnel who stole food before it even made it to the cafeteria. Fedor Nikitin, who shared Savinkov's suspicion that theft was systematic and highly coordinated, called pilfering "our Russian plague" and likened the "bread ladies" *(khlebnie babi),* bread cutters, and cafeteria directors to an enemy army, a "brotherhood in arms" *(bratstvo po oruzhiyu),* that was closing ranks against the *blokadniki.*[68] For Savinkov and Nikitin, these internal adversaries eclipsed the German besiegers. Of course, most Leningraders were not fully informed about the severity of the food crisis, which city authorities concealed. The Military Soviet of the Leningrad Front (VSLF) often neglected to adjust rations when there were dips in supply in order not to hurt morale or give the impression that the food crisis was worsening.[69] Leningraders were left to search for explanations of why they were shortchanged. They may have found it easier to blame the individuals they confronted every day instead of impersonal policies and circumstances.

The diarists' animosity was fueled by the fact that, according to them, bakery and cafeteria workers flaunted their criminality. They emerge from the journals as a kind of nouveau riche adorned in "gold rings and earrings" obtained from bartering stolen bread.[70] Young children also participated in conspicuous displays of privilege. In July 1942, Esfir' Levina recorded a conversation she overheard between three small boys comparing their bodies on a street corner. "The winner" explained his victory by announcing, "I look better than all of you because my dad [works] at a bread factory."[71] Such superior wealth and health made food workers appear alien to Leningraders. While Elena Kochina was aboard an evacuation convoy with her husband, Dima, and daughter, Lena, in April 1942, she observed that passengers "present[ed] a homogeneous mixture," except for "one young fellow and a girl" who stood out: "Both are robust and red-cheeked. They quickly sniffed one another out and got together. The guy jabbers on without stopping. Words fly out of his mouth, quickly running into one another. The result is a kind of leapfrog *[naskokivaia drug na druga]* that is impossible to follow. But the girl evidently understands him perfectly. Throwing her head back, she scatters laughter throughout the car. Together, they raise quite a hullabaloo." Kochina was struck not only by their impudence, but also by the distinct physicality and style of speech. Peculiar in its speed, energetic delivery, and mirth, this language was disturbingly human and incomprehensible to her. The pair gravitated towards each other and ignored the other passengers until Dima Kochin interrupted their conversation: "'Somehow you don't look like you went hungry,' Dima said tauntingly. 'I didn't go hungry. [. . .]

My father works in Leningrad in supply. During the blockade we ate better than before the war. We had everything.' 'Then why are you being evacuated?' 'I was bored in Leningrad. There wasn't anyone around to have a few laughs or go dancing.' [The girl] also spoke quite readily: 'I work in the supply department at Lake Ladoga. We ate whole boxes of butter and chocolate.' She said boastfully, 'Of course, before the war I didn't see that.' I felt indignation rising in me. Neither of them could begin to comprehend their tactlessness, telling this to the very people they had robbed."[72] Such incidents helped Kochina rationalize the times her husband stole food from neighbors, shops, and storehouses. "After all," Kochina reasoned, "the salespeople are really robbing us blind. In exchange for bread, they have everything they want. Almost all of them, without any shame at all, wear gold and expensive furs. Some of them even work behind the counter in luxurious sable and sealskin coats."[73] Kochina considered her family's thefts as necessary, but the accumulation of gold and other finery was sheer greed in her eyes. Although she tried to draw clear boundaries between food-service workers and her family, Kochina's remarks did point to the fluidity of social and moral categories under siege. Her account underscores how the diarists' visions of the social order were tied to personal claims of entitlement and exemption.

Another group, distinct in appearance and decorum, that secured a high place in the food hierarchy consisted of those who traded sexual favors for food. The diarists called them "cafeteria girls" *(devushka iz stolovoi)* or "blockade wives" *(blokadnaia zhena)*. Along with food, sex was a major currency under siege, as it typically is in circumstances of war, incarceration, and poverty. In Leningrad, only the well fed maintained their libido and could afford to give up food for sex. "A new term even has emerged to explain this: 'blockade acquaintanceship' *[blokadnoe znakomstvo]*," Ivan Savinkov explained.[74] The diarists instructed their potential readers in how to spot this type. "Using a special sense," Zelenskaia remarked, "your eye fishes out from these old, doomed people healthy blooming faces. They are mostly young women, and if they are not in military uniforms, then of course one can suspect them of being 'cafeteria girls,' the only stratum of the population this winter that has preserved its normal appearance, although without much honor for themselves."[75] Although she accepted that military personnel deserved more food, Zelenskaia considered healthy-looking civilians to be parasites living off the rest of the population. Their healthy and feminine appearance indicated a kind of inner debauchery. However, even as she underlined the reversal of these cues, Zelenskaia admitted, "you are just happy to see fresh, healthy young faces, like these young ladies," rather than the "numerous walking skeletons" of *blokadniki*.[76]

Most diarists gendered this social type female. Nina Klishevich depicted the "blockade wife" as heavily made up and oversexed—a stark contrast to the androgynous *blokadniki*.[77] Ivan Savinkov, however, reversed the usual pairing of female prostitute and male patron and explained that men also sold themselves to female food-service workers. Savinkov called these female patrons "the new Leningrad female aristocrats *[aristokratki]*" or "the aristocrats of the stove" *(aristokratki ot plity)*, smearing them as class enemies. Like Zelenskaia and Klishevich, Savinkov vilified the women, not the men, as overly sexualized and brazenly materialistic. The main difference between blockade wives and *aristokratki* was that the latter were marked by telltale plump physiques and conspicuous wealth. "This is first and foremost a fat, well-nourished carcass *[tusha]*, dolled up in silk, velvet, stylish boots, and shoes. There is gold in their ears, heaps of it on their fingers, piles, and of course a watch, stolen and, depending on its grandeur, golden or plain. When this type of '*aristokratka*' chats with us, it is necessary for her to look at the watch, shaking her wrist for a long time and keeping it at eye level. What an assured, insolent conversation [it is]—she thinks that she can buy you for a night for a plate of soup. And the conversation is only about food, about theft, [about] how and how much someone steals."[78] To Savinkov, the cafeteria worker was a fat, "greasy" *(zhirnyi)* "carcass," a piece of meat more than a human being, whose appetite for food, valuables, and men was insatiable.

Savinkov characterized these sexual transactions as elite affairs in which junior engineers like him could not participate. The *aristokratki* partnered with political and military elites who had less need for food but probably were more physically desirable. They had little to gain, he remarked with pride and bitterness, by choosing him. "Such an '*aristokratka* of the stove' does not want anyone lower than an engineer as her lover. 'My lady-killer *[ukhazher]*' supervising engineer is proud of this.

And so we enter into slavery under a cook, he goes [to her] in order not to die or freeze during winter. Such an acquaintanceship guarantees you food, firewood, and definitely a featherbed with a 'fat lady in it.' [. . .] Sailors and especially commanders are held in high esteem by the '*aristokratka* of the stove.' [. . .] I do not want to sell myself, and it is obvious, therefore, that I am a *distrofik*. I have been ill for nine months of 1942 and in bed for five of them. Oh war! What are you doing to people!"[79] Savinkov called himself a *distrofik* to convey his physical deterioration and marginal status but also his purity. *Distrofiia* was a highly malleable and politicized term that could be wielded as an insult to ostracize others or as a badge of suffering, a marker of insider status as a *blokadnik*. In this case, Savinkov drew on both of these meanings to describe the cook's rejection of him. He criticized himself for being unappealing and unwilling to do anything—including sell himself—for food, while gesturing toward his moral purity, especially compared to the *aristokratka* holding court in the canteen.

Vilification of food-service workers was also a major feature of the local press. *LP,* for instance, was mum about administrative blunders and miscalculated norms, but it published at least a dozen notices about food-service personnel tried for theft.[80] It also printed twenty-five articles demonizing cafeteria staff; all but two of them appeared in 1943 or later—after the previously quoted diary entries were written.[81] These articles, therefore, did not prompt Leningraders to implicate food workers, but they did reflect the widespread assumption that food workers stole, as well as the regime's misleading explanations of how much food was available. When hunger began to subside in 1943, *LP* began reporting on raids of canteens and investigations of corruption and theft.[82] That same year, it also resumed publication—after stopping when the siege began—of censorious letters to the editor, in which the signatories legitimized demands for better food and conditions by emphasizing their status as workers. They chastised cafeteria managers for "not improving the lives of working people" and ordered them "to deliver to the workers every gram that they are due."[83] Local NKVD reports list at least seventeen stoppages or slowdowns by workers protesting labor and canteen conditions.[84] Furthermore, when the Sovinformbiuro first openly discussed food shortages in 1944, it was also with regard to cafeteria problems, not general supply issues. This report opened with the declaration that "the cafeterias ought to feed the working people better."[85] The language of these grievances underscores the enduring privilege of workers in wartime Leningrad.

Under siege, as in the prewar period, industrial workers occupied a privileged position, socially and spatially. They usually had access to canteens inside their factories and to occasional food parcels sent from the front. Some moved into barracks at their work sites, which helped them conserve energy and warmth. In addition, during November 1941, when the food crisis became dire, Lengorispolkom slated workers at a hundred defensive plants to eat at their factories' cafeterias off-ration. In bakeries, their ration status granted them roughly twice as much bread as people in Categories II and III.[86] These practices were justified pragmatically and ideologically. Workers in heavy industry expended the most calories doing labor essential to the war effort. Moreover, they had long been privileged by the regime that seized power and ruled in their name. Workers at the city's power plants, the Stalin Metal Works, and the Kirov Factory had a 10–20 percent lower death rate than the general population did.[87] Of course, they still died at appalling rates.

Initially, some diarists praised the ration system as "necessary," "logical," and good for "discipline" because it upheld Soviet tenets and military priorities.[88] A Category II worker, Zelenskaia remarked that the decision to "support all those who were able-bodied" and "not feeding those who are dying" was "cruel" but "acceptable" in light of the immediate goal of winning the war.[89] Over time, however, she and other diarists grew critical of it. The diarists hotly disputed which workers were included in Category I. The distinction between Category I "workers" and Category II "service workers" was an artifact of the prewar period, but the blockade raised the stakes of this divide because food was so scarce and because the "worker" designation was granted to fewer residents, just 34 percent in the winter of 1941–42.[90] This excluded workers in lighter or non-war-related industries, many of whom considered themselves workers and deserving of equal status.[91] The 34 percent included, however, some political and cultural elites, who did not do heavy labor but whose clout earned them Category I cards.

Diarists in Category II claimed that the ration system devalued them in at least two ways. First, at the height of the food crisis, they received the same norms as people in Category III, as dependents who did not work. Since the 1930s, as Shelia Fitzpatrick has pointed out, Category II workers occupied a precarious position, as there was no clear service workers group in traditional Marxist categories.[92] These workers were less favored than the proletarian workers in Category I, and some of them felt offended to be fed the same as people in Category III. This resentment might be a holdover from the Civil War era, when this status was given to "nonlaboring, exploiting classes" and thus was a mark of dishonor. Indeed, some of this stigma endured during the siege. In an unpublished entry, the artist Anna Ostroumova-Lebedeva put it quite severely: "all these old people, dependents, and pensioners are useless and surplus mouths in Leningrad," so the authorities aimed "to get rid of them."[93] Category III norms were so small that the ration card was nicknamed the *smertnik,* or death certificate.[94]

Second, diarists in Category II often complained that Category I workers did not do enough labor to earn rations that were twice as large as theirs. Leningraders were not eating "each according to his labor." At the start of the war, the situation was quite different. After Germany invaded, city authorities extended the workday, raised production quotas, and increased the punishments for absenteeism.[95] However, by late November 1941, a lack of electricity, raw materials, and manpower began to cripple industry. That winter, the city closed 270 factories. Roughly half of all workers stopped going to work, and those who did occupied themselves with keeping warm, making repairs, and reading. Aleksandra Liubovskaia, a librarian (and Category II employee), described a typical day at the milling factory: "No one is seriously working. The head of the department, it is true, punctually comes to work at eight a.m. and literally sits with his hands folded on the table for an hour and then leaves." Workers crowded into the library. "They sit for two hours at our tables," reading newspapers, discussing the war until it was time for lunch.[96]

During the months when industry was largely inoperative, workers still received Category I rations.[97] Natal'ia Uskova, a philology student who took a munitions job in order to get Category I status, echoed this: "Right now it's not working because of the lack of electric energy. But all who have remained alive come to the office like it's their duty. [. . .] The big motivation is the cafeteria. From one to two o'clock, it's lunch, but the line on the stairwell toward the second floor already forms at twelve o'clock. Here they feed us every day, despite the fact that the factory is not working."[98]

In light of such inactivity, some diarists in Category II insisted that their work was comparable to the work of people in Category I. As Esfir' Levina sat in the cafeteria at the Architects' Union, she fumed that engineers were fed more than architects even though at that moment the difference in their jobs was negligible.[99] "We work or do nothing to the same extent," Irina Zelenskaia contended. "I am feeling like a victim of injustice. These horrors weaken one's will and, what is worse, one's principles."[100] These issues prompted her and others to reflect on what it meant to be a worker. Drawing on a wider range of criteria—including political attitudes, industriousness, and discipline—she argued that Category I workers lacked the proper consciousness to warrant such privilege. In the summer of 1942, when the electrical plant where she worked was fully operational, Zelenskaia claimed that the Category I workers were undisciplined. Even those who lived at the station overslept and missed their shifts. Work started two hours late and lasted only five hours total. When city authorities declared that 1 May and 2 May were mandatory workdays, the diarist remarked, "it is true with our doubtful discipline that, instead of two working days, we have five nonworking days."[101] The workers' apparent indifference to the party mission further discredited their special status. As a local party delegate, Zelenskaia tried to create equal enthusiasm for political activities as for the cafeteria, but without success. "We have been unable to organize something like the canteen in the red corner. The workers themselves talk less about these external conditions but always talk about whether or not there will be food."[102]

Zelenskaia's disdain for her Category I coworkers grew stronger when she joined the commission at Lenenergo in charge of feeding workers in its cafeterias. Now on the other side of the food counter, she leveled the same accusations against her coworkers that she once lodged against food-service workers.[103] Shortly after she assumed this position in late September 1941, she observed "my work could make you a misanthrope," surmising that that rudeness was the essence of human nature.[104] Over time, the animosity she felt for her coworkers in the cafeteria intensified. By October, one month into her position, Zelenskaia declared that she was "surrounded by swindlers."[105] She described the canteen as a "battle" *(bor'ba)* and a "siege" *(osada)*, in which she, behind the rampart of the bread counter, was surrounded and outnumbered.[106] An "onslaught" of "blows pour onto me," she despaired. These cafeteria wars eclipsed the actual war in Zelenskaia's account and perhaps in her mind. Accusations about class enemies flew from both sides of the counter. Workers wielded threats and slogans against her: "The people are becoming my personal enemies [. . .] By the end of the first half of the day, I had to hear that I should be thrown out, dragged out by my hair, that I 'am not working class,' and finally candid statements: 'right now they are squeezing us, but there will come a time when we shall squeeze them.' A representative of the 'working class,' a young *Komsomolka,* said this. But who are 'they,' and who are 'we'? One hears this division often. The bosses? The communists?" The categories of "us" and "them" were in flux as they battled to prove their authentic "working-class" status. And when she and other food-service personnel tried to defend themselves, explaining that the German blockade was to blame for the shortages, one party member retorted, "What does the war have to do with it?"[107] The cafeteria battles continued through December. "I practically have to engage in hand-to-hand fighting," Zelenskaia admitted.[108] The canteen provided a crucial setting in which Leningraders posited themselves as true members of the working class and tried to distinguish proletarians from class enemies, even though, as Zelenskaia's account suggests, these categories and their meanings were evolving.

If, in the eyes of some diarists, Category I workers did an insufficient amount of manual labor, then party officials did even less. Even so, they often received Category I cards and access to "closed" canteens and stores because of their work on the ideological front. According to NKVD records, 70 percent of party members received Category I rations and that during the deadly winter months of 1942, party members died at a rate of 15.1 percent. Compare this to the estimated 37 percent of the general population who died in the first eleven months of the siege.[109]

Most diarists, of course, had only a vague sense of the numbers, but they recorded rumors that at Smolny, the local party headquarters, "they are eating cake." A few got a more detailed view. In January 1942, Kseniia Matus heard from Zina, a fellow musician and friend, what fare was like in the Smolny cafeteria. Zina had been invited there as part of a musical ensemble, and she told Matus of the "600 grams of bread and three-course meal" that they shared with First Party Secretary Andrei Zhdanov.[110] Just reading about one of Stalin's diplomatic dinners in *LP* threw sixteen-year-old Elena Mukhina into a fit of rage: "It is just shameful how they stuff themselves like devils while we inhumanely do not even receive our piece of bread. There, they host extravagant events, and we live like cave people, like blind moles."[111]

The journal of Nikolai Ribkovskii offers a rare peek into elite party cafeterias. A union official from Vyborg, Ribkovskii fled to Leningrad in the summer of 1941. Now an unemployed refugee, he received a dependent's ration, and his health deteriorated that autumn. Ribkovskii's fortunes changed in December, however, when he became a political instructor for the city soviet. He was given a Category I card and access to party cafeterias. At a time when 2,000–3,000 Leningraders died daily, Ribkovskii reportedly ate goose, ham, turkey, and even caviar.[112] After eating too much too quickly, he spent a week recovering in the party's clinic, where the meals remained substantial. The clinic was "simply just a seven-day vacation house," where "the war hardly makes itself felt. [. . .] Yes, only under the Bolsheviks, only under Soviet power, it is only possible to have such rest under the conditions of war, of a prolonged siege of a city. [. . .] What could be better? We eat, drink, stroll about, sleep, or we just idly listen to the gramophone, tell jokes or play dominoes and cards."[113] The relaxed atmosphere of the party clinic transported Ribkovskii's attention far away from the circumstances of war and blockade, which he felt so acutely only months before. He documented this without shame or guilt. Perhaps his sense of relief trumped all other emotions. Ribkovskii's response, although extreme, mirrors that of other diarists who disputed the advantages of others without questioning or acknowledging their own.

Few diarists experienced party canteens as Ribkovskii did, but many sat near party members in factory canteens and noted the disparities in their portions. Diarists both inside and outside the party questioned whether their political leaders still deserved Category I cards if they denigrated Soviet values. Irina Zelenskaia painted Lenenergo's party elite as "sluggish, indifferent, and uninspired people" and more devoted to their own comfort than to their professional and political duties.[114] When she complained about the lack of discipline and productivity during a meeting of Lenenergo's party committee, she was given the absurd task of waking the station's party secretary at 7:55 a.m. so that he started to work on time.[115] Similarly, Savinkov declared that party and Komsomol workers at the Molotov Factory had the lowest morale and highest absenteeism. Far from model workers, the Komsomol members "killed the initiative to work." "I, however," Savinkov claimed, "demand more severe requirements for party members and Komsomol members since I consider them more disciplined. But they are just the opposite, they demand amnesty for their position. They need to go." Their willingness to abandon their posts, he noted, marked a reversal in Soviet priorities: "People do not understand. Now, the personal is taking precedent over the societal."[116] Individual survival had trumped one's commitment to the collective.

A more unusual critique of party privilege appears in the diary of Elizaveta Sokolova, who was an interim director of Istpart, the organization that encouraged Leningraders to keep diaries for its collection. Sokolova was a proponent of party privilege. Her objection was that she had not been granted access to the party's elite canteens and stores. Her diary documents how she worked tirelessly so that she and her staff could eat at a party cafeteria.[117] "Until nine in the evening yesterday, I had to make telephone calls in order to obtain a decision of the higher party organs," the diarist explained. "It requires a lot of energy to overcome various bureaucratic loopholes."[118] Once this access was granted, Sokolova cautioned her staff to behave like model workers in the Lengorkom canteen, lest there be any doubt that they deserved to eat there.[119] This warning echoed the observations of Levina, Nikitin, and others about the importance of table manners as markers of status and worthiness.

In November and December 1941, Sokolova set her sights on obtaining Category I rations for Istpart's staff, arguing that their scholarly work was essential to the lifeblood of the party.[120] But Nikolai Shumilov, the Lengorkom secretary of propaganda and editor in chief of *LP,* refused. According to Sokolova's paraphrase, he said "that it is impossible to do that, that in

Leningrad there is only enough bread for two days and that half a thousand people die from hunger every day." Sokolova countered that she would not have asked for him to bend the rules if he were not already doing so: " 'If you did not give [Category I cards] to anyone,' I said, 'then we also would not aspire [to them], but since you give them to local party committee workers, then you could support us too.' " From this unfolded a frank discussion about party privilege, in which Sokolova and Shumilov accused each other of being self-interested, not party minded. Sokolova reconstructed their conversation this way: " 'Well, there she goes again, harping on the same old thing,' Shumilov said discontentedly. 'Workers in the district party committee [raikom] are our foundational cadres, and if we do not give them [Category I] cards, then who will carry out the party work? We will have no one to rely on.' 'But,' I said, 'our workers also carry out great party work for the masses according to the line of the party raikom. [. . .] The raikom values our work, and it is surprised and outraged that you cannot help arrange Category I for us.' "[121] By casting doubt on Shumilov's support of Istpart's political work, Sokolova succeeded in obtaining Category I cards for her workers. This scene highlights the bureaucratic "loopholes" in the ration system and the moral flexibility they bred.[122] Sokolova might have been considered a savior by her coworkers but a thief by others. Indeed, once in a bomb shelter, a Category II worker confronted Sokolova about her relatively healthy appearance. The diarist retorted, "Why are you whining? What, [you think] others have it better or something? The distribution of goods applies to everyone equally."[123] Solokova recorded this statement without comment even though her previous entries reveal her intimate knowledge of how to manipulate the rules. After the "all clear," she sped to a "closed" cafeteria, where she received soup and two portions of kasha. "And this is a special canteen!" she exclaimed, wondering how much less was distributed at ordinary ones.[124]

Social Difference Laid Bare: The Bathhouse

Even more than queues and canteens, bathhouses starkly exposed the food-based hierarchy. In line, status was based on proximity to the front; in the canteen, it was determined by ration size and decorum. In the *bania,* it was inscribed on the body. Esfir' Levina darkly joked that a trip to the *bania* was a great "anatomy lesson," where the peculiar physiognomy of the *blokadnik* was laid bare.[125] As the diarists studied the bathers around them, they compared what they saw to memories or stories of the *bania* from the prewar period. In particular, they thought of the writer Mikhail Zoshchenko, whose vignettes present the *bania* as a microcosm of Soviet society. Familiar types—from zealous communists and careerists to lackeys—pass through the doors of Zoshchenko's bathhouse, and through the obstacles they encounter there, the reader glimpses the dynamics and problems of Soviet life in the 1920s. Like Zoshchenko, the diarists approached the *bania* as an emblem of blockade life.

In imperial and Soviet Russia, communal bathing had long helped build bonds of community.[126] The isolating conditions of the blockade endowed this act with new urgency. Through bathing, Leningraders could both commune with and learn about the public. The blockade *bania,* however, was very different from its prewar incarnation. Like most municipal services, most of the city's sixty-two bathhouses shut down during the winter of 1941–42. Only a handful reopened in spring 1942. City leaders endeavored to reopen them because the bathhouse was a public-health necessity. During the winter, the city's sanitary services broke down, and streets became littered with garbage, sewage, and corpses, but the freezing cold staved off an outbreak. During the spring thaw, however, bathhouses were one of the few safeguards against infectious disease.[127] The act of bathing may have eased Leningraders' minds about infection, but its hygienic effects were limited. The few bathhouses that opened were overcrowded and undersupplied. Most opened only one washroom, where men and women bathed together. Moreover, enemy bombardment and periodic freezes destroyed the city's water and sewage lines, depriving bathhouses of electricity and running water. *LP* published grievances about *bania* conditions and reported on a contest that awarded a cash prize to the bathhouse with the best facilities.[128]

The diaries contain very conflicted readings of the *bania,* which dramatically showcased the tensions between equality and privilege under siege. On a typical trip to the bathhouse, most diarists were impressed by the similarity of the bodies they saw. Men and women were barely distinguishable. Distinctions in age, social standing, education, or party affiliation were washed away. Emaciation overshadowed all other social signifiers. At the same time, the *bania* operated according to practices of privilege. Tickets to the bathhouse were distributed disproportionately to political, cultural, and industrial elites through their institutions. Moreover, with so few bathhouses in the region, there were times when outsiders with healthy bodies arrived to bathe with the skeletal *blokadniki*. Therefore, on any given day, the *bania* could foster a sense of equality or of stratification.

Leningraders waited in long lines for the bathhouse. Once inside, they arrived in the anteroom, where they struggled to undress and confront their bodies. Next, they entered the washroom, where their nakedness along with their inability to wield buckets of water and wash themselves was plain for all to see. "Yes," Ivan Savinkov wrote after a bath in late January 1942, "I wanted to describe the scene in the *bania,* horrible, only skeletons, not people. What will become of us?"[129] In the translator Aleksandra Liubovskaia's recounting of her son Igor's first trip to the *bania* in March 1942, she was struck by the uniformity of the bathers' bodies. As usual, she referred to him by the pseudonym "Iura" in her original entry. "The closest working *bania* from us is located on Il'ichevskii Sidestreet. Enormous line. Only one class is operating, the general one for men and women. Somehow no one paid attention to this. All the bathers, men and women, were so identical that you wished to stand out from them immediately. Everyone is shriveled, their breasts sunken in, their stomachs enormous, and instead of arms and legs just bones poke out through wrinkles, like an elephant's skin."[130] Igor' was alarmed at his own emaciation but even more so at the extent to which his body resembled those of other bathers, most of whom were women. Afraid of losing his identity, he "wished to stand out" from the sea of skeletons. Some diarists were misidentified because of this homogenization. Nikolai Aleksandrovich Berngardt, for instance, was arrested in the bathhouse and then promptly released; he had been mistaken for the wrong man. In his journal, Berngardt confessed that this frightening "incident at the *bania*" was "worse than the incident that M. Zoshchenko wrote about."[131]

In June 1942, Liubovskaia and her son were evacuated from Leningrad. When they reached Yaroslavl', they were required to wash before entering the clinic there.[132] It turned out that all the bathers were Leningrad refugees. Like Igor', Liubovskaia was struck by her own inability to decipher age, gender, or any distinguishing traits among the bodies: "Everyone, women and men, bathe together. One old man came toward me (but perhaps he was not an old man!) and held out a washrag."[133] Although horrified by what she saw, Liubovskaia also noted a certain naturalness in the mass of bathers. The siege had distorted their bodies, but the atmosphere of the washroom conjured an image of human innocence before "the fall." "Oh, holy shamelessness, without dirty thoughts, without the notion of sex! This is what sickness and suffering do! I wash Igor'. Automatically tears rush to my eyes. My poor, dear boy! How thin he is. Only bones are left. A sunken-in stomach, ribs jutting out pointedly, the bones of the pelvis are outlined sharply, and over all of this dark, blemished skin covered with small scurvy-induced blotches. My heart is so, so heavy!"[134] This scene has a sacred, chaste feel. Liubovskaia's description of washing Igor' recalls Mary cleansing the body of her crucified son. All around Liubovskaia, Igor' was mirrored by other bathers, rendered physically androgynous and amorphous by starvation. When viewed from inside washrooms like this, the blockade seemed a brutal equalizing force.[135]

However, there were moments when this apparent uniformity was belied by the presence of alien, healthy bodies. Some diarists speculated that these were the same enemies they saw in canteens and behind bread counters. In an entry that the artist Anna Ostroumova-Lebedeva cut from the published version of her diary, she noted how on a recent trip to the *bania*, a friend "was completely astounded by the large number of plump young women of a Rubenesque character with robust bodies and glowing physiognomies. They are all workers in bakeries, cooperatives, city canteens, and children's homes. In bakeries and cooperatives, they cheat unfortunate residents. They divide the best food among themselves."[136]

Similarly, the poet Ol'ga Berggol'ts' spotted a "blockade wife" in the *bania*. In *Daytime Stars,* a work based on her wartime notes, Berggol'ts described the woman this way:

> I had a look at women. Their dark female figures covered with rough skin—no, not even women—they ceased to be like women—their breasts had disappeared, their stomachs were sunken in, purplish and

blue spots, from scurvy, covered their skin. [. . .] And suddenly a
woman entered. She was smooth, white, glimmering with golden
peach fuzz. Her breasts were round, pert, with almost shame-
lessly erect pink nipples. [. . .] Her skin was like from Kustodiev's
paintings—its color unbearable when seen next to the brown, blue,
and spotted bodies. We wouldn't be more frightened if a skeleton
entered that room. Oh, how scary she was! Scary with her normal,
impeccably healthy, eternal female flesh. How all this could have
managed to survive? She was simply frightening to us.

   She was nauseating, repulsive, disgusting—with her round breasts,
created so that a man could press and squeeze them, panting in lust,
with her thighs created for fornication, for conception—for that sort
of thing that could not be now, that once was natural but became
now impossible, shameful, forbidden. [. . .] Insulted by this blas-
phemy, women whispered behind her back: healthy! rosy! fat! [. . .]
A frighteningly bony woman approached her, gave her a slight
smack on her butt, and said, "Hey, beauty—don't come here, we
might eat you!" [. . .] They spurned her as if she had leprosy, not
wanting to touch her silky, glowing skin. [. . .] The woman screamed,
threw away her bucket, and ran from the room.[137]

Like Liubovskaia, Berggol'ts evoked biblical imagery but to emphasize
the shamefulness of the healthy feminine body. The healthy woman was
a leper, a pariah, an abomination compared to the *blokadniki,* whose emaciated, sexless bodies had become normalized by the siege. The hungry
woman's threat to eat the interloper anticipates the healthy woman's terror
at the skeletal bathers around her. At the same time, the scene underscores
that the true horror in the washroom was the fact that a few Leningraders
somehow still had their prewar bodies.

   For the medical student Zinaida Sedel'nikova and the artist Nikolai
Byl'ev, the interlopers in the *bania* were not *blokadniki* but soldiers and
militia members stationed nearby. But the bathhouse staged the contrast
between their bodies, etiquette, and attitudes in equally dramatic fashion.
In November 1941, Sedel'nikova likened her trip to the bathhouse as a
kind of invasion experience. "Huge queues," combined with students'
low status, made the bathhouse "almost inaccessible" for them. Thank-
fully, the directors at the Second Leningrad Medical Institute, where
Sedel'nikova studied, "worked out an agreement with one *bania*."

Sedel'nikova and her classmates went to wash there. Only a few minutes after they had begun, they were ordered to vacate. The Red Army was coming. Although the warnings became louder and frequent, the bathers stayed put. Finally, an onslaught of soldiers burst into the crowded washroom.[138] Rather than eject the gaunt bathers, the soldiers helped them by carrying heavy buckets and scrubbing them. "I saw another man use a washcloth to rub the back of Tonia Deva, who was washing near the end," the diarist noted. What began as an invasion became a kind of rescue mission. Sedel'nikova and her classmates "were full of surprise, indignation, and laughter. The only thing we lacked was Zoshchenko."[139]

Byl'ev visited a bathhouse in January 1942 under much worse conditions of starvation. His account shares none of the humor of Sedel'nikova's. However, its depiction of the dynamic between insiders and outsiders is illuminating when read in conjunction with hers. Initially, Byl'ev was the intruder. He unwittingly stepped into a washroom full of Leningrad women. They were "bony, angular": "Their breasts hang down like little empty bags. I stood in the doorway in a sheepskin coat and car-flap hat—nobody paid any attention to me." Then, Byl'ev "noticed another steam room," which seemed empty. Perhaps he thought that this was the male side: "I enter and undress. Suddenly I hear loud voices. The door opens, and a gaggle of robust girls enter in their hats and sheepskin coats. They notice me and begin giggling: 'Come here, little chicken, we will wash you now!' These are militia women sent to Leningrad from the mainland. The second steam room was prepared for them. They make a striking contrast to what I've just seen behind the wall. I gaze at their full breasts, torsos, and arms as if at some kind of marvel. As if I found myself in Rubens's paintings."[140] The literary scholar Polina Barskova has argued convincingly that, by entering this washroom, Byl'ev stumbled across a critical conceptual divide. At first, this barrier seemed to separate male and female, but it proved to be the divide between the island and the mainland. The healthy, feminine women were beautiful yet grotesque, almost too human. They themselves drew attention to their humanity by calling Byl'ev "little chicken." Moreover, they giggled at his presence in their section of the bathhouse, not understanding that many gender- and class-based distinctions were fading in the city. Their reaction, even their mere presence, evoked boundaries that no longer existed.[141]

The 1941–42 bathhouses emblematized the horrors of starvation and stratification. They alerted many diarists to the widespread extent of suffering as well as brought them into contact with elites from within and without the city who embodied the persistence of inequality. As in line or in a canteen, the diarists presented themselves as disadvantaged and thus typical or true *blokadniki*. Their notions of distributive justice became inextricably linked with their emerging wartime identities.

During the siege, queues, cafeterias, and bathhouses became essential to Leningraders' survival and to how they envisioned society. The diarists were isolated from the Soviet Union and from their own community, and they hungered for insights about the city's changing demographics, hierarchies, and norms. They also were eager to gauge where they stood in the evolving social order. Although they tried to generalize about blockade society from their encounters in lines, cafeterias, and bathhouses, the diarists' entries underscore the very personal, particular nature of their perspective. Their impressions depended on where they stood—at the front or back of a line, before or behind a food counter—and next to whom they ate and bathed. Moreover, the operating logic and configuration of each locale informed the diarists' visions of the social order. The queue presented a highly linear social structure. The canteen exhibited a spectrum of social types, from *distrofiki* to food-service workers. The bathhouse displayed mass starvation but also exposed the satiated few. All three settings showcased the uneasy coexistence of multiple principles of distribution at work in blockade society, including "he who does not work does not eat," "first come, first served," "each according to his need," "each according to his labor," and so on. These sites also facilitated the diarists' impressions that these principles were being violated legally— by giving party workers or inactive laborers Category I status—or illegally through theft and prostitution.

The politics of location and consumption meld together in these accounts. Regardless of whether the diarists held a Category I, II, or III ration card or a party card, they were filled with suspicion that others unfairly received more than they did. That starving Leningraders complained about how food was distributed is hardly surprising. *How* they complained is telling. The diarists reconstructed the social and moral geography produced by the blockade and placed it in dialogue with ration policies, Soviet ideals, and wartime practices. They activated long-standing debates about class, equality, and entitlement and wielded their own understandings of Soviet values to identify which groups or individuals should be advantaged in the fight for life. In the process, they continually focused on internal adversaries and rarely mentioned the German besiegers, even during the period of greatest scarcity. The diaries indicate that starvation led them not to question Soviet tenets altogether but rather to mobilize them in order to advance their own entitlement claims and dispute those of others, including party leaders. And because Soviet practices of resource distribution were inconsistent during the prewar and wartime eras, they could be used to challenge wartime policies as much as to justify them.

Chapter Six

The City as Medical Laboratory

WHEN THE SIEGE BEGAN, Zinaida Sedel'nikova was in her third
year of medical school at Leningrad's Second Medical Institute.
A dedicated student and Komsomol member, she was determined to finish
her degree quickly so she could help the scores of wounded soldiers sent
to the institute's clinic for treatment. "I need to hurry, hurry," she wrote
in her diary. "I need to become a doctor because it is impossible to witness all this suffering . . ."[1] She longed to be out of the classroom and in
the field, especially during the autumn of 1941, when air raids disrupted
her classes. When the institute closed that November, Sedel'nikova took
a job as a nurse in Hospital 95 and was assigned to a ward of starving
civilians, now the majority of the city's infirm. The hospital became
Sedel'nikova's university. What she learned there shook her faith in the
power of medicine and in herself as a healer.

Sedel'nikova discovered during her first shift that her studies had prepared her poorly for the job. This was because, as she later reflected, the
work was "almost not medical."[2] Her duties entailed serving meals, wiping
patients' brows, turning them in their beds, and providing other basic
comforts. Yet she barely could perform these tasks. Her ward was supposed to be staffed by two nurses and two medical assistants, but because
"everyone [was] ill," Sedel'nikova had to manage fifty-three patients

alone.[3] The diarist described her first shift as a tragicomedy of errors: "It started with a hot water bottle that needed to be changed. I grabbed one from under the feet of a patient, and it turned out to be ice cold. I went down to the boiler room, filled it with hot water, and brought it to the patient. I immediately heard several voices asking for hot water bottles. As it turned out, there were only six, and I could not satisfy all the patients. I did not have enough strength to keep going down and back up to the third floor constantly."[4] An inexperienced caregiver, Sedel'nikova worked inefficiently, repeatedly climbing the stairs. The Category III rations she had been subsisting on for several months had depleted her energy. After the water-bottle incident, the twenty-one-year-old "did not have enough strength" to make morning rounds. Later that day, Sedel'nikova faced the "nightmarish" task of serving the midday meal. While she was handing out bread and plates of soup, "something unexpected happened": "From an indistinct, general noise I understood that one patient was asking for bread as though he had not received it. Then two others kept demanding seconds, seeing the remaining plates [of food] on the table. I got flustered. I started to point out, futilely, that the first [patient]'s claim was a mistake, at which point the doctor on duty entered. I took my own piece of bread from my case and gave it to the patient. But my distress did not subside. When I ended up with the doctor in the hallway, [. . .] [he] said that one dishonest person simply had taken advantage of my inexperience." Sedel'nikova completed the rest of her twenty-four hour shift on an empty stomach. "How thoughtlessly I gave my bread away."[5] Over the course of the workday, she registered fourteen new patients and certified four deaths. Sedel'nikova had become a nurse in hopes of preventing death, but instead she had become its record keeper. When she sat down to her diary after going off duty, she wrote of "the full difficulty of the work I have taken on."[6]

The blockade unleashed a public-health catastrophe unprecedented in Leningrad's history. It pushed the human organism and the city's medical establishment to the extreme. The rising tide of death overwhelmed both those who were giving and receiving medical treatment. It destabilized their body beliefs and upset their expectations about clinical care. In their diaries, caregivers and patients alike placed wartime medicine under a critical microscope. They scrutinized medical practitioners, bureaucracies, and theories—all of which they found sorely inadequate. The health crisis triggered a conceptual crisis.

By focusing on one particular setting, the clinic, we can reconstruct the diarists' shifting views of medicine. I use "clinic" but also include hospitals, medical points, and stations because the diarists used these terms inconsistently and sometimes interchangeably. Whether as patients, medics, or family caregivers, Leningraders spent considerable time in such treatment centers observing and interacting with medical professionals. In this way, the clinic facilitated the circulation of medically related rumors, terms, and theories around the island.[7] It became the focal point of biopolitics in blockaded Leningrad, the major site where medical knowledge and practices were contested.[8]

The health crisis peaked during the first ten months of the siege. During that time, professional medical teaching, research, and treatment broke down. Many of the city's medical schools and academies closed, evacuated, or operated in limited capacities. Because of this institutional collapse, there is a dearth of professional medical reports on the first months of the blockade.[9] The diaries therefore offer critical insight on those early days. Not only do they provide an intimate look at everyday medical practices; they reveal how Leningraders—increasingly skeptical of medical expertise—took it upon themselves to develop new theories and remedies. For them, the struggle to survive necessarily became a struggle for knowledge. The diarists not only hoped to discover better health strategies but also drew on medical discourse to classify, explain, and otherwise bring order to the incomprehensible devastation around them. The spirit of scientific inquiry even seized diarists who, by their own admission, had little interest in medicine before the war.

Like some nightmarish experiment, the blockade confined the population to a closed, somewhat controlled environment conducive to scientific study. As the doctor and siege survivor Svetlana Magaeva explained, the siege "conducted an experiment of terrible harshness in which more than two million Leningraders were brought to the limit of survival." This ordeal, however, also yielded "discoveries of fundamental importance to physiology and medicine."[10] Magaeva had professional research in mind, but such discoveries were not limited to elite scientists. Rank-and-file practitioners, as well as patients and observers with no medical expertise, carried out their own inquiries, using themselves and the people around them as test subjects. Before scholarship on Leningrad's health crisis began appearing in press in late 1942–early 1943, the diarists were recording their own observations about the practices of medicine and the pathogenesis of starvation.

The diarists' theories are impressionistic and—by the standards of medicine today—factually problematic. But they contributed new layers of meaning to wartime medical concepts. The diarists highlighted the inconstancy of medical terms and theories under siege, when "medicine" was food, "discharge" often meant death, and "clinic" became synonymous with "cafeteria" or "morgue."[11] Moreover, they unpacked the political and practical complexities of official categories like Level I Invalid or Stage III *distrofik*. Finally, they helped formulate disease constructs like nutritional dystrophy *(alimentarnaia distrofiia)*, moral dystrophy *(moral'naia distrofiia)*, and hunger psychosis *(golodnyi pskhikoz)*. The diaries capture how the politics of health were bound up with social and moral practices and thus embedded in larger networks of meaning that structured blockade life.

The Medical Crisis

When the war began, Soviet medicine was forced into a state of "frantic improvisation," as the historian Christopher Burton put it.[12] Cities like Leningrad faced shortfalls that were both material and informational in nature. Most medical facilities and personnel were mobilized for the front, leaving civilian clinics across the USSR undersupplied and understaffed. In 1941, there were 65 percent fewer hospital beds available to civilians than there had been in 1940, and the number of functioning Soviet medical institutes fell from seventy-four to forty-eight.[13] The need for doctors was so urgent that the remaining institutes tried to replenish their ranks by shortening the training program for doctors, nurses, and medics. Many went into the field with just two to four months of preparation.[14]

In Leningrad, public health had been in a tenuous state even before World War II. The city had been home to some of the country's best medical research and treatment centers. But the Winter War with Finland (1939–40) drained the city's medical and food resources, and infectious disease was on the rise.[15] Once the blockade began, Lengorkom and Leng-orispolkom mandated that new treatment centers be opened and well stocked, but these orders were difficult to execute.[16] Civilian clinics not only were overcrowded but were hit by shells and caught fire from nearby explosions. Inside, medics worked without electricity or hot water, making it impossible for them to deploy a full range of diagnostics, to sterilize instruments, or to keep patients warm. During the winter of 1941–42, mortality rates reached 70–80 percent in a few hospitals. Doctors and nurses themselves were starving and demoralized.[17]

By spring 1942, Leningraders gained a bit of a reprieve. The population had been reduced by death and evacuation such that more hospital beds and larger (although still insufficient) rations were available per person. Warmer weather, however, thawed the frozen human waste and filth that covered the city, raising concerns about infectious disease. Without sufficient food to "cure" hunger, medics focused on preventing the spread of illnesses through evacuation, quarantine, sanitation, and the production of vitamin supplements. And with the exception of tuberculosis, they prevented major epidemics.[18] This is a remarkable achievement in light of the conditions in which the medical community worked.

Hunger is a timeless phenomenon, and its general effects on the body are very familiar. So it is easy to forget that the international scientific community had a limited understanding of its pathogenesis in the 1940s. Huge progress in nutritional science was made during and after World War I, by which time the new Bolshevik state was embroiled in civil war. Soviet doctors in Petrograd in 1919–21 or in the region of the 1932–33 famine would have had direct knowledge of starvation. But for others, only a small number of publications on Petrograd were available.[19] Explicit discussion of hunger produced by collectivization was forbidden. As a result, most of Leningrad's doctors had only a general understanding of starvation when the siege began. At first, many failed to distinguish between undernutrition caused by a caloric deficit and malnutrition due to protein or vitamin deficiency.[20] They also misattributed shared symptoms, like swelling (edema) and diarrhea, which led to erroneous diagnoses and treatments.[21] Initially, Leningrad hospitals endorsed refeeding regimens based on high-calorie diets rather than on ones rich in proteins and vitamins. They added these dietary elements in February 1942.[22]

Moreover, as more food became available, some clinicians fed patients too much too quickly, inducing heart failure. Of course, the overarching problem was that doctors simply did not have enough food to feed Leningraders sufficiently, which made them appear helpless, even incompetent, to the diarists who observed them in clinics.

Inside the Clinic

Clinics had changed so dramatically from their prewar state that diarists likened them to two other institutions, cafeterias and morgues. They sometimes used the terms interchangeably. Leningraders spent considerable time in clinics because doctors had the authority to prescribe extra food and temporary work releases—the two main forms of treatment for starvation. Although neither measure ensured survival, their absence spelled almost certain death. Prescribed food was known as "curative food" *(lechebnoe pitanie),* or UDP. Because these extra rations were small and given to patients in dire condition, some joked darkly that UDP stood not for "increased supplementary food" *(usilenoe dopolnitel'noe pitanie)* but for "you'll die one day later" *(umresh' dnem pozzhe).*[23]

For doctors like Anna Likhacheva, medical practice revolved around food. Likhacheva, a physician in the Red Banner Factory clinic, summed up her "very interesting work" as "the observation and study of workers who have been approved for extra food at our factory's cafeteria."[24] Her job was to prescribe food, vitamins, salt acids, and bed rest to patients and, above all, to oversee the factory's kitchens and canteen. The cafeteria was the epicenter of treatment—so much so that Likhacheva built herself an examination room inside it. In truth, it was just a corner partitioned off by a few cabinets, a spatial testament to the blurred lines between food and medicine, treating and feeding.[25]

Excerpts from Likhacheva's diary were published in 1968 in a volume celebrating workers' and soldiers' defense of Leningrad. The excerpts begin in May 1942, skipping the worst period of the siege. However, Likhacheva depicted local officials and policies during this time in a manner that was far from heroic. She complained that food deliveries often arrived late and in amounts smaller than the promised norms. "Theoretically, the [official] caloric intake was the highest at 3,100, and the [cafeteria] menu listed a variety of items. But in practice—alas!—often the supply base is insufficient to distribute norms fully, and this hinders the distribution of food and the very effectiveness of its nourishment."[26] The cafeteria menu was a fiction. In addition, because of the city's stringent wartime labor norms, patients could be prescribed rest and extra food for only ten to fourteen days before they were returned to work. Not only was this "too brief a time" for them to recover, but patients often suffered "a rapid and acute loss of strength" upon discharge. As a result, Likhacheva always had a "hungry human stream," caught in a revolving door between the clinic and the shop floor.[27] These fluctuations in diet and in exertion taxed the workers' health further, offsetting the improvements Likhacheva and the other staff had made to their condition.

Their hands tied by policy and resource constraints, doctors lost efficacy in the eyes of many diarists. Leonid Gal'ko, for instance, was a political instructor at the Kirov Factory and later a decorated hero of Leningrad. In his diary, he used "clinic" and "cafeteria" interchangeably.[28] Gal'ko's journal appears in the same collection as Likhacheva's, and while his journal certainly praises the party, it assesses medicine critically. Gal'ko was desperate to help his ailing wife but dismissive of doctors' advice. "She received a doctor's certificate for sick leave, but what is the point? The doctors say (and I myself know this no less than they do), that she needs to eat; she needs bread and fats. But nowadays it is useless to talk about that."[29] Gal'ko himself declined a stay in the Kirov Factory's "so-called hospital" because, he wrote, "I need food, and there is none."[30]

Doctors' orders seemed commonsensical yet impossible to follow. After the writer Sof'ia Ostrovskaia heard one physician's advice for how to care for her brother, she had a good laugh: "The doctor says: 'Diet. Rice flour. White meat. White bread—and not fresh, but with rusks.' I chuckle. The doctor also laughs. Alas, the sick one does not laugh."[31] Such advice seemed absurd because it belonged to a different world. Ostrovskaia rehearsed this farce several months later when she consulted another doctor about how to save her mother. She was advised to " 'give her food, medicine, and peaceful surroundings. Then your mother will pull through.' The doctor speaks and knows: in the city, there is no medicine," to say nothing of food and tranquility. Ostrovskaia, herself struggling with edema and scurvy, pleaded with the doctor, explaining that she had only a bit of pea flour left to feed her mother: "'If in a normal time I fed my ailing family [only] peas, what would you say?' 'That consciously or deliberately you are committing a crime.' Yes. It seems there is little hope. Death stands nearby."[32] Doctor and diarist agreed that such neglect was tantamount to murder, but there was little they could do. As the diarist's mother drew nearer to death, Ostrovskaia decided to take her to the hospital anyway. At least she could be made comfortable there. "It will not help her with anything," Ostrovskaia surmised. "It will not return her to health or to life: it is only so that the care for her will be better."[33] That way, Ostrovskaia could concentrate on nursing her brother at home.

During the winter and spring of 1941–42, most *blokadniki* came to hospitals to die or after they were already dead. Leningraders often left the bodies of their loved ones outside local clinics; they were too weak to drag them to a cemetery. It is estimated that in January and February 1942 hospital mortuaries received an average of 566 corpses a day.[34] Bodies also lined the streets and lay in courtyards, making Leningrad "not a city, not people but ghosts, phantoms, [. . .] a panopticon, an open-air morgue," as Ostrovskaia put it.[35] The line between "hospital" and "morgue" grew faint. Eighteen-year-old Nina Mervol'f likened the elite Erisman Hospital of Leningrad's First Medical Institute to a morgue of living and dead corpses.[36] And from the poet Vera Inber's description of Erisman's facilities, Mervol'f's description is apt: "In other rooms, in the corridors, patients sit or lie as a matter of course. They are on benches, on stretchers, or simply on the floor, like corpses, only they are dressed. Only their eyes are alive. . . . Two female doctors move among them. They look like corpses themselves."[37] "The whole territory of the hospital is full of corpses," Inber continued. "Today they carried away 500, but there are 2,000 left."[38] Inber's husband, Il'ia Davidovich Strashun, was chairman of Erisman and director of Leningrad's First Medical Institute. According to her, he became so accustomed to directing new patients to the morgue that he sometimes forgot to make sure that they were in fact dead.[39]

The ominous "tomb-like silence" of Hospital 95 haunted Zinaida Sedel'nikova.[40] One of her main duties as a nurse was to take bodies to the hospital "morgue." This was just a mound of bodies in the hospital courtyard. "The scene is astonishing," Sedel'nikova remarked. "The corpses lay on top of each other, stacked up with plywood tags on their legs. . . . There is no one and no way to get them off to the cemetery." Too weak to haul the bodies by herself, she enlisted stronger patients to help her. From the window by her workstation, Sedel'nikova commanded a view of the makeshift mortuary. With one eye on the bodies inside the ward and the other on the corpses outside, she became mindful of the growing proximity between them. Hospital and morgue, doctor and patient, began to meld together. As she walked home in December 1941, she "could not get rid of a feeling of either guilt or dread of ending up as one of those 'stacked up' [sredi shtabelei]."[41]

Some diarists suspected that the clinic actually hastened death. Ivan Savinkov, for instance, studied his coworkers as they were discharged from the Molotov Factory clinic, and he became convinced that "they leave feeling worse" than when they arrived. The art historian Vladimir Makarov echoed, "The hospital is harmful to man. Of course this is true." Makarov was a patient in an elite ward at Sverdlovsk Hospital overlooking the Fontanka Canal. He noted that the doctors and nurses were very kind, but he still found the conditions intolerable: "What horrors there are at 52 Fontanka. If only I could never return here! Need to find a way out."[42] The sight of other patients eating, Makarov and Irina Zelenskaia observed, was emotionally devastating. "It is curious," Zelenskaia wrote in March 1942, "that, as a rule, our patients who are sent to the clinic to get well come down with diarrhea almost within a day. All of the treatment, all of the nourishing food, leads to nothing."[43] In several entries, Zelenskaia repeated her theory that "in the hospital, they get even sicker." She acknowledged that hunger was the underlying cause of death but blamed the clinic for delivering the fatal blow.

This perceived link between the clinic and death became one of Zelenskaia's core beliefs. She even pitched it to a physician, much to his chagrin.[44] She also began to draft case histories of her coworkers in which she replaced the official cause of death with what she considered to be the real one. In her analysis of "Aleksandr Aleks.," a friend, coworker, and fellow party member," Zelenskaia admitted that "scurvy and distrofiia took him" but insisted, "His time in the hospital knocked him out. I superstitiously have begun to fear the hospital atmosphere, and according to my theory, this evil consists of the fact that it acts by oppressing man and depriving him of courage and the will to resist, and this, not the disease, leads him to death."[45] If he had stayed at home, she reasoned, he would not have become infected with the despair of other patients. Sharing Zelenskaia's suspicions, the translator Aleksandra Liubovskaia tried to prevent her son, Igor', from interacting with other hospital patients, concerned that their morose attitudes might destroy his will to live. "I will fight for the life of my son in every way that I know. First and foremost, I must tear him away from depressing conversations and instill [in him] hope and interest in life."[46] Depression and apathy are common symptoms of starvation, but most diarists blamed the clinical environment more than hunger for infecting patients with these sentiments. They reasoned that, because hospitalized patients ate and rested more, they ought to have improved. When the patients did not, the diarists looked for other explanations. They did not realize how slowly small bits of "curative food" reversed the damage of prolonged starvation, if at all.

Other diarists held doctors personally accountable. In general, the diarists' depictions of doctors were overwhelmingly negative. Out of all the diarists featured in this book, only four characterized doctors and nurses as benevolent.[47] The reproaches are understandable in light of the desperate situation. It is impossible to ascertain if they stemmed from actual abuses by the staff, from diarists' frustrations with factors outside doctors' control, or from a combination of these. Whatever the reason, criticisms abound in the journals, which provided space for Leningraders to air their grievances.

The most frequent accusations against doctors were of favoritism, theft, neglect, and putting state interests ahead of those of patients. Aleksei Chernovskii, a historian at the Museum of the History and Development of Leningrad, was one of many diarists who complained that doctors favored elites. "I do not understand," he chided, "why the 'clinic' is basically a cafeteria for administrators."[48] Others hinted that doctors withheld food for themselves. The diarists may have witnessed this directly, heard about it from rumors, or read about it in *LP*, which published reports of doctors hawking food and medicine on the black market. An investigation by Leningrad's health department evidently confirmed these reports.[49] Recent research by Richard Bidlack and Nikita Lomagin suggests that pilfering was widespread. Although doctors received Category II rations, their access to extra food meant that only 2 percent of them died, compared to 37 percent of the general population. The NKVD also recruited informants from medical staff because they were well positioned to eavesdrop on patients; it rewarded them with extra food.[50]

The diarists' most common complaint about physicians was that they were passively killing their patients through negligence *(nebrezhnost')*. Christopher Burton has argued that there was no distinct concept of malpractice in Soviet medicine because doctors treated patients according to preset policies. However, they were prosecuted for negligence.[51] The diarists frequently levied this accusation themselves. The teacher Aleksandra Mironova, for instance, described one incident when a doctor refused to treat an orphan whom she rescued, claiming that his medical station was too crowded. When the little girl died two days later, Mironova reported him to the party.[52] Doctors' heavy reliance on *distrofiia* as a diagnosis also made them appear dismissive. "Doctors barely look at patients. Everyone mechanically gets a diagnosis—general *distrofiia*," Irina Zelenskaia proclaimed.[53] Mariia Konopleva developed the same impression while working in Clinic 22. During the war, she became a clerical assistant to the VTEK (Vrachebno-trudovaia ekspertnaia komissiia; Medical-Labor Expert Commission), which certified illnesses and authorized work releases. Konopleva wrote at length about one patient who spent hours moaning in the corridor and dipping in and out of consciousness. But the medical staff "paid little attention to this. The doctor approached her, listened to her heart, felt for a pulse, and left with a hopeless wave of his hand. And the medical assistant said, 'And why do they trudge here to die? They could have taken to their beds at home.'"[54] The perfunctory nature of this exam alarmed Konopleva more than the deathly pallor of the patient did. "Our attitudes toward death, this great mystery of our existence, has changed radically," she remarked.[55] Konopleva did not consider (on the page at least) that such apathy was a symptom of the doctors' own emaciation or perhaps an accurate assessment that nothing could be done. In an effort to rectify such dismissiveness, Konopleva penned detailed case histories of the patients she observed.

Biopolitics and Blockade Medicine

The diarists were not the only ones to accuse physicians of negligence. Leningrad's top officials also blamed them for the health crisis. When rations increased in spring 1942, state and party officials, like the diarists, expected the mortality rate to fall sharply. When it did not, Lengorispolkom fired the head of the city's health department and mandated that doctors reduce the mortality rate by a factor of eight. The Lengorispolkom chairman, Petr Popkov, publicly chastised health-care workers for not taking the initiative to ensure that the city had ample cafeterias and health facilities. "Had this matter been raised earlier," he insisted, "had appropriate material assistance been requested, it would have been given sooner. But what was manifested here was some sort of timidity or perhaps unwillingness to work." Popkov's claim that more food would have been supplied to ailing Leningraders had doctors requested it was preposterous, but it shifted blame away from circumstances or administrators and onto doctors. It blamed the health crisis on a treasonous "unwillingness to work."[56]

City authorities also reprimanded individual physicians for perceived negligence. Vera Inber wrote a series of terrified entries, which she not only omitted from publishing but also blackened out in her diary manuscript, relaying how the NKVD interrogated her husband, Il'ia Strashun, about the high mortality rate and appalling conditions at Erisman Hospital. On 3 February 1942, "the police chief Grushko came and saw the mountains (in the full sense of the word) of corpses, the piles of filth over the whole area of the hospital, the disassembled fences, and declared that all of this (especially the corpses) were counterrevolutionary and ordered an investigation. The doctors and the NKVD were already there. The *raikom* secretary [. . .] knew terrifically well what the situation was in the hospital and institute. Still, the secretary stood by silently while the police carried out their duties with characteristic 'Bolshevik flair.' [. . .] I was beside myself." For weeks, Inber expected her husband to be arrested at any moment. "Who knows how this will all end. It depends on the direction in which it will head. Here there is less than one step between unpleasantness and catastrophe . . . what will happen to me without I[l'ia] D[avidovich]? What will happen to him without me?" This prospect terrified her more than the horrors of war: "To perish not from a bomb, not from fire, and not even from hunger but from the cold cogwheels of the administrative machine, what could be more frightening than that? Never have things been as hard for me in Leningrad as they are now."[57]

In this way, the diaries testify to the enormous political pressure under which wartime physicians worked. Of course, this was not new. Since the revolution, Soviet medicine operated according to two, often competing, guidelines, which Michael Kaser has called the "district" and the "industrial" principles. The district principle dominated the 1910s and 1920s, when, despite a lack of resources, the regime promised open, free, and universal health care in every district. The industrial principle, which reigned during the first two Five-Year Plans (1928–37), stressed the necessity of a healthy workforce and led to the establishment of medical facilities in industrial centers that were specifically for workers. Between 1928 and 1941, 2,000 hospitals, twenty-four medical schools, and 224 research institutions were established under this model. Doctors worked with factories and unions to maximize productivity by improving sanitation and keeping injuries and absenteeism low.[58]

Thus, by World War II, the workplace was the main center of medical care for urban laborers. Illnesses and injuries that required time off had to be officially certified. Infirmity was defined and measured against what was considered its opposite: the capacity to work. As of 1932, "invalids," as they officially were called, were grouped into three categories based on labor capability. Individuals whose disabilities were so severe that they could not work were placed in Level I; those who could still perform a wide variety of jobs in Level III. Christopher Burton, who has traced the application of these categories over time, has argued that they were highly subjective and fluctuated as labor priorities and notions of able-bodiedness (or labor capacity) evolved.[59]

In the years before World War II, the state tightened its regulation of medicine and illness categories. Medical practitioners and inspectors were expected to enforce labor codes and grant time off sparingly. In August 1940, new inspection commissions, the VTEK, were established to examine patients and determine their level of infirmity according to the three invalid categories. Invalid status had to be recertified every six months.[60] Doctors, like their patients, were under close scrutiny and could be tried as class enemies if it was suspected that they put "welfare objectives" ahead of the state's economic goals. The city's health department was one of the organizations purged as a result of such suspicions.[61] By the same token, there was no Hippocratic oath in the USSR until 1969, as doctors were instructed to privilege the collective good over individual patients. Doctor-patient confidentiality did not exist either.[62]

The blockade intensified the pressure on doctors to make Leningrad's workforce productive. In February 1942, one of the deadliest months, Lengorispolkom tried to increase the labor force by requiring recertification of all illnesses and by fining or imprisoning those who missed work but did not have a current exemption. "State doctors no longer have the right to issue illness certifications to the nonworking—that is, to dependents," Sof'ia Ostrovskaia remarked.[63] Too weak to work but denied an exemption, Nina Mervol'f despaired: "They do not at all take into account that everyone is worn out, emaciated, and weakened. This Popkov wants the remaining Leningrad inhabitants to die. Labor conscription hangs over my head like the sword of Damocles."[64] Enforcement of the mandatory labor requirement fueled some diarists' suspicions that doctors essentially served state interests and not those of their patients.

At the same time, the diaries suggest—often inadvertently—that doctors were not blindly obedient to state directives. Rather, they worked within and against the system to provide care.[65] They could manipulate medical certifications and invalid categories to benefit patients, not labor quotas. Mariia Konopleva observed this at Clinic 22, where she served as secretary for the VTEK. She noted that, as ration and evacuation policies fluctuated, certain statuses became more "desirable" and thus more frequently granted than others. In winter and spring of 1942, even the sickest patients begged doctors to certify them fit for work and put them down as Level III invalids. They did this because then they might be eligible for Category I rations. Moreover, "doctors, like the patients," Konopleva observed, also secured this status for themselves because "only through work can one receive 'high-calorie food' in the cafeterias and thus lessen starvation to a degree." She continued, "In order to save those patients who can still stand up and who themselves want this, doctors transfer them from Invalid Level II, where they are not given the right to work, to Level III."[66] The situation reversed itself in summer 1942, when the sickest Leningraders, unable to contribute to the war economy, were evacuated. Now everyone wanted to be designated a Level I "invalid."[67] Classifications and definitions of illness could change in response to military conditions or the efforts of doctors.

The doctor Anna Likhacheva admitted that she adjusted diagnoses and certificates in order to help workers in the Red Banner Factory who were beset with high labor quotas. She kept certifying them as ill, authorizing them for multiple two-week hospital stays after short stints on the shop floor. "I managed to push through especially valuable workers for a second time. I hope that in the month of June we will have managed to fill all of the plant's workers with food a second time."[68] Likhacheva took advantage of the vagaries behind official labels to intervene for the dying and at least postpone their deaths. As her diary suggests, physicians walked a tightrope between professional and political obligations, each of which harbored different notions of proper care.

Like doctors, city authorities manipulated medical classifications and standards to suit their objectives. Out of growing concern that the number of Level II invalids was ballooning, A. Ia. Averbakh of the Commissariat of Health ordered VTEK commissions across the Soviet Union to reduce the number by 12 percent in 1943 and by 17.8 percent by 1944. The certification of illness was tightened and the notion of labor capacity expanded accordingly.[69] The health department found other ways to improve public health, at least on paper. In April 1942, the city municipal and political authorities began closing workplace medical clinics and stations, claiming that they would be replaced by more and better supplied canteens.[70] An unstated goal, however, must have been that this would make workers more productive. The clinic treating Irina Zelenskaia's coworkers at Lenenergo was liquidated in April 1942.[71] Gesel' Gel'fer's clinic closed in May, Anna Likhacheva's clinic in June. "They are not registering new patients," she dismayed. "It is really too bad that there is no possibility now of bringing people to a normal state." This included doctors as well. In her diary, the doctor submitted her own medical history as evidence that these high-level decisions bore no relation to any actual measure of recovery: "The deficits of fat and sugar are making themselves felt, but the ration issued to us healers has decreased. Before they gave us up to 60 grams of sugar and 40 of fats a day. [. . .] Now we get only 10 grams per day of fats and 10–20 grams of sugar or glucose. [. . .] I tried begging to be evacuated, but the District Health Department turned me down: I am needed here because of the shortage of doctors. One must have a Level II illness in order to leave the city."[72] Likhacheva was caught in the same bind as her patients. She was too ill to work but not enough to be evacuated. She both profited from and fell victim to the inconsistent way medical designations could be applied and enforced.

In the clinic, therefore, the diarists confronted what they perceived to be the diminishing power of medicine. They attributed its apparent inefficacy to bureaucratic constraints, indifferent caregivers, insufficient resources, and inadequate expertise. Their accounts highlight the inconstancy and politicization of medical knowledge, especially with regard to the classification, diagnosis, and treatment of the dying. But the public-health crisis ignited their interest in medicine rather than dampening it. Fueled by their new familiarity and dissatisfaction with medicine, many diarists began to formulate their own explanations and remedies. If the blockade clinic faltered as a center of patient care, it succeeded in providing ample opportunities for the diarists to conduct observational research.

Medical Observation

One of the lesser-known legacies of the blockade is its contribution to the science of starvation. Along with the Holocaust and the Dutch Hunger Winter, the siege sparked a great deal of research on hunger, especially among people of European descent.[73] On the island, there were over a million human subjects trapped in a closed environment for nearly three years. In the West, researchers disseminated the discoveries of Leningrad scientists and drew on their findings when designing studies like the Minnesota Hunger Experiment of 1944–45. In 1943, the American-Soviet Medical Society was founded in New York and began to publish a journal, the *American Review of Soviet Medicine,* in order to disseminate the discoveries of Soviet doctors to their American counterparts.[74]

In Leningrad, both elite researchers and general practitioners collected invaluable data. As early as December 1941, many began meeting through their district health departments in order to coordinate their investigations.[75]

Doctors evaluated patients' bodies and behaviors, took blood samples, measured vital signs, and analyzed atrophied organs and tissues through autopsies. They worked to discern the pathogenesis of starvation as well as treatments for chronic hunger and related conditions like vitamin deficiency and hypertension. Most formal research ventures began after the winter of 1941–42. In 1943, Leningrad's Medical Publishing House produced a *Great Medical Encyclopedia*. Shortly after the siege was lifted in 1944, the USSR established an Academy of Medical Sciences, a testament to the surge in medical research during the war.[76]

At the same time that professional researchers were studying starvation, diarists conducted observational research of their own. A few, like Anna Likhacheva and Ol'ga Peto, were doctors, but most had no medical expertise at all. And yet they found themselves adopting a clinical gaze. Daily survival in Leningrad, Sof'ia Ostrovskaia suggested, necessitated daily experimentation. Ostrovskaia was "busy with a research experiment" based on two queries: "can a human being live without bread, without sugar, without fats, without meat, without vegetables, and how will he feel throughout this?"[77] Her own gaunt body was an ideal study specimen: "A medical [chekhovskii] student could prepare for an examination in anatomy based on me. All my ribs can be detected, and each bone can easily be defined by its sonorous Latin name."[78]

One might assume that individuals exceptional enough to keep diaries also were exceptional in their devotion to medical observation. However, there is some evidence to suggest that Leningraders, not just diarists, displayed a burgeoning interest in medicine. Wartime librarians noted that books and journals on basic biology, first aid, and home remedies were among the most requested items by patrons. Leningrad's presses regularly printed pamphlets and manuals on nutrition and hygiene.[79] Meanwhile, *LP* announced regular lectures and exhibitions on creative food preparation, sanitation, and edible local plants.[80] Such events provided another route through which medical concepts and terms entered public usage and acquired meanings beyond the control of the professional practitioners.

The city became a living laboratory. For Zinaida Sedel'nikova, medical examination became so automatic that she did it in passing. While walking home from Hospital 95, she cast discerning glances at the corpses lining her route, registering how many had died and from what. "I automatically looked back once or twice . . . the cause of death is the same—hunger and cardiac exhaustion."[81] The pathologist Vladimir Garshin, who did not keep a diary but published a short memoir in 1944, explained how he scrutinized his "new body and new soul" like the "hidden corners" of an "unfamiliar flat." Garshin dissected bodies in Erisman Hospital's morgue, and as Anna Reid has argued, he was both fascinated by these "beautiful specimens" and revolted by the human suffering they represented.[82]

Sedel'nikova and Garshin already had a strong interest in medicine, but others, like the philology student Natal'ia Uskova and the art specialist Mariia Konopleva, took jobs in clinics only to earn better rations. They were surprised to discover how fascinating the new work was. Uskova even had second thoughts about her plan to pursue a career in literature. After she seated patients for examination or surgery, she often stayed nearby to watch. "Letting such an opportunity go would be a sin," she explained. "The entire surgery I stood by the operation table as though bewitched. They were removing an appendix. It's extremely interesting! I probably made a mistake in my day by not entering a medical institute. I love medicine, and it is possible that this is what I am meant to do."[83] At Clinic 22, Konopleva followed patients into examination rooms, studied their bodies, and interviewed their relatives in order to write their medical histories.[84] Those who had artistic training, like Ol'ga Matiushina and Aleksandr Nikol'skii, drew corpses. Evgeniia Mikhailovna, Matiushina wrote of her alter ego, "could not help sketching them."[85] Irina Zelenskaia inspected Lenenergo's dormitories and clinic as well as helped to clear out the corpses. "One comes across amazing things," she marveled. Zelenskaia confessed that she had "a wild desire" to go to Smolensk cemetery and see the bodies: "all with my own eyes."[86] The more time Zelenskaia spent in the clinic, the more she adopted a medical gaze. "I was so struck, from a medical point of view, by these numerous deaths that often defy explanation." She recounted one "curious conversation with a doctor" who proposed that hunger had weakened Leningraders' hearts to such a degree that "the slightest nervous blow" could lead to "cardiac arrest and infectious disease." "The explanation fascinated me," Zelenskaia remarked.[87] In her next entry, however, she rejected the doctor's hypothesis because she had observed "another interesting phenomenon: the exceptionally low incident rate of the normal winter illnesses" like typhus, influenza, and pneumonia. "[Leningraders'] susceptibility to infection has not been determined, but I am quite ready to deny it. The situation is not like that," Zelenskaia concluded.[88]

Such claims hint at the range of ideas about illness that circulated on the island. Perhaps because of the diarists' nonexpert status or perhaps because they recorded these observations in private journals, they tended to emphasize personal and contextual factors that precipitated siege maladies. They focused not only on physical symptoms but also on identities and social relations associated with them.

Anatomy of an Illness: *Distrofiia*

"In the winter months," Lidiia Ginzburg observed, "the desire to eat was like a disease; satiety represented the ending of an illness."[89] Ginzburg couched this as a metaphor, but the notion that hunger was a disease, rather than a sociopolitical or environmental condition, became widespread under siege. That disease was dubbed nutritional dystrophy *(alimentarnaia distrofiia)*. It is an unusual term. Composed of Greek and Latin roots, it is not Russian at all. According to the historian Rebecca Manley, *dystrophy* first appeared in Russian in 1937 in a dictionary of foreign medical terms.[90] However, "nutritional dystrophy" rarely appears outside the Russian and Soviet contexts and is closely associated with the blockade and, by 1944, the gulag. Even gulag prisoners were known to have called it "the Leningrad illness."[91]

Distrofiia also is a controversial term. Hunger was a regular occurrence in Russia and the USSR, so why was a new name needed? Some scholars argue that the novelty of wartime discoveries about starvation, especially as it disrupted vital bodily systems, warranted, in the eyes of researchers, the coinage of a new term to replace "from inanition" *(ot istoshchenii)*.[92] Others, mindful that the term developed in the blockade and gulag, where the state distributed, even manufactured, hunger, consider it a euphemism that emphasized "natural" causes in order to deemphasize political, military, and bureaucratic factors that precipitated mass starvation. By pathologizing hunger, the regime may have hoped to limit investigations of it to the medical field.[93]

There is some truth to both views. In one of the first publications on *distrofiia,* the doctor Mikhail Vasil'evich Chernorutskii provided evidence for each side. On the one hand, Chernorutskii stated plainly that "it is completely clear" that *distrofiia* stemmed from "the lack of food for the population." The presence of hunger was undisguised. But its causes were. Chernorutskii referred vaguely to "the pathological conditions that have been observed in the winter of 1941–42" as the reason for this mass starvation.[94] It is likely the term appealed to scientists and officials for different reasons, for its power to reveal and to conceal, respectively. The diaries help bridge these views by addressing both scientific and sociopolitical aspects of *distrofiia.* In the process, they underscore how the concept obscured as much as it explained.

Distrofiia became an almost universal diagnosis in blockaded Leningrad, but not right away. At first, doctors favored other concepts like inanition *(istoshchenie)* and vitamin deficiency *(avitaminoz).* But *distrofiia* began cropping up in medical and diary accounts around the same time, in late November 1941. It was approved by the city health department on 7 December 1941 and soon became a mainstay of Leningraders' vocabularies.[95] "The term *'distrofiia'* has become very widespread," Aleksei Chernovskii observed, and he gave a few examples: "'a Stage III *distrofik,'* 'a *distrofik* needs such and such,'" and so on.[96] The term was slower to be accepted by the Kremlin. The first reports identifying *distrofiia* as the main cause of hospital deaths were submitted to the Leningrad health department in January 1942, but the Commissariat of Health listed it as a cause of death only in late 1942.[97] By early 1943, the first major scientific papers on *distrofiia* were published, and the Leningrad health department established a special committee of researchers to coordinate studies and publications about it.[98]

Diarists often learned about the symptoms and stages of *distrofiia* from the considerable time they spent in clinics. On Zinaida Sedel'nikova's first day at Hospital 95, as she accompanied doctors on rounds, she "understood that the diagnosis for all the patients is the same, Stage II or III *distrofiia.* The main treatment consists of food three times [daily]." Three days later, Sedel'nikova began her own study of the condition, especially its effects on her patients' elimination and digestion systems.[99] As her remarks indicate, the pathogenesis of *distrofiia* was divided into three stages or levels of severity. The scientific descriptions of each stage are very detailed, but in general terms, individuals who experienced notable weight loss, fatigue, muscle pain, and acute hunger pangs were classified as Stage I. In Stage II, patients suffered severe weight loss, fatigue, and pain; they also experienced drops in body temperature, heart rate, and protein and sugar levels in the blood. Many exhibited swelling (edema), and most were bedridden. Stage III was terminal. Such individuals were cachectic and their bodies irreversibly damaged.[100]

Almost immediately, the concept of *distrofiia* and its stages obtained usage and meaning outside the clinic. Like the three "invalid" categories, the diarists wielded *distrofiia* categories freely and in accordance with their own interpretations of them. Esfir' Levina, for instance, instructed her readers how to identify *distrofiia* when recounting a chance meeting she had with a friend, Doctor S.N. When she was unable to identify him, he asked,

> "Do you recognize me?"
> "Aren't you a *distrofik?*"
> Suspicion in his eyes: "what could I be if not a *distrofik?*"

> All of Leningrad is ill with *distrofiia*. The strongest part of the population is thin, exhausted, but psychologically fine. *Distrofiia* I—this is not yet an illness. *Distrofiia* II is already a sickness: they lie around, sluggish, indifferent or mean; with the appropriate routine and food they can be saved. *Distrofiia* III, this is the end. Easy death.[101]

Levina supplied her own definitions to these official categories, especially emphasizing *distrofiia*'s capacity to alter personalities, behaviors, and relationships. Like most diarists, she tended to focus on the starving, the *distrofiki,* more than on *distrofiia* as a condition. More than a medical concept, *distrofiia* provided another way for Leningraders like Levina to make sense of their changing identities and emotions under siege.

Similarly, the physicians Ol'ga Peto and Anna Likhacheva grounded *distrofiia* in the personal and situational as much as in the medical. Likhacheva diagnosed herself with *distrofiia* and *istoshchenie* (she used both terms) and used her diary to work out the symptoms, stages, and attendant illnesses of her condition. At that point, her entries increasingly resembled installments of a medical case file. "I survived all the stages of emaciation *[istoshchenie]*, even crossing over into the third [stage]. It started simply with wasting away *[iskhudanie]* and shortness of breath, slowed mental processes. On 12 December 1941, the dysentery began. [. . .] Then everything began to rapidly deteriorate. The darkness, horrible cold, hunger, the lack of strength to stand in line at night for the daily ticket we needed to receive food—this doomed me and my whole family and led to the loss of my husband and son."[102] Likhacheva listed her symptoms not with the detached tone of a clinician but with the emotional anguish of a patient, wife, and mother.

Peto's diary also blends the intimate and the clinical. Between 1942 and 1943, Peto worked for the local NKVD to find abandoned youths and bring them to "child reception centers," or DPRs *(detskii priemnik raspredelitel').*[103] She kept a journal of the ten children she found. This unusual diary reads like a series of case histories even though it also includes Peto's daily routines and personal reflections. Each entry is labeled with the name of a child she rescued and the date she found him or her. Peto wrote in two columns, creating two distinct texts. The main text, on the left side, paints a personal portrait of the waifs she rescued: their appearance, physical condition, background, and familial circumstances. The children's voices and perspectives shine through her descriptions. The right-hand column or margin comments on the children from a detached scientific perspective and draws a composite sketch of the "child-*distrofik.*" Thus, her narrative oscillates between emotional and detached, personal and professional, particularizing and generalizing.

Peto's first entry, titled "January 1943. Galia, 8 Sovetskaia Street, 54," relays how she found Galia lying in a heap of dirty laundry in the dark corner of a freezing apartment. When she opened the door, the diarist noticed that "a pile of rags stirred." She spotted "a little creature that appeared about six or seven years old and with a little gray face and enormous eyes." At this point, Peto broke from her narrative and, broadening the lens of her analysis, noted in the right-hand column, "the characteristic face of a child *distrof.*" Then, retightening her focus on Galia, Peto elaborated on the moment she first saw the child: "She was wrapped in rags full of lice. [. . .] The girl stood silently, indifferently, saying nothing. She neither asked nor answered any questions." Here again, Peto shifted back to her analytical mode, noting in the right margin, "characteristic indifference."[104] After a meal and a rest at the DPR, Galia finally spoke. "Responding to repeated questions in a monotone voice, she quietly answered 'I am Galia. I am thirteen years old.'" In the margin, Peto explained, "this is how all *distrofiki* spoke." Slowly, Galia shared her story. She had no father; her mother left for work a month ago but never returned. A few days later, her ration card was stolen. For a while, she survived on rusks given to her by a generous stranger, but before long, the starving child returned to her dark, empty apartment: "I gathered together all clothes in the room, covered myself up, and lay down to die."[105] By directly quoting the children, Peto captured their unique voices and situations. At the same time, her annotations remind the reader that the girl's tragic story and physical deterioration were typical symptoms of pediatric *distrofiia*.

Every child's story is told from these dual perspectives. In each entry, Peto the diarist was stunned by a child's physical deterioration, whereas Peto the doctor reminded her implied reader that all *deti-distrofiki* looked this way. In her entry for "Fania (Feofan) January 1943," Peto was taken aback by the child's "tiny, gray little face, dark blue lips and nose. Enormous, infinitely sad eyes. He asked for nothing. He just looked melancholy as only a deeply unhappy child can look."[106] Peto similarly was stunned by Vova's "gray face" and "enormous eyes," by Mania's "gray face" and "enormous eyes," and so on.[107] The same was true for age. Peto knew from experience that it was difficult to tell the ages of *deti-distrofiki* from their appearance. In all ten cases, she incorrectly guessed their ages by a huge margin. Valia, whom Peto found lying next to her dead mother, appeared to be four when she was actually ten; thirteen-year-old Galia appeared to be six or seven; nine-year-old Mania only five. The physician commented in the margin, "*deti-distrofiki* seem so much younger than they are."[108] Peto always presented her guesses along with the actual ages, highlighting the contrast between her personal and professional perspectives. In this way, she captured the particularities of the children's experiences while extrapolating a clinical picture of pediatric *distrofiia.* Her entries bring together personal and theoretical, situational and biological aspects of the starvation experience.

Peto and Likhacheva emphasized personal and situational facets of *distrofiia,* but not to the exclusion of medical ones. Neither doctor questioned its status as a disease. Other diarists, by contrast, increasingly used the term to characterize people, objects, and situations outside a medical context and even outside the blockade.[109] Small objects, such as meager rations or the diminutive cigarettes manufactured during the war, were pronounced "dystrophic" (*distroficheskii*). A lapse in focus or memory might indicate "*distrofiia* of the brain." The term became a dynamic and powerful metaphor. The school inspector Lidiia Zabolotskaia used this phrase when she lost her train of thought in the middle of a diary entry. "When I say *distrofiia* of the brain," she wrote in October 1942 after the worst period of starvation had subsided, "everybody laughs. But a year ago it was absolutely, actual *distrofiia* of the brain that I felt then."[110] Indeed, the meaning of *distrofiia* had expanded to such a degree that, the schoolteacher Aleksandr Vinokurov explained, it could be applied to any aspect of life. "The words '*distrofiia*' and '*distrofik*' were not known to citizens of Leningrad before, but now you can hear them everywhere: in offices, lines, and streetcars. These words are used both with and without purpose and gradually are losing their original meanings and acquiring new ones. They compare a slow-moving streetcar not to the turtle now but to a *distrofik*. [. . .] Several years ago, in order to insult somebody you'd call this person '*kolkhoznik*' (collective farmer), but now a new pejorative term emerged—'*distrofik*.'"[111] Like Zabolotskaia, Vinokurov penned these lines in the autumn of 1942, by which time *distrofiia* acquired a myriad of meanings, most of them negative. Entries from that time describe the *distrofiki* as an underclass of blockade society, one considered slow, grotesque, even anti-Soviet.

At first, the opposite had been true. During the winter of 1941–42, when *distrofiia* became the default diagnosis, *distrofik* became synonymous with *blokadnik*. Diarists commented off-handedly that "everyone is a *distrofik*" and readily applied the term to themselves. For example, in April 1942, Aleksei Kozlovskii, a former director of Lenenergo and the wartime director of the North Cable Factory, explained, "The factory is organizing a medical station for *distrofiki,* and everyone is a *distrofik.* They feed us a little."[112] Slippage between *blokadnik* and *distrofik* occurred outside the city as well. A red banner that welcomed Leningrad evacuees as they crossed Lake Ladoga proclaimed, "Warm greetings, Leningrad *distrofiki!*" At that time, *distrofiia* was a marker of shared identity based on shared suffering.[113]

But the term's connotations evolved as rations increased. Improvements to the food supply and the dwindling population made this increase possible. This in turn shaped official and personal expectations that public health soon would recover and the city would become productive again. In spring 1942, as local authorities closed hospitals and restricted work releases, they also mandated that *distrofiia* diagnoses be limited.[114] Sof'ia Ostrovskaia discovered this when her brother and mother—who had been diagnosed with *distrofiia* that winter—lost the designation. The diarist noted how one doctor carefully omitted the term while making a house call: "She replaced '*distrofiia*' *(istoshchenie)* with other words. She answered my puzzled question [this way]: the words '*distrofiia*' and '*istoshchenie*' are categorically forbidden for use. As it turns out, by order of the powers that be, there are no *distrofiki* and no *istoshchennye* in Leningrad. It follows, then, that everyone can work. [. . .] In connection with this unexpected discovery of the 100 percent health of Leningraders, they are beginning to close the clinics for *distrofiki,* where for ten to fourteen days they gave out extra food, which in truth was surprisingly meager. Since everyone is healthy, who needs extra food?"[115] This restriction of diagnoses occurred shortly after *distrofiia* was approved as an official cause of death. Thus, according to personal accounts at least, no sooner had *distrofiia* been approved than its usage was circumscribed in order to give the impression—at least on paper—that the city was recovering. Rumors of this phenomenon reached the poet Ol'ga Berggol'ts when she was in Moscow in March 1942. She recorded a friend's news that "the word '*distrofiia*' now has been banned—death results from other factors, but not from hunger!"[116] *Distrofiia* went from being an almost universal Leningrad condition to a disease in decline. To be sure, the mortality rate was quite high in spring and summer 1942, but—according to personal accounts—diagnoses changed by decree.

Official and societal pressures contributed to the marginalization of the *distrofiki*. A stigma against *distrofiki* emerged in tandem with this official taboo. According to the diaries, some Leningraders came to detest the *distrofiki* who stubbornly lingered on. "It is strange: a foundational mass of people," Sofia Ostrovskaia observed, "look at the *distrofiki* coldly, even without curiosity, with disgust and malice (beasts after all do not love sick beasts). They do not forgive them: because they have not gotten well on time or because they have not died on time. The faces of the *distrofiki*, therefore, are guilty."[117] As Leningraders grew healthier, they did not like to look upon *distrofiki* and be reminded of the tenuous state of their own recovery. The public, Irina Zelenskaia claimed, loathed their "improbably thin legs and fingers, or just the opposite, swollen pillars" for appendages. "People have become agitated and evil. [. . .] You feel this way yourself," she admitted.[118] "'*Distrofik*' has turned into a curse word," Aleksandr Boldyrev echoed. "*Distrofiki* are despised, persecuted, beaten into the ground. If you are applying for a job, the first requirement is to not look dystrophic. These are the morals of the second year of the siege."[119] Thus, while the usage of *distrofiia* declined in the medical realm, it flourished in the sociocultural one.

Blokadniki and *distrofiki* who once were intermingled now stood on opposite sides of a divide between the recovering and the dying or—as Esfir' Levina put it—between "the cruel" and "the weak."[120] Some diarists drew on scientific explanations to justify this separation, describing *distrofiki* as members of a lesser species. For instance, doctors in Clinic 22 taught Mariia Konopleva how to spot the *distrofiki* by their supposedly animalistic features. "One doctor, looking at such a patient, told me how clear the symptoms of the *distrofiki* are, evidence of man's affinity 'with the monkey!' It is terrible to see these 'monkey-like' symptoms on the faces of young people, obviously doomed, as well as on old people."[121] Sof'ia Ostrovskaia also commented on the "monkey-like" features of the *distrofiki*. Not unlike an anthropologist who reconstructs ancestry from bone fragments, she identified what she considered to be their distinct cranial features: "their skulls break through, [one can see] an outline of a skull under skin the color of wood, dirty wood."[122] They were inferior, primitive, and no longer fully human. By summer 1942, the *distrofik* came to resemble other figures of the living dead, such as the *muselmann* of the Nazi death camps or the *dokhodiaga* (goner) of the gulag.[123]

Some diarists chalked up the apathetic, inhumane affect of the *distrofik* to a personal failing, not just to starvation. This judgment was termed "moral dystrophy." The concept of moral dystrophy is even more polysemic than nutritional dystrophy. Siege diarists, survivors, and scholars have defined it differently over time. During the war, it generally referred to a lack of mental fortitude. Those who were suffering from moral dystrophy had "lost heart" or contracted "a special blockade-induced malaise of the will" *(osobaia blokadnaia bolezn' voli)*.[124] Moral dystrophy, the diaries suggest, manifested itself through opposite affects. It took the form of apathy and acquiescence to death or of emotional volatility, which produced panic, despair, and obsessive behavior. In both cases, it was defined against the ideal of the New Soviet Person, whose steely body was matched by strong determination and complete self-possession. Esfir' Levina argued that her colleagues cited moral dystrophy to excuse a variety of lapses: "There is a new term: *'moral'naia distrofiia'*—many people use it as a screen for justifying filth and laziness. It is hard to find the line between suffering and speculation in this atmosphere. Voslinskii came to work in tatters, soot on his face, sobbing loudly, smearing dirty tears. Rubanenko yelled at him, 'Aren't you ashamed of yourself'; he stopped crying and then whined, asking to be taken home. For the second month, the workers have been given medical certifications on their service workers' cards. Many of them have been excused from work."[125] Levina resented how their weakness was rewarded with extra food and work exemptions. However, she admitted, "it is difficult to distinguish between the *distrofiki* (moral ones) and actual emaciation."[126] The artist Nikolai Byl'ev echoed this point, differentiating between the "authentic type of blockade *distrofiki*" and other, presumably false or *moral'nye distrofiki*.[127]

For Levina, moral dystrophy came to index lethargy and wantonness, which could be construed as political, not just personal, failings. As the historian Nikita Lomagin has shown, party leaders occasionally used the term to label certain individuals as ineffective or defeatist because they fixated on the city's problems. Aleksei Kuznetsov, Second Secretary of Lengorkom, branded officials who "start speaking about the people's hunger, about emaciation, about how it is impossible to do anything" as moral dystrophics. "The *moral'nyi distrofik*," he continued, "masks his own inactivity and lack of desire to organize anything with these conversations." Such characterizations, Rebecca Manley has argued, demonstrate how some Leningraders associated the illness not only with irresponsibility but with insufficient patriotism. It was a political crime.[128] Moreover, after the war, *distrofik* was used to denigrate East Germans as politically and physically degenerate and by Stalin to deride Soviet officials he felt were overly concerned about famine victims in Moldavia and Ukraine.[129]

Viewed from a different perspective, the concept of moral dystrophy reflects a general optimism—one characteristic of but not unique to Soviet culture—that, with enough determination, an individual can overcome any obstacle. Aleksei Kozlovskii was one of many diarists who clung to this hope, drawing more on folk wisdom than on Soviet slogans, although both probably influenced him. "Things are hard, but I am not losing spirit. There is a wise saying: 'in a healthy body lies a healthy spirit.' I cannot deny that my body is lacking, but my spirit is healthy."[130] A firm belief in mind over matter provided the foundation for Irina Zelenskaia's theories about death and her survival strategies. Although she did not evoke the term *moral'naia distrofiia*, she used phrases like "losing heart" and emotional "atrophy" to suggest that moral, not bodily, weakness was the chief cause of death in the city.[131] Without discounting the importance of eating "until full, often, and—when you can manage it—regularly," Zelenskaia argued that nourishing the spirit was more important.[132] She began formulating this theory during the first days of the blockade as she watched Leningraders panic during air raids. She expanded it during the famine. If everyone was hungry, why did some people live and others die? "The whole difference," she explained, "is only that some fight and gather together their strength while others, based on the same data, consider themselves sick, lie down, and after that they already can consider themselves doomed and many never get up again."[133] Like Zelenskaia, there were Leningrad doctors who claimed that active individuals avoided death even though they expended more calories.[134] It is easy to see how such a theory might appeal both to party workers intent on boosting productivity and to residents. It gave them hope that a resolute attitude and consistent activity might help them survive.

Zelenskaia not only lived by this principle but used it to diagnose others around her. She monitored her coworkers for what she called "moral demobilization" and sometimes wrote case histories of individual *blokadniki*.[135] She penned a detailed account of the death of Mina Gertselevna, a friend and coworker. Officially, Mina died of asthma and cardiac complications, but Zelenskaia insisted that she actually perished from "spiritual depression," which weakened her to such a degree that two *proximate* factors, asthma and a heart condition, ended her life: "much later this was joined by a heart condition," Zelenskaia explained. Generalizing from Mina's case to the population, she surmised, "I have noticed this with a lot of people."[136] Firm in her convictions, Zelenskaia pitched this theory to others. On 18 January 1942, she described a debate she had with a friend that created "unexpected antagonism" between them. "He still explains everything in terms of physical reasons. I have resituated the center of the problem onto man's inner, willful makeup, and we cannot find common ground or a way to relate these reasons for the countless deaths."[137] The considerable time that Zelenskaia spent in clinics increased her exposure to medical theories but ultimately strengthened her prior belief that hunger was necessary but insufficient to explain "the countless deaths" of Leningraders. Her diary underlines how the political, personal, and medical together informed notions of health and illness.

Regardless of whether moral dystrophy manifested itself as emotional volatility or indifference, it became associated with speech. Again, it took the opposite forms of either speaking obsessively (especially about food) or an inability or unwillingness to speak at all. One example of this effect appeared in a 1942 story published in the journal *Leningrad*. In it, Soviet troops at the Leningrad front have captured German prisoners of war and are interrogating them for military secrets. When the Germans refuse to speak, the Soviet soldiers call them *distrofiki*—a sign of how the term was applied widely and pejoratively.[138] Another twist on the association between *distrofiia* and constrained speech comes from the famed siege documentarian Lidiia Ginzburg. According to the Slavic studies scholar Irina Sandomirskaya, Ginzburg viewed *distrofiia* not as a siege illness but as a condition that afflicted all Soviet intellectuals who hungered to express themselves freely but were trapped in a world of impoverished ("dystrophic") language. Sandomirskaya has argued that Ginzburg understood the twentieth-century writer as a figure "always already besieged: the faceless object of biopolitical and ideological manipulation."[139] To overcome *distrofiia,* from this perspective, was to regain wholeness and authentic expression. More permutations of moral dystrophy as aphasic developed in the postwar period. In *A Book of the Blockade,* Adamovich and Granin applied the term to describe, first, the reluctance of survivors to speak about grim aspects of the siege and, second, members of younger generations who expressed doubt or disinterest in survivors' testimonies.[140] Lisa Kirschenbaum has echoed the point, arguing the symptoms associated with *moral'naia distrofiia* provided survivors with a strategy for reducing the stigma of starvation. They remained silent about their experiences of hunger and instead emphasized their war wounds, which linked them to soldiers and other heroes of war.[141]

The diaries demonstrate how Leningraders helped to define *distrofiia* and how the term in turn furnished them with ways to describe not only starvation but also the identities, characteristics, and stigmas associated with it. Moreover, the diaries spotlight the historicity of *distrofiia,* especially its evolution from a marker of shared suffering to one of derision. Through their broad usage of the term, we can glimpse various conceptualizations of normalcy, pathology, and humanness that circulated at the time. These concepts were bound up with Soviet ideals about health and willpower but also with general human tendencies to judge an individual's personal and political merit by his or her appearance. In this way, *distrofiia* illuminates the slippage not just between hungry bodies and diseased bodies but also between diseased bodies and politically dubious ones.

Siege Psychoses

Moral'naia distrofiia was one example of how the diarists appropriated medical terms to articulate hunger's emotional and psychological assault. Soviet wartime medical researchers approached this theme of hunger-related psychopathy more cautiously.[142] The Soviet medical establishment rarely broached the topic in the prewar era. During World War II, it acknowledged that the incidence of mental illness had increased but emphasized that such disorders were induced physiologically (as by brain injury) or were signs of moral weakness, cowardice, and malingering.[143] In Leningrad, doctors were less hesitant to discuss the psychological toll of war. According to the researcher Pavel Vasil'ev, in 1942–43 there were several conferences on the subject held at the Institute of Postgraduate Education for Physicians and at the V. M. Bekhterev State Psycho-Neurological Institute. In 1942, the psychiatrist B. E. Maksimov of the Bekhterev Institute announced that "the siege increased the frequency and above all the acuteness of mental disease," which could alter "the entire neuro-psychic organization of both the individual and the entire social group" of *blokadniki*. Although psychological symptoms frequently were observed in Leningrad, psychopathologies rarely were diagnosed. In 1943, the First Leningrad Medical Institute reported that only two out of 128 *distrofiki* who were studied in spring 1942 suffered any psychiatric disturbances.[144]

By contrast, the diarists frequently and liberally diagnosed Leningraders with psychological disorders, especially with two conditions: bomb psychosis and hunger psychosis. Unlike *distrofiia*, which was used as a diagnostic category during the postwar occupation and the 1946–47 famine, neither of these terms gained a foothold in wartime or postwar medical literature. They were popularly conceived afflictions that shaped and were shaped by Leningraders' personal experiences of trauma.

During the first months of the war, when the city was under intense bombardment, diarists began to liken Leningraders' reactions to a kind of psychosis. Indeed, German forces designed and timed their bombing and shelling to maximize their disruption of life inside the city. In September 1941, there were as many as twelve air raids a day, some lasting up to eighteen hours. The journals articulate a fairly widespread belief that German troops used bombardment as a psychological weapon to destroy Leningraders' mental stability as much as the city itself. The physical damage each shell inflicted was localized, but the psychological damage might encompass the whole population. Many diarists referred to German explosives as "psychological bombs" and air raids as "psychological attacks." "The Germans 'psyche us out' [*'psikhovali' nas* (sic)]," Aleksandra Zagorskaia claimed.[145] Irina Zelenskaia called the raids "German jokes" and explained that the pauses between explosions were intended "to fool" Leningraders into a false state of security. A December 1941 article in *LP* on the "lessons of war" also claimed that "the school of war began" with "psychological" bombs as the first lesson.[146]

While the diarists generally agreed about the intentions behind these attacks, they conceptualized bomb psychosis differently depending on how they experienced it. Some understood bomb psychosis to be a problem of sensory hyperactivity. Mariia Konopleva concluded from studying herself and others during raids that Leningraders not only misjudged explosives' paths of trajectory but also hallucinated bombs, shells, and sirens that did not exist. Konopleva argued that the Germans deliberately cultivated such delusions by bombing at night, depriving the *blokadniki* of sleep and mental clarity.[147] Others, however, claimed that bomb psychosis was rooted in misperception. The core traumatic experience was the fear that every shell was aimed directly at them. For this reason, Zinaida Sedel'nikova claimed that, despite the danger, it was better for her mental health to watch air raids in "an open space" rather than to wait in a shelter, where her imagination was "prone to exaggeration."[148] Aleksandra Liubovskaia had an additional reason to classify bomb psychosis as misperception. She was deaf and had an especially difficult time judging the trajectory of falling explosives. Still, Liubovskaia wrote in general terms, suggesting that all *blokadniki* misjudged them in a similar way: "The Germans just dropped 'psychological bombs.' Their specialness consists in that, for the whole time that a bomb is flying, it howls with such terrifying strength that, no matter where it ends up, it seems as if it were falling right on your head."[149] In a later entry, she continued, "You cannot help feeling that you are living directly at the front and that right before your nose shells explode with such intensity as if this were artillery fire preparing an infantry attack and hand-to-hand combat right there on the Mars Field."[150] On one occasion in November 1941, Liubovskaia and her children (who were not hearing impaired) became convinced that an explosive had detonated by their apartment, but, she wrote, "as we found out the next day, the psychological bomb fell two kilometers from our building."[151] Bomb psychosis, the tense state of living if not in fear then in anticipation of fear, encapsulated the trauma of the first months of the siege as well as the summers of 1942 and 1943, when aerial attacks were relentless.

Lidiia Ginzburg also considered bomb psychosis a form of perceptual misjudgment. In her wartime notes, she argued that fear of bombardment rearranged Leningraders' perceptual worlds to such a degree that
the laws of time and space and of cause and effect seemed not to apply.
"Man thinks that everything will happen in order," Ginzburg observed.
"There will be a whistle, then an explosion, which he'll see from the
side, then something will happen to him." Instead, bombs fell without
warning and landed in unexpected places. All of this gave the *blokadnik*
"a mad sensation of things being overturned," of being "turned inside
out."[152] These attacks assaulted not just one's body but also one's understanding of reality, of the connection between sights, sounds, and
spaces. The concept of bomb psychosis lent coherence to the perceptual and emotional restructuring that the diarists underwent during the
blockade.

The diarists referred to bomb psychosis less frequently in the winter
of 1941–42, when hunger became a much greater concern. Bombing and
shelling decreased, and by then, Ol'ga Matiushina claimed, these "psychological flights" had "train[ed] the nerves of Leningraders" such that
they no longer reacted.[153] Liubovskaia echoed this point, noting, "the
shooting has ceased to act on the psyche of the people."[154] Bomb psychosis
was eclipsed by the trauma of starvation. The diarists referred to the latter
using similar terms. They called it "hunger psychosis" *(golodnyi psikhoz)*,
"psychotic" or "psychological hunger" *(psikhicheskii golod)*, and "starvation trauma" *(golodnaia travma)*. As with bomb psychosis, scientific
investigations and personal testimonials diverge on the issue of hunger-
induced psychosis. Wartime researchers in Leningrad, France, the United
States, and elsewhere determined that there were few psychotic symptoms of hunger, although psychological ones, like depression and anxiety,
were common.[155] A few Soviet medical professionals used "starvation
psychosis," but the term seldom appears in scholarly publications. Most
concluded that emaciation induced trauma but rarely psychosis. V. M.
Miasishchev of Leningrad's Neurological Institute did note that symptoms of psychosis stemmed from hunger-related events like eating toxic
plants, industrial or food poisoning, sleep deprivation, and infectious
disease.[156] But he and others held firm that hunger did not cause psychosis
directly. Psychiatrists at the Bekhterev Institute and leading theorists

of *distrofiia,* like M. V. Chernorutskii and M. I. Khvilitskaia, affirmed that they observed a minimum of psychotic symptoms.[157]

By contrast, many who starved in Leningrad, in German death camps, and in prisoner-of-war camps during World War II testified that they experienced delusions as well as cognitive and memory disruptions.[158] The siege diarists wielded "hunger psychosis" liberally as though it was a common affliction. Even young children, the journals suggest, learned to identify and diagnose it. The teacher and orphanage worker Aleksandra Mironova described how one of her former students, Tolia, voluntarily came to the orphanage where she worked and asked to be admitted. "Mama has hunger psychosis," he explained. Mironova understood his anguish, replying that her brother also was stricken with "hunger psychosis."[159] Similarly, now fourteen-year-old Dima Afanas'ev applied the concept to himself in 1942 when he began to obsessively read and copy out recipes from Elena Malakhovets's classic cookbook *A Gift to Young Housewives.* "Mama said that it is a type of psychosis. Nevertheless I decided to finish this work. After all, I am doing it for myself." "Never was Malakhovets's book used with such huge success as in Leningrad in 1941–42," Esfir' Levina remarked.[160]

The medical student Zinaida Sedel'nikova learned about hunger psychosis from patients and colleagues, not from medical textbooks. At Hospital 95, she watched the ill come to blows, accusing each other of stealing the food they had hallucinated into being.[161] But her schoolbooks did facilitate her understanding of hunger psychosis, in a way. In December 1941, she was reading a section on anatomy when she was flooded by visions of food. "It is sad," the diarist observed of her studies, "that this task has given way to hallucinations. I study pathology of the liver, but I [think of] how it, the liver, crackles in a skillet . . . even my head begins to whirl from the smell."[162] What began as a theoretical lesson became a frightening tutorial in psychosis as she fantasized about the delicious aroma of sizzling liver. Sedel'nikova continued to mingle medical study with self-study by analyzing her digestive system during meals. "I pinch off a crumb, suck on it, it immediately melts in saliva and is swallowed, but I accompany this with the thought, 'Well, already my stomach juices have thrown themselves on this crumb because the rumbling has grown stronger . . .,' and still more it gnaws at the pit of the stomach."[163]

Most diarists had less specific knowledge about hunger's psychological properties, but they were keen observers of its effects. Eighteen-year-old
Nina Mervol'f, a dramaturgy student at the Leningrad Theatrical Conservatory, admitted that she did not understand the medical jargon that
now peppered everyday conversation, but she meticulously chronicled her
father's crippling delusions, which also included—like Sedel'nikova's—
images of devouring oneself:

> He has been diagnosed with Stage III *distrofiia,* the cachectic kind
> (I don't know what that means, but they say that it is the worst kind
> of *distrofiia,* from which it is impossible to recover, even through
> healthy food). He is really just terrible. He is completely withered,
> his face is yellow and puffy, and his eyes are glazed. Above all, he is
> completely changed through and through; he has become deranged.
> All day he lies around [. . .] indifferent to everything. Or he begins
> to cry or scream from hunger and says that he will eat kindling, that
> he is prepared to eat himself. His voice rings in my ears, "Give me
> something to chew on! Give me something to chew on!" [. . .] Some-
> times he starts saying all sorts of absurd things: "Where is my body?
> I don't know what happened to me. I don't understand what's going
> on with me. Where is my body?" It is difficult and also irritating to
> look at him. This is not Papa, it is simply not him—this is a dirty, lice-
> infested, half-insane person, almost not even a person.[164]

Here, starvation's dual assault on mind and body is imagined quite literally. Just as a starving body is forced to cannibalize itself in order to remain alive, Mervol'f's father expressed the desire to devour himself in
order to save himself. But hunger was far ahead of him in disappearing
his body. At first, Mervol'f noted, he could not feel or even find it. Then
he experienced the unimaginable ordeal of being devoured alive.

Natal'ia Uskova's diary provides a firsthand testament of terrifying
hunger-induced delusions. Weak from malnutrition and scurvy, the philology student was lying in bed, listening to a Ukrainian folk song on the
radio, when suddenly "a wild image arose in [her] head": "Cold air, brittle
and blue, pink smoke arises from pipes, and to this happy little song, crin-
kling and ringing their little bones, skeletons are galloping to a cemetery
and lying down, row by row, in the trenches. What is this, hallucinations?
I fall into a kind of oblivion for a while and again a voice on the radio:

'The enemy will be destroyed, victory will be with us.' I am taken by a strange feeling, strange and scary. Slowly my head expands more and more. And now it is of such a size that it fills the entire room. In terror I scream, 'Turn on the light, quickly, my head will burst any moment now.' In the light, the apparitions disappear. Am I losing my mind?"[165] In contrast to the cautious tone of wartime medical literature, diaries like Uskova's vividly present the trauma of starvation as a form of psychosis because it rendered the diarists' sensory and perceptive systems unreliable, here to the point of hallucination. The skeletons that danced and laid down in mass graves were harbingers of Uskova's future. The cheerful music and patriotic promises seemed equally fantastical. After experiencing these incongruous images of mass death and a victorious future together, Uskova began to question her sanity. Her mind literally swelled to such a size that it threatened to overtake her.

While Sedel'nikova, Afanas'ev, and Mervol'f understood hunger psychosis as an obsession with food, Irina Zelenskaia, Aleksandra Liubovskaia, and others described it as a psychological inability to stop eating or to feel full. Many diagnosed themselves with this type of hunger psychosis in the spring of 1942, when rations increased. They overestimated how quickly larger rations could reverse months of severe starvation. When Zelenskaia discovered eating more increased her appetite, she worried that she was mentally ill. "I experienced a curious presence of psychotic/psychological hunger *[psikhicheskii golod]* from fear that hunger would return and would lead [me] to physically devour everything edible. This is what just happened, and worst of all, I again ate my bread ration for tomorrow."[166] Here, the anticipation of hunger, as much as hunger itself, triggered her symptoms, making it similar to bomb psychosis. Both kinds of psychosis, like the various forms of *distrofiia*, were formulated in contradistinction to certain assumptions of normalcy, so that the diarists' inability to control their bodies, emotions, appetites, or recovery processes, they feared, was pathological. Despite Zelenskaia's self-assurance, this was not her last attack of "psychotic/psychological hunger." The thought of a second siege winter, which threatened to be an "incommunicable nightmare," induced another episode.[167]

Similarly, Aleksandra Liubovskaia diagnosed herself with "torturous hunger psychosis" when her appetite became more insatiable under larger rations.[168] She gave herself regular "checkups" until finally she saw a doctor, who diagnosed her with Stage II *distrofiia* and prescribed three weeks of "curative food." Both the extra nourishment and official confirmation brought relief. By June, the diarist observed, "Today, I am perfectly energetic. Besides that, there is a noticeable decrease in 'hunger psychosis.'" She continued, in a medical tone, "Since winter and spring, the organism has somewhat replenished its exhausted reserves of fats, proteins, carbohydrates, and other elements. It is necessary only to maintain this condition in order not to waste away again."[169]

As the diarists examined themselves and others, they turned to pathology in order to name the physiological, emotional, and cognitive upheaval they endured. They worked within and against the prevailing medical discourse to understand starvation and its attendant conditions. The siege maladies that they helped to conceptualize underscore how notions of health and disease are as cultural and political as they are medical. They also are historically specific. *Distrofiia* and *psychosis* acquired new meanings and political valences over time as the siege and public-health expectations changed. Some of the diarists' contributions, especially to nutritional dystrophy and moral dystrophy, have outlasted both World War II and the USSR.

World War II inaugurated a new phase in health care and medical research in many nations, including the Soviet Union. Most Soviet and post-Soviet scholarship emphasizes Soviet medicine's many advances, especially in surgery, blood transfusion, the treatment of wounds, and the manufacture of penicillin. Some accounts that reported medical crises and missteps were sometimes censored. The overwhelmingly positive literature repeatedly cites two statistics to encapsulate these strides: roughly 70 percent of wounded and 90 percent of ill soldiers returned to active duty.[170] It is unclear whether these figures are accurate. But their ubiquity does capture the postwar scholarly literature's focus on soldiers rather than on civilians and on disease and injury, not hunger.

Doctors associated with the city and front of Leningrad were celebrated on similar grounds. Long before the blockade was lifted, they received commendations from all sides—from the city party boss Andrei Zhdanov, from numerous articles in *LP,* and from the selection committees that awarded them the coveted medal "For the Defense of Leningrad."[171] While the city was still under siege, Istpart prepared a series of volumes heralding Leningrad's Academy of Sciences for developing new medicines and surgical methods. As its 1943 tome *Heroic Leningrad, 1917–1941* proclaimed, "In the difficult days of the blockade, Leningrad medics worked tirelessly in the creative scientific thought, developing much in the area of healing war wounds."[172] All of these sources emphasize the medical community's service to frontline hospitals, to research laboratories, and to wounded civilians, giving little attention to starvation. A perfect example is S. Ezerskii's 1943 paean to seven Leningrad doctors. Five perform surgeries, and two treat diseases. Hunger is only mentioned once, as a complication that made surgical operations riskier.[173] Similarly, the Soviet press provided greater coverage of wounded Leningraders than of starved Leningraders. Emaciated bodies raised troubling questions about the failure of state officials to stockpile and secure sufficient food resources.[174]

The growing stigma surrounding *distrofiia* strenghtened the taboo about publicizing the full extent of starvation in Leningrad. One of the diarists who experienced this taboo was Zinaida Sedel'nikova. She continued to care for her charges in Hospital 95 until she completely exhausted herself. In March 1942, Sedel'nikova barely escaped with her life by evacuating on a medical convoy headed for Belorechensk.[175] She kept treating evacuees until she was put on bed rest. The nurse became the patient. The diarist wrote bitterly that she and the other Leningrad patients were hidden from locals and treated in secret. "They do not want us to show anyone how painfully frightening we all look."[176]

Diaries like Sedel'nikova's provide a very different picture of wartime medicine. They certainly do not negate the achievements of frontline medicine, but they shift the frame of analysis from battle scars to scars of deprivation, from research facilities to makeshift clinics. During the winter of 1941–42, the period of most extreme hunger, Leningrad's First and Second Medical Institutes operated in limited capacities. Local clinics and medical stations became increasingly important centers of medical learning. There, professionals and amateurs alike collected data on those who were giving and those who were receiving care. The diaries, which detail these clinical encounters, shed light on how Leningraders grappled with the medical crisis by interrogating doctors, policies, theories, and practices.

During the blockade, medical categories and concepts based on previous understandings of the body came under fire. Medicine, as a body of knowledge and as an approach to healing, was in crisis. This situation only encouraged the diarists to engage with it more fully. By placing both institutions and individuals under a critical microscope, the diarists developed new ideas about hunger disease, its causes, symptoms, and remedies. They wielded medical terms, wrote case studies, and conducted observational research. Their criticisms and discoveries often were inflected with the language of Soviet ideology or informed by expectations and reassurances voiced in official propaganda and the press. At times, they were at odds with Soviet officials over the policies regarding curative food, hospital stays, and work exemptions. At other times, they operated under similar assumptions about illness and willpower. But the diarists were not passive recipients of labels and behavioral norms prescribed by scientific and political elites. On the contrary, they worked to name, classify, diagnose, and otherwise make sense of the medical nightmare in which they were trapped. Unquestionably, the blockade was an enormous and devastating tragedy. However, it was also a moment of opportunity for the diarists to discover new and—in their view—more meaningful notions of health and infirmity.

Chapter Seven

In the Mirror of History

IN DECEMBER 1942, while Leningraders endured a second brutal winter and Soviet troops ground out a victory at Stalingrad, the acclaimed writer Aleksei Tolstoy urged his compatriots to take up a new weapon, one that would give them a decisive military edge: history. "The admirable force of the Russian people's historical resistance," Tolstoy declared, was a power "great enough to withstand the German-fascist armies." But until Soviet citizens became better students of history, they could not wield this weapon successfully: "There is no denying it, [we] do not know ourselves well enough. That is a pity, for to know one's own history, one's own good qualities and faults and to be aware of one's own possibilities, means being twice as strong and ten times more resolute."[1] Despite Tolstoy's exigent tone, the celebration of Russia's glorious past already was a critical part of the Soviet strategy of inspiring the people toward victory.[2] It was a central theme of Molotov's 1941 speech announcing the German invasion and of Stalin's speech marking the anniversary of the October Revolution several months later. Since then, Soviet citizens had been flooded with journalism, fiction, and scholarship dedicated to historical themes. This official prompting, along with their personal experiences of war, heightened the historicist consciousness of many. Soviet citizens were acutely aware that the fate of their county, of their lives, and of Marxist-Leninist theories of history all hung in the balance. And while the devastating first months of fighting cast doubt on the regime's reassurances that socialism inevitably would triumph over fascism, the first victories aroused hope and quickly were added to the annals of Russian military glory.

Although Leningraders were isolated from the mainland, they also were inundated with historical references in wartime speeches, media, and scholarship. Diaries suggest that such public discussions of history prompted many *blokadniki* to consider their plight in light of Russia's past and to integrate the blockade into developing narratives of Russian and Soviet history. Equally as powerful in piquing their historicist consciousness were the primitive conditions of siege life, which catapulted them back to an archaic world. In the midst of their struggle for survival, the diarists contemplated, read, and wrote history. Leningraders "who found themselves in the midst of 'unprecedented' events had a habit of searching for precedents, for frameworks, of understanding," the historian Lisa Kirschenbaum has observed.[3]

As the diarists attempted to write histories of their present moment, they encountered both narrative and conceptual challenges. Their engagement with history raised questions about local leaders, contemporary war policies, official interpretations of the past, and the likelihood of a Soviet victory. Especially during the chaotic and devastating years of 1941 and 1942, when official narratives of the war were still being scripted, the diarists interrogated and even reworked predominant narratives of Russian and Soviet history. During this period of relative freedom from a hard-line historical orthodoxy, they endeavored to make sense of the past in order to come to terms with a shocking new present.

Three specific events preoccupied the diarists: the War of 1812, the Civil War of 1918–22, and the Crimean War of 1854–56.[4] Their reflections did not converge around these moments accidentally; journalists, scholars, and propagandists encouraged Leningraders to consider 1812, 1918, and 1854 as inspiring analogues to their present struggles. With no apparent intention to be adversarial, the diarists responded to these analogies with confusion and doubt, drawing different lessons from those the regime's journalists, propagandists, and historians intended to impart.

Living History

The anachronistic and brutal qualities of siege warfare accentuated the diarists' historicist consciousness. Scarcity, bombardment, and isolation seemed to transform the city into an archaic version of itself. "In the middle of the twentieth century, history is taking a frightening step backward!" the historian Georgii Kniazev exclaimed.[5] The theatrical director Aleksandr Dymov called the blockade "a fantasy time machine," which "hurled" *blokadniki* back "to the early eighteenth century."[6] The darkness, the lack of basic necessities, and the difficulty of maintaining good health and hygiene prompted many diarists to dub their existence premodern or even "prehistoric."[7] "I did not hear the [news] summary, I did not read the newspaper, I forgot when I last cleaned my teeth, today I did not wash my face, there is no water," Ivan Savinkov remarked. "I have turned into a caveman and where? In the center of the city of Leningrad."[8] "We are like cave dwellers," the sixth grader Dima Afanas'ev echoed, "waiting to see the sun."[9]

When the sun arrived in spring 1942, it illuminated how life in the metropolis had reverted to one of a bygone era. Local efforts to increase the food supply converted the city into a patchwork of rural and urban as kitchen gardens sprouted among the ruins. The defunct public transit system meant all distances had to be traversed on foot. In the absence of mechanized vehicles, people walked in the center of the street as they had a century before. As Lidiia Ginzburg later observed, "we have once again obtained what was lost to modern man: the reality of city distances, long ago swallowed up by trams, buses, cars and taxis."[10] The siege transformed not only the cityscape but also the diarists' perceptions of near and far, rural and urban, modern and archaic. Leningraders returned to older ways of growing food, doing housework, and crafting home remedies, as most methods relying on imports or modern technology now were irrelevant. According to city librarians, patrons scoured antiquarian and historically themed books for practical information on how to build stoves, how wild grasses and roots could be prepared and eaten, how medical materials could be created from household items, and so on. To meet readers' demands, Leningrad's wartime presses published survival guides in unprecedented numbers. Istpart even produced pamphlets on Russian military history into which they infused practical information about safety, sanitation, and the like. This was a new hybrid genre, the historical survival guide. Under siege, historical thinking had both conceptual and practical significance. [11]

The tedium of blockade life also prompted the diarists to reflect on history. The siege dragged on, seemingly defying time's forward march. This was especially true during the first six months, when schools and factories closed, clocks and other mechanized timekeepers failed, and the dark winter days and nights melded together. Leningraders described time as moving in circles, in reverse, or remaining at a standstill. Some worked against this temporal disorientation by measuring the passage of time in new ways—through biorhythms, seasonal changes, or personal events. Others quantified time by the number of air raids or bombs dropped, or periodized it by deaths in the family or changes to rations. "We do not live by the calendar," the ballerina Vera Kostrovitskaia explained. "We are aware of the days and dates only through small square-shaped paper coupons [marked] with the number 125."[12] Weeks were eclipsed by the ten-day cycles *(dekada)* on which the ration system operated. As Leningraders struggled to stretch their food reserves from *dekada* to *dekada,* they partitioned their futures into ten-day segments. Earlier efforts to establish a ten-day week, which had failed in revolutionary France and in the early Soviet period, gained traction under siege.

The diary itself was a key weapon against temporal disorder. With its name derived from the word *day,* the diary's oldest use was as a timekeeper and aide-mémoire. Some *blokadniki* began journaling primarily to keep track of the day and date.[13] Others kept diaries to sharpen their vision of the recent past. They reread their accounts regularly to identify events and shifts that might otherwise be obscured by the monotony of siege life. The engineer Ivan Savinkov, for instance, studied his previous entries in order to predict when a decisive break in the German lines might occur. A typical example can be found in his entry for 12 December 1942, when he declared, "I would like to compare [today] with 18 December of last year." After consulting his entries for the previous year and noting that rations had increased, factories were working, and the radio and post were operational, he concluded, "That means that life in the country has been restored, and this is a sign that Russia will be victorious over Germany. It seems to me that now our army is stronger than it was at the beginning of the war."[14] War correspondents also tried to track changes in the besieged city, mostly for the purposes of highlighting improvements and thus boosting morale. A principal example is Nikolai Tikhonov's "Leningrad Year," which was written concurrently with the blockade and published in installments in *Star*. "Leningrad Year" begins in May 1942 after the worst period of the siege was over and when signs of progress presumably were easier to detect. Still, improvements were rather subtle, Tikhonov admitted, especially hard for diarists to notice: "If one were to write a daily chronicle of the city," he noted, "it would seem that November differs very little from October. The monotonous autumn takes the place of a monotonous summer, and even the war does not produce any particularly tragic impressions. In reality, however, this is not so."[15] Still, in "Leningrad Year," he attempted to graft siege time back onto chronological, "calendar" time, all the while conceding that they did not really coincide.[16]

Eleven-year-old Nikolai Ivanovich Vasil'ev's journal provides a striking example of the diary's function as timekeeper. Vasil'ev inscribed his fourteen-page account directly onto a calendar, each page of which was imprinted with inspirational quotes from Stalin and Lenin and with reminders about what important past events occurred on that date. Next to these texts, Vasil'ev wrote his entries, his own version of "on this day in history," which effectively juxtaposed life inside and outside the ring. A tragic entry about his father losing his ration card, for instance, appears beside a quotation of Stalin promising victory. The calendar reports the births and deaths of great men like Goethe, Stalin, and Newton, whereas the diary observes the deaths of less-known figures: Vasil'ev's mother, father, and brother. Above the printed reminder that today "Chekhov was born," Vasil'ev scrawled, "Lesha (my brother), sixteen years old, died at 5:30 a.m."[17] Moreover, Vasil'ev signed his name at the bottom of each entry, so his prose and the printed quotations of Lenin and Stalin resemble parallel citations.

At times, Vasil'ev forced these two historical narratives to intersect by commenting on the calendar's imprinted claims. His entry for 10 January 1942 is written beside an inspiring reference to Aleksei Tolstoy, who was born on that date in 1883. Here Vasil'ev scribbled, "he is a bad writer *[pisatil (sic)]*."[18] He also challenged the calendar's declaration that "Leningrad is the city of great victories and honors," noting, "L[eningrad] is the city of the Great October Revolution, a city of glory. But what has become of it? Life has died out. It is as if *[butto (sic)]* the city were empty. [. . .] Everything is as if *[butto]* it were dead."[19] As a schoolboy, he penned his entries in a rough hand and with spelling and punctuation mistakes. As a diarist, Vasil'ev played the historian, linking his own life to historical time and amending official claims in light of his personal experiences.

Disoriented by the archaic, brutal conditions of the siege, these Leningraders looked to diary writing as a way to illuminate their moment against the shadows of the past. For them, keeping a journal became, in part, a historical exercise.

Writing History

Regardless of whether the diarists were children or adults, workers or intellectuals, most of them kept journals with some historical objective in mind. They wrote to track change over time, to communicate with their children or future descendants, or to document the blockade for posterity. Nearly all were aware that they were witnessing a monumental event and that their accounts might someday provide critical evidence to scholars. "I felt myself to be Herodotus," the art historian Georgii Lebedev observed, "with that kind of historical responsibility."[20] Another art expert, Mariia Konopleva, strove to record as much "historically useful" information as she could and, in 1943, sent her diary to the State Literary Publishing House (Goslitizdat) and urged it to publish her 180 pages of data on "the conditions of everyday life in blockaded Leningrad."[21]

Historians and literary scholars have shown that Russia has been home to a strong tradition of historicism, one that has colored the personal and political writings of the intelligentsia since the nineteenth century.[22] Drawing on this tradition, the Soviet intelligentsia strongly argued for the interconnectedness of personal, political, and historical development and encouraged Soviet people to see themselves as "conscious historical subjects."[23] During the 1930s, members of the Soviet political and cultural elite viewed the diary as one tool through which Soviet people could cultivate a historicist and revolutionary consciousness. "The decisive quality of the New [Soviet] Man," Jochen Hellbeck has argued, was "the ability to see the laws of history and comprehend one's potential as a subject of historical action."[24] In the future-oriented Soviet Union, this fostered a sharper vision of the future than of the past. Many diaries of the 1930s, Hellbeck notes, "barely exhibit a sense of, let alone a longing for the past, and their reflections on the present are embedded in an almost exclusive orientation toward the future."[25] From this perspective, the diary was intended not as a place of historical refuge but as a tool for overcoming the past. The events and rhetoric of World War II, however, shifted this orientation, placing a premium on history as a source of Soviet identity and strength. Blockade diarists reveal a stronger orientation toward the past than toward the future. At a time when the future held the frightening prospect of death, they looked backward, sometimes out of nostalgia, sometimes out of a desire to better understand their current predicament.

Members of Leningrad's party organization encouraged this historicist mind-set by asking its besieged residents to keep diaries. When Secretary V. S. Efremov of the Kirov *raikom* first proposed such a campaign, he argued that unofficial accounts were needed to counterbalance official histories, which tended to gloss over personal experiences or "correct" the actions of wartime leaders.[26] By calling on citizens to chronicle the siege, members of the party granted authority both to them and to the place of intimate experience in history. However, neither the party nor Istpart, which eventually oversaw the campaign, specified how Leningraders should take up this task, except to suggest that they document "historical episodes that characterize our epoch" or the "historic atmosphere" of the city.[27] As a result of these open-ended recommendations, there is great variety in how the diarists—both those who participated in this campaign and those who wrote independently of it—approached the task. Some concentrated on reporting international or military news, others on personal events. Some placed a premium on facts and figures, others on personal impressions and experiences. What most diarists shared, however, were deep misgivings about which approach was best. They often shifted between methods and frequently apologized to future readers for any digressions and inconsistencies. Nearly all expressed a desire that their accounts be "historically useful," but they were unsure of what material future scholars might need.

The diarists grappled with three challenges in particular. First, how might they write a history of the blockade without hindsight, perspective, or sufficient information? Even diarists who had better access to information, such as Elizaveta Sokolova, an acting director of Istpart, complained that they did not know enough about current events to keep accurate accounts.[28] And the diarists, as both makers and observers of their historical moment, lacked hindsight and scholarly detachment. Second, the siege pushed the limits of representation even for authors of considerable talent. How could they, mostly amateur writers, convey the nightmare of blockade life? Third, they struggled to find the right balance between recording personal incidents and shared experiences. On the one hand, individual and world-historical struggles had become intertwined during the war. On the other hand, the diarists worried that intimate accounts might be dismissed as subjective or self-indulgent. Professional writers confronted these same difficulties. In a November 1943 article for *Star*, the correspondent Il'ia Ehrenburg summarized all three challenges: "War is complex, obscure, and dense, like an impenetrable forest. It does not resemble its descriptions; it is both simpler and more complicated. It is felt, but not always understood by its participants, and it is understood, but not felt by later investigators." Ehrenburg noted that the historian "correctly evaluat[es] the significance" of events, but he erroneously "dress[es] up" past events rather than presenting them as they really were. By contrast, those who experience the war directly "know what the war looks like [. . .] but it is difficult for the participants of the war to appreciate the historical significance of what was taking place."[29] These fundamental questions about the practice and purpose of history were a daily source of concern for those who kept diaries under siege.

Let's take a closer look at how three diarists grappled with these questions. All three are male diarists, who tended to dwell at greater length on methodological concerns than female ones. Anisim Prokof'evich Nikulin was a party delegate and manager of an integrated industrial plant in the October District. Nikulin felt obliged to keep a diary because of his party position, but he often regretted that decision. "I work a lot and do not have time to make observations. I am not used to observations. It's a bit boring." He tried to ease his burden with alcohol. "In the course of [making] observations twice, I stopped by pubs even though I don't like them. Drank a bit too much."[30] Nikulin's diary is filled with apologies for the halfhearted and haphazard way he wrote, with no clear narrative in mind. He wrote almost as much about his search for a proper method of diary writing as he did about the siege itself. "Yes, excuse me, reader, perhaps after some time I myself will find that my notes are useless, not needed by anyone, of no value; I know that one should not write like this. After all, I am only making notes without any kind of plan, without selecting facts, unsystematically."[31] Through these admissions, Nikulin underscored the challenges of writing a diary as history. The diary is supposed to be written spontaneously and concurrently with events and so resists a coherent structure. But that was exactly the kind of narrative Nikulin felt he needed to provide.

In addition to apologizing for his unsystematic approach, Nikulin asked his potential reader to pardon his limited literary skills, which, he worried, prevented him from conveying the complexity of life on the island: "I am no writer, and the pen in my hand will not be able to capture all of reality. My limited thoughts will not be able to write with enough color to depict the reality of the besieged city of Lenin. This is why I am not attempting to switch to a brush and create a picture on a big canvas. I note down what I experience myself, what I see and observe."[32] Nikulin tried to limit his literary ambitions by recording only firsthand experiences rather than trying to document the siege as a whole. Still, he questioned whether his personal life should be made part of the historical record. Whenever he mentioned his family or his declining health, he apologized as though this was an indulgence. For example, in January 1942, he wrote, "Forgive me, whoever might look over my notes some day, if that happens at some point, but I want to say one word about myself. In the past few days, I have started to lose weight catastrophically. There is almost nothing on my ribs, only skin and bones remain."[33] Conflicted over what and how to write, Nikulin left large gaps between entries. In the end, he penned a few, retrospective reflections and mostly inserted documents— telegrams, announcements, speeches, and work reports—to do the historical record keeping for him.[34]

One might assume that more experienced historians handled these challenges with greater ease. But professionals wrestled with similar concerns about how to keep a "historically useful" diary. The historians Aleksei Alekseevich Chernovskii and Georgii Aleksandrovich Kniazev also questioned and adjusted their approaches to diary writing, especially as their sense of historical significance evolved. Kniazev was an archival director at the Historical Institute of Leningrad's branch of the Academy of Sciences. During his career, he created several archives, including one on the Soviet navy and another on the Academy itself. He also oversaw the publication of twenty-one volumes documenting the Academy's work.[35] Throughout the war, Kniazev compiled materials for a collection on the siege. In recognition of his many accomplishments, he received the Order of Lenin and the Order of the Red Banner.[36]

Kniazev had kept a diary off and on since he was eight years old. His reasons for writing evolved with his interests. They shifted from "self-analysis" to preparing "a psychological novella" to writing the "history of everyday life," as he did during the siege. During the war, he addressed his entries to a "faraway friend" *(dal'nii drug)*, a Soviet reader from a future and, he hoped, a happier time. He titled them "Days of Great Suffering. War with Germany. Impressions of My Small Radius," which captures the intimate and yet wide-reaching aspirations of his wartime journal.[37]

Kniazev was constantly concerned with how to select material in a way that balanced the big picture of the siege with the small "radius" of his life. Three days after the invasion, he decided his priority should be to document personal incidents, so that future generations might understand how an ordinary person experienced this extraordinary event: "If they do reach you, my faraway friend, these pages of mine—perhaps in fragments, scorched ones—you will experience with me what I, your unfortunate predecessor, had to live through, I who lived in a 'prehistoric' era and at the dawn of true human history. You, faraway friend, will remove all that is extraneous or repetitive. In the official documents preserved for you, you will find the material for a scholarly history, but in my notes you will feel the beating pulse of the life of one small person who, within his own small radius, lived out a life that was big, boundless, complexly tragic, and full of contradictions . . ."[38] Even though he was a historian interested in a larger horizon of events, Kniazev decided to contribute this way in part because he lacked the necessary distance and information to do otherwise: "As contemporaries, we must not and cannot know all that will be known to historians. But how contemporaries experienced events, how they comprehended them will not always be clear to historians. My notes, perhaps, can partially serve this [purpose]."[39] Kniazev's experiential approach set his diary apart from both professional historiography and local media coverage: "The newspapers are full of articles about battles with the enemy on the outskirts of Leningrad," he wrote in September 1941. "They will be in the hands of readers and preserved in libraries. But the newspapers do not convey the hues or 'nuances' of the experiences of individual people. They report about heroism or about criminal acts or about something out of the ordinary. And here, in these pages, I try to convey plainly what is experienced by most ordinary people, including me."[40] In this diary-cum-history of everyday life, he implored his "faraway friend not to forget the little people" like himself and his coworkers.[41]

However, Kniazev frequently second-guessed his personal approach. Like Nikulin, he worried that his "radius" was too narrow, boring, and unsystematically studied to be useful to future generations. Kniazev also suspected that his notes were full of "repetitions, digressions, mistakes, and contradictions."[42] To make his diary more relevant, he began summarizing official news reports but admitted that this gave his journal generic and redundant qualities. Frustrated, Kniazev questioned whether he should continue his diary practice at all. As he wrote in November 1941, "Shall I take my notes any further? They are taking on the overly monotonous character of a catalogue of the destruction caused by bombardment from enemy planes. As a contemporary, I cannot get a real grasp of events, and my radius is too restricted to offer a full and varied description of them. I am trying to broaden my radius to include general information, gathered from newspapers, but do I need to do this? After all, in these notes, I don't really take upon myself the role of historian or war correspondent or something of that sort. The newspaper is a peculiar document. All that can be said about propagandistic literature has been said long ago. Should I jot this down or not?" Like Nikulin, Kniazev struggled to differentiate the role of the diarist from the role of the historian.

Moreover, Kniazev worried that his personal, experiential approach to history might be misconstrued as self-aggrandizement: "Should I be writing about myself, about my own experiences? I might seem to be showing off: 'Look at our hero, stoically and courageously enduring all these ordeals?' I do endure them stoically, but I endure them dialectically, with great contradictions, as a thinking person does. [. . .] Will you, my faraway friend, read with interest these not heroic but sincere notes kept by a contemporary of terrifying events?"[43] Did the "ordinariness" of his life make it historically valuable or irrelevant to scholars? Kniazev was unsure. His own life story was too small, inconsistent, and—as he put it in ideologically inflected terms—dialectical to warrant hero status. He seemed uneasy about being the protagonist of his own diary when the collective struggle held far more weight. This attitude points to the premium placed on the collective in Soviet historiography as well as to the personal shyness of the diarist. Both augmented Kniazev's anxiety over how to capture the siege for posterity.

Subsequent entries illustrate that Kniazev continued to both summarize news reports and describe personal experiences. Like Nikulin, Kniazev apologized repeatedly: "My faraway friend, when reading these notes, will you discard or skip whatever he [sic] finds uninteresting or unnecessary? And I can't tell exactly what will be needed and what will not."[44] It was not until February 1942, the height of the famine, that Kniazev made peace with writing more instinctively. "I am writing down everything that I see, think, and experience. Now, spontaneously, without worrying about any contradictions, long-windedness, or repetition. Because such is real life."[45] If his notes were jumbled, this made them all the more reflective of the fractious and chaotic nature of life under siege.

Aleksei Chernovskii chose to do the opposite. He focused on the collective story, not his own. Chernovskii was a professional historian and a senior staff member at the Museum of the History and Development of Leningrad. There, he helped draft historical articles inspired by World War II as well as lectured, published articles, and curated exhibitions on war-torn Petrograd and Leningrad.[46] He also kept a diary and gave it over to the museum for its growing archive of siege materials in spring 1942. Istpart's staff acquired it in 1948.[47]

Perhaps from a combination of ideological, professional, and personal convictions, Chernovskii viewed history as an impersonal enterprise. To create a historically "useful" diary, he filled his account with excerpts from newspapers and leaflets, charts, and hand-drawn maps from which readers might piece together the blockade experience. He did not do this interpretive work for them. Chernovskii also quoted radio broadcasts, political speeches, and the conversations of his coworkers verbatim. Kniazev did this too, but his voice still dominated the narrative. Chernovskii, however, privileged the voices of other people over his own. He quoted them numerous times and, as a good scholar, cited his sources by putting the informant's last name in parentheses after each reference. For Chernovskii, history was what happened to other people.

In fact, Chernovskii seemed to consider his diary's historical value as inversely related to the amount of personal content it contained. He took pride in making "many important omissions" about his personal life except when it matched the collective experience. "In keeping this diary as an authentic document of a great historical epoch, as material for historians of Leningrad, I meticulously avoid registering personal experiences as best I can, and, if I dwell on some minor facts about my family, food and so on, then it is only because I consider it part of the typical picture, reflecting the unique conditions of life in our city. I think that keeping these daily notes will be useful in the future."[48]

Despite Chernovskii's intentions, he struggled to restrain himself from making personal reflections, especially as the siege intensified. He could not help expressing despair about how to feed his children or about his own deterioration, even though he worried that such concerns damaged his spirits and the scholarly merit of his account. "Right now it is very important not to engage in analyzing my physical condition," he wrote. "My head, the feeling in my stomach, the taste in my mouth, the weakness of my legs, my weight loss, and so on. In general, I need to devote myself to happy news, hope, expectations, and to an inevitably improved future."[49] When he did indulge in private confessions, Chernovskii either chastised himself or found professional justification for the lapse—other Leningraders shared his hardships. This internal struggle to censor himself endured to the very last entry, which begins with the declaration,

"I will not talk anymore about my illness; this is not the place." But then Chernovskii proceeded "just to note" some observations about his own condition, which comprised the bulk of the entry.[50] Like Nikulin, Chernovskii devoted nearly as much text to outlining what he ought to say as to actually writing on the topics he found acceptable. When his health and spirits greatly declined in early 1942, he offered his notes to the Museum of the History and Development of Leningrad. In a letter dated 18 February 1942, he explained, "Since 22 June, I have been keeping a diary as part of my museum work. The entries have all been made comprehensively, in great detail. Will I survive—I do not know, but this diary, this document for the history of the city, will. It reflects these exceptional days (of course with some subjectivity)," he admitted.[51]

Nikulin, Kniazev, and Chernovskii are three of many diarists who agonized over how to keep journals that were both personally satisfying and historically useful. Methodological questions occupied professional and amateur historians alike. Such concerns in turn led the diarists to reflect on what history was and how it should be crafted. As a form, the diary preserves the inconsistencies and reversals in their thinking. Nikulin's apologies, Kniazev's apprehensive intimacy, and Chernovskii's omissions demonstrate, if not the successful implementation of a historical approach, then the difficulty of developing one and adhering to it.

Waging the "Historical Front"

Similar fluctuations mark the public writings of Soviet academicians, writers, and agitators who rushed to interpret the historical significance of the war. Especially during the chaotic early years of fighting, there was no consensus about how exactly to accommodate current events into established historical narratives. Disputes over the "historical front" have been well documented by scholars, especially David Brandenberger and Katharine Hodgson.[52] They have shown how uncertainty about the war's outcome kept the official historical line hazy in 1941–42. This in turn created inconsistency and flexibility in how the war was presented. Building on prewar trends, correspondents and academics tended to stress the same general themes of Russian nationalism, German barbarism, the certainty of victory, and the cult of the individual hero. In terms of specifics,

however, they varied. [53] In 1944, the Central Committee summoned historians, journalists, and propagandists to a conference hoping, as leading
Politburo member Georgii Malenkov explained, "to develop a set of
principle positions for all historians." However, no resolution was reached.
The historical line did not crystallize until the end of the war.[54]

Despite this haziness, a consistent feature of Soviet wartime historiography and propaganda was the glorification of Russia's prerevolutionary
past. "Nowadays, they frequently write 'Russia,' 'Russian' instead of
'Soviet Union' in the newspapers. There is not a peep about the International, about Soviet socialist Europe. Now, they only talk about the
motherland, about patriotism," Georgii Kniazev observed.[55] Lisa Kirschenbaum has demonstrated in her study of the blockade's legacy how, just
days after the invasion, Leningrad political and cultural leaders began to
plan exhibitions, monuments, and films that would encourage the
blokadniki to see themselves in the shadows of Russia's glorious past.
Leningrad's Russian Museum and the Museum of the Revolution mounted
exhibitions titled *The Great Fatherland War* and *The Heroism of the
Great Russian People.* Party cells, hospitals, and libraries hosted lectures honoring the city's imperial and revolutionary past. Several of the
diarists studied here gave historically themed talks.[56] In addition, impe-
rial-era heroes who had vanquished foreign invaders, like Aleksandr
Nevskii, Mikhail Kutuzov, and Aleksandr Suvorov, were honored anew.
Military orders for each of them were established in July 1942. Suvorov
became the subject of a suite by the Leningrad composer Boris Asaf'ev,
and Kutuzov of a 1943 film. Sergei Eisenstein's 1938 film *Aleksandr
Nevskii,* which had been banned when the Molotov-Ribbentrop Pact was
signed, was rereleased in 1941 and shown widely, even in bomb shelters.[57] Furthermore, traces of the tsarist era reappeared as Leningraders
began referring to prominent thoroughfares and squares by their pre-
Soviet names. Several were readopted officially in January 1944.[58]

While these events and publications encouraged historicism, it is also
likely that some Leningraders cultivated it through private reflections,
conversations, and reading. Local correspondents like Vera Ketlinskaia,
Nikolai Tikhonov, and Aleksandr Fadeev characterized the *blokadniki* as
voracious readers. The diaries also suggest that Leningraders scoured libraries, bookstores, and kiosks for historical works that might offer insight

into how the present conflict would unfold.[59] It is unclear how available books were inside the city. Reports on the city's libraries, bookstores, and presses fluctuate between bemoaning the lack of available reading material and trumpeting high print runs and sales.[60] On the one hand, during the first year of the blockade, the flow of new works into Leningrad ground to a halt, and the city's book production fell. Libraries fell into disrepair as books were damaged, sold, or burned as fuel. On the other hand, once Leningrad was cut off, newly printed books could not be delivered and so stayed in the city. The premier bookshop, Book House (*Dom knigi*), was one of a dozen bookshops and kiosks that remained open and fairly stocked. This fact, combined with a robust market for used books, created the impression that there was an abundance of print.[61]

The available data on print runs suggests that in Leningrad, works of history and historical fiction were produced in high numbers relative to other genres.[62] Among the most printed books were E. V. Tarle's books on the Napoleonic and Crimean Wars *Napoleon, Nakhimov*, and *The Defense of Sevastopol'*, as well as his tracts "Two Great Fatherland Wars" and "The Fatherland War of 1812 and the Defeat of Napoleon's Empire."[63] Other historically-themed works such as Sergei Borodin's *Dmitrii Donskoi*, Sergei Sergeev-Tsenskii's *The Ordeal of Sevastopol'*, K. Osipov's (the pen name of Osip Kuperman) *Suvorov*, and Boris Kochakov's *Aleksandr Suvorov* and *Mikhail Kutuzov* were also produced in large numbers. In addition, historical fiction by Aleksandr Pushkin, Mikhail Lermontov, and Leo Tolstoy enjoyed renewed popularity. Although *War and Peace* already graced the shelves of most personal and public libraries, 100,000 new copies were printed in the besieged city alone.[64] Excerpts of *War and Peace* were read aloud at performances of Tchaikovsky's *1812 Overture*, and Boris Asaf'ev composed new music based on the novel.[65]

How did Leningraders respond to this deluge of historically themed materials? David Brandenberger has argued that Russian public reception was positive. In general, Russians "adopted the language of the official Soviet wartime line."[66] The blockade diaries suggest a more ambivalent picture, at least during the first years of the war. Party efforts to cultivate greater interest in history—as shown by officially sanctioned events, publications, and print runs—opened the door to a multitude of interpretations. The diarists did engage critically with historical analogies suggested by official publications, especially Napoleon's invasion of 1812, the siege of Petrograd during the Civil War of 1918–22, and the siege of Sevastopol' in 1854. From their unusual position on the island, the diarists raised questions and insights about those wars that sometimes conflicted with official views and seemed to bring the blockade's incomparable and unique features into sharper relief.

Two Great Fatherland Wars

The moment the Soviet regime announced the German invasion, it suggested the attack marked a continuation of Russia's 1812 "great fatherland war" or "great patriotic war" against Western imperialism. Viacheslav Molotov used this epithet in his radio address of 22 June 1941, and it endures to this day.[67] Even though 1812 was not as deeply connected to Leningrad's history as it was to Smolensk's or Moscow's, Leningrad broadcasts, posters, and newspapers reminded residents of local sites connected to 1812, and they offered point-by-point comparisons between partisans, civilians, and military leaders in 1812 and in 1941.[68] The diarists readily adopted 1812 as the central historical touchstone for understanding World War II. They referred to Napoleon's invasion more frequently than to any other historical event, albeit rarely by the phrase "great fatherland war."[69] They also unearthed points of contention when making this comparison.

One issue pertained to the spirited celebration of the battles of Borodino and Moscow. In the wartime press, Aleksei Tolstoy and Il'ia Ehrenburg and, in academia, the historian E. V. Tarle of Leningrad's branch of the Academy of Sciences tried to recast Borodino and Moscow as moral victories, but the diarists could not overlook the fact that Russia surrendered both cities to Napoleon.[70] The Russian imperial army's abandonment of these cities also contradicted the Soviet regime's mandate against retreat. How, then, could the memory of such battles strengthen Leningraders' resolve never to capitulate? In the autumn of 1941, the former *LP* writer Ksaverii Sel'tser observed that Red Army commanders were retreating so much that they were starting to resemble Kutuzov or even surpass him: "If we, according to the announcement by the [Sov]informbiuro, will resist the fascists for many more days, covering the battlefield with their corpses, seizing mountains of tanks and other weaponry, then why have we not only *not* thrown off the enemy, *not* chased him off, but we retreat and retreat? It is just incomprehensible! Among the people the words 'betrayal' and 'treason' are circulating. Everything has a limit. Even Kutuzov retreated to a certain degree . . . or—I don't want to believe this—do our commanders want to copy Kutuzov and give even Moscow to the enemy?!"[71] Although ultimately victorious in the war, Kutuzov's extensive use of tactical retreat in early battles meant that one had to proceed carefully in celebrating him. Articles in *LP* referred to Kutuzov's tactical retreats in veiled terms as "concealing" the army, "skillful maneuvering," "flexibility," or simply "moving troops from one position to another" for the "preservation and care of the Russian army."[72] Likewise, Tarle presented Kutuzov's order to retreat as a brave, honorable act because it put the welfare of the troops first.[73] He won the Stalin Prize in scholarship in 1943 for his efforts. This led some Leningraders to ask why, then, Soviet commanders were not following Kutuzov's example and saving more civilian lives. "He pitied the soldiers," Liudmila El'iashova observed. "And our commanders? Were we ourselves ready to give up Leningrad?"[74]

The timeline of events in 1812 also weighed on many diarists' minds as they tried to predict the second "great fatherland war" on the basis of the first. Not surprisingly, this comparative tendency marks the diaries of historians like Kniazev. On 14 August 1941, he recalled, "Smolensk fell [on 18 August] in 1812. The Battle of Borodino was fought on 26 August. In September, Napoleon entered Moscow. How will events unfurl this time?"[75] All signs indicated an even greater military disaster: "Can it be that the fascists have arrived in Yaroslavl' province?" asked Elizaveta Sokolova, an interim acting director of Istpart, in August 1941. "It was not even like that under Napoleon."[76] "In October 1812, the expansion and retreat of Napoleon's army from Moscow had begun. What will happen with Hitler's army by October 1941?" the art specialist and archivist Mariia Konopleva wondered. Answering her own question, she retorted, "Matters turned out to be otherwise." Not only were the Germans advancing, but also evacuations were done haphazardly if at all. "This evacuation was badly organized; truly it was not organized at all."[77] The 1812–1941 parallel framed Konopleva's expectations and criticisms of Leningrad authorities' management of the population.

Prediction was a common pastime of Ivan Savinkov, a brigade leader at the Molotov Factory. Referencing historians like Ernst Herni and E. V. Tarle, Savinkov declared, "Everything is repeating itself. All that Napoleon did, Hitler is doing."[78] Savinkov applied his understanding of the Third Coalition to the Soviet Union's relationship to its allies, and from this, he predicted that England, not Russia, would prove the most decisive of the belligerents. Perhaps mindful of Tilsit, when Russia abandoned its ally Britain, Savinkov warned that Hitler would meet the same fate as the French emperor: "this is no Napoleon, but nevertheless England will win the war."[79] Subsequently, much of Savinkov's diary details his disappointment when his predictions failed to come true. While Napoleon's men had begun to retreat in October 1812, Hitler's troops were taking vast swaths of Soviet territory in October 1941. England's delay in opening a second front frustrated Savinkov, as it did many Soviet citizens, and it reminded him of how Russia eventually bore the brunt of Napoleon's Grand Armée. "Oh, how trying it is for us to fight Europe all alone. History is repeating itself again. For the second time Russia is fighting with all of Europe. [. . .] Again, England, using our Russians, will win the second fatherland war," he surmised in October 1942, holding to the same analogy one year later.[80]

Diarists also feared a recurrence of the devastation wrought by Napoleon's troops. Elizaveta Sokolova, for example, prayed for "no repeat of 1812."[81] To describe the human costs of the blockade, the schoolboy Dima Afanas'ev drew on the 1812–1941 parallel, but in an unusual way. He likened Leningraders to the hungry, devastated French army. In spring 1942, Afanas'ev observed that "under the sunny light," Leningraders "looked rather frightening: gaunt, yellow, with drooping eyes, dirty, all bundled up in whatever was available, like soldiers of the Napoleonic army in 1812 . . . what a tenacious creature is man!"[82] To him, the defenders of the city of Lenin resembled a defeated army. Both Sokolova's and Afanas'ev's interpretations suggest how diarists could draw unorthodox and potentially subversive conclusions from the 1812–1941 pairing.

Most diarists based their views about the Napoleonic campaign on Leo Tolstoy's depiction in *War and Peace*. When Maria Konopleva began gathering documents and images for a wartime exhibition on "the Great Fatherland War of 1812" in July 1941, she sat down "to reread *War and Peace* with great attention."[83] Despite initial ideological reservations about the novel and its author, Soviet leaders began to herald *War and Peace* in the 1930s as a literary masterpiece and a testament to the heroism of the Russian people. The celebration of the novel reached new heights during World War II. Three weeks after the German invasion, four reissues of Tolstoy's works were slated for publication.[84] Because soldiers had little time to read, *Pravda* printed 150,000 copies of part 4 of the novel, which describes heroic peasants attacking French soldiers; the state publishing house also released 100,000 reprints of the sections on Borodino and Schöngraben.[85] The diarists noticed that the novel was appearing in new formats, including a portable, one-volume edition and as a play for the Leningrad stage.[86]

The most famous articulation of the novel's importance to *blokadniki* comes from the opening lines of Ginzburg's retrospective *Notes of a Blockade Person:* "During the war years, people used to read *War and Peace* avidly, comparing their own behavior with it (and not the other way around—no one doubted the accuracy of Tolstoy's response to life). The reader would say to himself: right, I've got the proper feeling about this. So then this is how it should be. Whoever had energy enough to read, used to read *War and Peace* avidly in besieged Leningrad."[87] According to Ginzburg, Leningraders reread the novel in order to corroborate their feelings and experiences, fully expecting them to match those of Tolstoy's characters. But comparing their lives to those of the characters furnished the diarists with as many questions as insights. The architect Esfir' Levina lingered over the moments when the characters revealed their naïveté about war, such as the famous scene when the protagonist, Pierre, foolishly wears white on the battlefield. "I am rereading *War and Peace*. Pierre Bezukhov is on the Borodino battlefield, in a caftan and white hat. They ask him, 'Are you a doctor?'—No, not a doctor, I'm just . . . ,' and he moves on. I think about Sevastopol', Stalingrad, and it seems that all people at that time were children. Leaving Moscow to escape the French, the Rostov family loaded up twenty-eight carts. I think about the hundreds of thousands of people on the endless roads of our motherland," destitute by comparison.[88] Compared to Soviet models of heroism, Pierre Bezukhov and the Rostovs seemed far cries from Levina's steely, battle-hardened compatriots. As she pointed out, nowhere was this more apparent than in the country's besieged cities: Stalingrad, Leningrad, and Sevastopol'. Thus, in a way, the novel inadvertently provided her comfort by suggesting that the Russian people had evolved and were now more prepared to withstand the onslaught.

While Levina focused on civilian characters, the art critic Georgii Lebedev compared his predicament to that of Tolstoy's soldiers. He wrote about them fondly even though he did not seem to identify with the characters any more than Levina did. Still, Lebedev *wished* that he could. How much better it would be to exist in this familiar and fictional world.

> I am rereading *War and Peace*. Captain Tushin, of course, remains unharmed. Nikolai Rostov, of course, will continue to be occupied with the affairs of his squadron. The buzz of bullets and fierce hand-to-hand fighting—these are only episodes from which the one and the other emerge whole and unharmed. It is quite another situation for a person who is not a character of literary creation. The plot of his life is still not rounded off. The hero is not sure of anything. The novel might not even be written. At the current moment, for example, while I write these lines, I don't know what could happen in half an hour, in an hour, in the course of a day. Danger hangs over my head constantly. My diary might be broken off midsentence.[89]

The characters' struggles paled in comparison to the actual uncertainty of Lebedev's existence. Their fates—however tragic—were known, their stories written. For Lebedev, this fact alone made the two worlds incomparable. He longed to finish the chapter of his blockade life and to know the outcome of this ordeal. *War and Peace* reminded Lebedev of how tenuous his situation actually was.

In sum, several diarists did read about the Napoleonic Wars in order to "check" their own experiences of war, but 1812 mostly seemed to magnify the rapid advance of the Wehrmacht, the brutality of Soviet policies, the failure to evacuate or otherwise save civilians, and the agony of the unknown future. The 1812–1941 analogy did inspire them but to feelings other than confident triumphalism.

Starving Petrograd, Starving Leningrad

The invasion of 1812 was regarded as a sacred touchstone and counterpart to 1941 all across the Soviet Union. In Leningrad, however, another moment had almost as much resonance with the diarists. This was the Russian Civil War of 1918–22. In October 1919, their city—then called Petrograd—was starved and nearly encircled by the coalition of anti-Bolshevik "White" forces.[90] The diarists did not need a Tolstoy to capture the experience of the Civil War; many remembered it vividly. Nor did they need much official prompting toward this comparison, although there was plenty of that.

As early as August 1941, Leningrad's party organization created pamphlets reminding Leningraders of the steadfast bravery of Petrograders who had refused to surrender their city in 1919. Istpart prepared a series of historical essays, "On Our City's Military Tradition," which brought encircled Petrograd and besieged Leningrad together. They bore such titles as "To Defend Petrograd to the Death," "The Failure of the German Occupation of the Pskov Region (1918)," and "Petrograd Workers on the Front of the Civil War."[91] Similarly, *LP* reprinted headlines, posters, and slogans from the Civil War to remind Leningraders that "neither hunger nor cold nor blockade could break the spirit of proletarian Petrograd. Like an impregnable rock, Red Petrograd has towered all of these years and still remains the first citadel of Soviet power."[92] If Soviet citizens demonstrated equal courage, the correspondent Il'ia Ehrenburg prophesied, "1943 might become 1918."[93] Through these texts, historians and correspondents hoped the 1918–1941 parallel would remind Leningraders of Bolshevism's triumph over a hostile West, and they took care to emphasize the international composition of the White forces and of Germany's invasion during the Civil War.[94] Moreover, these sources presented Petrograd in much the same way as 1812, stressing heroism, sacrifice, patriotism, and the Russian people's unrivaled ability to outlast and oust foreign invaders. Also like 1812, the Civil War narrative was amended during World War II to make it a more inspirational point of comparison. It was forgotten that, when White general Nikolai Iudenich reached Pulkovo, Lenin spoke of deserting Leningrad. In addition, Leningrad's wartime press gave Stalin a more prominent role in Petrograd's defense.[95]

The diarists' memories of the Civil War, however, were deeply conflicted and bound up with numerous personal and political factors. These ranged from the memories of youth to the mythos of the revolution to the return of material hardships. Although it is difficult to generalize about these entries, they do follow a pattern. Diarists expressed some nostalgia for the Civil War in the first months of the war but increasingly became averse to comparing these blockades, because of both their similarities and differences. Initially, they hoped the Civil War had prepared them to face their current struggles. Elizaveta Sokolova drew on the earlier conflict to inspire her husband as he left for the front in September 1941: "If at any time you feel afraid during battle, remember that you already were in two wars—the imperial war and the Civil War and you remained alive[;] in the third war and you will not perish! I have faith in your gumption and your experience."[96] Aleksandra Zagorskaia, chair of the Red Case-maker artel, found solace in city structures that outlasted the Civil War and would survive the Germans' assault on them. The Narva Arch particularly inspired Zagorskaia. First built in 1814 to greet Russian soldiers returning victorious from France, Narva was an architectural rebuttal to Napoleon's Arc de Triomphe. "Now, as it was then in the days of 1917–18," it "stood strong, undefeated." "Now, the Narva pickets stand up with the pride of defending our city from the fascist hordes."[97] Zagorskaia's spirited vision of the Civil War rarely faltered—a rarity among diarists.

When starvation began to grip the city, most diarists discarded their memories of the Civil War as naïve or romanticized. Sixteen-year-old Maia Bubnova was too young to experience the Civil War herself, but 1941 still upset her idealized image of 1918. That November, Bubnova recalled how she and her friend Zoia, both devoted Komsomol members, used to envy the Civil War fighters and "imagined it [war] in a romantic light without those practical inevitabilities, which exist now." In light of her current situation, Bubnova admitted that the "heroic fairytale" of 1918–22 that she had learned in her youth was misguided.[98] This passage was removed when Istpart published her diary in 1947.

The return of acute shortages raised for most diarists vivid memories of blockaded Petrograd. For this reason, they often evoked the year 1919—the time when Petrograd was in greatest peril—as opposed to 1918, which was shorthand for the Civil War as a whole. Objects frequently triggered their recollections. The makeshift, potbellied *(burzhuiki)* stoves and the wick *(koptilki)* lamps that graced their homes in 1919 returned in 1941. The site of Leningraders sitting indoors and bundled in "felt boots, ear-flapped hats, padded jackets, greatcoats" conjured for Georgii Lebedev "a still frame from a blessed memory of 1919–1920."[99] "Thoughts carry me back to recollect the analogous deprivations from 1919–20," the translator Aleksandra Liubovskaia similarly noted, "when we sat without candles or kerosene and only with the meager illumination from the *burzhuika* around which the whole family or collective of workers gathered."[100] Survival depended on how well the diarists could revive the skills they used during the Civil War. In Petrograd, they had learned how to make *burzhuiki,* to cope with breadlines, and to save and savor food, although most noted that the quantity and quality of bread was far better in 1919 than in 1941.[101] Those who could not retrieve such skills from memory learned them from books. According to the librarian Mariia Sadova, patrons devoured materials published during 1919–20 that addressed first aid, edible native plants, street fighting, and so on.[102]

The relative advantages of the Civil War period stood out sharply to the diarists. In Leningrad, shortages were more severe and enduring, and there were fewer possibilities for procuring food than in "Starving Petrograd."[103] Aleksandra Liubovskaia was trudging through the frozen city toward the Neva River "to get some water" in January 1942 when she "observed the enormous lines at the bakery": "Automatically one recalls a drawing from the cover of the journal *Little Flame (Ogonëk)* in 1918—'the modern circles of Dante's hell'—a long, winding line, ending somewhere far away. But in 1942 the situation is incomparably worse," she continued, "if only because in the blockaded city it is impossible to leave, whereas in 1918 all who wanted to could leave and go to any Russian city. Besides, it was possible to buy a few food products."[104] The *blokadniki* could not flee to the city's rural outskirts or trade with local farmers for food, as Petrograders could. The memory of Petrograd, therefore, brought the unprecedented material hardships in Leningrad into sharp relief. The theatrical student Nina Mervol'f declared that "hunger now is much worse than in '18" even though she had not been alive to experience it. This was the conventional wisdom of her parents' and teachers' generation by January 1942.[105] The writer Sof'ia Ostrovskaia even scorned the comparison: "Hunger? Hunger. Real? Real. I knew hunger during the Civil War (for our house[hold]—the end of 1918 through the spring of 1922) and hunger in the epoch of collectivization and the epoch of Torgsin. But that was not hunger—not in either one of these epochs. Real hunger has come now. [. . .] can no longer we go hungry romantically *[romanticheski golodat']* the way that Anna Akhmatova was doing in 1919, lying in bed and admiring a rose that she bought with her last bit of money. We have even been robbed of the romanticism that adorns death. [. . .] Who cares about roses at this moment! Who cares about adornment!"[106] For Ostrovskaia, the extremity of hunger during the blockade made it distinct from the Civil War, from collectivization, or from the 1930s. Some members of the intelligentsia, Lisa Kirschenbaum explains, recalled hunger during the Civil War as an ascetic experience that was cleansing and inspiring.[107] Here, Sof'ia Ostrovskaia made reference to that phenomenon by insisting that the ascetic aesthetic of 1918 did not apply to "real" hunger," under which it was impossible to find beauty. The only "adornments" of siege life were the brief joys of savoring one's soup, tea, or meager rations.

Others saw parallels not just in the shortages but in the social tensions they created. Mariia Konopleva remarked that, along with *burzhuiki* stoves, the "disorganization of life" and infighting in Petrograd had returned to Leningrad.[108] Already in the first month of the siege, Konopleva noticed a new atmosphere in the canteen at the factory where she worked. She had to eat standing up, without a fork, and constantly vying for space with a hostile crowd of coworkers. "Recalling the years 1919–20," she observed, "how quickly in the days of war our cafeterias have sunk to this level! The same, familiar dried fish *[vobla]*, [. . .] the same old angry, greedy crowd!"[109] Konopleva presented the Civil War not as a struggle of proletarians versus anti-Bolshevik "Whites" but as one between workers for resources. The 1919–1941 comparison also sharpened Ostrovskaia's vision of strife and indifference on the island. In 1919, she noted, gravediggers still dug graves for free; speculators were "kind spirited." "Here is the difference: In '19, the streets were strewn with the bodies of dead horses. People walked by, they stopped and were taken aback. In '41–42, the bodies of dead people are scattered about. People walk right by, not stopping and unsurprised."[110] For her, 1919 only elucidated the widespread indifference to suffering and death in Leningrad. While official presentations of the Civil War tended to emphasize its international and class dimensions, many diarists recalled moments of conflict between residents or between them and the fledgling Bolshevik state.

In 1918, Bolshevik power had just taken root in the city and was struggling to quell the chaos of war and revolution. Recollections of this period raised questions for a few diarists about current Soviet authorities and their ability to organize a strong defense of Leningrad. Diarists at opposite ends of the political spectrum evoked the revolution and Civil War in order to suggest that the leadership in 1941–42 was just as feeble, if not worse. Party members like Irina Zelenskaia declared that the preparations and safety exercises in Leningrad were a sham: "Rescue, in the style of 1918, will hardly be necessary. That means the only thing that remains is just inconvenience and the waste of strength for the sake of military decorum."[111] It was not just that local leaders were disorganized, insisted Elizaveta Sokolova, another party member, but that they did not trust Leningraders with the supplies and information they needed to protect themselves. At least during the Civil War, Sokolova claimed, Lenin took the people into his trust and appealed to them for help, whereas "now the enemy stands at the doors of Leningrad, but the communists do not know what to do. No one has weapons, even hunting rifles have been confiscated. Among the populace, rumors about betrayal are beginning to spread."[112]

Similar criticisms appear in the diary of the vehement anticommunist Lidiia Osipova. Her journal contains the most biting critiques of Soviet power of any siege diary I have seen. She welcomed the Germans as liberators and, after several months in Leningrad, escaped to the nearby city of Slutsk (Pavlovsk), where she worked for the Nazi occupiers. Before she left, she couched the mounting tensions between Leningrad residents and authorities as a return to the early days when Bolshevik authority hung in the balance. Civilians conscripted into digging trenches and preparing fortifications, she claimed, "insist that this Egyptian toil has been created on purpose so that people do not take it into their heads to repeat what happened in Petrograd during World War I. The government does not trust the people and is afraid of uprisings." By forcing Leningraders to do defensive labor, "first, surveillance of the population is made considerably easier, and second, the conditions of labor are not conducive for [the workers to have] any other kind of thoughts," especially thoughts of revolting against Soviet power.[113] Thus, like Zelenskaia and Sokolova, Osipova claimed that these defensive measures were a ruse to mask how poorly protected Leningrad actually was. Of course, as an opponent of the regime, Osipova hopefully listened for criticisms of it, predicting excitedly that "the end is coming soon."[114] Still, it is notable that she framed this claim with a historical comparison between the two periods.

Months later, in early 1942, labor brigades were reorganized and tasked with removing snow and human waste from the city. And for the twenty-one-year-old student Nina Mervol'f, they ignited thoughts of 1918. Mervol'f, too young to have experienced the Civil War, held a romantic view of it. She identified the demoralization of city workers as a point of *contrast* between 1918 and 1941. In Leningrad, she remarked, there was nothing of the esprit de corps she imagined between workers defending Petrograd: "Everything here in Leningrad is so horrid, such absurd organization, such bungling around. There is nothing of the spirit of the '18 era. I think and I know that everyone has boiled over with rage, that there is absolutely nothing of that original romanticism, of brutal fighting and with it the honorable and morally pure spirit that there was in '18 under the first, real Bolsheviks, during the time of Lenin, Sverdlov, Dzerzhinskii, during the time of the Cheka and the Russian Telegraph and News Agency's display windows. Everything is completely different."[115] Mervol'f's criticisms of Leningrad authorities were based on her idealized vision of the "real Bolsheviks" of 1918. Her remarks intimate that such sentiments were citywide and created a lack of resolve or military discipline among residents. Suspended in the uncertain state of siege, Mervol'f longed for "brutal fighting" that was "honorable" and "purifying."

Regardless of the diarists' political views, they tended to frame social tensions in Leningrad through this historical analogy. Their memories and images of the emergent Bolshevik state heavily informed their visions of 1941, and vice versa. In particular, the Civil War raised questions about the extremity of hunger and deprivation in Leningrad, about internal conflicts, and about the ability of municipal authorities to provide sufficient resources and protection. Above all, it drew the diarists' attention to what they considered to be far worse material and leadership conditions in Leningrad.

Sevastopol', City of Sieges

The Crimean War has been called "the forgotten war," and in light of the Russian empire's defeat in 1856, it is easy to see why such a memory lapse occurred. Even Soviet officers in Vasilii Grossman's epic novel about World War II *Life and Fate* were incredulous to learn that Leo Tolstoy did not fight in the Napoleonic Wars himself, forgetting that he actually participated in the Crimean conflict.[116] With the Nazi invasion, however, this forgotten war was resurrected in the Soviet press and in journals of Leningraders, albeit not to the same degree as 1812 or 1918. In reportage on the "the second defense of Sevastopol'," Leonid Sobolev was fond of heralding the present-day residents and soldiers of the city-fortress as "the great-grandchildren of Admiral Nakhimov's marines." The triumvirate of Crimean heroes, Kornilov, Nakhimov, and Istomin, joined Nevskii, Suvorov, and Kutuzov in the Soviet regime's pantheon of heroes. Once again they were celebrated in wartime radio broadcasts, in the pages of *Leningrad, LP,* and historical monographs.[117]

If any city rivaled Petrograd/Leningrad in the Soviet imagination as a besieged city, it was Sevastopol'. Sevastopol' suffered a 349-day siege between 1854 and 1855 and a 250-day siege between 1941 and 1942. These sieges provided the foundation for pairing Sevastopol' and Leningrad together as kindred cities. Correspondents and journalists inside and outside Leningrad emphasized the resemblances between them as heroic city-fronts. *Blokadniki* and *sevastopol'tsy* (people of Sevastopol') were given almost identical heroic profiles. Depictions of them emphasized their unwavering discipline, endurance of staggering deprivations, and success in stalling the German army and frustrating its military plans.[118] According to Il'ia Ehrenburg, these besieged communities shared a similar outlook and vocabulary; both were stranded on "islands" and referred to the rest of the Soviet Union as the "mainland."[119] The Leningrad writer Nikolai Tikhonov similarly stressed the affinity between these cities but also reassured Leningraders that their batteries or defenses were superior to those of Leningrad's Crimean counterpart. Interestingly, in these comparisons, Tikhonov sometimes neglected to specify whether he meant Sevastopol' in 1854–55 or in 1941–42.[120]

Because Sevastopol' fell both times, wartime journalists and historians went to great lengths to depict the Crimean defeat as a moral victory, much like Borodino and Moscow in 1812. In a collection of stories on the 1941 siege of Sevastopol', a Soviet version of Leo Tolstoy's *Sebastopol Sketches*, prominent correspondents including Ehrenburg, A. Tolstoy, M. Turovskii, and Sobolev laid the "foundation for the new epic Sevastopol'" as the city-fortress, the "hard nut" the Germans would regret taking.[121] Although the city fell after eight months, Leonid Sobolev explained, "Sevastopol' will remain an unconquerable city. Sevastopol' is unconquerable because its achievements, courage, and endurance have long since risen high above any narrow territorial or geographic conception. [. . .] Far from being a victory, on the contrary it is a grave setback for the German Army." The exemplary valiance and resistance of its troops and civilians made Sevastopol' a model to emulate. The journalist's declaration of a moral victory was corroborated by Vice Admiral F. S. Oktiabr'skii, who composed his own piece claiming that surrender did not mean defeat: "Although we evacuated Sevastopol', we were victorious in this unparalleled struggle."[122]

As with 1812, Leningrad's correspondents and diarists identified Tarle and Tolstoy as twin authorities on 1854. Barely a week into the war, the city's branch of the state publishing house published 150,000 new copies of Tolstoy's *Sebastopol Sketches*, and excerpts were broadcast over Leningrad radio.[123] Although Tarle was best known for strengthening the association between the "two great fatherland wars" of 1812 and 1941, he also was a chief author of the myth of Sevastopol'. His two-volume, Stalin Prize–winning *The Crimean War* linked 1854 and 1941 together as two unjust, imperialist wars initiated by Western aggression. The affinity between Sevastopol' and Leningrad was enhanced by the fact that the first volume of this work was printed in Leningrad during the winter of 1941–42. The workers' perseverance in producing the book came to symbolize the importance of the Crimean city to the *blokadniki*.[124] Tarle was presented with a souvenir copy of his work along with a note that proudly declared, "This book was edited and published in besieged Leningrad during the harsh winter of 1941–42. The hungry and suffering workers turned the presses by hand. [. . .] A few workers fell by their machines, being worn out from a lack of food," but they persisted until the work was done.[125]

For the diarists, however, the association of Sevastopol' with Leningrad created more concern about defeat than confidence in victory. Accepting a certain kinship between Petrograd/Leningrad and Sevastopol' as besieged cities, they watchfully monitored the battle for Sevastopol' by reading these celebrated works, reviewing daily news reports, and making their own comparisons. When discussing Sevastopol', diarists tended not to distinguish between the city's 1854 and 1941 sieges either, treating them as two acts of the same drama. The diarist Aleksandr Buianov, for instance, closely followed reports of the Germans' assault on Sevastopol' and reread historical accounts of the battles of the Alma and Sevastopol' in 1854 in order to discern any parallel causes of the city's demise. As he served on watch duty at the district party committee's headquarters, Buianov became engrossed in S. N. Sergeev-Tsenskii's Stalin Prize–winning novel *The Ordeal of Sevastopol'*. In his journal, Buianov pondered whether Sergeev-Tsenskii's stress on incompetence, military leadership as either "stupid" or "swindlers," held true for either Sevastopol' or Leningrad in 1941 and whether this might seal their fate.[126]

The inspired works of Tolstoy, Tarle, and others notwithstanding, the diarists tended to regard Sevastopol' as a harbinger of events to come. Numerous entries about the fall of Sevastopol' indicate that there was a fairly widespread fear, if not assumption, that Leningrad would meet the same demise. Once "small, heroic Sevastopol'" and its "mythical titans" met their demise, Natal'ia Uskova predicted, Leningrad was next to be "stormed": "We will see much sorrow."[127] Vera Inber and Sof'ia Ostrovskaia echoed Uskova's despondency: "The fall of Sevastopol' reduced still further the spirit of the hungry people of this besieged city," Ostrovskaia wrote. "The conversations are the same everywhere: Leningrad is awaiting the same fate as Sevastopol', and soon it will be the same for us; we are doomed."[128]

Several diarists treated Sevastopol' as a model of what might befall besieged Leningrad. The engineer Gesel' Gel'fer called this "the Sevastopol' variant" of his city's possible fates. "Since the fall of Sevastopol'," he observed, "there is very little hope for our existence left. All rumors are about the Sevastopol' variant [happening] in Leningrad. Whether such talk is justified or not, it is hard to say, but we must understand that it [Sevastopol'] did not stay a blockaded city. Battles are coming, brutal fighting, and bloody too, and who knows whether or not we have enough forces to defend the city. The evacuation of women and children, the old, and the infirm was done in an organized, obligatory, and massive fashion. This already suggests the Sevastopol' variant."[129] Based on the Sevastopol' model, Gel'fer read panic, not protection, in the summertime evacuations of Leningraders. They indicated that an invasion was imminent.

Vera Inber believed that the fates of the cities were so intertwined such that the destiny of one could be predicted from the fate of the other. She recalled that during the nineteenth-century siege of Sevastopol', new measures of time were used: one month was counted as a year. In 1941–42, a few correspondents again proposed that each day in Sevastopol' be counted as a year.[130] Similarly, Inber argued for a new system for quantifying time spent inside Leningrad citing the precedent set for this in 1854: "Six years have been spent here, if one counts a month for a year, as was done during the defense of Sevastopol' in the Crimean War, not this one. No, it must be counted more here," she observed in February 1942.[131] After considering the analogy, Inber concluded that the Leningrad siege was extraordinary and unprecedented even compared to its Crimean counterpart.

The factory worker Ivan Savinkov also regarded Sevastopol' as a litmus test for Leningrad. In the eighth month of the blockade, Savinkov reflected, "Sevastopol' held on for a nine-month [*sic*] siege. How many months can we hang on?"[132] He tried to calculate Leningrad's future on the basis of Sevastopol' but complained that the Sovinformbiuro had not supplied enough information about Leningrad for him to make an accurate prediction. Plunging ahead with this goal, Savinkov left blanks where missing details could be filled in later. None of the blanks ever were filled: "The Germans have 300,000 [in Sevastopol'], but we have ____ of this number. And this sends my mind thinking that about the same number of people died for Sevastopol' as did in the Napoleonic army, but for Leningrad a whole million need to die. Eh, life is only worth a kopek," he remarked, giving up on his calculations.[133] Here, Savinkov fused the sieges of Sevastopol' together with the two fatherland wars. Even without knowing this figure, he assumed that Leningrad's casualties must be three times worse. Was this because Leningrad was doomed to a more tragic fate or destined to hold out longer than the Crimean city? It is unclear. What is clear is that some Leningraders took seriously the affinity between the cities suggested by scholars, journalists, and novelists. They too believed the fates of these two cities to be closely related and so often arrived at terrifying conclusions that were opposite of what the regime had intended.

History—both past events and the act of writing about them—played a critical role in how the diarists understood the blockade. Their accounts articulate enthusiasm and skepticism about history, its methods, and its reigning narratives. During the siege, the diarists looked to the past in order to make sense of their present circumstances. The peculiar circumstances of the blockade piqued their historicist consciousness. An archaic, protracted style of warfare, the siege seemed a throwback to a bygone era. As the diarists' lives began to revolve around the hunt for food, shelter, and warmth, they likened themselves to Neolithic people. They turned to their journals again and again to make sense of their circumstances and the sense of historical return they fostered.

Along with these situational factors, the diarists' writing and reading practices encouraged them to view their lives in historical terms. They used their journals as calendars, memory aids, chronicles, and avenues through which to inscribe their own experiences onto the historical record. Moreover, they periodically reread their journals in hopes of elucidating how the blockade had progressed over time and what would come next. In addition, the diarists expressed a keen interest in reading historical studies and novels like *War and Peace* for inspiration, information, and guidance about the experience of living through war. And despite the fact that the diarists' knowledge of and perspectives on the past varied widely, they all focused on three moments, 1812, 1854, and 1918, as they worked to situate the blockade vis-à-vis the Russian and Soviet past. Soviet journalists and scholars bombarded the Soviet people with references to those events in hopes of boosting morale through stories of victory and heroism. The diary accounts illustrate that some Leningraders took the analogies very seriously, trying to predict specific aspects of Leningrad's fate based on examples from Petrograd, Sevastopol', or imperial Moscow. By suggesting these historical parallels, the regime inadvertently invited scrutiny of its selective reading of past events. The diarists did not come to these analogies with a subversive agenda or with deliberate skepticism. Even so, some offered unorthodox interpretations of them, like comparing starving Leningraders to Napoleon's beleaguered army or emphasizing internal conflicts and the party's weaknesses in 1918. The diarists also brought nuances and ambiguities of past events to the fore. They questioned whether hallowed moments like Borodino or figures like Kutuzov were appropriate analogues to celebrate in 1941–42.

In the end, most diarists seemed dissatisfied with these historical analogies. The act of comparison ultimately alerted them to the unique, incomparable aspects of the siege. "Nothing parallel exists in world events," Irina Zelenskaia concluded. It had no proper analogue. "I am no historian," Ansim Nikulin conceded, "and I cannot pretend to have a deep knowledge of history. But I read a lot of historical literature, and it seems to me that the situation in Leningrad and of Leningraders has no contenders in history."[134] With no discernable beginning or end, the ring seemed to defy historicization.

Of course, through its campaign to gather diaries and other materials, members of Leningrad's party organization aspired to do just that, to prepare the future historicization of the blockade. In 1943, after Istpart assumed control of these collection efforts, its staff held a meeting to discuss the campaign and why it was so important. Echoing the statement of Aleksei Tolstoy that opened this chapter, Istpart's staff pronounced the history of the Great Fatherland War to be "a powerful military weapon for fighting great battles, present and future."[135] This remark proved prophetic. In a few years, as the final chapter explains, Istpart became embroiled in a violent struggle over how to tell the history of the blockade.

Conclusion

After the Ring Broke

Berta Zlotnikova had just completed the tenth grade when war erupted. The young teenager longed for a career in theater or journalism, but within a week of the German invasion, she reluctantly took a position in the Northern Press Factory. She subsequently tried a number of other jobs including medical aide and Pioneer troop leader.[1] This range of experiences would have told a fascinating story, but Zlotnikova hardly commented on work or on events at the front. Instead, she chronicled her inner struggles with pain, loneliness, and despair. "I am becoming an animal," she declared. "There is no worse feeling than when all your thoughts are on food."[2]

Then, in the winter of 1942–43, something changed. The diarist made no mention of what event, if any, precipitated it, but striking alterations in the substance and style of her journal indicate that a fundamental shift took place. During that second, brutal winter, Zlotnikova stopped meditating on the grim realities of her life and began occupying herself with inquiries into the nature of love, freedom, and happiness.[3] She engaged these age-old themes with new urgency, turning her diary into a set of philosophical notes. Her dated entries gave way to pages of aphorisms and insights.

Zlotnikova's chief investigation was into the nature of freedom. In the process of working through this theme, she gradually removed blame from any polity or power for Leningraders' state of confinement. What really held them hostage, she came to suggest, were certain habits of mind. True freedom could only come from within, and so it was from within that the *blokadniki* had to liberate themselves: "Only the mind can set a person free. The less thoughtful a human life is, the less free it is. You asked, what pathway leads to freedom? For this, you must learn to distinguish good from evil but not based on the whims of the crowd. Become attached to this famous idea, almost like a pillar that is fastened in the ground. Man measures his freedom by the length of his tether, but those who attach themselves to the idea of goodness for all will enjoy much greater freedom. [. . .] Freedom cannot be given to a person. Every man, and he alone, must free himself."[4] Every individual was responsible for his own imprisonment and his own liberation. Those who mistook freedom of mobility—or "the length of their tether"—for true freedom would never obtain it. Liberty was not physical or material; it was obtained "in the quest for truth."[5] This was an insight that Zlotnikova repeated often, and she considered her diary a place where she could practice such transformational thinking.

Liberation from within is a familiar, even commonplace, notion, but considering the circumstances under which Zlotnikova came to embrace it, the insight seems remarkable. After being immobilized physically, emotionally, and intellectually for over a year, the diarist began to break through these barriers on the page. She worked to transcend her hunger for food and freedom through dictums like, "Whoever is drawn in by the passionate flames of yearning, whoever thirsts for pleasure and enjoyment, his yearning will grow and he will imprison himself in chains. Whoever thinks only about the happiness of peace [. . .] will break the chains of death and toss them aside forever." By fixating on material needs, she suggested, Leningraders had imprisoned themselves. The path to freedom resided in spiritual, not nutritional, sustenance. Zlotnikova played with the concept of satiety often to underscore that inner peace was the only true source of satisfaction and that "the person who is truly empty is the one who is full of himself." Here and throughout her journal, the diarist paraphrased various philosophical traditions but never evoked a specific religion or ideology. "You must be your own savior," she insisted.[6]

Zlotnikova's account is extraordinary in many respects. At the same time, its interpretive bent and quest for conceptual clarity mark the tattered pages of numerous blockade diaries. In their own unique ways, they tell the story of how individuals living in extremis struggled to break free from the "self-siege" imposed on them by profound isolation, disorientation, and loss. The violence of war and starvation tore into Leningraders' lives, radically altering their bodies, identities, relationships, and assumptive worlds. The diarists' perspectives—starting with the physical act of perception and extending to their views of self and society—were shattered. In an effort to adapt to the world of the ring, the diarists were compelled to reckon with habits of mind, personal relationships, and the sociopolitical milieu that structured their lives. From these deeply inquisitive accounts, the blockade emerges as a moment not only of tremendous crisis but also of intellectual inquiry. Scholars have understandably stressed the siege's devastation but have not sufficiently attended to the conceptual ambiguities it left in its wake. To focus on destruction alone is to discount how the extreme uncertainty that pervaded the siege experience created space for the development of new meanings and perspectives.

Cut off from regular and reliable sources of information, some diarists worried that their notes might not be accurate or useful to future readers. And while their journals are not always factually correct in their documentation of the world outside—the facts and figures of battle, for instance—they provide tremendous insight about the battles that raged within. Of course, the diarists were keenly aware of their military enemies, and they cursed Hitler and his armies; but they devoted more narrative attention to looking inward for the authors of their pain. The internal combatants that the diarists faced ranged from their own ravenous stomachs and paralyzing doubts to local elites, relatives, and municipal policies. And although the journals are personal and unique to their authors, they converge around shared questions and concerns regarding the body, self, family, social hierarchy, medicine, and history. Pushed to new intellectual horizons, diarists with no preexisting knowledge of health care wrote case histories and developed disease constructs. Those without children earnestly studied the blockaded family. Nonprofessional historians steeped themselves in historical debates and reworked narratives of the Russian and Soviet past. The tumult of war threw many narratives, personal and official, into crisis, and it "awoke in [Soviet] people the capacity to think in unaccustomed ways," the historian Elena Zubkova has argued. "The social psychology of the war years shaped all of postwar life." Zubkova surmises further that the mental shifts incurred by war became one source of critical public opinion in the postwar Soviet Union.[7] Isolation from the mainland indeed afforded the siege diarists a critical distance from which to view Soviet life. They scrutinized the local press, political leadership, and policies regarding the distribution of food and of medical care. They also reconsidered prevailing ideas about human corporeality, class warfare, and historical change in light of their wartime experiences. In this way, the diarists' reflections on the extraordinary events of the blockade are equally revealing of their everyday lives in the Soviet Union. Their interpretations of the blockade were embedded in a mesh of personal associations, ideological principles, social patterns, practices, and policies, which helped to structure their prewar lives.

The diarists' remarks could occasionally be construed as subversive, but in general they were not anti-Soviet. Many of the diarists studied here were party members who seemed unaware that their insights might fall afoul of the shifting party line. Moreover, most of the entries cited above were penned during the first two years of the blockade. This was while the master plot of the blockade myth still was being scripted, before themes of heroism and victory edged out grief and loss, before celebrating the solidarity of "we" took precedence over lamenting the shattered "I." The earnest way that the diarists probed proclamations and policies from local leaders and press organs demonstrates that they did not merely respond to official cues. Instead, they looked to additional explanatory frameworks—philosophical, medical, or literary—in order to understand and articulate their wartime predicament. The diarists tackled universal questions about the human condition as much as political ones. As they fought for their lives, they reconsidered what it meant to live. Berta Zlotnikova and her search for inner freedom is but one example of the diarists' tremendous intellectual reach.

One of the main themes of these personal accounts is the siege's assault on concepts and expressions of self. But the projects of purging and refashioning the self, which have been closely associated with Soviet diary-writing practices of the 1930s, do not seem to have been the main preoccupations of the siege diarists. Rather, the imperative of survival, of preserving or at least documenting traces of one's self, seemed a more powerful motor of diary writing. The true nature of the "I" they evoked, and whether it was liberal or illiberal, seems impossible to ascertain. The "I" became a mystery to the diarists themselves, especially as the siege experience exposed them to new dimensions of bodily consciousness, social consciousness, and historical consciousness. What is clear is that daily practices of life writing and storytelling became critical, life-affirming tools in the fight for survival. As Rachel Langford and Russell West have noted, diary writing is "a mode of creating meaning in a meaningless world, and thus of maintaining subjectivity in the face of its annihilation."[8]

The diarists not only experimented with ways to represent the self; they also wrote stories, novels, ethnographic field notes, medical case studies, and historiographies. In order to articulate their horrific predicament, they drew on elements from an array of genres and analytical frameworks. Their accounts underscore the flexible quality of the diary mode in general as well as showcase the diverse forms and functions that Soviet diary writing adopted during World War II. This diversity is exemplified by siege diaries drawn from both private and party collections. Zlotnikova's journal, for example, testifies to the wide range of diaries gathered by Istpart. She deposited it there in 1943 after the ring finally broke.

The Ring Breaks, 1943

Zlotnikova strove to liberate herself by cultivating inner freedom. But how did she and other diarists respond when Leningraders were physically freed from the military blockade? During the winter of 1942–43, when she was crafting her theory of freedom from within, the Leningrad front quieted once more. Worried that the silence indicated inactivity, not peace, many diarists despaired that more months of blockade lay ahead. So when strong cannon fire erupted in mid-January 1943, they rejoiced at the sound. "Today I decided to write something," the journalist Boris Lesin explained after a considerable hiatus. "Maybe the chronicles will consider 14 January 1943 the initial date for the breaking of the blockade. [. . .] Well, my dear diary, it is possible that I will delight you with exceptional entries. I want to believe that this is the beginning of the end of the sausage-makers' [kolbasniki] [assault] on Leningrad."[9] The sounds of fighting intensified, and on 18 January, the radio announced, "the blockade is broken." Soviet armies on the Leningrad and Volkhov fronts had united and pierced the ring. They created a break nine miles long and six wide along the southern coast of Lake Ladoga. This corridor was wide enough for trains to bring supplies in and carry people out. The first one arrived on 7 February, the 517th day of the blockade.[10]

Both diaries and official reports on the public mood (svodki) suggest that Leningraders interpreted the news in the most optimistic of lights, as an indication that the siege essentially was over. "Breakthrough! Breakthrough!" the artist Anna Ostroumova-Lebedeva exclaimed. "What happiness, what joy! The whole city did not sleep all night. No one slept. Some cried from happiness, others kissed each other, others simply yelled loudly. The city rejoiced. We are no longer cut off from the motherland! Our hearts beat as one!"[11] "THE BLOCKADE IS BROKEN!" the engineer Mikhail Krakov proclaimed in block letters. "The joy is difficult to express, everyone is shocked to the core! Laughter and tears on their faces." "And now the word 'mainland' has lost its meaning," he continued. "We are also the 'mainland!'" Krakov went on to give a synopsis of the radio broadcast on the piercing of "the ring."[12] Around this time, many diarists devoted themselves to news summaries, as they had done in summer 1941. They increasingly used clippings to narrate this period or, assuming that the siege essentially was over, stopped journaling altogether.[13] Of the 125 unpublished diaries informing this book, only eleven describe that final period, fewer in any detail.[14] The journals ended as abruptly as they began, so we lack crucial data about how the diarists regarded their accounts in the postwar period. It is unclear whether their wartime discoveries and transformations were lasting.

Although most diaries wound down at this time, other efforts to document and memorialize Leningrad were in full swing. The puncturing of the ring touched off numerous celebrations and commemorations in which Leningraders became intimately involved. These commemorative activities have been described in detail elsewhere, so I touch on them only as they pertain to the postwar fate of the diarists and diaries.[15]

The break in the ring brought greater notoriety to Leningraders. In the spring of 1943, thousands of soldiers and civilians, including a dozen of the diarists studied here, were decorated for their wartime contributions. The break also brought greater oversight to how Leningraders depicted the blockade. Of course, residents had been depicting it as early as the summer of 1941. In the fall and winter of 1941, many more took up the task, encouraged by local party representatives to keep diaries. By spring 1942, organizations like the Academy of Sciences' Institute of History, Istpart, and the Museum of the History and Development of Leningrad started gathering materials on the siege. Some of their staff also kept diaries. However, it was only after the break of 1943 that Leningrad's party organization centralized these efforts.

Through a joint resolution passed on 3 April 1943, Leningrad's city and regional party organizations established a commission "For the Collection of Materials and for the Preparation of a Chronicle on 'Leningrad and the Leningrad Region in the Patriotic War against the German-Fascist Invaders.'"[16] Through this campaign, they would systematize and control the collection of materials about the blockade. Interestingly, throughout 1942, the Academy of Sciences repeatedly petitioned Lengorkom to lead such a campaign. Ultimately, however, the city and regional party committees entrusted the documentation effort to party organizations under their jurisdiction. They established a leadership committee chaired by Lengorkom's secretary of propaganda, A. I. Makhanov, to oversee the commission and placed Istpart in charge of gathering, cataloging, and transcribing the materials. Under the direction of S. I. Avvakumov and his successor K. G. Sharikov, Istpart's staff worked with party and soviet delegates from each district to amass thousands of photographs, letters, leaflets, and brochures as well as many recollections and diaries, which Avvakumov noted were of particular value.[17]

Thus, Istpart continued to solicit diaries, as it had done since late 1941, but now with official approval and oversight. It also began to collect oral and written reminiscences based on prescribed themes and questions developed by its staff. Despite this standardization, the staff affirmed that these recollections "must highlight these issues in the form of a living story" and that the memoirists, like the diarists, should use their own words. "People need to bring to the story as much as possible."[18] In this way, Istpart continued to allot personal narratives a privileged place among the sources it gathered in order to prepare future histories of the siege. Unlike the reminiscences, the diaries that Istpart acquired were crafted with little official input regarding what they should include. This may account for some of the critical and unorthodox comments the journals contain. In fact, there are hints that Istpart's staff was aware that some intellectual shift had occurred under siege. Judging from the minutes of one staff meeting, there was some consensus that diarists and memoirists "should tell about or write down that which they lived through, 'reconsidered' [peredumali], heard and saw directly."[19]

Many of those who were involved in the 1943 commission, including Makhanov and Avvakumov, also helped establish a Museum of the Defense of Leningrad that same year. The museum grew out of several early exhibitions in 1942 and 1943, which honored Leningrad's soldiers and civilians and prominently featured German weapons as trophies of war.[20] Istpart transferred many of the artifacts it collected, although not diaries or memoirs, to the museum for display.[21]

These commemoration efforts added to the impression that the siege was ending. However, it would still be a year before the blockade was lifted completely. The ring had been pierced, but this was only the beginning of the Red Army's twelve-month offensive to retake Leningrad. The few journals that document 1943 characterize it as a time of extremes: relief and anxiety, euphoria and despair. Many diarists confessed to feeling more ill and depressed than they had under siege. Perhaps they began to feel fully all of the tragedies of 1941 and 1942 only after they were no longer caught up in the struggle for survival. Liberation may have created emotional space for them to grieve. Moreover, they were beset by similar material shortages and restrictions as before the break. This may also explain the diarists' expressed disappointment.

Hunger still dominated the diarists' lives and entries. On the day the break was announced, Mikhail Krakov flipped to an entry he had written one year previously and read his remarks "on culinary 'experiments,'" on "hopes for an increase in the bread ration, on how it is too quiet on the Leningrad front . . . but it is not so today!" he rejoiced.[22] Many expected convoys of food to stream into Leningrad through the corridor created by the break. But only a few arrived. German troops heavily bombed the channel, and the railroad line had to be patched 1,200 times. Initially called "the road of victory," this passage earned the moniker "the corridor of death."

Contrary to Krakov's expectations, his entries from February 1943 closely resembled those from February 1942.[23] Rations increased, but they were slow to reverse the physical and psychological damage wrought by a year and a half of acute starvation. Hunger, theft, and rumors of cannibalism all continued. The poet Vera Inber called the first half of 1943 the "most unfortunate half year" she had experienced since World War II began. It was one of both physical torment and "spiritual collapse."[24] After euphorically declaring in January, "The blockade is broken. Leningrad is free," by February she admitted, "No, Leningrad's difficulties still are not over. And this break of the blockade . . . it is also not finalized."[25] Inber's entries from the summer and autumn of 1943 ruminate on her failing eyesight, neuralgia, tremors, cardiac pains, respiratory problems, and toothaches.[26] Her discussion of these concerns was dramatically reduced in the published version of the diary. The ballerina Vera Kostrovitskaia described this physical anguish on behalf of the collective. "We *distrofiki*," she explained, using a term that implied continuity between 1941–42 and 1943, still longed for death in August 1943, but "contrary to all laws of medicine," their bodies refused to die. "Every morning, you open your eyes and again and again you realize with horror that you are still alive. Can you really judge us, the survivors? [Can you] watch with contempt the ghost of a person who licks the saucer under his cup clean?"[27] Here, Kostrovitskaia struck preemptively at her readers' assumption that Leningraders' bodies and behaviors normalized after the break. Even by summer 1943, she suggested, little had changed.

Along with hunger, air strikes continued. The first occurred just two days after the break. The engineer Ivan Savinkov noted how much more distressing these late air raids were than those of fall 1941, marveling that he must have aged a hundred years since then.[28] "Why is my mood so rotten?" the journalist Boris Lesin echoed in March 1943. "Perhaps because the night before last an unexploded shell fell in our courtyard or because for the last ten days, without interruption, the Germans have been flying over and bombing our city, and their bombs have destroyed the buildings on the street neighboring ours? No, no, we are already used to this, we have already been through this. But I feel, more so than usual, that I cannot stand waiting anymore."[29] Raids not only continued but intensified. More artillery shells were fired at Leningrad in autumn 1943 than at any earlier point of the war. "Hell has returned to Leningrad," the schoolgirl Anna Kechek proclaimed.[30]

The diarists' optimism that the break would rapidly improve their situation made the continued difficulties even more painful to bear. "Outwardly, everything seems so beautiful, good," Aleksandra Zagorskaia observed, "but not internally."[31] Lesin described feeling a similar disjuncture between expectation and experience. During one air raid, he marveled, "How long it lasts. And this is ruining my mood. Outwardly, it seems that I live better, but in fact [life] is very, very sad. Now it feels particularly acute, and so I pick up my diary."[32] A few months later, Lesin gave his journal to Istpart. Zagorskaia did so after the siege was lifted on 27 January 1944.

The Siege Ends, 1944

When the siege finally ended, a full year after the break, the few diarists who kept writing greeted the news more cautiously. As in 1943, they took to the streets, but this time they conferred with their neighbors before celebrating. Their trepidation is evident in their reactions to the celebratory fireworks known as the Leningrad Salute. When they heard the ceremonial rockets explode, some worried it was another raid. The artist Ostroumova-Lebedeva watched the salute and "felt, as everyone, as the poor children did, nervous shock and stress. A lot of time will have to pass before Leningraders return to a normal state."[33] Judging from the journals, this took longer than expected. Air strikes continued in 1944, adding a sense of anticlimax to the liberation. During one raid in February of that year, Ostroumova-Lebedeva "suffered a terrible feeling of hopelessness" that she might never live without the threat of death overhead.[34] Municipal authorities were forced to reinstate prior restrictions on transportation, theater, cinema, and community events for the sake of public safety.[35]

Leningraders were slow to regain their freedom of mobility in other ways too. The military and the municipal soviets limited the movements of Leningraders in and out of the city, especially curtailing how many evacuees could return home. Many had to wait a year, until the summer or fall of 1945. In the interim, the NKVD intercepted thousands of Leningraders—13,000 in the first three months of 1944—who tried to return illegally.[36] These delays, the historian Rebecca Manley has explained, were designed in part to maintain a productive industrial workforce in the rear and in part because most housing stock was either damaged or occupied by new residents. As one *LP* article noted in 1945, "when the great Leningrad family began to reassemble, not everyone found their corner free."[37] Returnees also competed with Leningraders and demobilized soldiers for housing and food. Theft and strife over living space escalated. By summer 1944, the city soviet stationed guards in residential sections to curb criminal activity.[38]

Food, supplies, and evacuees were slow to reach Leningrad, as they were to many liberated Soviet cities.[39] However, commendations arrived with astonishing alacrity. In May 1945, Leningrad was the first Soviet city to be named a "hero city." It also was granted the Order of Lenin. Local architects drafted plans to restore Leningrad to even greater grandeur; temporary monuments, including three wooden triumphal arches, quickly were erected to honor the city's defenders. Exhibits in the newly refurbished Museum for the Defense of Leningrad showcased the sacrifices of soldiers and workers. The museum devoted several galleries to hunger but avoided darker themes of cannibalism, murder, and familial betrayal mentioned in the diaries. Still, the museum became a critical site for the *blokadniki* to honor and to teach returnees and newcomers about their wartime ordeal. Smaller exhibits also sprang up across the city. The public library mounted forty-seven exhibitions in 1944 alone and created a new collection on "Leningrad in the Patriotic War."[40]

By October 1944, Istpart had accumulated 57,830 items on wartime Leningrad, including 536 reminiscences and thirty diaries. Its collection of journals swelled to more than a hundred by 1946.[41] The institute had to hire more staff in order to transcribe diaries, a task it never completed. Its holdings remain a combination of handwritten manuscripts and typed transcripts. The diarists themselves proofread the transcripts, making mostly stylistic and typographical corrections, and then signed off on them. If a diarist had died, a relative or spouse did this on his or her behalf. Istpart memoranda stressed that it needed these signatures to verify that the journals were authentic. Plus, it did not want to hold accounts for which "no one was responsible."[42] The dates affixed to the signatures fall between 1943 and 1946.

Istpart used the tens of thousands of artifacts it amassed to craft and publish many brochures and at least ten volumes on wartime Leningrad between 1943 and 1947. Most of these tomes were collections of documents. In the introductions to these works, the editors presented themselves as merely relaying the testimonies of heroic Leningraders, allowing them to narrate the siege and battle of Leningrad themselves. The foreword to *Leningrad in the Days of the Blockade,* for instance, describes the contents as "the straightforward *[bezyskusstvennye]* notes" of "simple Soviet people, [. . .] notes that were made during a time when shells and bombs still were tearing into the city streets, when the enemy was still at the city [gates]." It explains that the sources were collected between 1942 and 1943 and selected "to show people of different professions" whose labor was instrumental to the defense of the city and front.[43] However, despite the institute's long-standing goal of providing a people's history of wartime Leningrad, these volumes mostly contain material from the press and from official speeches given by the city's top leaders, including Andrei Aleksandrovich Zhdanov, Aleksei Aleksandrovich Kuznetsov, Iakov Fedorovich Kapustin, and Petr Sergeevich Popkov.[44] Few civilian diaries were used.

The early publications center around two major themes. First, they emphasize the uniqueness of blockade, its devastation, magnitude, and duration. Readers frequently encounter declarations that "never in the history of mankind has it been that besieged troops, hungry, exhausted, and tormented by blockade, could have amassed so much energy and fought with such an unquenchable offensive spirit as in Leningrad."[45] This statement also underlines the works' second major theme: they highlight the defense of Leningrad more than the blockade. They depict soldiers and civilians as two armies working in tandem to defeat the enemy. Leningraders' active resistance of the German troops overshadows their battles against hunger, isolation, and grief. This can be gleaned from one of the few civilian diaries featured in an Istpart publication, the journal of the eighth grader Maia Bubnova. The printed version is heavily redacted; passages are missing, rearranged, and curiously added. That is to say, they were not in her manuscript. Most of the cuts were designed to reduce the eighth grader's descriptions of citywide hunger and to remove her criticisms of the party and Komsomol.[46] Additional themes that pervade Bubnova's and many other diaries, like the ordeal of confinement, the loss of perspective, and the rise in social tensions inside the ring, also were edited out.

Diaries not in Istpart's collection but published in the 1940s were subject to comparable pressures and edited to privilege similar themes. Vera Inber, for example, decided to publish her siege diary after the ring was pierced in 1943. In 1944, she went through her manuscript, marking it with *X*s, cross-outs, and brackets to designate what should be cut from the published version. Notably, she removed passages describing her profound disorientation, physical and emotional anguish, and disapproval of officials and policies. Inber did not fabricate new expressions of patriotism and optimism. She simply removed the material that detracted from a positive portrayal of the siege. Inber also added in subject headings and references to military events to anchor her personal experiences. These infused her manuscript with a sense of temporal progression and left the impression that she not only focused on military events but also could anticipate their future significance.[47] Moreover, despite doubts about the veracity of official information—expressed through offhand remarks like "if one believes the *[Sov]Informbiuro*"—Inber included figures, quotations, and slogans from *LP*. She knew how to edit her journal for publication because she "knew precisely how to write for the newspapers," having contributed many articles and poems to *LP*.[48]

Inber's diary appeared in *Banner (Znamia)* in January 1945 under the title "Almost Three Years" and then as a freestanding volume in November 1946. It became a bestseller and foundational text of the blockade myth. However, it met stiff opposition from leading members of the Writers' Union including Pavel Gromov and Dmitrii Polikarpov, who claimed that the diary was too focused on death and everyday life to give readers "a panoramic, generalizing picture of the whole" or "a feeling of the heroic atmosphere—labor and military—of the honorable city," as Gromov put it. "Who needs these clinical descriptions" of *distrofiki*, he asked.[49] Similarly, Polikarpov complained that too much of the text described Leningraders' "everyday hardships" such that it "obscured, overpowered" their military struggles and victories. "Through the prism of the diary, the reader wants to feel and to comprehend the gigantic scope and internal tensions of the heroic work of the wider circle of Leningrad residents. But the diary just does not convey this."[50]

Inber managed to weather these attacks with minimal changes to her diary, but her fellow writers were not so fortunate. Fellow writers Ol'ga Berggol'ts, Vera Ketlinskaia, and Vsevolod Vishnevskii also were accused of presenting blockade life in a manner too dark and too removed from the mainland.[51] When performances of Vishnevskii's 1943 play *The Walls of Leningrad* were suspended pending rewrites, he observed in his diary, "The tragic days of September 1941 should appear on the stage in ordinary colors, all 'cleaned up' (*chisto*) . . . it grates on their eyes and ears to show openly trials, trauma, difficulties, and how they were overcome. Perhaps this is understandable from the perspective of 1943," he admitted.[52] Thus, Leningraders did help write the blockade's legacy but under considerable pressure and within prescribed limits. "It has been impossible," one writer proclaimed in the journal *Star*, "to write the truth about the days of the blockade since 1944, that is, from the time when the canals of literature and criticism filled with people who did not experience the blockade. They interpret every attempt to portray the blockade realistically as slander against Leningraders."[53] Victory, in short, was fraught with ambiguity. On the one hand, reunion with the mainland granted Leningrad national recognition for the horrific siege it had suffered. On the other hand, it restored Kremlin authority over the city and placed tighter restrictions on expression.[54]

Andrei Zhdanov, Leningrad's wartime party boss and a member of the Politburo, orchestrated many of the attacks on Leningrad writers. Between 1946 and 1948, his name became synonymous with a wave of repression known as *zhdanovshchina*. Zhdanov acted under pressure from the Politburo and from Stalin directly, especially the general secretary's concern that Soviet soldiers and civilians had been ideologically contaminated by foreign influence during the war.[55] What emerged as a result was a violent purge of party, state, military, industrial, and cultural leaders, especially those who had played prominent roles during the war. Leningrad certainly was not the only city to suffer from postwar terror, but repressions there were particularly brutal.[56] Because of the crackdown, most of the journals used in this study languished in archives or were privately hidden away until long after Stalin's death.

The Leningrad Affair, 1949–53

There is considerable debate about what triggered this crackdown on a city that had just suffered 872 days of unparalleled hardship. Cold War tensions, political rivalries, the wartime isolation of Leningrad's party organization, and the battle to control the blockade narrative all played a role.[57] According to some scholars, Stalin was eager to reestablish his dominion over territories that had been occupied or detached from Kremlin authority during World War II, and Leningrad had been isolated from it longer than any other city. Rumors circulated that Leningrad, empowered by its relative independence or its hero-city status, might demand greater autonomy or even stage a putsch.[58] And with the dawning of the Cold War, Stalin felt compelled to keep all Soviet citizens disciplined, obedient, and united for the struggles ahead.

Other scholars attribute the affair to a rivalry between two factions in the Politburo, one associated with Andrei Zhdanov and Aleksei Kuznetsov and the other with Georgii Malenkov and Lavrentii Beriia.[59] After World War II, Zhdanov and many of his Leningrad protégés were promoted to new posts in the Politburo and Central Committee. Kuznetsov and Petr Popkov were among those who benefited. Meanwhile, Stalin curbed the authority of Malenkov, Beriia, and Molotov. After Zhdanov died on 31 August 1948, Beriia and Malenkov moved to reassert themselves by various intrigues and provocations. In February 1949 a secret Politburo resolution denounced Kuznetsov, Popkov, and other former Leningrad officials for "erect[ing] a barrier between the Central Committee and the Leningrad organization" and for acting independently of Kremlin authority.[60] Kuznetsov and Popkov were shot. Between 1949 and 1953, 214 of Kuznetsov's associates were arrested. Twenty-three were executed.

A few days later, not long after the five-year anniversary of Leningrad's liberation, Malenkov went to inspect Leningrad on the Politburo's suspicion that members of the city's governing organs had formed an "anti-party group." The group was linked to several counterrevolutionary acts, including the promotion of a narrative that emphasized Leningrad's unique suffering and prolonged isolation from the Kremlin. In fact, these themes *were* featured regularly in *LP,* Istpart's publications, and blockade diaries, which emphasize internal struggles and rarely mention the central governing bodies of the USSR. Commissions arrived from Moscow to inspect local affairs in Leningrad, and "they looked everywhere for blockade 'sedition.'"[61] Many works about the siege, especially those published by Istpart and the Academy of Sciences, were removed from circulation. This was necessary, explained the main Soviet censorship bureau, the Chief Directorate for the Protection of State Secrets in the Press (Glavlit), because "during the Great Fatherland War, bibliographic files were not subjected to inspection." The censor, in other words, had lost control over the war narrative. Between 1946 and 1950, Glavlit removed 900,000 items "full of quotations and portraits of enemies of the people" from Soviet libraries. In Leningrad, the local censorship bureau identified 5,000 books and journals to be pulled because they honored "enemies of the people" from either the prewar or wartime eras. Indeed, nearly all of Istpart's siege-related publications either quoted the speeches of or were dedicated to Kuznetsov and Popkov who had been shot as "enemies of the people."[62] These books were removed in 1949.

In 1946, Istpart started to scale back its collection efforts, working with diaries and memoirs but "not with the same intensity."[63] By 1949, the situation became dire. Istpart's internal memoranda ominously refer to the destruction of large parts of its archive. They also allude to "several principles and practical reasons" that necessitated the termination of certain projects on the blockade. These were replaced by new publications, which bore titles like "Comrade Stalin—the Inspiration and the Organizer of the Defeat of Nazi Troops near Leningrad" or "The Road to Life: The Ice Highway Created by Stalin's Initiative."[64] Finally, Istpart's wartime director, S. I. Avvakumov, his successors K. G. Sharikov and P. A. Tiurkin, and deputy director N. Kruzhkol were accused of supporting the "anti-party" group and arrested. S. P. Kniazev, who replaced Tiurkin in late

1949, spent his first six months on the job—as he put it—"disclos[ing] and eliminat[ing] the consequences of the activities of the institute's former enemy leadership." He fired fifty people, almost the entire staff.[65]

Istpart was not alone. Editors at the publishing house Lenizdat, journalists from the local branch of the newswire service, the Telegraph Agency of the Soviet Union (TASS), and academics and administrators from Leningrad State University and the Historical Institute of the Academy of Sciences were fired. About 2,000 Leningraders lost their positions. The Museum for the Defense of Leningrad, which Kuznetsov and Popkov had helped to organize, suffered a worse fate than Istpart. When *zhdanovshchina* revved up in 1946, the museum also was pressured to accentuate Stalin's role in saving Leningrad and deemphasizing the city's isolation. By 1949, tours were rerouted to avoid passing beneath the portraits of Popkov and Kuznetsov. Eventually, the paintings were removed. The museum was formally denounced for fostering a myth of Leningrad's special victimhood and heroism, "a myth designed by traitors trying to diminish the greatness of Comrade Stalin." Museum workers were accused of overemphasizing, especially through their selection of photographs, the brutal 1941–42 winter.[66] Another point of concern was that the weapons displayed in the museum might be used in an act of terrorism or insurrection against the Kremlin. The museum closed, and its director was arrested. In 1953, its collections were "liquidated."[67]

The Leningrad Affair silenced the local, insular, particularistic myth of the blockade and erased many siege stories from public view.[68] In this repressive climate, the diaries and materials Istpart had collected became, in the words of the historian Andrei Dzeniskevich, "practically unavailable to historians." Some of them may have been destroyed.[69] Since the second month of the siege, Leningraders had been encouraged to keep diaries and record reminiscences, but once they were liberated and reunited with the mainland, they lost the authority to craft the story of the blockade in their own way, as a unique and horrifying ordeal they endured in isolation from the rest of the USSR. This political environment also helps to explain why, until recently, the collection of diaries and recollections was not widely known to scholars. The blockade practically was erased from the 1952 *Great Soviet Encyclopedia* and excluded from most

Soviet historiography on World War II for almost a decade.[70] *LP* also quieted, mentioning important anniversaries of blockade events only in passing or sometimes not at all.[71]

After Stalin's death in 1953, the Soviet Supreme Court rehabilitated those who were repressed during the Leningrad Affair, but scholars and survivors remained reluctant to publish on the blockade. A few cautious volumes appeared in the 1950s and took care to stress the role of the Central Committee as "the soul of the defense of Leningrad."[72] It was not until after Nikita Khrushchev initiated widespread destalinization in 1956 that scholars and survivors broke their silence. Several diaries were published in the 1960s.[73] Under Leonid Brezhnev's tenure as general secretary, World War II obtained cult status; a deluge of books on the siege appeared, and commemorative events multiplied.

The trend has continued through the post-Soviet era. To date, hundreds of books have been published on the siege. Memorials, tributes, and survivors groups have sprung up across the former Soviet Union, and a host of commemorative events are held every year. Still, in the midst of so many discussions of the blockade, strong taboos remain. These silences are a legacy of those brutal years when local efforts to make ordinary Leningraders the siege's chief documentarians were crushed. This book recovers some of those lost narratives of the blockade. It endeavors to give voice to a few of the individuals who expended enormous effort not only to survive the siege but to interpret its meaning, for themselves and for Soviet society.

Notes

Selected Bibliography

Acknowledgments

Illustration Credits

Index

Notes

ABBREVIATIONS

Archives

ARAN   Arkhiv rossiiskoi akademii nauk, Sankt-Peterburg (Archive of the Russian Academy of Sciences, St. Petersburg)

GMMOBL   Gosudarstvennyi memorial'nyi muzei oborony i blokada Leningrada, Sankt-Peterburg (State Memorial Museum of the Defense and Blockade of Leningrad, St. Petersburg)

HIA   Hoover Institution Archive, Stanford University, Stanford, California

MNM   "A Muzy ne Molchali": Shkol'nyi-narodnyi muzei, shkola No. 235 im. D. D. Shostakovicha, Sankt-Peterburg ("The Muses Were Not Silent": The People's School Museum of the D. D. Shostakovich School No. 235, St. Petersburg)

OR RNB   Otdel' rukopisei, Rossiiskaia natsional'naia biblioteka, Sankt-Peterburg (Manuscript Division, Russian National Library, St. Petersburg)

RGALI   Rossiiskii gosudarstvennyi arkhiv literatury i iskusstva, Moskva (Russian State Archive of Literature and Art, Moscow)

TsGAIPD   Tsentral'nyi gosudarstvennyi arkhiv istoriko-politicheskikh dokumentov Sankt-Peterburga (Central State Archive of Historical-Political Documents, St. Petersburg)

TsGALI   Tsentral'nyi gosudarstvennyi arkhiv literatury i iskusstva Sankt-Peterburga (Central State Archive of Literature and Art, St. Petersburg)

Archival Notations

d. (plural: dd.)	file
f.	collection
k.p.	register of accessions
l. (plural: ll.)	sheet
ob.	obverse
op.	inventory

Epigraph: Nikolai Tikhonov, ed., *The Defence of Leningrad: Eye-witness Accounts of the Siege* (London and New York: Hutchinson and Co., 1943), 71–72.

INTRODUCTION

1. Georgii Alekseevich Kniazev, entry for 29 November 1941, ARAN SPb, f. 929. Because Kniazev's manuscript was only partially accessible during my research, I quote from Kniazev, *Dni velikikh ispytanii, dnevniki 1941–1945,* ed. N. P. Kopaneva (St. Petersburg: Nauka, 2009), 327 (hereafter "Kniazev").

2. Kniazev, entry for 13 October 1941, 224. Like Kniazev, scholars also identify World War II as a watershed moment for the USSR, one eclipsing the revolution. A seminal formulation of this idea appears in Amir Weiner, "The Making of a Dominant Myth: The Second World War and the Construction of Political Identities within the Soviet Polity," *Russian Review,* 55, no. 4 (1996): 638–60.

3. Kniazev, entry for 22 February 1942, 499–501.

4. Aleksei Alekseevich Chernovskii, "Dnevnik. V Leningrade, 1941–42," TsGAIPD, f. 4000, op. 11, d. 119 (hereafter "Chernovskii").

5. Aleksandr Matveevich Buianov, "Dnevnik," entry for 30 January 1942, TsGAIPD, f. 4000, op. 11, d. 19, ll. 11–110b (hereafter "Buianov"). The archive lists this diarist as "Buianov," but in his file his name occasionally appears as "Vuianov," perhaps with a letter transposed.

6. Diaries feature prominently in the work of several other researchers, including the literary scholar Polina Barskova, the sociologist Jeffrey Hass, and the historians Sergei Iarov, Richard Bidlack, and Nikita Lomagin. See Barskova, *Besieged Leningrad: Aesthetic Responses to Urban Trauma* (DeKalb, IL: Northern Illinois University Press, forthcoming); Hass, "Fields of War, Survival, and Suffering: The Human Condition under Siege in the Blockade of Leningrad, 1941–1944" (unpublished manuscript); Bidlack and Lomagin, *The Leningrad Blockade, 1941–44: A New Documentary History from the Soviet Archives* (New Haven, CT: Yale University Press, 2012). During my research (2007–14), scholars at the Historical Institute of RAN St. Petersburg published several of the diaries used in this study.

7. The anthropologists Veena Das and Arthur Kleinman argue that, across cultures, everyday life supplies the main tropes for articulating suffering. Veena Das and Arthur Kleinman, "Introduction," in *Violence and Subjectivity,* ed. Veena Das, Arthur Kleinman, Mamphela Ramphele, and Pamela Reynolds (Berkeley: University of California Press, 2000), 14–15; Kleinman, "The Violences of Everyday Life: The

Multiple Forms and Dynamics of Social Violence," ibid., 226–41; Das, *Life and Words: Violence and the Descent into the Ordinary* (Berkeley: University of California Press, 2007).

8. Scholars estimate civilian deaths were between 800,000 and 1.5 million. See the range of figures in Bidlack and Lomagin, *Leningrad Blockade*, 1–2; David M. Glantz, *The Siege of Leningrad, 1941–1944: 900 Days of Terror* (London: Cassell, 2001), 230–31; Leon Goure, *The Siege of Leningrad* (Stanford, CA: Stanford University Press, 1962), 218.

9. John Barber, "Introduction: Leningrad's Place in the History of Famine," in *Life and Death in Besieged Leningrad, 1941–44*, ed. John Barber and Andrei Dzeniskevich (London: Palgrave Macmillan, 2005), 1.

10. Bidlack and Lomagin, *Leningrad Blockade*, 38.

11. Rebecca Manley, *To the Tashkent Station: Evacuation and Survival in the Soviet Union at War* (Ithaca, NY: Cornell University Press), 56.

12. Phrase from Hitler's directive of 22 September 1941. Scholars debate whether Hitler besieged Leningrad intentionally or whether he was forced to by a military stalemate. Arguments in favor of the former are in Bidlack and Lomagin, *Leningrad Blockade*, 35–36; Lizzie Collingham, *The Taste of War: World War II and the Battle for Food* (New York: Penguin, 2012), 184–226; Albert Pleysier, *Frozen Tears: The Blockade and Battle of Leningrad* (New York: University Press of America, 2008), 37. Arguments for the latter are in Glantz, *Siege of Leningrad*, 48, 220; Goure, *Siege of Leningrad*, 85–87; J. Bowyer Bell, *Besieged: Seven Cities under Siege* (Philadelphia: Chilton Books, 1966), 123.

13. Pleysier, *Frozen Tears*, 42; Bidlack and Lomagin, *Leningrad Blockade*, 38.

14. Heather Jones, "Blockades," in *The Encyclopedia of War* (Wiley Online Library, November 2011), http://onlinelibrary.wiley.com/doi/10.1002/9781444338232.wbeow071 /abstract?deniedAccessCustomisedMessage=&userIsAuthenticated.

15. I put these terms in quotation marks to underscore that they are from the diaries, not my own invention. Incidentally, gulag prisoners also favored this island-mainland analogy to convey their estrangement from mainstream society. See Jacques Rossi, *The Gulag Handbook: An Encyclopedia Dictionary of Soviet Penitentiary Institutions and Terms Related to the Forced Labor Camps*, trans. William A. Burhans (New York: Paragon House, 1989), 29.

16. Alexander Werth, *Leningrad* (New York: Knopf, 1944), 128; E. I. Bolubeva and A. A. Krestinskii, *Risunut deti blokady* (St. Petersburg: Avrora, 1994), 10–11.

17. Pleysier, *Frozen Tears*, 42–43; Bidlack and Lomagin, *Leningrad Blockade*, 262–63.

18. In January and February 1942, Category 1 workers received 707 calories a day and everyone else 423–73. Nicholas Ganson, "Food Supply, Rationing, and Living Standards," in *The Soviet Union at War, 1941–1945*, ed. David R. Stone (Barnsley, UK: Military Pen and Sword, 2010), 83.

19. Bread recipe in TsGAIPD, f. 4000, op. 10, d. 839, l. 6. The VSLF initially established rations in conjunction with State Defense Committee (Gosudarstvennyi komitet oborony or GKO), which oversaw rationing across the USSR.

20. References to self-devouring in Gesel' Aizikovich Gel'fer, "Dnevnik," entry for 26 January 1942, TsGAIPD, f. 4000, op. 11, d. 24, l. 6ob (hereafter "Gel'fer"); Vera Mikhailovna Inber, "Dnevnik voennykh let," entries for 22 January, 19 October 1942, OR RNB, f. 312, dd. 44, 46 (hereafter "Inber"). These passages were cut from her published diary.

21. Elaine Scarry, *The Body in Pain: The Making and Unmaking of the World* (New York: Oxford University Press, 1985), 356–57. The psychiatrist Colin Murray Parkes, who coined "assumptive world," defined it as "a strongly held set of assumptions about the world and the self that is confidently maintained and used as a means of recognizing, planning, and acting." Parkes, "What Becomes of Redundant World Models? A Contribution to the Study of Adaption to Change," *British Journal of Medical Psychology* 48 (1975): 132. See Jeffrey Kauffman, ed., *Loss of the Assumptive World: A Theory of Traumatic Loss* (New York: Brunner-Routledge, 2002); Das et al., *Violence and Subjectivity;* Veena Das, Arthur Kleinman, Margaret Lock, Mamphela Ramphele, and Pamela Reynolds, eds., *Remaking a World: Violence, Social Suffering, and Recovery* (Berkeley: University of California Press, 2001).

22. I owe a great intellectual debt to existing scholarship on the blockade, especially Glantz, *Siege of Leningrad;* Nikita A. Lomagin, *Neizvestnaia blokada,* 2 vols. (St. Petersburg: Neva, 2002–4); Richard Bidlack, "The Political Mood in Leningrad during the First Year of the Soviet-German War," *Russian Review* 59 (January 2000): 96–113; Bidlack, "Workers at War: Factory Workers and Labor Policy in the Siege of Leningrad," in *The Carl Beck Papers in Russian and East European Studies* (Pittsburgh: University of Pittsburgh Press, 1991); Bidlack, "Survival Strategies in Leningrad," in *The People's War: Responses to World War II in the Soviet Union,* ed. Robert W. Thurston and Bernd Bonwetsch (Urbana: University of Illinois Press, 2000), 84–107; Cynthia Simmons and Nina Perlina, *Writing the Siege of Leningrad: Women's Diaries, Memoirs, and Documentary Prose* (Pittsburgh: University of Pittsburgh Press, 2002); S. V. Iarov, *Blokadnaia etika: Predstavleniia o morali v Leningrade v 1941–1942* (St. Petersburg: Nestor-Istoriia, 2011); Barber and Dzeniskevich, *Life and Death;* Lisa A. Kirschenbaum, *The Legacy of the Siege of Leningrad, 1941–1995: Myths, Memories, and Monuments* (Cambridge: Cambridge University Press, 2006); M. V. Loskutovoi, ed., *Pamiat' o blokade: Svidetel'stva ochevidtsev i istoricheskoe soznanie obshchestva* (Moscow: Novoe, 2006). For an insightful study that poses some parallel questions to wartime diaries of Japanese soldiers, see Aaron William Moore, *Writing War: Soldiers Record the Japanese Empire* (Cambridge, MA: Harvard University Press, 2013).

23. Zhdanov quotation published in *Leningrad* 4–5 (1942): 25.

24. Kirschenbaum, *Legacy;* Loskutovoi, *Pamiat' o blokade;* Tatiana Voronina, "Sotsialisticheskii istorizm: Obrazy leningradskoi blokady v sovetskoi istoricheskoi nauke," *Zhurnal'nyi Zal,* http://magazines.russ.ru/nz/2013/1/v15.html; Dieter De Bruyn and Michel De Dobbeleer, "Mastering the Siege: Ideology and the Plot of the Leningrad Blockade and the Warsaw Uprising in Adamovich and Granin, and Białoszewski," *Ljubljana* 32, no. 2 (2009): 53–76.

25. Aleksandra Pavlovna Liubovskaia, "Leningrad, 1941–42: Zapiski zhitelia blokadnogo goroda" (text courtesy of Igor' Liubovskii), 201 (hereafter "Liubovskaia"). Kirschenbaum argues convincingly that official and personal siege narratives were mutually constitutive. She also argues that Leningraders accepted—though not unconditionally—the official "myth of the heroic city" promoted in the press as "a template for understanding and remaking personal experiences." In the diaries, I see less "commitment to the theme of heroic Leningrad" at least in 1941–42 (Kirschenbaum, *Legacy,* 45, 54–56, 95–96).

26. Liubovskaia, entry for 16 November 1941, 11.

27. Lidiia Ginzburg, "Zapiski blokadnogo cheloveka," in *Prokhodiashchie kharaktery: Proza voennykh let, zapiski blokadnogo cheloveka,* ed. Andrei Zorin and Emily Van Buskirk (Moscow: Novoe, 2011), 325. Ginzburg reworked this text, dating it "1942– 1962–1982." Translation from Ginzburg, *Blockade Diary,* trans. Alan Myers (London: Harvill, 1996), 76.

28. Bell, *Besieged,* 123, 161, 282–87; Charles Carlton, "Sieges during the British Civil Wars," in *Situazioni d'Assedio/Cities under Siege: Conference Proceedings,* ed. Lucia Carle and Antoinette Fauve-Chamoux (Montalcino, Italy: Pagnin E. Martinelli, 1999), 241–44; Geoffrey Parker, "Introduction: The Western Way of War," in *The Cambridge History of Warfare,* ed. Geoffrey Parker (Cambridge: Cambridge University Press, 2005), 6–7; Victor Davis Hanson, "From Phalanx to Legion," in Parker, *Cambridge History of Warfare,* 33; Bernard S. Bachrach, "On Roman Ramparts," in Parker, *Cambridge History of Warfare,* 71–83; Christopher Allmand, "New Weapons, New Tactics," in Parker, *Cambridge History of Warfare,* 89–100; Geoffrey Parker, "The Gunpowder Revolution," in Parker, *Cambridge History of Warfare,* 108, 111; Parker, "Dynastic War," in Parker, *Cambridge History of Warfare,* 148–57. On starvation in siegecraft, see Hans Delbrück, *History of the Art of War: Within the Framework of Political History,* vol. 1, *Antiquity,* trans. Walter J. Renfroe Jr. (Westport, CT: Greenwood, 1975), 126, 153.

29. Carlton, "Sieges during the British Civil Wars," 241; Bell, *Besieged,* 287.

30. Rocco Coronato, *"King John* and the Siege as Hermeneutics," in Carle and Fauve-Chamoux, *Situazioni d'Assedio,* 353; see also Bruce Allen Watson, *Sieges: A Comparative Study* (London: Praeger, 1993), xi.

31. Ales' Adamovich and Daniil Granin, *Blokadnaia kniga* (St. Petersburg: Pechatnyi dvor, 1994), 102; translation from Adamovich and Granin, *A Book of the Blockade,* trans. Hilda Perham (Moscow: Raduga, 1983), 134.

32. In this way, the diaries support a growing body of research suggesting that World War II fostered self-assertiveness and a questioning outlook among Soviet citizens rather than cementing their loyalty and legitimizing the regime. See Amir Weiner, *Making Sense of War: The Second World War and the Fate of the Bolshevik Revolution* (Princeton, NJ: Princeton University Press, 2001); Mark Edele, *Soviet Veterans of the Second World War: A Popular Movement in an Authoritarian Society, 1941–1991* (Oxford: Oxford University Press, 2008); E. S. Seniavskaia, *1941–1945: Frontovoe pokolenie. Istoriko-psikhologicheskoe issledovanie* (Moscow: Institut istorii RAN, 1995); Elena Zubkova, *Russia after the War: Hopes, Illusions, and Disappointments, 1945–1957,* trans. Hugh Ragsdale (Armonk, NY: M. E. Sharpe, 1998); A. A. Danilov and A. V. Pyzhikov, *Rozhdenie sverkhderzhavy: SSSR v pervye poslevoennye gody* (Moscow: Rosspen, 2001).

33. Jochen Hellbeck, *Revolution on My Mind: Writing a Diary under Stalin* (Cambridge, MA: Harvard University Press, 2006); Igal Halfin, *Terror in My Soul: Communist Autobiographies on Trial* (Cambridge, MA: Harvard University Press, 2003); Oleg Kharkhordin, *The Collective and the Individual in Russia: A Study of Practices* (Berkeley: University of California Press, 1999). Other scholars stress public identity and self-presentation rather than the "self" per se: Shelia Fitzpatrick, *Tear Off Masks! Identity and Imposture in Twentieth-Century Russia* (Princeton, NJ: Princeton University

Press, 2005); Fitzpatrick, *Everyday Stalinism: Ordinary Life in Extraordinary Times; Soviet Russia in the 1930s* (New York: Oxford University Press, 1995); Stephen Kotkin, *Magnetic Mountain: Stalinism as Civilization* (Berkeley: University of California Press, 1995).

34. Rachel Langford and Russell West, "Introduction: Diaries and Margins," in *Marginal Voices, Marginal Forms: Diaries in European Literature and History,* ed. Rachel Langford and Russell West (Atlanta: Rodopi, 1999), 9.

35. N.I. Sinitsyna, MNM, k.p. 6513, f. 3, d. 2318; Aleksandr Sergeevich Nikol'skii, OR RNB, f. 1037, dd. 900–901 (hereafter "Nikol'skii").

36. Vladimir Andreevich Lukin and Tamara Petrovna Nekliudova, "Delo Lukina, V. A. i ego zheny T. P. Nekliuovoi," GMMOBL, f. RDF, op. 1L, d. 238; Tat'iana Grizova-Rudykovskaia, "Dnevnik," GMMOBL, f. RDF, op. 1R, d. 1, punkt 7, (hereafter "Rudykovskaia").

37. Irina Paperno, "What Can Be Done with Diaries?" *Russian Review* 63, no. 4 (2004): 561–62, 572; Felicity A. Nussbaum, "Toward Conceptualizing a Diary," in *Studies in Autobiography,* ed. James Olney (New York: Oxford University Press, 1988), 134. Philippe Lejeune has aptly defined diaries and other autobiographical genres not by their formal elements but by the expectations that readers and writers bring to them. On this "autobiographical pact," see Lejeune, "The Autobiographical Contract," in *French Literary Theory Today: A Reader,* ed. Tzvetan Todorov (Cambridge: Cambridge University Press, 1982), 192–222; Lejeune, *On Diary,* ed. Jeremy D. Popkin and Julie Rak (Honolulu: University of Hawai'i Press, 2009). On the diary's fragmentary, flexible structure, see K. Eckhard Kuhn-Osius, "Making Loose Ends Meet: Private Journals in the Public Realm," *German Quarterly* 54 (1981): 173; Harriet Blodgett, *"Capacious Hold-All": An Anthology of Englishwomen's Diary Writings* (Charlottesville: University Press of Virginia, 1991).

38. Vladimir Grigor'evich Mantul, entries for 29 November 1941, 4 January 1942, TsGAIPD f. 4000, op. 11, d. 67, ll. 30b, 4–40b.

39. On historians' approaches to diaries, see Mary Jo Maynes, Jennifer Pierce, and Barbara Laslett, *Telling Stories: The Use of Personal Narratives in the Social Sciences and History* (Ithaca, NY: Cornell University Press, 2008); Suzanne L. Bunkers and Cynthia Huff, eds., *Inscribing the Daily: Critical Essays on Women's Diaries* (Amherst: University of Massachusetts Press, 1996). On diaries as coping methods, see Wendy J. Wiener and George C. Rosenwald, "A Moment's Monument: The Psychology of Keeping a Diary," in *The Narrative Study of Lives,* vol. 1, ed. Ruthellen Josselson and Amia Lieblich (London: Sage, 1993), 30–58. On the diary in sociological research, see John Goodwin, ed., *Sage Biographical Research,* vol. 3, *Other Forms of Life Writing: Letters, Diaries, and Auto/Biography* (London: Sage, 2012); Ken Plummer, *Documents of Life 2: An Invitation to Critical Humanism* (London: Sage, 2001).

40. Gel'fer, entry for 18 July 1942, 27. He made these reflections when starting a second diary notebook. Here and throughout, I have placed brackets around all ellipses I have inserted to truncate a quotation. Ellipses that are not in brackets appear in the original texts.

41. Philippe Lejeune, "How Do Diaries End?," *Biography* 24, no. 1 (2001): 99–112. On this phenomenon in Holocaust diaries, see Alexandra Garbarini, *Numbered Days: Diaries*

and the Holocaust (New Haven, CT: Yale University Press, 2006), 5; Amos Goldberg, *Holocaust Diaries as "Life Stories"* (Jerusalem: Yad Vashem, 2004), 13–18.

42. Iura Ivanovich Riabinkin, entry for 11 December 1941, in Ales' Adamovich and Daniil Granin, *Leningrad under Siege: First-hand Accounts of the Ordeal,* trans. Clare Burstall and Vladimir Kisselnikov (Barnsley, UK: Military Pen and Sword, 2007), 142–43 (hereafter "Riabinkin").

43. TsGAIPD, f. 25, op. 10, d. 330, l. 82; TsGAIPD, f. 4000, op. 1, d. 233, ll. 1–35; TsGAIPD, f. 4000, op. 1, d. 196, l. 1.

44. TsGAIPD, f. 25, op. 10, d. 330, ll. 82–84. Diarists who mentioned journaling at the party's bequest include Aleksandra Nikiforovna Borovikova, TsGAIPD, f. 4000, op. 11, d. 15, l. 1 (hereafter "Borovikova"); Lidiia Korlovna Zabolotskaia, "Dnevnik Shkol'nogo inspektora Sverdlovskogo Raionnogo Otdela Obrazovaniia," TsGAIPD, f. 4000, op. 11, d. 30, ll. 29–30 (hereafter "Zabolotskaia"); Aleksandra Nikolaevna Mironova, TsGAIPD, f. 4000, op. 11, d. 71, l. 1 (hereafter "A. Mironova").

45. TsGAIPD, f. 4000, op. 1, d. 129, ll. 1–8. Lengorkom already planned to entrust Istpart with the collection process by July 1942. On this collection, see Andrei Dzeniskevich, "O sozdanii obshchegorodskoi komissii po sboru materialov dlia istorii oborony Leningrada," in *Leningradskaia nauka v gody Velikoi Otechestvennoi Voiny,* ed. V. A. Shishkin (St. Petersburg: Nauka, 1995), 129–39; Nina Borisovna Lebedeva, "Kollektsiia dokumentov po istorii Velikoi Otechestvennoi Voiny v fonde Leningradskogo Instituta Istorii Partii," in *Bitva za Leningrad: Problemy sovremennykh issledovanii* (St. Petersburg: Sankt-Peterburgskii Universitet, 2007), 117–24. Moscow had a similar campaign, with less emphasis on diaries, in summer 1942 (TsGAIPD, f. 4000, op. 1, d. 148, l. 11).

46. TsGAIPD, f. 4000, op. 10, d. 776, ll. 1–18.

47. Ibid., 7, 18.

48. Ibid., 8–11.

49. Propaganda and Agitation Department for the Moscow district *raikom,* "Dnevnik otdela propagandy i agitatsii RK VKP(b) Moskovskogo raiona," TsGAIPD, f. 4000, op. 11, d. 124 (hereafter "PAD"); Komsomol organization of North Cable Factory (Sevkabel'), TsGAIPD, f. 4000, op. 11, d. 130.

50. TsGAIPD, f. 4000, op. 10, d. 776, l. 13.

51. One diary that alludes to the vague party guidelines is PAD, entries for 22 December 1942, 3 January 1943, 19 140b, 180b.

52. An example in Vera Sergeevna Kostrovitskaia, "May [1942]," TsGALI, f. 157, op. 1, d. 28, l. 40 (hereafter "Kostrovitskaia"). This diary was written on loose-leaf paper and recopied by the author in 1969. Entries are labeled as months or seasons.

53. Borovikova, entry for 26 August 1941, 23.

54. Luise White, *Speaking with Vampires: Rumor and History in Colonial Africa* (Berkeley: University of California Press, 2000), 5.

55. Donna M. Budani, *Italian Women's Narratives of their Experiences during World War II* (Lampeter, UK: Edwin Mellen, 2003), 4–6. Useful "sense-making" approaches can be found in Marianne Gullestad, *Everyday Life Philosophers: Modernity, Morality, and Autobiography in Norway* (Oslo: Scandinavian University Press, 1996); James Young,

Writing and Rewriting the Holocaust: Narrative and the Consequences of Inter-pretation (Bloomington: Indiana University Press, 1988); Garbarini, *Numbered Days.*

56. On diaries as practices, see Philippe Lejeune, "The Practice of the Private Journal: Chronicle of an Investigation (1986–1998)," in Langford and West, *Marginal Voices,* 185–211; and Anne Roche, "The Practice of Personal Writing by Non-writers: Memory, History, and Writing," ibid., 175–84.

57. Ginzburg, "Zapiski blokadnogo cheloveka," 358.

58. Quoted in John Barber, "War, Public Opinion, and the Struggle for Survival, 1941–45: The Case of Leningrad," in *Russia in the Age of Wars, 1914–1945,* ed. Silvio Pons and Andrea Romano (Milan: Feltrinelli Editore, 2000), 272.

59. Aleksandr Vinokurov, "Blokadnyi dnevnik uchitelia Vinokurova," entry for 7 January 1942, in *Blokadnye dnevniki i dokumenty,* ed. Stanislav Konstantinovich Bernev and Sergei Vladimirovich Chernov (St. Petersburg: Evropeiskii Dom, 2004), 240 (hereafter "Vinokurov"); Sof'ia Kazimirovna Ostrovskaia, entry for 18 February 1942, OR RNB, f. 1448, d.11, l. 13 (hereafter "Ostrovskaia").

60. Lidiia Osipova, entry for 12 December 1941, HIA, Box 1, 80033-10.V, 27 (hereafter "L. Osipova").

61. The 1920s magazine *Sparrow* was renamed the *New Robinson.* Evgeny Steiner, *Stories for Small Comrades,* trans. Jane Ann Miller (Seattle: University of Washington Press, 1999), 53. I have not seen a similar fixation on Robinson Crusoe in *Leningradskaia Pravda* or other periodicals during the siege.

62. Tat'iana Nikolaevna Glebova, entry for 7 December 1941, "Risovat', kak letopisets: stranitsy blokadnogo dnevnika," *Iskusstvo Leningrada* 2 (1990), 15–16.

63. Arkadii A. Lepkovich, "Dnevnik Arkadiia Lepkovicha, 1/XII/41–20/IX/1942," entry for 3 January 1942, TsGAIPD, f. 4000, op. 11, d. 85, l. 14 (hereafter "Lepkovich"). In citing specific diary entries, newspaper articles, and works that contain exact dates, I have adhered to the Russian-language format, placing the day first, then the month (often written in Roman numerals), and finally the year.

64. Gel'fer, entry for 3 February 1942, 90b.

65. Elena Skriabina, *V blokade: Dnevnik materi,* entry for 25 February 1942 (Iowa City: Herausgeber, 1964), 90 (hereafter "Skriabina"). If they were Robinsons, then they were closer to the "Soviet Robinsons" satirized so vividly in Il'ia Il'f and Evgenii Petrov, *Kak sozdavalsia Robinzon: Fel'etony i rasskazy* (Moscow: Tekst, 2007).

66. Berta Abramovna Zlotnikova, "Dnevnik," entries for 15, 16 November 1942, TsGAIPD, f. 4000, op. 11, d. 39, ll. 13–14ob (hereafter "Zlotnikova").

1. THE RING TAKES SHAPE

1. *Sankt-Peterburg XX Vek: Chto, gde, kogda?* (St. Petersburg: Paritet, 2000), 204.

2. Elena Vladimirovna Mukhina, entry for 5 June 1941, TsGAIPD, f. 4000, op. 11, d. 72, l. 8 (hereafter "Mukhina").

3. Natal'ia Borisovna Uskova, entry for 30 June 1941, MNM, k.p. 6518, f. 1, d. 5577, ll. 1–2 (hereafter "Uskova"). Here and throughout, any parentheses included in quotations appeared in the original text.

4. Aleksei Fedorovich Evdokilov, entry for 14 September 1941, GMMOBL, f. RDF, op. 1R, d. 30, l. 68.

5. Riabinkin, entry for 22 June 1941, 8 (translation modified for clarity); Mukhina, entries for 22, 23 June 1941, 120b, 13.

6. Lisa A. Kirschenbaum, *The Legacy of the Siege of Leningrad, 1941–1995: Myths, Memories, and Monuments* (Cambridge: Cambridge University Press, 2006), 43.

7. Richard Bidlack and Nikita Lomagin, *The Leningrad Blockade, 1941–44: A New Documentary History from the Soviet Archives* (New Haven, CT: Yale University Press, 2012), 39, 42.

8. Uskova, entry for 16 July 1941, 4. In a section not included in the published version of her diary, the poet Vera Inber also commented that this common phrase "had a whole other meaning in Leningrad" (Inber, entry for 31 May 1943, 720b). People aged fifteen and older were recruited starting in August 1941.

9. Esfir' Gustanovna Levina, "Pis'ma k drugu," in *Leningradtsy v dni blokady: Sbornik,* ed. Ia. I. Klebanov and A. N. Pazi (Leningrad: Lenizdat, 1947), 198; A. Mironova, entry for 12 September 1941, 90b.

10. Bidlack and Lomagin, *Leningrad Blockade,* 41–42.

11. Rebecca Manley, *To the Tashkent Station: Evacuation and Survival in the Soviet Union at War* (Ithaca, NY: Cornell University Press, 2009), 36–37, 55–56.

12. A. Mironova, entries for 29–30 June, 25 July, 3 August 1941, 2–30b, 6, 7; Nina Georgievna Gorbunova, "Dnevnik 22/VI/41–11/V.43. Leningrad," entries for 4, 28, 31 July, 2–4 August 1941, TsGAIPD, f. 4000, op. 11, d. 27, ll. 2–50b (hereafter "Gorbunova").

13. Bidlack and Lomagin, *Leningrad Blockade,* 49.

14. Diary of Dmitri Vladimirovich Afanas'ev, entry for 23–24 August 1941, 44–45. (Text courtesy of Natal'ia Aleksandrovna Afanas'eva) (hereafter "Afanas'ev"). Excerpts are published in Tamara Staleva, *Vechnye deti blokady: Dokumental'nye ocherki* (Moscow: Author, 1995).

15. Ibid., entry for 22 June 1941, 7.

16. Ibid., entry for 6 July 1941, 10.

17. Examples in Bubnova, entry for 2 September 1941, "Iz dnevnika Maii Bubnovoi," in Klebanov and Pazi, ed. *Leningradtsy v dni blokady* (Leningrad: Lenizdat, 1947), 222–223. This entry is not in the archival version of her diary, which begins in October; Mukhina, entries for 24, 25, June, 5 July, 4, 12 September 1941, 140b, 150b–170b, 190b–20, 46–47. Note that Mukhina may have meant to write "October" instead of "September" for these last two entries.

18. Uskova, entry for 15 July 1941, 2. Cross-out in original. On the metronome, see Kirschenbaum, *Legacy,* 64.

19. Bidlack and Lomagin, *Leningrad Blockade,* 38.

20. A. M. Melua, *Blokada Leningrada* (Moscow: Gumanistika, 1999), 644.

21. Nicholas Ganson, "Food Supply, Rationing, and Living Standards," in *The Soviet Union at War, 1941–1945,* ed. David R. Stone (Barnsley, UK: Military Pen and Sword, 2010), 81–83.

22. Fedor Mikhailovich Nikitin, "Dnevnik," entry for 12 September 1941, MNM, k.p. 6920, f. 1, d. 5580, l. 23 (hereafter "Nikitin").

23. Irina Dmitrievna Zelenskaia, entries for 9 July, 25 November 1941, TsGAIPD, f. 4000, op. 11, d. 35, ll. 20b, 36 (hereafter "Zelenskaia").

24. Liubovskaia, entry for 19 November 1941, 12.

25. Examples in Mariia Sergeevna Konopleva, "V blokirovannom Leningrade: Zapiski," entry for 20 May 1942, OR RNB, f. 368 (hereafter "Konopleva"); Nikolai Punin, "Blokadnyi dnevnik," entry for 26 August 1941, *Zvezda* 1 (1994): 97 (hereafter "Punin"); Kniazev, entry for 15 July 1942, 19; Elena Kochina, "Blokadnyi dnevnik," entry for 20 February 1942, in *Pamiat': Istoricheskii sbornik,* vol. 4 (Moscow and Paris: YMCA Press, 1979–81), 196 (hereafter "Kochina").

26. Ol'ga Konstantinovna Matiushina, "Dnevnik," TsGAIPD, f. 4000, op. 11, d. 68, ll. 42–43, 46, 65 (hereafter "Matiushina, Diary"); Uskova, entries for 15 December 1941, 15 March 1942, 29, 50. Most of the entries in Matiushina's diary, like this one, are undated. I include exact dates in the notes only when one is provided in her manuscript.

27. Bidlack and Lomagin, *Leningrad Blockade,* 39. This policy was extended across the USSR.

28. Ales' Adamovich and Daniil Granin, *Leningrad under Siege: First-hand Accounts of the Ordeal,* trans. Clare Burstall and Vladimir Kisselnikov (Barnsley, UK: Military Pen and Sword, 2007), xiii; M. M. Krakov, "Dnevnik," entry for 17 January 1943, TsGAIPD, f. 4000, op. 11, d. 55, l. 52 (hereafter "Krakov"). Vasilii Timofeev, M. M. Krakov, Irina Zelenskaia, Aleksandra Zagorskaia, Georgii Kniazev, Gesel' Gel'fer, Elizaveta Sokolova, and Ivan Savinkov were among the diarists who moved into their workplaces.

29. Bidlack and Lomagin, *Leningrad Blockade,* 189–97.

30. Uskova, entry for 4 January 1942, 40. Another example is Riabinkin, entry for 26 October 1941, 97.

31. On 1 February 1942, Category I was subdivided to favor laborers in war-related industries like steel, gas, chemicals, and transportation. On rationing, see Elena Osokina, *Our Daily Bread: Socialist Distribution and the Art of Survival in Stalin's Russia, 1927–1941,* ed. Kate Transchel (New York: M. E. Sharpe, 2001), xv, 69, 83, 197; Lars T. Lih, *Bread and Authority in Russia, 1914–1921* (Berkeley: University of California Press, 1990); William Moskoff, *The Bread of Affliction: The Food Supply in the USSR during World War II* (Cambridge: Cambridge University Press, 1990).

32. Provisions for children and pregnant women are discussed in "Protokol No. 50, Zasedaniia biuro Lengorkom VKP(b)," 3/I/42, TsGAIPD, f. 25, op. 2, d. 4408, l. 25; "Protokol No. 52, Zasedaniia biuro Lengorkom VKP(b)," 19/I/42, TsGAIPD, f. 25, op. 2, d. 4433, l. 6.

33. N. V. Sedova, "Shkola v gody voiny," in *Zhenshchina i voina: O roli zhenshchin v oborone Leningrada: 1941–44,* ed. M. I. Bozhenkova, A. I. Burlakov, A. R. Dzeniskevich, A. N. Rubtsov, T. A. Postrelova, I. D. Khodanovich (St. Petersburg: Izdatel'stvo Sankt-Peterburgskogo Universiteta, 2006), 98–99; Valerii Nikolaevich Selivanov, *Stoiali kak soldaty: Blokada. Deti. Leningrad* (St. Petersburg: Ego, 2002), 18, 22, 76.

34. Valia Peterson, "Dnevnik," entry for 9 October 1941, TsGAIPD, f. 4000, op. 11, d. 86, l. 2 (hereafter "Peterson"); Maia Aleksandrovna Bubnova, "Dnevnik," entry for 27 November 1941, TsGAIPD, f. 4000, op. 11, d. 16, l. 66 (hereafter "Bubnova").

35. Mukhina, entry for 1 December 1941, 60ob.

36. Anatolii Vladimirovich Molchanov, "Ia na voine byl shkol'nikom blokadnym: vospo- minaniia" (text courtesy of Evgeniia Alekseevna Molchanova), 27.

37. Glafira Nikolaevna Korneeva, entry for 13 September 1942, TsGAIPD, f. 4000, op. 11, d. 51, l. 33 (hereafter "Korneeva").

38. Peterson, entry for 25 December 1941, 6ob-7; Vinokurov, entry for 7 May 1942, 261.

39. John Dunstan, *Soviet Schooling in the Second World War* (London: Macmillan, 1997), 89; Sedova, "Shkola v gody voiny," 101, 107.

40. Ginzburg, "Zapiski blokadnogo cheloveka," 325; translation from Ginzburg, *Blockade Diary*, 24.

41. Kniazev, entry for 25 June 1941, 33.

42. Steven M. Maddox, *Saving Stalin's Imperial City: Historic Preservation in Leningrad, 1930–1950* (Bloomington: Indiana University Press, 2015), 68–69. Different figures are provided in Edward Bubis and Blair A. Ruble, "The Impact of World War II on Len- ingrad," in *The Impact of World War II on the Soviet Union,* ed. Susan J. Linz (Totowa, NJ: Rowman and Littlefield, 1985), 189.

43. Matiushina, Diary, 31.

44. Nikitin, entry for 23 September 1941, 30.

45. Skriabina, entry for 9 September 1941, 34. Skriabina reworked this diary before pub- lishing it.

46. Ginzburg, "Zapiski blokadnogo cheloveka," 325; translation from Ginzburg, *Blockade Diary*, 24–25.

47. Skriabina, entry for 24 June 1941, 12.

48. Matiushina, Diary, 143; Bidlack and Lomagin, *Leningrad Blockade,* 38. This strategy also was used during the Civil War. Julie Hessler, *A Social History of Soviet Trade: Trade Policy, Retail Practices, and Consumption, 1917–1953* (Princeton, NJ: Princeton University Press, 2004), 45.

49. Vera Inber, "Vremia vozvrashchaetsia," 1944, OR RNB, f. 312, d. 5, l. 1. This article originally was titled "Prishlo vremia."

50. Konopleva, entries for 31 October, 6–8, 30 November, 1 December 1941, 85–86, 154– 55, 187–88, entries for 26–27 October 1942, 30 31.

51. Borovikova, entry for 11 January 1942, 99ob-100.

52. Nina Nikolaevna Erokhana, "Blokadnyi dnevnik Niny Nikolaevny Erokhanoi," entry for 14 November 1941, GMMOBL, f. RDF, op. 1L, d. 490, l. 29 (hereafter "Erokhana"). Klishevich was her maiden name.

53. Karel Berkhoff, *Motherland in Danger: Soviet Propaganda during World War II* (Cam- bridge, MA: Harvard University Press, 2012), 21.

54. Erokhana, entry for 25 November 1941, 31. Tram service resumed on 15 April 1942.

55. Bidlack and Lomagin, *Leningrad Blockade,* 248–49.

56. Berkhoff, *Motherland in Danger,* 12–14.

57. Ibid., 30. Excerpts of radio programming are provided in: *Radio, blokada, Leningrad* (St. Petersburg: Spetsial'naia literatura, 2005).

58. Ibid., 35. One example is in Zinaida Sergeevna Sedel'nikova, *279 dnei voiny: Blokadnyi dnevnik* (Volgograd: Volgogradskii Komitet Popetchi, 1995), 28 (hereafter "Sedel'nikova").

59. Zelenskaia, entry for 9 July 1941, 20b.

60. Arguments that Leningraders were comforted by the press are in A. Rubashkin, *Golos Leningrada: Leningradskoe radio v dni blokady* (St. Petersburg: Neva, 2005); Kirschenbaum, *Legacy,* 43–45, 54; Michael K. Jones, *Leningrad: State of Siege* (New York: Basic Books, 2005), 157–59, 266–68.

61. Liubovskaia, undated fragment, 36ob.

62. Sedel'nikova, entry for 22 January 1942, 68.

63. Afanas'ev, entry for 19 February 1942, 113.

64. On public criticism of wartime media, see John Barber, "War, Public Opinion, and the Struggle for Survival, 1941–45: The Case of Leningrad," in *Russia in the Age of Wars, 1914–1945,* ed. Silvio Pons and Andrea Romano (Milan: Feltrinelli Editore, 2000), 265–76; James von Geldern, "Radio Moscow: The Voice from the Center," in *Culture and Entertainment in Wartime Russia,* ed. Richard Stites (Bloomington: Indiana University Press, 1995), 47–50.

65. Zelenskaia, entry for 25 July 1941, 5. On delayed radio updates, see von Geldern, "Radio Moscow," 46.

66. Zelenskaia, entry for 16 September 1941, 15ob–16; Elizaveta Aleksandrovna Sokolova, "Dnevnik," entries for 20, 26 August 1941, TsGAIPD, f. 4000, op. 11, d. 109, ll. 7–7ob, 10 (hereafter "Sokolova").

67. Richard Bidlack, "Propaganda and Public Opinion," in Stone, *Soviet Union at War,* 55–56.

68. Kniazev, entries for 15, 30 August 1941, 4 February 1942, 124, 149, 447. Other examples are in Liubovskaia, entry for 31 January 1942, 71; Esfir' Gustavovna Levina, "Dnevnik. 12/I–24/XI/42," TsGAIPD, f. 4000, op. 11, d. 57, l. 17 (hereafter "Levina"); Konopleva, entry for 13 September 1941, 80.

69. Korneeva, entry for 9 September 1942, 31. On such euphemisms, see Berkhoff, *Motherland in Danger,* 36–40; Jeffrey Brooks, "*Pravda* Goes to War," in Stites, *Culture and Entertainment,* 12–13.

70. Afanas'ev, entry for 14 August 1941, 36.

71. Ibid., entry for 11 March 1942, 33.

72. Ivan Alekseevich Savinkov, "Dnevnik, 1941–45," entry for 4 July 1941, TsGAIPD, f. 4000, op. 11, d. 99, l. 20b (hereafter "Savinkov"). For another example, see ibid., entry for 14 February 1942, 22, 27ob.

73. Brooks, "*Pravda* Goes to War," 11, 16–19. Brooks argues that this method of championing individual valor strongly appealed to Soviet readers.

74. Buianov, entry for 13 February 1942, 16.

75. Afanas'ev, entries for 8, 15 July 1941, 14–16.

76. *LP,* 1/XI/42, no. 260 (8366).

77. Afanas'ev, entry for 26 September 1941, 61.

78. Buianov, entry for 19 June 1942, 35–35ob. He was responding to Fadeev's article in *Pravda* (no. 144), 19/VI/1942.

79. Zelenskaia, entry for 30 August 1942, 96ob.

80. Ibid.

81. Bidlack and Lomagin, *Leningrad Blockade,* 415–16.

82. The first articles in *LP* on hunger, blaming thieves, are 20/XI/41, no. 277 (8070), 4; no. 303 (8096), 2. For discussions of hunger outside the USSR, see the following issues of *LP*: 23/V/42, no. 121 (8227), 2; 9/VIII/42, no. 188 (8294), 2; 15/IX/42, no. 219 (8325), 4; 9/X/42, no. 240 (8346), 4. On euphemisms for hunger, see *LP*, 2/XII/42, no. 285 (8391), 2. On starving German rats, see *LP*, 25/XII/42, no. 304 (8410), 3. In the national press, one article in *Komsomol Pravda* (*Komsomol'skaia Pravda*) from 17 December 1941 mentioned starvation in Tosno and Liuban' of the Leningrad region (*oblast'*) but not in Leningrad itself. A second article, this time in *News* (*Izvestiia*) from 10 July 1942 finally mentioned hunger in Leningrad. See Mariia Petrovna Tokareva, "Pytka golodom: naselenie okkupirovannykh nemtsam raionov vymiraet ot istoshcheniia," *Komosomol'skaia Pravda* 17 / XII / 41, no. 296 (5082), 2; William Moskoff, *The Bread of Affliction: The Food Supply in the USSR during WWII* (New York: Cambridge University Press, 1990), 204.

83. For example, *osada* and *blokada* appear in these *LP* articles: 7/XI/41, no. 266 (8059), 3; 12/XI/41, no. 270 (8063), 1; 19/VI/42, no. 144 (8250), 2. *Blokada* first appeared in a headline on 20 January 1943 (*LP*, no. 16 [8431], 1), on 4 March 1943 (*LP*, no. 52 [8467], 3), and on 28 January 1944, when the siege ended (*LP*, no. 24 [8748], 1).

84. Aleksandr Pavlovich Grishkevich, undated entry, TsGAIPD, f. 4000, op. 11, d. 29, l. 24 (hereafter "Grishkevich").

85. Sedel'nikova, entry for 11–12 January 1942, 65. Also see ibid., entry for 15–16 January 1942, 65–66.

86. Kniazev, entry for 4 February 1942, 448.

87. Erokhana, entry for 26 January 1944, 61.

88. Konopleva wrote this on an index card dated 9 July 1943 and placed it in her diary.

89. Levina, "Pis'ma k drugu," 198; Levina, entry for 12 January 1942, 1 (this is one of three passages that appear in both of Levina's accounts); Zelenskaia, entry for 22 December 1941, 330b.

2. BECOMING NEW PEOPLE

1. Borovikova, entry for 14 December 1941, 88–89.

2. Ibid., entry for 25 March 1942, 121ob.

3. In Moscow, workers in heavy industry received 800 grams, service workers 600 grams, and dependents 400 grams of bread daily versus 300, 250, and 125, respectively, in Leningrad. Nicholas Ganson, "Food Supply, Rationing, and Living Standards," in *The Soviet Union at War, 1941–1945,* ed. David R. Stone (Barnsley, UK: Military Pen and Sword, 2010), 83.

4. Other mirror scenes in Sedel'nikova, entries for 14, 22 January 1942, 65, 68; Krakov, entry for 27 January 1942, 8; Sof'ia Gorkhart, "Leningrad. Blokada," in *Dve sud'by v velikoi otechestvennoi voine,* ed. V. L. Vikhnovicha (St. Petersburg: Gumanitarnaia Akademiia, 2006), 57–58. Mirror scenes are prominent in Holocaust literature, including the final scene of Elie Wiesel's memoir *Night* when his image is reflected back as a corpse. Wiesel, *Night,* trans. Stella Rodway (New York: Bantam Books, 1986), 109.

5. Buianov, entry for 26 October 1942, 56–56ob.

6. Leonid Pavlovich Gal'ko, "Iz dnevnika Gal'ko Leonida Pavlovicha," entry for 12 January 1942, in *Oborona Leningrada, 1941–1944: Vospominaniia i dnevniki uchastnikov,* ed. E. G. Dagin (Leningrad: Nauka, 1996), 516 (hereafter "Gal'ko").

7. Kochina, entry for 12 December 1941, 171.

8. Mukhina, entry for 25 May 1942, 134ob.

9. Svetlana Magaeva, "Physiological and Psychosomatic Prerequisites for Survival and Recovery," in *Life and Death in Besieged Leningrad, 1941–44,* ed. John Barber and Andrei Dzeniskevich (London: Palgrave Macmillan, 2005), 150–51.

10. Studies that stress the disfiguration of Leningraders' bodies include Lisa A. Kirschenbaum, "'The Alienated Body': Gender, Identity and the Memory of the Siege of Leningrad," in *Gender and War in Twentieth-Century Eastern Europe,* ed. Nancy M. Wingfield and Maria Bucur (Bloomington: Indiana University Press, 2006), 220–37; Polina Barskova, "The Corpse, the Corpulent, and the Other: A Study in the Tropology of Siege Body Representation," *Ab Imperio* 1 (2009): 361–86.

11. This was not unique to Leningrad. Doctors in the Warsaw ghetto began to reconceptualize human physiology on the basis of their emaciated patients. See Julian Fliederbaum, "Clinical Aspects of Hunger Disease in Adults," in *Hunger Disease: Studies by the Jewish Physicians in the Warsaw Ghetto,* ed. Myron Winick, trans. Martha Osnos (New York: Wiley, 1979), 15.

12. Antoine de Baecque, *The Body Politic: Corporeal Metaphor in Revolutionary France, 1770–1800,* trans. Charlotte Mandell (Stanford, CA: Stanford University Press, 1997), 4–6, 129–37.

13. Jochen Hellbeck, "Working, Struggling, Becoming: Stalin-Era Autobiographical Texts," *Russian Review* 60, no. 3 (2001): 351–53.

14. Toby Clark, "The 'New Man's' Body: A Motif in Early Soviet Culture," in *Art of the Soviets: Painting, Sculpture, and Architecture in a One-Party State, 1917–1992,* ed. Matthew Cullerne Brown and Brandon Taylor (Manchester: Manchester University Press, 1993), 33; Keith A. Livers, *Constructing the Stalinist Body: Fictional Representations of Corporeality in the Stalinist 1930s* (Lanham, MD: Lexington Books, 2004); Lynne Attwood, *The New Soviet Man and Woman: Sex-Role Socialization in the USSR* (Bloomington: Indiana University Press, 1990), 36–39.

15. Clark, "'New Man's' Body," 33–35, 44–46; Livers, *Constructing the Stalinist Body,* 5. On Soviet science's approach to cultivating the New Man, see Frances L. Bernstein, "Envisioning Health in Revolutionary Russia: The Politics of Gender in Sexual-Enlightenment," *Russian Review* 57, no. 2 (1998): 191–217; Raymond Bauer, *The New Man in Soviet Psychology* (Cambridge, MA: Harvard University Press, 1968); David Joravsky, *Russian Psychology: A Critical History* (Oxford, UK: Blackwell, 1989); Loren R. Graham, *Science and Philosophy in the Soviet Union* (New York: Knopf, 1972).

16. Tricia Starks, *The Body Soviet: Hygiene, Propaganda, and the Revolutionary State* (Madison: University of Wisconsin Press, 2008).

17. Beate Fieseler, "Soviet-Style Welfare: The Disabled Soldiers of the 'Great Patriotic War,'" in *Disability in Eastern Europe and the Former Soviet Union: History, Policy,*

and Everyday Life, ed. Michael Ransell and Elena Iarskaia-Smirnova (New York: Routledge, 2014), 18–41; Lilya Kaganovsky, *How the Soviet Man Was Unmade: Cultural Fantasy and Male Subjectivity under Stalin* (Pittsburgh: University of Pittsburgh Press, 2008). An alternative argument is made in Claire Louise Shaw, "Deaf in the USSR: 'Defect' and the New Soviet Person, 1917–1991" (Ph.D. diss., University College London, 2011), 128–35.

18. Nikolai Tikhonov, "Liudi goroda Lenina," *LP,* 22/VI/42, no. 147 (8253), 3; Tikhonov, *Cherty sovetskogo cheloveka. Leningradskie rasskazy* (Moscow: Pravda, 1942).

19. Aleksandr Fadeev, "Chto ia videl v Leningrade," *LP,* 19/VI/42, no. 144 (8250), 2. Also see N. Kuropatkin, "Sila sovetskogo cheloveka," *LP,* 16/XII/43, no. 296 (8711), 2.

20. Boris Skomorovsky and E. G. Morris, *The Siege of Leningrad* (New York: Dutton, 1944), 117–18.

21. Liubovskaia, entries for 7, 30 January 1942, 43, 71.

22. Inber, entry for 1 December 1941, 41.

23. Kochina, entry for 10 December 1941, 170.

24. There are numerous statements of this in Lenin's writings. For an early example, see the 1899 "Development of Capitalism in Russia" and for a later example the 1920 *Pravda* article "To the Working Woman," in *The Emancipation of Women: From the Writings of V. I. Lenin* (New York: International Publishers, 1969), 13, 79.

25. Zelenskaia, entry for 6 January 1942, 49–50.

26. Igor Kozlov and Alla Samsonova, "The Impact of the Siege on the Physical Development of Children," in Barber and Dzeniskevich, *Life and Death,* 174–96. Doctors in the Warsaw Ghetto also observed this phenomenon. See Anna Braude-Heller, Israel Rotsbalsam, Regina Elbinger, "Clinical Aspects of Hunger Disease in Children," 55.

27. The female death rate caught up by March 1942. Cynthia Simmons and Nina Perlina, *Writing the Siege of Leningrad: Women's Diaries, Memoirs, and Documentary Prose* (Pittsburgh: University of Pittsburgh Press, 2002), 2–3; Nadezhda Cherepenina, "Assessing the Scale of Famine and Death in the Besieged City," in Barber and Dzeniskevich, *Life and Death,* 46.

28. Richard Bidlack, foreword to Simmons and Perlina, *Writing the Siege,* xii; Simmons and Perlina, *Writing the Siege,* 2–11. On national gender disparities, see John Erikson, "Soviet Women at War," in *World War 2 and the Soviet People,* ed. John Garrard and Carol Garrard (New York: St. Martin's Press, 1993), 51–54.

29. Kniazev, entry for 4 February 1942, 447–48. Also see ibid., entry for 3 January 1942, 382–83.

30. Levina, entry for 10 February 1942, 7.

31. Uskova, entry for 19 March 1942, 51–52.

32. Ol'ga Freidenberg, "Osada cheloveka," *Minuvshee,* vol. 3 (Paris: Athenaeum, 1987), 7–44; Ginzburg, "Zapiski blokadnogo cheloveka"; M. Iu. Sorokina, "Kratkoe opisanie materialov lichnogo arkhiva O. M. Freidenberg," in *Mif i literatura drevnosti* (Moscow: RAN, 1998), 781; Emily Van Buskirk, "Reality in Search of Literature: Lydia Ginzburg's In-Between Prose" (Ph.D. diss., Harvard University, 2008), 315, 405–15.

33. On the typically masculine qualities of the Soviet New Person, see Thomas G. Schrand, "Socialism in One Gender: Masculine Values in the Stalin Revolution," in *Russian Masculinities in History and Culture,* ed. Barbara Evans Clements, Rebecca Friedman, and Dan Healy (New York: Palgrave 2002), 195–204; John Haynes, *New Soviet Man: Gender and Masculinity in Stalinist Soviet Film* (Manchester: Manchester University Press, 2003); Eliot Borenstein, *Men without Women: Masculinity and Revolution in Russian Fiction, 1917–1929* (Durham, NC: Duke University Press, 2000).

34. Pat Simpson, "Parading Myths: Imaging New Soviet Woman on Fizkul'turnik's Day, July 1944," *Russian Review* 63 (April 2004): 187–211. Women displaying gender ambiguity were celebrated during the New Economic Policy (NEP) when female sexuality was seen as wild and irrational. Eric Naiman, *Sex in Public: Incarnation of Early Soviet Ideology* (Princeton, NJ: Princeton University Press, 1997).

35. Aleksandr Fadeev, *Leningrad v dni blokady: Iz dnevnika* (Moscow: Sovetskii Pisatel', 1944), 85; translation from *Heroic Leningrad: Documents, Sketches, and Stories of its Siege and Relief* (Moscow: Foreign Languages Publishing House, 1945), 49.

36. Ibid., 8–9, 12–13; translation from *Heroic Leningrad,* 37–39.

37. Anna Krylova, *Soviet Women in Combat* (Cambridge: Cambridge University Press, 2010), 12.

38. "Zhenshchiny ovladevaiut muzhskimi spetsial'nostiami," *LP,* 9/VII/41, no. 161 (7954), 3; O. Smirnova, "Prostye sovetskie devushki," *LP,* 8/X/41, no. 240 (8033), 3; "Nashi devushki," and "Russkie zhenshchiny," *LP,* 25/VI/41, no. 149 (7942), 3; "Geroizm sovetskikh zhenshchin," *LP,* 23/VII/41, no. 174 (7967), 4; "Geroicheskie zhenshchiny goroda Lenina," *LP,* 25/XII/41, no. 307 (8100), 1. A full page of articles on women appeared in *LP,* 21/X/41, no. 251 (8044), 3.

39. Vera Inber, *Dusha Leningrada: izbrannoe* (Leningrad: Lenizdat, 1979), 42–44. An exception is a stanza of Inber's "Pulkovskii Meridian," which refers to women's barren breasts (Inber, *Pulkovskii meridian* (Moscow: Ogiz, 1944), 15). On the theme of gender in Inber's work, see Cynthia Simmons, "Lifting the Siege: Women's Voices on Leningrad (1941–1944)," *Canadian Slavonic Papers* 40, nos. 1–2 (1998): 47.

40. Aleksandr Dymov, entry for 17 January 1942, in Ales' Adamovich and Daniil Granin, *Blokadnaia kniga* (St. Petersburg: Pechatnyi dvor, 1994), 302; translation from Adamovich and Granin, *A Book of the Blockade,* trans. Hilda Perham (Moscow: Raduga, 1983), 380–81.

41. Liubovskaia, entry for 9 February 1942, 80. More examples in A. Mironova, entry for 27 February 1942, 19–190b; Savinkov, entry for 26 August 1942, 53.

42. Nikolai Mikhailovich Byl'ev (Protopopov), "Otryvki iz blokadnikh zapisei, 1941–2," TsGALI, f. 109, op. 1, d. 9, l. 1–2 (hereafter "Byl'ev").

43. Vasilisa Petrovna Malysheva, entry for 7 August 1942, TsGAIPD, f. 4000, op. 11, d. 65, ll. 12–13.

44. From an interview with Ol'ga Nikolaevna Mel'nikova-Pisarenko in Adamovich and Granin, *Blokadnaia kniga,* 162. On hunger-induced hair growth, see Fliederbaum, "Clinical Aspects of Hunger Disease in Adults" and Anna Braude-Heller, Israel Rotsbalsam, and Regina Elbinger, "Clinical Aspects of Hunger Disease in Children," 17, 48.

45. Ol'ga Richardovna Peto, "Deti blokady: Deti Leningrada, 1942–1943," OR RNB, f. 1273, d. 52, ll. 16, 5–6, 14 (hereafter "Peto").

46. Levina, entry for 1 July 1942, 25.

47. Dymov, entry for 17 January 1942 in *Blokadnaia kniga*, 302; translation from Adamovich and Granin, *A Book of the Blockade*, 380–81.

48. On the eve of World War II, there was an unprecedented number of Soviet psychological studies on sensation and perception as the bases of human apprehension (Bauer, *New Man*, 118).

49. Recently, scholars have argued for a historically and culturally contingent approach to the senses. See Martin Jay, "In the Realm of the Senses: An Introduction," *American Historical Review*, April 2011, 307–8; and the articles in part 2 of *Empire of the Senses: The Sensual Cultural Reader*, ed. David Howes (Oxford, UK: Berg, 2005), 55–139.

50. Ginzburg, "Zapiski blokadnogo cheloveka," 349; Lidiia Ginzburg, "Otrezki blokadnogo dnia," in *Prokhodiashchie kharaktery: proza voennykh let, zapiski blokadnogo cheloveka*, ed. Andrei Zorin and Emily Van Buskirk (Moscow: Novoe, 2011), 444.

51. P. F. Gladkikh, *Zdravookhranenie i voennaia meditsina v bitve za Leningrad glazami istorika i ochevidtsev: 1941–1944* (St. Petersburg: Dmitrii Bulanin, 2006), 31.

52. Ibid., 31–32; Josef Brožek, Samuel Wells, and Ancel Keys, "Medical Aspects of Semi-starvation in Leningrad," *American Review of Soviet Medicine* 4, no. 1 (1946): 77; World Health Organization, "Neurological Disorders Associated with Malnutrition," 115, http://www.who.int/mental_health/neurology/neurodiso/en/index.html.

53. Examples in Zelenskaia, entry for 26 January 1942, 58; Nina Rudal'fovna Mervol'f, entry for 14 March 1942, MNM, k.p. 6580, f. 2, d. 5579, l. 57. Doctors in the Warsaw Ghetto saw hunger induce cataracts and edema around the eyelids. Szymon Fajgenblat, "Ocular Disturbances in Hunger Disease," in Winick, *Hunger Disease*, 199–200.

54. Ostrovskaia, entry for 1 February 1942, 2–20b.

55. Ibid., entry for 9 October 1941, 1070b.

56. Zelenskaia, entry for 6 May 1942, 790b.

57. Lidiia Ginzburg, "Zapisi i dni blokady," in *Prokhodiashchie kharaktery: proza voennykh let, zapiski blokadnogo cheloveka*, ed. Andrei Zorin and Emily Van Buskirk (Moscow: Novoe, 2011), 435, 437; translation from Ginzburg, *Blockade Diary*, 97–98, 100.

58. Ol'ga Matiushina, *Pesn' o zhizni: avtograficheskaia povest'* (Leningrad: Molodaia Gvardiia, 1946), 2.

59. Ibid., 91–93. On Matiushina's conflicting reports on her vision and how it was lost, see Matiushina, "Zapiski," *Zvezda* 2 (1943): 56, 71; Ol'ga Matiushina, "'Ia ochen' plokho vizhu,' Interv'iu ili vystuplenie," OR RNB, f. 1059, op. 2, d. 113, l. 1; Ol'ga Matiushina, "Pochemu ia pishu," stat'ia, 1949–60, OR RNB, f. 1059, op. 2, d. 86, ll. 1–2.

60. Matiushina, *Pesn' o zhizni*, 93.

61. Matiushina, Diary, 42, 44–45, 61–67, 77–78. Contrast this with the novella: Matiushina, *Pesn' o zhizni*, 102–3.

62. Matiushina, Diary, 37–38. An almost identical version is in Matiushina, "Zapiski," 60.

63. Matiushina, *Pesn' o zhizni*, 96–97.

64. Ol'ga Matiushina, "Pochemu ia pishu," stat'ia, OR RNB, f. 1059, op. 2, d. 86, ll. 2, 15, 21; Ol'ga Matiushina, "Mne khochetsia ob'iasnit'," stat'ia (1945), OR RNB, f. 1059, op. 2, d. 81, l. 2; Ol'ga Matiushina, "Mysli o knige," stat'ia, OR RNB, f. 1059. op. 2 d. 87, ll. 2–3.

65. Matiushina, Diary, 95. Also in OR RNB, f. 113, op. 1, d. 86, l. 2.

66. Matiushina, Diary, 110–11. For an interpretation of the blockade as an auditory experience, see Vladimir Lapin, *Peterburg: zapakhi i zvuki* (St. Petersburg: Evropeiskii Dom, 2007), 261.

67. Andrei Dzeniskevich, "Medical Research Institutes during the Siege," in Barber and Dzeniskevich, *Life and Death,* 104. This research was published in *Sbornik trudov LNII po bolezniam ukha, nosa, gorla, i rechi,* volumes 7 (1944) and 8 (1947).

68. Kniazev, entries for 2, 26 July 1941, 18 August 1942, 15, 37, 191.

69. Anna Ivanovna Likhacheva, "Iz dnevnika Likhachevoi Anny Ivanovny," entry for 20 June 1942, in Dagin, *Oborona Leningrada,* 688 (hereafter "Likhacheva").

70. An example in Levina, entry for 10 April 1942, 17.

71. Konopleva, entries for 4, 13, 19, 26 July, 22, 24 September, 5–9 October, 13 November 1941, 1–3, 10–11, 20–21, 24, 98–101, 126–33, 164; entries for 20 April, 4 July 1942, 60–63, 1–2.

72. Zelenskaia, entries for 2, 16 September 1941, 11, 150b; Vera Inber, "Dnevnoi kontsert" and "Govoriat zentiki," *Zvezda* 1–2 (1942): 51.

73. Konopleva, entries for 30 August, 1 September, 20 November 1941, 175–76, 52–55; entries for 17, 19 April, 28 June 1942, 59–60, 88–89. The phrase "regimes of listening" is from Peter Szendy, *Listen: A History of Our Ears,* trans. Charlotte Mandell (New York: Fordham University Press, 2008), 15–23.

74. Zelenskaia, entry for 13 October 1941, 23.

75. Liubovskaia, undated entry, 4–50b; ibid., entry for 17 December 1941, 30.

76. Ibid., entries for 15, 19 November 1941, 11–12.

77. Levina, entry for 2 April 1942, 16; Ginzburg, "Zapiski blokadnogo cheloveka," 355–57. I treat taste and smell together because they are closely related; olfaction accounts for roughly 70 percent of taste.

78. Liubovskaia, entry for 12 January 1942, 51.

79. Gel'fer, entry for 30 January 1942, 7–8.

80. Priscilla Parkhurst Ferguson, "The Senses of Taste," *American Historical Review,* April 2011, 370–72, 375, 381.

81. Likhacheva, entry for 15 May 1942, 682.

82. Kochina, entry for 17 December 1941, 173.

83. Ginzburg, "Zapiski blokadnogo cheloveka," 351; translation from Ginzburg, *Blockade Diary,* 65.

84. Uskova, entry for 29 December 1941, 38–39.

85. Ibid., entry for 28 January 1942, 49.

86. Ibid., entry for 25 July 1942, 59–60.

87. Ostrovskaia, entry for 30 March 1942, 1.

88. Brožek, Wells, and Keys, "Medical Aspects of Semi-starvation in Leningrad," 77.

89. Inber, entries for 1 November 1942, 8 February 1943, 46ob, 100; Ginzburg, "Zapiski blokadnogo cheloveka," 318.

90. Ginzburg, "Zapiski blokadnogo cheloveka," 314.
91. Matiushina, *Pesn' o zhizni,* 121; Matiushina, Diary, 154–57.
92. Liubovskaia, entry for 6 March 1942, 114–15.
93. Ibid., entries for 27 December 1941, 3 March 1942, 22 July 1942, 33, 111, 188.
94. Ibid., entry for 19 May 1942, 155.
95. Savinkov, entry for 23 February 1942, 23; also see ibid., entry for 4 January 1942, 15–15ob.
96. Ibid., entry for 7 January 1942, 15ob.
97. Ibid., entries for 11, 12, 16–18 March 1942, 25–26ob.
98. Uskova, entry for 25 March 1942, 95.
99. Sedel'nikova, entries for 18, 21 November, 22–23 December 1941, 42–43, 58.
100. Matiushina, *Pesn' o zhizni,* 121, 125.
101. Zelenskaia, entry for 2 September 1941, 11.
102. Ibid., entries for 18, 22 September 1941, 16ob–17ob, 18.
103. Ibid., entry for 22 September 1941, 18–18ob.
104. Ibid., entry for 12 December 1941, 41ob–42.
105. Savinkov, entry for 16 April 1942, 31ob.
106. Dymov, entry for 25 January 1942, in Adamovich and Granin, *Blokadnaia kniga,* 304; modified translation from Adamovich and Granin, *A Book of the Blockade,* 384–85.
107. Uskova, entry for 23 December 1941, 33.
108. Zelenskaia, entry for 6 May 1942, 79ob.
109. Ostrovskaia, entry for 13 August 1942, 80.
110. Ibid., entry for 8 May 1942, 275.
111. Sedel'nikova, entry for 19 December 1941, 53–54.
112. Ostrovskaia, entry for 20 February 1942, 14ob.
113. Elsewhere in the diary, Ostrovskaia rued Russians' proclivity, inherited from the Scythians, to endure hellish conditions because it prevented them from surrendering (ibid., entry for 3 October 1942, 92).
114. Ibid., entry for 20 February 1942, 14ob, underlining in the original changed to italics. Ostrovskaia also referred to Aleksandr Blok's 1918 poem "Skify," which describes the battle between west and east as one between Germanic "steel machines" and "the wild Tatar horde." On this, see Ekaterina Bobrinskaia, " 'Skifstov v russkoi kulture nachala XX veka i skifskaia tema u russkikh futuristov," *Rannii russkii avantgard v kontekste filosofskoi i khudozhestvennoi kultury rubezha vekov: Ocherki* (Moscow: Gosudarstvennyi institut iskusstvoznaniia, 1999).
115. This is paraphrase of Elizabeth D. Harvey, "The Portal of Touch," *American Historical Review,* April 2011, 386.

3. THE ELUSIVE I

1. Levina, entry for 14 April 1942, 18.
2. M. V. Chernorutskii, "Problemy alimentarnoi distrofii," *Raboty leningradskikh vrachei za god Otechestvennoi voiny* 3 (1943): 3–13.

3. Paul John Eakin, *Living Autobiographically: How We Create Identity in Narrative* (Ithaca, NY: Cornell University Press, 2008), 154–55. Antonio Damasio summarized his research on the self and consciousness for a general audience in *The Feeling of What Happens: Body and Emotion in the Making of Consciousness* (New York: Harcourt Brace, 1999) and *Self Comes to Mind: The Conscious Brain* (New York: Pantheon Books, 2010).

4. Kniazev, entry for 17 November 1941, 312.

5. Scholarship on the self is quite extensive, too much to summarize here. I draw from Charles Taylor, *Sources of the Self: The Making of Modern Identity* (Cambridge, MA: Harvard University Press, 1989); Alex Aronson, *Studies in Twentieth-Century Diaries: The Concealed Self* (Lewiston, NY: Edwin Mellen, 1991); Deborah Martinson, *In the Presence of Audience: The Self in Diaries and Fiction* (Columbus: Ohio State University Press, 2003); Katherine P. Ewing, "The Illusion of Wholeness: Culture, Self, and the Experience of Inconsistency," in *The Art of Medical Anthropology: Readings,* ed. Sjaak van der Geest and Adri Rienks (Amsterdam: Het Spinhuis, 1998), 296–310.

6. For another example of a diarist mentioning her incorporation of "literary elements," see Kostrovitskaia, "February [1942]," 25. I do not make a hard distinction between fiction and nonfiction. Some fictionalization is to be expected from the act of narration. For a treatment of this phenomenon in documentary prose from the gulag, see Leona Toker, *Return from Archipelago: Narratives of Gulag Survivors* (Bloomington: Indiana University Press, 2000). The creation of a fictionalized self and the insertion of novels also occurred in diaries of the 1930s. See Boris Wolfson, "Escape from Literature: Constructing the Soviet Self in Yuri Olesha's Diary of the 1930s," *Russian Review* 63, no. 4 (2004): 609–20; Jochen Hellbeck, *Revolution on My Mind: Writing a Diary under Stalin* (Cambridge, MA: Harvard University Press, 2006), 285–345.

7. On diarists' tendency to incorporate fiction in order to gain control over their lives and stories, see Steven E. Kagle and Lorenza Gramegna, "Rewriting Her Life: Fictionalization and the Use of Fictional Models in Early American Women's Diaries," in *Inscribing the Daily: Critical Essays on Women's Diaries,* ed. Suzanne L. Bunkers and Cynthia Huff (Amherst: University of Massachusetts Press, 1996), 38–55; Trevor Field, *Form and Function in the Diary Novel* (London: Macmillan, 1989).

8. Jeffrey Kauffman, "Safety and the Assumptive World: A Theory of Traumatic Loss," in *Loss of the Assumptive World: A Theory of Traumatic Loss,* ed. Jeffrey Kauffman (New York: Brunner-Routledge, 2002), 208, italics in original.

9. Hellbeck, *Revolution on My Mind,* 5, 10, 13.

10. V. M. Koval'chuk, A. I. Rupasov, and A. N. Chistikov, "Kommentarii" and "Neobkhodimoe posleslovie: kak byla vosstanovlena biografiia Leny Mukhinoi" in *Sokhrani moiu pechal'nuiu istoriiu . . . : Blokadnyi dnevnik Eleny Mukhanoi* (St. Petersburg: Azbuka, 2011), 323, 355–58.

11. Mukhina, entry for 27 November 1941, 590b.

12. Ibid., entry for 29 August 1941, 30.

13. Ibid., entry for 10 February 1942, 820b.

14. Ibid., entry for 3 April 1942, 99. Letters and jokes appear in her entries for 5 March, 12 April 1942, 890b, 104–5.

15. Ibid., entries for 22, 26 April 1942, 110, 1120b–13. Literary scholars have noted how the diary can function as a mode of social interaction, in part by fusing diary writing with letter writing, as Mukhina did. See Philippe Lejeune, "The Practice of the Private Journal: Chronicle of an Investigation (1986–1998)," in *Marginal Voices, Marginal Forms: Diaries in European Literature and History,* ed. Rachel Langford and Russell West (Atlanta: Rodopi, 1999), 201; Jerome Bruner, "The Autobiographical Process," in *The Culture of Autobiography: Constructions of Self-Representation,* ed. Robert Folkenflik (Stanford, CA: Stanford University Press, 1993), 38–56; Robert Folkenflik, "Self as Other," in Folkenflik, *The Culture of Autobiography,* 215–34; Elizabeth W. Bruss, *Autobiographical Acts: The Changing Situation of a Literary Genre* (Baltimore: Johns Hopkins University Press, 1976), 4–32.

16. Mukhina, entry for 23 November 1941, 58. On the insertion of fiction into diaries, see Lorna Martens, *The Diary Novel* (Cambridge: Cambridge University Press, 1985); H. Porter Abbott, *Diary Fiction: Writing as Action* (Ithaca, NY: Cornell University Press, 1984); Andrew Hassam, *Writing and Reality: A Study of Modern British Diary Fiction* (Westport, CT: Greenwood, 1993).

17. Mukhina, entry for 22 October 1941, 57. In light of the surrounding entries, the diarist may have meant to date this 22 November.

18. Ibid., 57ob.

19. On the practice of staging dialogue between aspects of the self, see Philippe Lejeune, "Autobiography in the Third Person," *New Literary History* 9, no. 1 (1977): 28, 35–41; Folkenflik, "Self as Other," 233.

20. Mukhina, entry for 23 November 1941, 58. Mukhina had trouble focusing on her studies: "Studying is the last thing you think about when you have only a glimmer of life in you" (ibid., entry for 10 January 1942, 76).

21. Ibid., entry for 10 December 1941, 64.

22. Roger Cardinal, "Unlocking the Diary," *Comparative Criticism* 12 (September 1990): 80, 78.

23. Mukhina, entry for 28 April 1942, 115–150b.

24. Ibid., 115.

25. Ibid., entry for 22 October 1941, 550b–56.

26. Ibid., entry for 30 April 1942, 117.

27. Ibid., entries for 22, 10 April 1942, 110, 100.

28. Folkenflik, "Self as Other," 218–33.

29. Lejeune, "Autobiography in the Third Person," 32.

30. Eckhard Kuhn-Osius, "Making Loose Ends Meet: Private Journals in the Public Realm," *German Quarterly* 54 (1981): 173. On the use of stock scenes and characters in diaries and autobiographical novels, see Roy Pascal, *Design and Truth in Autobiography* (Cambridge, MA: Harvard University Press, 1960), 171; Martinson, *In the Presence of Audience,* 33.

31. Mukhina, entry 2 May 1942, 1190b.

32. For additional examples, see ibid., entries for 3–11 May 1942, 1200b–30.

33. Ibid., entry for 1 May 1942, 117ob–18. It is not clear if Mukhina was referring to her biological or adoptive mother.

34. Ibid., entry for 2 May 1942, 120.
35. Ibid., entry for 4 May 1942, 121–22.
36. Ibid., entry for 25 May 1942, 134ob.
37. Ibid., 135.
38. Mukhina was evacuated with Vera Vladimirovna Miliutina, an artist and friend of Bernatskaia from the Small Operatic Theater (*Malyi Opernyi Teatr*) who cared for her after she was orphaned (Koval'chuk, Rupasov, and Chistikov, "Neobkhodimoe posleslovie," *Sokhrani moiu pechalnuiu istoriiu,* 356–58).
39. Biographical information from Sof'ia Vinogradova, E. A. Giliarova, and M. Ia. Razumova, "Korotko ob avtorakh," *Leningradki: Vospominaniia, ocherki, dokumenty* (Leningrad: Lenizdat, 1968), 408–9.
40. Several entries for November 1941 are inserted into the section on February 1942.
41. Martinson, *In the Presence of Audience,* 12. A version of "Notes" also appears as "Zapiski Leningradki," in *Zhenshchiny goroda Lenina: Rasskazy i ocherki o zhenshchinakh Leningrada v dni blokady,* ed. A. F. Volkova (Leningrad: Lenizdat, 1944), 143–53.
42. Matiushina later reworked and published the novella in 1970. This edition contains many alterations. "Autobiographical" was removed from the subtitle, but a new afterword states that the piece was based on her "diary notes" *(dnevnikovye zapisi).* Matiushina's references to Stalin are pared down significantly, and she removed the pseudonyms used for her friends. See Ol'ga Matiushina, *Pesn' o zhizni: Povest'* (Leningrad: Lenizdat, 1970).
43. Compare Matiushina, *Pesn' o zhizni* (1946), 113–14; Matiushina, *Pesn' o zhizni: Povest'* (1970), 103–4, 228–30, 196–97.
44. Matiushina, Diary, 124–25.
45. Ibid., 54, 169.
46. Ibid., 102. For a large section of recorded conversations, see ibid., 102–7.
47. A. Girard, *Le Journal intime* (Paris: Presses universitaires de France, 1963), 19; translated and quoted in Field, *Form and Function,* 147.
48. Matiushina, Diary, 17, 34–35.
49. Ibid., entry for 23 June 1941, 1.
50. Ibid., entry for 22 June 1941, 3, 6–7.
51. Matiushina, "Zapiski," 56.
52. Matiushina, *Pesn' o zhizni* (1946), 62.
53. Matiushina, Diary, 19, 9.
54. Ibid., 56–58.
55. Wendy J. Wiener and George C. Rosenwald, "A Moment's Monument: The Psychology of Keeping a Diary," in *The Narrative Study of Lives,* vol. 1, ed. Ruthellen Josselson and Amia Lieblich (London: Sage, 1993), 31–35.
56. Hellbeck, *Revolution on My Mind,* 30–33, 352–56.
57. A recent study arguing this is Bunkers and Huff, *Inscribing the Daily,* 43.

4. FAMILY LIFE AND STRIFE

1. Zelenskaia, entry for 22 November 1941, 330b–34.
2. Wendy Z. Goldman, *Women, the State and Revolution: Soviet Family Policy and Social Life, 1917–1936* (Cambridge: Cambridge University Press, 1993), 296–343;

Judith Harwin, *Children of the Russian State: 1917–1995* (Aldershot, UK: Ashgate, 1996), 18–22.

3. Lisa A. Kirschenbaum, *Small Comrades: Revolutionizing Childhood in Soviet Russia, 1917–1932* (New York: Routledge Falmer, 2001).

4. David Hoffman, *Stalinist Values: The Cultural Norms of Soviet Modernity, 1917–1941* (Ithaca, NY: Cornell University Press, 2003), 88–117; Hoffman, "Mothers in the Motherland: Stalinist Pronatalism in Its Pan-European Context," *Journal of Social History* 34, no. 1 (2000): 35–54; Catriona Kelly, *Children's World: Growing Up in Russia, 1890–1991* (New Haven, CT: Yale University Press, 2007), 115–19, 243–44. Anton Makarenko was among the major Soviet theorists of childrearing and education who made this shift. See his 1937 manual *The Collective Family: A Handbook for Russian Parents,* ed. Robert Daglish (New York: Doubleday and Company, Inc., 1967), 1–17.

5. Valerii Nikolaevich Selivanov, *Stoiali kak soldaty: Blokada. Deti. Leningrad* (St. Petersburg: Ego, 2002), 163; Lisa A. Kirschenbaum, "'Our City, Our Hearths, Our Families': Local Loyalties and Private Life in Soviet World War II Propaganda," *Slavic Review* 59, no. 4 (2000): 827–28, 837–38; Ilya Ehrenburg, *Russia at War* (London: Hamish Hamilton, 1943), 251, 266. See these issues of *LP:* 16/VII/41, no. 168 (7961), 3; 11/IX/41, no. 217 (8010), 3; 21/IX/41, no. 226 (8019), 3.

6. Cathy A. Frierson and Semyon S. Vilensky, *Children of the Gulag* (New Haven, CT: Yale University Press, 2010), 260–70.

7. Kelly, *Children's World,* 242–43.

8. Harwin, *Children of the Russian State,* 20.

9. Quoted in Lisa A. Kirschenbaum, *The Legacy of the Siege of Leningrad, 1941–1995: Myths, Memories, and Monuments* (Cambridge: Cambridge University Press, 2006), 54, 76.

10. Fadeev, *Leningrad v dni blokady,* 15.

11. Boris Skomorovsky and E. G. Morris, *The Siege of Leningrad* (New York: Dutton, 1944), 37.

12. For presentations of family solidarity and altruism under siege, see the diary-memoir of Andrei Kriukov and the following scholarship: Kriukov, *Muzyka v efire voennogo Leningrada* (St. Petersburg: Kompozitor, 2005), 309–42; Ales' Adamovich and Daniil Granin, *Blokadnaia kniga* (St. Petersburg: Pechatnyi dvor, 1994), 121; Anna Reid, *Leningrad: The Epic Siege of World War II, 1941–1944* (New York: Walker and Company, 2011), 240–41; Richard Bidlack and Nikita Lomagin, *The Leningrad Blockade, 1941–44: A New Documentary History from the Soviet Archives* (New Haven, CT: Yale University Press, 2012), 51; Sergei Iarov, "'Pishite sirotam.' Leningradskaia sem'ia v 1941–1942: Sostradanie, uteshenie, liubov'," in *Bitva za Leningrad: Diskussionye problemy,* ed. Nikita Lomagin (St. Petersburg: Evropeiskii Dom, 2008), 137–72. More mixed evaluations of familial solidarity appear in Vladimir L. Piankevich, "The Family under Siege: Leningrad, 1941–44," *Russian Review* 75, no. 1 (2016): 107–37; Jeffrey Hass, "Norms and Survival in the Heat of War: Normative Versus Instrumental Rationalities and Survival Tactics in the Blockade of Leningrad," *Sociological Forum* 26, no. 4 (2011): 921–49. Hass rightly stresses that Leningraders were much more likely to cooperate and empathize with their kin than with strangers. This does not mean that they seldom vied with loved ones or contemplated betraying them. Alternatively, John Barber

argues that personal documents recount more instances of competition than of altruism in Leningrad. See Barber, "War, Public Opinion, and the Struggle for Survival, 1941–45: The Case of Leningrad," in *Russia in the Age of Wars, 1914–1945,* ed. Silvio Pons and Andrea Romano (Milan: Feltrinelli Editore, 2000), 272–74.

13. See Mervol'f, entry for 10 January 1942, 11; Skriabina, entries for 6–8 October 1941, 38–40.

14. Tat'iana Glebova, entry for 5 November 1941, "Risovat', kak letopisets: stranitsy blokadnogo dnevnika," *Iskusstvo Leningrada* 1 (1990), 31.

15. Zelenskaia, entry for 3 December 1941, 37ob–38ob.

16. Liubovskaia, entry for 24 February 1942, 99.

17. Rudykovskaia, entries for 9, 12–19 February, 27 May, 15 June, 14 July 1942, 5–6, 15, 16, 22.

18. "Young Avengers of the City of Lenin," *Smena* 7–8 (April 1944): 8–9; Stanislav Kotov, *Detskie doma blokadnogo Leningrada* (St. Petersburg: Politekhnika, 2005), 4; Selivanov, *Stoiali kak soldaty,* 124–25, 149–67, 173–74; N. V. Sedova, "Shkola v gody voiny," in *Zhenshchina i voina: O roli zhenshchin v oborone Leningrada: 1941–44,* ed. M. I. Bozhenkova, A. I. Burlakov, A. R. Dzeniskevich, A. N. Rubtsov, T. A. Postrelova, and I. D. Khodanovich (St. Petersburg: Izdatel'stvo Sankt-Peterburgskogo Universiteta, 2006), 100–101.

19. Iurii Voronov, "V blokadnykh dniakh my tak i ne uznali," *Skorb' i radost' popolam* (St. Petersburg: Vesti, 2006), 13.

20. Rudykovskaia, entries for 15 June 1942, 2 August 1942, 18 September 1942, 5 April 1943, 9 October 1943, 16, 20, 29, 45, 52.

21. Zelenskaia, entry for 8 April 1943, 116ob–17.

22. Ibid., entry for 5 April 1943, 114ob–15.

23. Ostrovskaia, entry for 27 November 1941, 118.

24. Ibid., 117–18.

25. Ibid., 118. For a fictionalized depiction of Lidiia Ginzburg's strained relationship with her mother during the siege, see Ginzburg, "Rasskaz o zhalosti i zhestokostii," in *Prokhodaishchie kharaktery*, 17–59.

26. Liubovskaia, entry for 19 May 1942, 155.

27. Ibid., entry for 14 February 1942, 86.

28. Ibid., entry for 9 April 1942, 137.

29. Riabinkin, entry for 9–10 November 1941, 102.

30. Ibid., entry for 2 December 1941, 128; translation modified for clarity.

31. Ibid., entry for 9–10 November 1941, 105.

32. Ibid., entry for 2 December 1941, 128.

33. Ibid., entry for 28 November 1941, 109.

34. Ibid., entry for 3 January 1942, 151–52; translation modified for clarity. Diarist N. Sudakova also referred to herself as a blockade parasite. See Sudakova, entry for 1 March 1942, "Dnevnik, 22 / I / 41-15 / IV / 42," TsGAIPD, f. 4000, op. 10, d. 1387, l. 6ob.

35. Kseniia Matus, entry for 31 December 1941, MNM, k.p. 4153, f. 2, d. 2804, ll. 23–24 (hereafter "Matus"). Exceptions include Elena Skriabina and Georgii Kniazev, who

described having happy marriages under siege. Skriabina, 8 October 1941, 39; Kniazev, 3 January 1942, 330.

36. Marina Aleksandrovna Tikhomerova, "Dnevniki (1943–57)," entry for 8 December 1943, TsGALI, f. 510, op. 1, d. 38, l. 9.

37. Kochina, entries for 5 July 1941, 6 January 1942, 159, 181.

38. Ibid., entry for 9 January 1942, 181; translation modified from Elena Kochina, *Blockade Diary,* trans. Samuel C. Ramer (Ann Arbor, MI: Ardis, 1990), 70.

39. Lepkovich, entry for 31 December 1941, 14.

40. Ibid., entry for 10 February 1942, 16.

41. Ibid., entry for 21 February 1942, 17.

42. Ibid., entry for 27 March 1942, 17. On the police, see ibid., entry for 20 May 1942, 18.

43. Liubovskaia, undated diagram, 2; Kniazev, 5 July 1942, 54–55.

44. Ibid., entry for 20 May 1942, 18–18ob.

45. Ibid., entry for 20 September 1942, 200b–21.

46. Kochina, entries for 25, 26 November 1941, 166–67.

47. Levina, entry for 19 January 1942, 17–18.

48. Peterson, entry for 29 December 1941, 7ob–8. On her stepfather, see ibid., entries for 25, 29 December 1941, 60b–70b.

49. Riabinkin, entry for 28 November 1941, 109–10; translation modified to clarify and smooth out the English.

50. Ibid., entry for 15 December 1941, 146–48. Also see ibid., entry for 11 December 1941, 141.

51. Ales' Adamovich and Daniil Granin, *Leningrad under Siege: First-hand Accounts of the Ordeal,* trans. Clare Burstall and Vladimir Kisselnikov (Barnsley, UK: Military Pen and Sword, 2007), 199–202; Adamovich and Granin, *Blokadnaia kniga,* 378–82.

52. Matiushina, *Pesn' o zhizni,* 142.

53. Matiushina, Diary, 126–30, 134–36.

54. Ibid., 127.

55. Levina, entry for 16 January 1942, 2–3. Also see Gel'fer, entry for 19 January 1942, 20b; Kochina, entries for 9, 20, 26 December 1941, 17 January 1942, 174–77, 186.

56. Levina, entry for 19 January 1942, 5.

57. Ibid., entry for 4 March 1942, 12. For more examples, see ibid., entry 26 August 1942, 29; Mukhina 28 December 1941, 68–69.

58. Lepkovich, entry for 24 December 1941, 11–11ob.

59. Grishkevich, undated entry, 3–3ob. Also see Zelenskaia, entry for 9 January 1942, 500b.

60. *LP,* 28/XI/41, no. 284 (8077), 1; *LP,* 9/I/42, no. 7 (8113), 1; S. Voinov, "Priznanie Liudoedov (kak oni obstrelivali Leningrad)," *Leningrad* 6–7 (1944): 22–23; Ilya Ehrenburg, "A Pile of Skulls," in *Russia at War,* 70–71.

61. Bidlack and Lomagin, *Leningrad Blockade,* 315–23. Boris Belozerov has offered a lower figure, 1,380 arrests. Belozerov, "Crime during the Siege," in *Life and Death in Besieged Leningrad, 1941–44,* ed. John Barber and Andrei Dzeniskevich (London: Palgrave Macmillan, 2005), 223.

62. Bidlack and Lomagin, *Leningrad Blockade,* 316–19.

63. Grishkevich, undated entry, 40b. On famine's assault on the family and its relationship to cannibalism, see Cormac Ó Gráda, *Eating People Is Wrong and Other Essays on Famine, Its Past, and Its Future* (Princeton, NJ: Princeton University Press, 2015), 19–21.

64. A. Mironova, entry for 25 February 1942, 19.

65. Levina, entry for 3 February 1942, 6.

66. Zelenskaia, entry for 12 April 1942, 74ob–75.

67. Ibid., entry for 15 March 1942, 69.

68. Matiushina, Diary, 158–59.

69. There were great disparities among orphanages. Those designated for children of military personnel or with high-profile sponsors were better supplied. Mariia R. Zezina, "Without a Family: Orphans of the Postwar Period," *Russian Studies in History* 48, no. 4 (2010): 65–67. On famine and child abandonment, see Robert Dirks, "Social Reponses during Severe Food Shortages and Famine," *Current Anthropology* 21, no. 1 (1980): 30.

70. Korneeva, entry for 6 October 1942, 50–51.

71. Lewis Siegelbaum and Andrei Sokolov, *Stalinism as a Way of Life: A Narrative in Documents* (New Haven, CT: Yale University Press, 2000), 389–402.

72. Selivanov, *Stoiali kak soldaty,* 30, 50–59; Mariia R. Zezina, "The System of Social Protection for Orphaned Children in the USSR," *Russian Social Science Review* 42, no. 3 (2001): 49; Kelly, *Children's World,* 243, 246. According to Kelly, between 1941 and 1947, the number of orphanages in Soviet Russia more than doubled, from 1,661 to 3,900, and the number of their residents grew from 187,780 to 422,600.

73. Kelly, *Children's World,* 242–43.

74. One example is Petr Andreevich's short story "Life." Elizabeth White, "After the War Was Over: The Civilian Return to Leningrad," *Europe-Asia Studies* 59, no. 7 (2007): 1147; Zezina, "Without a Family," 63.

75. A. Mironova, entry for 20 December 1941, 14. Before the war, Mironova worked at School No. 14. After that school was converted into a hospital, she taught at School No. 6 until it closed in December 1941.

76. Ibid., "January 1942," 15ob.

77. Ibid., "Postscript," 30–30ob.

78. Aleksandra Nikolaevna Mironova, "Iz dnevnika Mironovoi Aleksandry Nikolaevny," in *Oborona Leningrada, 1941–1944: Vospominaniia i dnevniki uchastnikov,* ed. E. G. Dagin (Leningrad: Nauka, 1996), 754–61. This edition lacks all entries before September 1941, most between November and February 1942, and all from 1944. Some sections are rearranged.

79. A. Mironova, entry for 18 January 1942, 16.

80. Ibid., entry for 27 December 1941, 14–14ob.

81. Ibid., entry for 4 March 1942, 22–22ob.

82. Ibid., entry for 22 January 1942, 16–16ob. In the published version, this passage appears in the entry for 20 January 1942 (A. Mironova, "Iz dnevnika").

83. Ibid., entry for 31 February 1942, 20–20ob.

84. A. Mironova, entry for 28 January 1942, 17.

85. Ibid., entry for 25 February 1942, 19.

86. Kelly, *Children's World,* 246–47. Kelly notes that this decree was ineffective because of the lack of inspectors.

87. Korneeva, entries for 6, 8 October 1942, 50–51, 55.

88. Ibid., entries for 27 December, 31 February 1942, 14–14ob, 200b–21. (Entry dated 31/II/42 in manuscript, but author may have intended to write 3/III/42 and transposed the hyphen.)

89. Gorbunova, entries for 10, 15 April 1943, 320b, 330b–34.

90. Ibid., entry for 27 November 1942, 16–16ob. For other examples, see ibid., entries for 2, 8 December 1942, 2 March 1943, 18, 290b.

91. Ibid., entry for 27 November 1942, 16–16ob.

92. Ibid., entries for 1 December 1942, 7 May 1943, 170b, 370b–38.

93. Ibid., entry for 29 November 1942, 17.

94. Ibid., "Jan.–Feb. 1942," 70b.

95. For examples, see ibid., entries for 23 February, 8 March 1943, 29, 30.

96. Ibid., entry for 25 February 1943, 29–290b. Also in Savinkov, entry for 9 February 1943, 780b–800b.

97. Gel'fer, entry for 11 February 1942, 120b–13.

98. Ibid., entry for 19 January 1942, 40b, 20b.

99. Ibid., entries for 21, 26 January, 3 February 1942, 5, 60b,10.

100. Ibid., entries for 9, 16, 27 March 1942, 140b–150b, 18.

101. Ibid., entry for 29 April 1942, 20.

102. Ibid., entry for 12 May 1942, 210b–22. There is a similar reaction to the lack of letters in ibid., entry 22 April 1942, 19.

103. Ibid., entries for 3 July, 14 August 1942, 250b, 280b.

104. Krakov, entry for 17 January 1943, 51–52.

105. Examples in Buianov, undated entry, 58–60; Mervol'f, entry for 6 May 1942, 66–68.

106. Examples in Aleksandra Pavlovna Zagorskaia, entries for 19 September 1941, 12–18 October 1941, 12, 26 January 1942, 4 February 1942, 2–3 April 1942, TsGAIPD, f. 4000, op. 11, d. 33, ll. 3, 60b, 7, 100b–110b, 130b, 170b–19.

107. Ibid., entry for 4 March 1942, 16. More on her returned letters in ibid., entry for 23–26 March 1942, 180b–19.

108. Ibid., entry for 20 May 1942, 22.

109. Ibid., entry for 22 June 1942, 24.

110. Ibid., entry for 22 June 1943, 300b–31.

111. Vladimir Kuz'mich Makarov, entries for 16 October, 6 December 1942, OR RNB, f. 1135, d. 55, l. 40b (hereafter "Makarov, Diary"). Z. P. Annenkova rewrote the diary to be more legible. The original manuscript, in his hand, is in OR RNB, f. 1135, d. 54.

112. Makarov, Diary, entry for 17 October 1942, 5–7.

113. This can be seen from the addresses Makarov used. Vladimir Kuz'mich Makarov, "Pis'ma (84) Zinaide Pavlovne Annenkovoi," letters of 31 March, 21 February, 5, 6 March 1945, OR RNB, f. 1135, d. 475, ll. 9–11, 64 (hereafter "Makarov, Letters").

114. Makarov, Letters, 12, 17 March 1945, 26–27, 34.

115. Makarov, Letters, 29 March, 5, 13 April 1945, 60, 80, 84.

116. Makarov, Diary, entries for 12 February, 28 March 1945, 123ob–24. On unsent letters written to maintain family bonds, see Albert Pleysier, *Frozen Tears: The Blockade and Battle of Leningrad* (New York: University Press of America, 2008), 94–109.
117. Makarov, Letters, 12 March 1945, 26–27ob.
118. Ibid., 6 March, 9 May 1945, 6–7, 140.
119. Ibid., 14 April 1945, 94. The nickname "Konti" appears throughout and in Romanized script.
120. Makarov, Diary, entry for 15 February 1945, 124.
121. Ibid., entry for 29–30 April 1945, 130ob.
122. Ibid., entry for 15 November 1945, 144.
123. Ibid., entry for 9–11 November 1945, 143ob, original underlined. For more examples, see ibid., entries for 3 June, 10 August 1945, 132–32ob, 136.
124. Makarov, Letters, 17 April 1945, 100.
125. Ibid., 2 April 1945, 70.
126. Ibid., 30 May 1945, 162. "Somov-like" may refer to Orest Somov, who painted the city in an eighteenth-century style.
127. Ibid., 7 May 1945, 136ob.
128. Although different, these accounts are not mutually exclusive. Levina claimed that both were accurate, declaring, "I did not add anything to what I wrote down in the days of the siege" (Levina, "Pis'ma k drugu," 195).
129. Ibid., 200–202, 210, 217.
130. Ibid., 204.
131. Ibid., 217, 213.
132. Ibid., 214–15.
133. Zezina, "Without a Family," 59.
134. White, "After the War," 1145–61; Rebecca Manley, *To the Tashkent Station: Evacuation and Survival in the Soviet Union at War* (Ithaca, NY: Cornell University Press), 246, 259–60.

5. THE HIERARCHY OF LIVES

1. Kniazev, entry for 4 February 1942, 447.
2. Afanas'ev, entries for 12 May, 13 June 1942, 140, 156; Mukhina, entries for 16, 22 October, 7, 9, 17 December 1941, 500b–510b, 56ob, 59–72.
3. Levina, entry for 1 February 1942, 5–6.
4. Examples in Levina, entries for 27 January 1942, 27 September 1942, 4–5, 30.
5. Levina, entry for 18 October 1942, 32.
6. Erokhana, entry for 13 June 1943, 56–57.
7. Levina, entry for 21 February 1942, 10; Ginzburg, "Zapiski blokadnogo cheloveka," 355–57.
8. Likhacheva, entry for 16 May 1942, 684.
9. Erokhana, entry for 26 January 1944, 61.
10. I emphasize these sites because of their prominence, but they were not the only settings of social activity and observation. Also critical were street corners and markets,

the latter of which are analyzed by Jeffrey Hass in *Fields of War, Survival, and Suffering* (unpublished manuscript).

11. As the sociologist Jane Roj Zavisca explains, "Class identities are forged in the process of making sense of the relationship between what is produced and what is consumed, what is deserved and what is distributed. Class identifications also operate as status claims." Zavisca, "Consumer Inequalities and Regime Legitimacy in Late Soviet and Post-Soviet Russia" (Ph.D. diss., University of California, Berkeley, 2004), ii. On the conflation of status and class, see Richard B. Dobson, "Socialism and Social Stratification," in *Contemporary Soviet Society: Sociological Perspectives,* ed. Jerry G. Pankhurst and Michael Paul Sacks (New York: Praeger, 1980), 88–114; Shelia Fitzpatrick, "Ascribing Class: The Construction of Social Identity in Soviet Russia," *Journal of Modern History* 65, no. 4 (1993): 745–70; Jean-Paul Depretto, "Stratification without Class," *Kritika* 8, no. 2 (2007): 380; Mauricio Borrero, *Hungry Moscow: Scarcity and Urban Society in the Russian Civil War, 1917–1921* (New York: Peter Lang, 2003), 120–38.

12. Similar debates transpired in other national contexts. See Louise A. Tilly, "Food, Entitlement, Famine, and Conflict," in *Hunger and History: The Impact of Changing Food Production and Consumption Patterns on Society,* ed. Robert I. Rothberg, Theodore K. Rabb, and Esther Boserup (Cambridge: Cambridge University Press, 1985), 135–52; Ina Zweiniger-Bargielowska, "Fair Shares? The Limits of Food Policy in Britain during the Second World War," in *Food and War in Twentieth-Century Europe,* ed. Ina Zweiniger-Bargielowska, Rachel Duffett, and Alain Drouard (Farnham, UK: Ashgate, 2011), 125; Mark Roodhouse, "Popular Morality and the Black Market in Britain, 1939–1955," in *Food and Conflict in Europe in the Age of the Two World Wars,* ed. Frank Trentmann and Just Flemming (New York: Palgrave Macmillan, 2006), 243–65.

13. Here I refer to the *klassovoi paek* and *trudovoi paek.* On the evolution of the class and labor rations in Moscow and Petrograd, see Borrero, *Hungry Moscow,* 115–17; Mary McAuley, *Bread and Justice: State and Security in Petrograd, 1917–1922* (Oxford, UK: Clarendon, 1991), 285–90. Also see Julie Hessler, *A Social History of Trade: Trade Policy, Retail Practices, and Consumption, 1917–1953* (Princeton, NJ: Princeton University Press, 2004), 63; Elena Osokina, *Our Daily Bread: Socialist Distribution and the Art of Survival in Stalin's Russia, 1927–1941,* ed. Kate Transchel (New York: M. E. Sharpe, 2001), xv, 69, 83, 197.

14. Zavisca, "Consumer Inequalities," 41. Lenin articulated this doctrine in *State and Revolution,* specifically in chapter 5, "The Economic Basis of the Withering Away of the State." V. I. Lenin, *Essential Works of Lenin: "What Is to Be Done" and Other Writings,* ed. Henry M. Christman (New York: Dover, 1987), 340–43.

15. Borrero, *Hungry Moscow,* 116.

16. Ginzburg, "Vokrug 'Zapisok blokadnogo cheloveka,'" in *Zapisnye knizhki. Vospominaniia. Esse,* ed. A. S. Kushner (St. Petersburg: Iskusstvo, 2002), 725; translation from Ginzburg, *Blockade Diary,* 81.

17. Kostrovitskaia, "September, October, 1941," 2.

18. Richard Bidlack and Nikita Lomagin, *The Leningrad Blockade, 1941–44: A New Documentary History from the Soviet Archives* (New Haven, CT: Yale University Press, 2012),

154; Stephanie Steiner, "The Food Distribution System during the Siege of Leningrad" (M.A. thesis, San Jose State University, 1993), 45–49.

19. Zelenskaia, entry for 6 January 1942, 49–49ob. For useful analyses of Soviet line culture, see Hessler, *Social History of Trade,* 40–41, 138–40; V. G. Nikolaev, *Sovetskaia ochered' kak sreda obitaniia: Sotsiologicheskii analiz* (Moscow: RAN, 2000), 8–69.

20. Kostrovitskaia, "September, October 1941," 2.

21. Nikitin, entry for 21 November 1941, 64; Konopleva, entry for 25 December 1941, 12–13; Punin, entries for 25 September, 20 November 1941, 98.

22. Kostrovitskaia, "September, October 1941," 3; Kochina, entries for 4 December 1941, 13 January 1942, 30 March 1942, 167–68, 184, 204–5.

23. Boris Apollonovich Lesin, "Dnevnik Borisa Apollonovicha Lesina," entry for 28 June 1942, TsGAIPD, f. 4000, op. 11, d. 61, l. 15 (hereafter "Lesin"); Savinkov, entry for 30 May 1942, 390ob–40.

24. Ginzburg, "Zapiski blokadnogo cheloveka," 333–35; translation modified from Ginzburg, *Blockade Diary,* 38–40. On line waiting as imprisonment, see Richard C. Larson, "Perspectives on Queues: Social Justice and the Psychology of Queuing," *Operations Research* 35, no. 6 (1987): 897.

25. Levina, entry for 16 January 1942, 2. For additional examples, see Kochina, entry for 9 January 1942, 181; Vera Inber, entry for 25 December 1941, in *Pochti tri goda* (Moscow: Sovetskaia Rossiia, 1968), 4 (this entry does not appear in the manuscript of Inber's diary).

26. Levina, entry for 16 January 1942, 2. The reference is to Popov's speech of 13 January 1942, in which he claimed, "All of the worst is behind us. Ahead of us lies the liberation of Leningrad and the deliverance of Leningraders from death by starvation."

27. Zelenskaia, entry for 6 January 1942, 49ob–50. She cited diminutives for food, like "lovely little meatballs *[kakleta]*" (which mimics how a child mispronounces the word *kotleta*) and *kashka,* meaning "lovely little porridge."

28. Ginzburg, "Zapiski blokadnogo cheloveka," 333–39; translation modified from Ginzburg, *Blockade Diary,* 38–46. Ginzburg studied line chatter as a form of self-assertion when conversation became more prevalent in summer 1942.

29. Afanas'ev, entry for 11 November 1941, 77.

30. Ginzburg, "Zapiski blokadnogo cheloveka," 333–36; translation from Ginzburg, *Blockade Diary,* 38–40.

31. On how lines make all markers of privilege other than position irrelevant, see Erving Goffman, *Relations in Public: Microstudies of the Public Order* (New York: Basic Books, 1971), 36–37. On the line as "a miniature social system," see Leon Mann, "Queue Culture: The Waiting Line as a Social System," *American Journal of Sociology* 75, no. 3 (1969): 340–54.

32. Levina, entry for 3 February 1942, 6.

33. Sociologists and psychologists have suggested that social comparison is a primary activity of line waiting. Leon Festinger, a pioneer of social comparison theory, found that people tend to "compare upwardly" to the person ahead of them. Festinger, "A Theory of Social Comparison Processes," *Human Relations* 7 (1954): 117–40. On when and why people compare downwardly, see Joanne V. Wood, Shelley E. Taylor, and Rosemary R. Lichtman, "Social Comparison in Adjustment to Breast Cancer," *Journal of Personality and Social Psychology* 49 (1985): 1169–83; Rongrong Zhou and

Dilip Soman, "Looking Back: Exploring the Psychology of Queuing and the Effect of the Number of People Behind," *Journal of Consumer Research* 24, no. 4 (2003): 518.

34. Kochina, entry for 4 December 1941, 167–68; translation from Kochina, *Blockade Diary*, 49.

35. Levina, entry for 3 February 1942, 6.

36. Kostrovitskaia, "September, October 1941," 2.

37. Kniazev, entry for 22 December 1941, 358–59.

38. Matus, entry for 26 December 1941, 16.

39. Riabinkin, entry for 9–10 November 1941, 104. Rudykovskaia noted how "a big girl" stole her ration card in line (entry for 10 September 1942, 23–24).

40. Levina, entry for 3 February 1942, 6; Matus, entry for 29 January 1942, 46–47 (she mistakenly wrote "January 1941").

41. Konopleva, entries for 23 July, 22, 24 September, 1941, 29, 98–101.

42. Levina, entry for 3 February 1942, 6.

43. Kochina, entries for 13, 27 January 1942, 184, 191.

44. On solidarity and altruism in lines, see Sof'ia Gorkhart, "Leningrad. Blokada," in Vikhnovicha, ed., *Dve sud'by,* 47–48; Ales' Adamovich and Daniil Granin, *Blokadnaia kniga* (St. Petersburg: Pechatnyi dvor, 1994), 113–25. On the distinction between cooperation and solidarity in German and Soviet concentration camps, see Tzvetan Todorov, *Facing the Extreme: Moral Life in the Concentration Camps,* trans. Arthur Denner and Abigail Pollak (New York: Metropolitan Books/Holt, 1996), 82–84.

45. Kochina, entry for 25 January 1942, 191; translation from Kochina, *Blockade Diary,* 83. The two other main examples of altruism that I have found in diaries are N. Sudakova, "Dnevnik, 22 / I / 41-15 / IV / 42," entry for 1 April 1942, TsGAIPD, f. 4000, op. 10, d. 1387, l. 7; Sedel'nikova, entry for 2 February 1942, 71.

46. Matus, entry for 19 January 1942, 42.

47. Richard Bidlack and John Barber have suggested that protests erupted in Moscow because Soviet officials were evacuated at the same time that conditions and supplies were at their worst. These events did not coincide in Leningrad. See Barber, "War, Public Opinion, and the Struggle for Survival, 1941–45: The Case of Leningrad," in *Russia in the Age of Wars, 1914–1945,* ed. Silvio Pons and Andrea Romano (Milan: Feltrinelli Editore, 2000), 266–67; Barber, "The Moscow Crisis of October 1941," in *Soviet History 1917–1953: Essays in Honour of R. W. Davies,* ed. Julian Cooper, Maureen Perrie and E. A. Rees (Basingstoke, UK: Macmillan, 1995), 201; Richard Bidlack, "Propaganda and Public Opinion," in *The Soviet Union at War, 1941–1945,* ed. David R. Stone (Barnsley, UK: Military Pen and Sword, 2010), 57.

48. For rare mentions of "closed stores," see Erokhana, entry for 4 November 1941, 27; *LP,* 31/III/44, no. 78 (8802), 3. On closed canteens, see Hessler, *Social History of Trade,* 65–67.

49. On the extensive use of canteens in Moscow and Petrograd during the Civil War, see Mauricio Borrero, "Communal Dining and State Cafeterias in Moscow and Petrograd, 1917–1921," in *Food in Russian History and Culture,* ed. Musya Glants and Joyce Toomre (Bloomington: Indiana University Press, 1997), 162–76. On Soviet canteens during World War II, see Aleksandr Liubimov, *Torgovlia i snabzhenie v gody velikoi otechestvennoi voiny* (Moscow: Ekonomika, 1968), 112–23.

50. On the expansion of canteens and food stores, see these issues of *LP*: 26/X/41, no. 256 (8049), 4; 7/V/42, no. 107 (8213), 2; 17/V/42, no. 116 (8222), 2; 26/IX/42, no. 229 (8335), 2; no. 6 (8421), 4; 20/X/42, no. 275 (8381), 4; 21/IV/42, no. 93 (8199), 4.

51. Nikitin, entry for 21 November 1941, 67; Levina, entry for 5 August 1942, 28; Zelenskaia, entry for 13 November 1941; Gal'ko, entry for 28 November 1941, 513.

52. Levina, entry for 14 April 1942, 18. For other examples, see Nikitin, entry for 21 November, 1941, 67; Zelenskaia, entries for 18 November, 12, 23 December 1941, 330b, 420b, 460b–47.

53. Levina, entry for 5 August 1942, 28.

54. Ginzburg, "Zapiski blokadnogo cheloveka," 345.

55. Nikitin, entry for 21 November 1941, 67; Lepkovich, entry for 13 December 1941, 60b–7.

56. Mary Douglas and Baron Isherwood, *The World of Goods: Towards an Anthropology of Consumption* (New York: Routledge, 1996), 68; quoted in Zavisca, "Consumer Inequalities," 23.

57. On class and conduct as two ways to display worthiness, see Amir Weiner, "Nature, Nurture, and Memory in Soviet Utopia: Delineating the Soviet Socio-Economic Body in the Age of Socialism," *American Historical Review* 104, no. 4 (1994): 1115. On *kul'turnost'* and individual consumption, see Vera Dunham, *In Stalin's Time: Middle Class Values in Soviet Literature* (Cambridge: Cambridge University Press, 1976); Catriona Kelly, "*Kul'turnost'* in the Soviet Union: Ideal and Reality," in *Reinterpreting Russia*, ed. Geoffrey Hosking and Robert Service (Oxford: Oxford University Press, 1999), 198–213. A classic argument on how manners display one's worthiness to belong to a society, class, or nation is in Norbert Elias, *The Civilizing Process: Sociogenetic and Psychogenetic Investigations* (Oxford, UK: Blackwell, 2000).

58. Liubovskaia, entry for 17 May 1942, 153.

59. Levina, entry for 17 October 1942, 31.

60. Liubovskaia, entry for 20 January, 1942, 56. On "upward" comparison in Civil War canteens, see Borrero, *Hungry Moscow,* 158.

61. Matus, entry for 29 January 1942, 47. She accidentally dated this entry 1941.

62. Zelenskaia, entries for 22 September, 3 December 1941, 18, 370b–380b.

63. Ibid., entry for 21 May 1942, 810b–82.

64. Richard Bidlack, "Workers at War: Factory Workers and Labor Policy in the Siege of Leningrad," *Carl Beck Papers in Russian and East European Studies,* no. 902 (1991): 24; Bidlack and Lomagin, *Leningrad Blockade,* 289, 161–62, 309–13. Bidlack and Lomagin offer the most recent statistics on theft: between December 1941 and March 1942, when the "Road to Life" was active, 818 people were arrested for stealing from food trucks.

65. Another example of a critique from diarists who benefited in Afanas'ev, entries for 7 November 1941, 23 December 1941, 3 January 1942, 76, 85, 89.

66. Savinkov, entry for 25 February 1942, 24.

67. Ibid., entry for 22 September 1942, 59. For more examples, see Riabinkin, entries for 9–10 November 1941, 102–3; Uskova, entry for 10 January 1942, 46.

68. Nikitin, entry for 28 November 1941, 68. For another example, see Anna Petrovna Ostroumova-Lebedeva, entry for 22 May 1942, OR RNB, f. 1015, d. 58, l. 31 (hereafter

"Ostroumova-Lebedeva"). On criminal rings of cooks, bookkeepers, and stockroom workers, see Bidlack and Lomagin, *Leningrad Blockade,* 161–62, 309–13.

69. Steiner, "Food Distribution System," 25, 72.
70. Nikitin, 28 November 1941, 68. Also see Kostrovitskaia, "January 1942," 20.
71. Levina, entry for 21 July 1942, 27.
72. Kochina, entry for 5 April 1942, 206; translation from Kochina, *Blockade Diary,* 106–7.
73. Kochina, entry for 23 November, 1941, 166; translation modified from Kochina, *Blockade Diary,* 47.
74. Savinkov, entry for 22 September 1942, 59–59ob.
75. Zelenskaia, entry for 22 August 1942, 96. For another example, see Kostrovskaia, "May [1942]," 38.
76. Zelenskaia, entry for 22 August 1942, 96. This discussion on the relationship between physical and moral purity harks back to debates over how party members (especially women) should look in the years after the 1921 famine. As Eric Naiman demonstrates, thin women who lacked strong secondary sexual traits were considered exemplars of discipline and ideological purity. Naiman, *Sex in Public: Incarnation of Early Soviet Ideology* (Princeton, NJ: Princeton University Press, 1997), 214–15.
77. Erokhana, entry for 13 June 1943, 57.
78. Savinkov, entry for 22 September 1942, 59–59ob.
79. Ibid.
80. On theft, see these issues of *LP*: 20/XI/41, no. 277 (8070), 4; 13/XII/41, no. 297 (8090), 4; 13/I/42, no. 10 (8116), 2; 9/IV/42, no. 83 (8189), 2; 2/VI/42, no. 129 (8235), 2; 31/VII/42, no. 180 (8286), 4; 5/VIII/42, no. 184 (8290), 2; 13/VIII/42, no. 191 (8297), 2; 15/IX/42, no. 219 (8325), 4; 14/X/42, no. 244 (8350), 3; 15/IX/43, no. 218 (8635), 2. Berkhoff argued that this practice of blaming locals, not the ration system, occurred across the war-torn USSR (Berkhoff, *Motherland in Danger,* 98, 101–3).
81. *LP*'s first article on hunger in Leningrad appeared on 20 December 1941. It tried to reassure readers of the effectiveness of city canteens, while conceding long lines, a lack of utensils, and "no shortage of swindlers who are not averse to profiting at the consumer's expense." A second appeared nearly a year later, in October 1942. On exposés of canteens, see *LP*, 20/XII/41, no. 303 (8096), 2; *LP*, 16/X/42, no. 246 (8352), 4.
82. *LP*, 20/XII/41, no. 303 (8096), 2; *LP*, 16/X/42, no. 246 (8352), 4.
83. *LP*, 20/II/43, no. 42 (8457), 2. For more examples, see these issues of *LP*: 24/XI/42, no. 278 (8384) 3; 2/XII/42, no. 285 (8391), 2; 19/I/43, no. 15 (8430), 3; 6/VII/43, no. 157 (8572), 3; 3/IX/43, no. 208 (8623), 3; 8/X/43, no. 238 (8653), 3; 25/XI/43, no. 273 (8693), 3; 30/XI/43, no. 282 (8697), 3; 10/XII/43, no. 291 (8706), 3; 13/II/44, no. 38 (8762) 3; 31/III/44, no. 78 (8802), 3; 20/VI/44, no. 146 (8870), 3; 13/VII/44, no. 166 (8890), 3; 29/VII/44, no. 180 (8904), 3; 25/VIII/44, no. 203 (8927), 3; 12/X/44, no. 244 (8968), 3; 18/X/44, no. 249 (8973), 3; 29/XI/44, no. 284 (9008), 3.
84. Bidlack and Lomagin, *Leningrad Blockade,* 346.
85. *LP*, 6/X/44, no. 239 (8963), 1.
86. Bidlack and Lomagin, *Leningrad Blockade,* 292.

87. Bidlack, "Workers at War," 20–21, 24–25. Bidlack notes that the data from other factories is sparse and that figures may be skewed because most workers were men and so died at higher rates during the first winter.

88. Anisima Prokof'evicha Nikulin, "Dnevnik i drugie materialy Anisima Prokof'evicha Nikulina," entry for 1–10 July 1941, TsGAIPD, f. 4000, op. 11, d. 80, ll. 1ob–2 (hereafter "Nikulin").

89. Zelenskaia, entry for 19 March 1942, 70.

90. Dmitri V. Pavlov, *Leningrad 1941,* trans. John Clinton Adams (Chicago: University of Chicago Press, 1965), 77. More workers received Category I rations when industry resumed. On similar disputes about workers' rations in wartime Germany and France, see Kenneth Mouré, *"Réalités Cruelles,* State Controls and the Black Market in Occupied France," in Zweiniger-Bargielowska, Duffett, and Drouard, *Food and War,* 125–28, 174–73; Lizzie Collingham, *Taste of War: World War II and the Battle for Food* (New York: Penguin, 2012), 367.

91. On petitions for and fluctuations in Category I, see Bidlack and Lomagin, *Leningrad Blockade,* 297.

92. Fitzpatrick, "Ascribing Class," 751.

93. Ostroumova-Lebedeva, entry for 22 May 1942, 33.

94. Borrero, *Hungry Moscow,* 121; Aleksandr N. Boldyrev, *Osadnaia zapis': Blokadnyi dnevnik,* entry for 29 March 1942 (St. Petersburg: Evropeiskii Dom, 1998), 78 (hereafter "Boldyrev").

95. Bidlack and Lomagin, *Leningrad Blockade,* 188–89; Bidlack, "Workers at War," 16–23, 29.

96. Liubovskaia, entry for 16 November 1941, 11–12. Some factories ordered workers to read to prevent mental idleness (Bidlack and Lomagin, *Leningrad Blockade,* 52n86).

97. Bidlack and Lomagin, *Leningrad Blockade,* 294–96.

98. Uskova, entry for 15 March 1942, 49–50.

99. Levina, entry for 3 August 1942, 25.

100. Zelenskaia, entries for 9 October, 9 April 1942, 102–3, 73.

101. Ibid., entry for 2 May 1942, 78ob.

102. Ibid., entry for 27 September 1941, 20.

103. Ibid., entry for 24 September 1942, 18ob–19.

104. Ibid., entries for 23, 24 September 1941, 18ob.

105. Ibid., entry for 11 October 1941, 22ob.

106. Ibid., entries for 24 October, 1 November 1941, 25–26ob.

107. Ibid., entry for 1 November 1941, 26ob.

108. Ibid., entry for 23 December 1942, 46ob–47.

109. Bidlack and Lomagin, *Leningrad Blockade,* 29, 299–301. On the controversy over allowing party members to move from Category II to Category I during the Civil War, see Borrero, *Hungry Moscow,* 120, 137.

110. Matus, entry for 18 January 1942, 40.

111. Mukhina, entry for 3 January 1942, 72ob.

112. Ribkovskii, quoted in Natalia Kozlova, ed., *Sovetskie liudi: Stseni iz istorii* (Moscow: Evropa, 2005), 264–67.

113. Ribkovskii, quoted in ibid., 268–69.

114. Zelenskaia, entry for 5 September 1942, 98–98ob.

115. Ibid., entry for 17 August 1942, 95–96.

116. Savinkov, entry for 25 October 1941, 8–9.

117. Sokolova, entry for 27 October, 23–23ob.

118. Ibid., entry for 1 November 1941, 25ob.

119. Ibid., entry for 24 December 1941, 35–35ob.

120. Ibid., entry for 28 November 1941, 32ob. The question of whether party members should receive extra rations (and be more active) or receive the same as other citizens recalls debates after the 1921 famine (Naiman, *Sex in Public,* 210–14).

121. Sokolova, entry for 24 December 1941, 34ob.

122. Shumilov later championed "the exceptional role" played by Istpart. When naming its heroic staff, he did not mention Sokolova. Nikolai Shumilov, *V dni blokady* (Moscow: Mysl', 1974), 28–29, 50.

123. Sokolova, entry for 28 November 1941, 30. Similarly, Shumilov claimed in his postwar account that "communists, like all residents, endured the deprivations and hardships of the blockade" (Shumilov, *V dni blokady,* 109).

124. Sokolova, entry for 28 November 1941, 32ob.

125. Levina, entry for 25 March 1942, 15. For useful studies on the body incarnating status, see Nancy Scheper-Hughes and Margaret M. Lock, "The Mindful Body: A Prolegomenon to Future Work in Medical Anthropology," *Medical Anthropology Quarterly* 1, no. 1 (1987): 6–41; Bryan S. Turner, *The Body and Society: Explorations in Social Theory* (London: Sage, 1996), 112.

126. On the *bania,* especially as a gendered space, see Ethan Pollock, "'Real Men Go to the Bania': Postwar Soviet Masculinities in the Bathhouse," *Kritika* 11, no. 1 (2010): 46–70; Nancy Condee, "The Second Fantasy Mother, or All Baths and Women's Baths," in *Russia, Women and Culture,* ed. Helena Goscilo and Beth Holmgren (Bloomington: Indiana University Press, 1996), 3–30.

127. I am indebted to Lisa Kirschenbaum's and Polina Barskova's research on various aspects of the blockade *bania*—survivors' guilt, sense memory, blurred distinctions between soldier and civilian, and notions of an aesthetic and the "anesthetic" siege body. Kirschenbaum, "'The Alienated Body': Gender, Identity and the Memory of the Siege of Leningrad," in *Gender and War in Twentieth-Century Eastern Europe,* ed. Nancy M. Wingfield and Maria Bucur (Bloomington: Indiana University Press, 2006), 229–31; Barskova, "The Corpse, the Corpulent, and the Other: A Study in the Tropology of Siege Body Representation," *Ab Imperio* 1 (2009): 370–86.

128. Bathhouse 16 in the Dzerzhinskii District won. *LP,* 3/VIII/43, no. 181 (8596). For an example of a letter to the editor complaining about *bania* conditions, see *LP,* 7/VIII/43, no. 3 (8600), 3.

129. Savinkov, entry for 26 January 1942, 19.

130. Liubovskaia, entry for 1 March 1942, 109.

131. Nikolai Aleksandrovich Berngardt, entry for 4 August 1941, TsGAIPD, f. 4000, op. 11, d. 1807, ll. 24–27.

132. Liubovskaia, entries for 10, 16 July 1942, 173, 183.

133. Ibid., entry for 16 July 1942, 183.
134. Ibid.
135. For similar imagery of washing as a form of healing, see Zelenskaia, entry for 6 February 1942, 61–61ob.
136. Ostroumova-Lebedeva, entry for 22 May 1942, 31–33.
137. Ol'ga Berggol'ts, "Dnevnye zvezdy," in *Vstrecha* (Moscow: Russkaia Kniga, 2000), 199–201.
138. Sedel'nikova, entry for 5 September 1941, 18.
139. Ibid.
140. Byl'ev, "Iz dnevnika," in *Khudozhniki goroda-fronta: Vospominaniia i dnevniki leningradskikh khudozhnikov,* ed. Iosif Anatol'evich Brodskii (Leningrad: Khudozhnik RSFSR, 1973), 337; this passage is not in the manuscript of his diary.
141. Barskova, "Corpse, the Corpulent, and the Other," 370–86.

6. THE CITY AS MEDICAL LABORATORY

1. Sedel'nikova, entry for 9 October 1941, 28.
2. Ibid., entry for 4 March 1942, 80. She made this comment about wartime medicine while working at an evacuation center.
3. Ibid., entry for 18 December 1941, 53.
4. Ibid., 52–53.
5. Ibid.
6. Ibid., entries for 18, 19 December 1941, 53.
7. On the clinic as a site of political negotiation, see Laurinda Abreu and Sally Sheard, eds., *Hospital Life: Theory and Practice from the Medieval to the Modern* (Oxford, UK: Peter Lang, 2013).
8. "Biopolitics," based on Michel Foucault's "biopower," has been used in many disciplines to describe practices of protecting and regulating life. Foucault's notion of biopower and elaborations of it by Giorgio Agamben, Michael Hardt, and Antonio Negri argue that a sovereign state's ultimate power is to govern the lives of its population through the regulation of medical meaning, expertise, and intervention. I evoke biopolitics loosely to highlight the relationship between biological, social, and political structures. I concentrate on the development of body beliefs by both professionals and amateurs. Of this vast literature, I particularly consulted Paul Rabinow and Nikolas Rose, "Biopower Today," *Biosocieties* 1, no. 2 (2006): 195–217; Majia Holmer Nadesan, *Governmentality, Biopower, and Everyday Life* (New York: Routledge, 2008), 8–9; Thomas Lemke, *Biopolitics: An Advanced Introduction,* trans. Eric Frederick Trump (New York: New York University Press, 2011). Classic formulations of biopolitics include Michel Foucault, *The Birth of the Clinic* (London: Tavistock, 1973); Foucault, *Discipline and Punish: the Birth of the Prison* (London: Allen Lane, 1977); Foucault, *The History of Sexuality* (London: Allen Lane, 1979); Giorgio Agamben, *Remnants of Auschwitz: The Witness and the Archive* (New York: Zone Books, 1999); Agamben, *State of Exception* (Chicago: University of Chicago Press, 2005); Michael Hardt and Antonio Negri, *Empire* (Cambridge, MA: Harvard University Press, 2000).

9. The best survey of medical research during the siege is Andrei Dzeniskevich, "Medical Research Institutes during the Siege," in *Life and Death in Besieged Leningrad, 1941–44,* ed. John Barber and Andrei Dzeniskevich (London: Palgrave Macmillan, 2005), 86–122. Most of the studies Dzeniskevich cites are from spring 1942 or later.

10. Svetlana Magaeva, "Physiological and Psychosomatic Prerequisites for Survival and Recovery," in Barber and Dzeniskevich, *Life and Death,* 156–57. I am indebted to the studies of professional medical research in Barber and Dzeniskevich, *Life and Death;* P. F. Gladkikh, *Zdravookhranenie i voennaia meditsina v bitve za Leningrad glazami istorika i ochevidtsev: 1941–1944* (St. Petersburg: Dmitrii Bulanin, 2006).

11. Substitutions in Gal'ko, entry for 11 December 1942, 532; Aleksei Kornil'evich Kozlovskii, "Iz dnevnika Kozlovskogo Alekseia Kornil'evicha," entry for 28 January 1942, in *Oborona Leningrada, 1941–1944: Vospominaniia i dnevniki uchastnikov,* ed. E. G. Dagin (Leningrad: Nauka, 1996), 575 (hereafter "Kozlovskii").

12. Christopher Burton, "Medical Welfare during Late Stalinism: A Study of Doctors and the Soviet Health System, 1945-1953" (Ph.D. diss., University of Chicago, 2000), 27.

13. V. O. Samoilov, "Leningradskie fiziologi v gody Velikoi Otechestvennoi voiny," in *Leningradskaia nauka v gody Velikoi Otechestvennoi Voiny,* E. M. Balashov, E. A. Tropp, V. A. Shishkin, ed. (St. Petersburg: Nauka, 1995), 50–54; N. G. Ivanov, A. S. Georgievskii, and O. S. Lobastov, *Sovetskoe zdravookhranenie i voennaia meditsina v Velikoi Otechestvennoi Voine 1941–45* (Leningrad: Meditsina, 1985), 200; Burton, "Medical Welfare," 62, 219.

14. Christopher Burton, "Soviet Medical Attestation and the Problem of Professionalisation under Late Stalinism, 1945-1953," *Europe-Asia Studies* 57, no. 8 (2005): 1218. Burton argues that the postwar professionalization of medicine was spurred by suspicions that the doctors who received this truncated training were incompetent.

15. Mary Schaeffer Conroy, *Medicines for the Soviet Masses during World War II* (Lanham, MD: University Press of America, 2008), 20–21, 40–47; Nadezhda Cherepenina, "The Demographic Situation and Health Care on the Eve of the War," in Barber and Dzeniskevich, *Life and Death,* 18–19.

16. "Protokol No. 50 zasedaniia biuro Lengorkom VKP(b), II chast'," 10/XII/41–9/I/42, TsGAIPD, f. 25, op. 2, d. 4408, l. 20; Gladkikh, *Zdravookhranenie,* 28.

17. Before the Health Department issued its first comprehensive report in April 1942, hospital mortality rates were unclear. Some records did not distinguish between patients discharged and deceased. The average hospital mortality rate in 1942 was 24.43 percent, ranging from 40.8 percent at the start of the year to 3.7 percent at the end. In Karl Marx Hospital, the death rate climbed to 84 percent in January 1942. Nadezhda Cherepenina, "Assessing the Scale of Famine and Death in the Besieged City," in Barber and Dzeniskevich, *Life and Death,* 46–48. G. L. Sobolev gives a 72 percent mortality rate for hospitals in 1942. Sobolev, *Uchenye Leningrada v gody velikoi otechestvennoi voiny, 1941–1945,* ed. V. M. Koval'chuk (Moscow: Nauka, 1966), 66. On clinicians' morale, see "Stenogramma Prof. Lopotko Ignatiia Anatol'evicha, direktora instituta po bolezniam ukha, gorlo, nosa, i rechi, 20/II/43," TsGAIPD, f. 4000, op. 10, d. 353, ll. 10–20.

18. On vitamin C manufacture, see Protokol No. 53, Zasedaniia biuro Lengorkom VKP(b), 18/II/42–9/III/42, TsGAIPD, f. 25, op 2, d. 4445, l. 9. On efforts to teach Leningraders about edible plants, vitamins, and cooking, see the following issues of *LP:* 29/V/1942, no. 126 (8232), 2; 2/X/1942, no. 234 (8340), 4; 20/XI/1942, no. 275 (8381), 4; 2/X/42, no. 234 (8240), 4; 16/XII/42, no. 296 (8402), 2. On efforts to control disease, see Donald Filtzer, *The Hazards of Urban Life: Health, Hygiene, and Living Standards, 1943–1953* (Cambridge: Cambridge University Press, 2010), 149–56.

19. Soviet research on the Petrograd famine is reviewed in Ancel Keys, Josef Brožek, Austin Henschel, Olaf Mickelsen, and Henry Longstreet Taylor, *The Biology of Human Starvation,* 2 vols. (Minneapolis: University of Minnesota Press, 1950), 2: 789–818.

20. For analyses of undernutrition and malnutrition for a general audience, see John R. Butterly and Jack Shepherd, *Hunger: The Biology and Politics of Starvation* (Hanover, NH: Dartmouth College Press, 2010), 124–77.

21. Misdiagnoses are discussed in M. I. Slonim, "Alimentarnaia distrofiia v usloviikh voennogo vremeni," in *Izbrannye raboty* (Tashkent: Akademiia Nauk USSR, 1949), 39–40.

22. Josef Brožek, Samuel Wells, and Ancel Keys, "Medical Aspects of Semi-starvation in Leningrad," *American Review of Soviet Medicine* 4, no. 1 (1946): 83–85.

23. William Moskoff, *The Bread of Affliction: The Food Supply in the USSR during World War II* (Cambridge: Cambridge University Press, 1990), 196.

24. Likhacheva, entry for 15 May 1942, 682.

25. Ibid., entry for 21 May 1942, 685–86.

26. Ibid., entry for 16 May 1942, 684. Hospitals were supposed to provide Leningraders 2,400 calories and up to sixty grams of protein a day, but few could (Brožek, Wells, and Keys, "Aspects of Semi-starvation," 78).

27. Likhacheva, entries for 16, 21 May 1942, 685–86. For a worker's experience of this "revolving door," see Mantul, entry for 4 January 1942, 4–4ob.

28. See Gal'ko, entry for 11 December 1942, 532.

29. Gal'ko, entry for 18 January 1942, 517.

30. Ibid., entry for 12 January 1942, 517.

31. Ostrovskaia, entry for 3 November 1941, 111. For a similar example, see Kostrovitskaia, "September, October [1941]," 6.

32. Ostrovskaia, entry for 25 April 1942, 54.

33. Ibid., entry for 8 May 1942, 62ob.

34. Cherepenina, "Assessing the Scale of Famine," 47.

35. Ostrovskaia, entry for 27 April 1942, 55ob.

36. Mervol'f, entry for 9 June 1942, 82–83.

37. Inber, entry for 5 January 1942, 34ob. In published editions, this passage is included in her entry for 6 January 1942.

38. Ibid., entry for 3 February 1942, 4–5. This entry only appears in the diary manuscript.

39. Ibid., entry for 12 June 1942, 32.

40. Sedel'nikova, entry for 22–23 December 1941, 57.

41. Ibid., entries for 19, 30–31 December 1941, 53, 60. More examples in Uskova, entries for 27 July, 6, 13 August 1941, 11, 20–21.

42. Savinkov, entry for 25 February 1942, 23ob–24; Makarov, entry for 10 December 1942, 8.

43. Zelenskaia, entry for 4 March 1942, 66. For other examples, see Makarov, entries for 30–31 December 1942, 5, 8 January 1943, 16–16ob, 17–18, 32ob–33; Zelenskaia, entry for 19 March 1942, 70.

44. Zelenskaia, entry for 4 March 1942, 66ob.

45. Ibid., entry for 5 September 1942, 97ob. For a similar example, see Gal'ko, entry for 3 May 1942, 522. Zelenskaia correctly observed that hospital mortality rates increased that spring without realizing that the overall death rate had fallen. More Leningraders were dying in hospitals as the famine decimated the population, making more hospital beds available (Cherepenina, "Assessing the Scale of Famine," 49).

46. Liubovskaia, entry for 16 July 1942, 184.

47. These are Liubovskaia, Konopleva, Likhacheva, and Makarov. Conversely, official media portrayed the relationship between medics and patients as close and familial. Lisa A. Kirschenbaum, "'Our City, Our Hearths, Our Families': Local Loyalties and Private Life in Soviet World War II Propaganda," *Slavic Review* 59, no. 4 (2000): 841.

48. Chernovskii, entry for 6 February 1942, 88.

49. For an example, see A. Mironova, entry for 15 February 1942, 17ob. This entry appears only in the diary manuscript. Also see *LP*, 14/X/42, no. 244 (8350), 3; Boris Belozerov, "Crime during the Siege," in Barber and Dzeniskevich, *Life and Death*, 218.

50. Richard Bidlack and Nikita Lomagin, *The Leningrad Blockade, 1941–44: A New Documentary History from the Soviet Archives* (New Haven, CT: Yale University Press, 2012), 246, 300–301.

51. Burton, "Medical Welfare," 326–27.

52. A. Mironova, entry for 25 February 1942, 19. This was cut from the published edition of her diary.

53. Zelenskaia, entry for 6 February 1942, 61ob.

54. Konopleva, entry for 22 May 1942, 73–74.

55. Ibid., entry for 22 May 1942, 74.

56. Quoted in Cherepenina, "Assessing the Scale of Famine," 51.

57. Inber, entry for 3 February 1942, 49–49ob.

58. Michael Kaser, *Health Care in the Soviet Union and Eastern Europe* (Boulder, CO: Westview, 1976), 39–40; Christopher Davis, "The Economics of the Soviet Health System: An Analytical and Historical Study, 1921–1978" (Ph.D. diss., Cambridge University, 1979), 42. Burton, "Medical Welfare," 30–38.

59. Sarah D. Phillips, "'There Are No Invalids in the USSR!': A Missing Soviet Chapter in the New Disability History," *Disability Studies Quarterly* 29, no. 3 (2009), http://dsq-sds.org/article/view/936/1111; Beate Fieseler, "Soviet-Style Welfare: The Disabled Soldiers of the 'Great Patriotic War,'" in *Disability in Eastern Europe and the Former Soviet Union: History, Policy, and Everyday Life,* ed. Michael Rasell and Elena Iarskaia-Smirnova (New York: Routledge, 2014), 23–26; Burton, "Medical Welfare," 268, 271.

60. Burton, "Medical Welfare," 266–67, 278. VTEK developed from VKK (Vrachebnaia konsul'tativnaia komissiia; Medical Consultative Commission).

61. Christopher Williams, "Soviet Public Health: A Case Study of Leningrad, 1917–1932" (Ph.D. diss., University of Essex, 1989), 278–79.

62. Richard T. DeGeorge, "Biomedical Ethics," in *Science and the Soviet Social Order,* ed. Loren R. Graham (Cambridge, MA: Harvard University Press, 1990), 208–9; Mark G. Field, *Doctor and Patient in Soviet Russia* (Cambridge, MA: Harvard University Press, 1957), 40; Henry E. Sigerist and Julia Older, *Medicine and Health in the Soviet Union* (New York: Citadel, 1947), 26, 41; Michael Ryan, *The Organization of Soviet Medical Care* (Oxford, UK: Blackwell, 1978), 160.

63. Ostrovskaia, entry for 4 April 1942, 42–42ob.

64. Mervol'f, entry for 28 February 1942, 46.

65. Historians of science have called for a more dynamic view of the interactions between scientists, doctors, and the Soviet state as opposed to an opposition- or obedience-based framework: Frances L. Bernstein, Christopher Burton, and Dan Healy, eds., *Soviet Medicine: Culture, Practice, and Science* (DeKalb, IL: Northern Illinois University Press, 2010); Mark B. Adams, "Science, Ideology, and Structure: The Kol'tsov Institute, 1900–1970," in *The Social Context of Soviet Science,* ed. Linda L. Lubrano and Susan Gross Solomon (Boulder, CO: Westview, 1980), 173–99; Ethan Pollock, *Stalin and the Soviet Science Wars* (Princeton, NJ: Princeton University Press, 2006).

66. Konopleva, entry for 22 May 1942, 74–75.

67. Ibid., entry for 24 August 1942, 9.

68. Likhacheva, entry for 21 May 1942, 686.

69. Burton, "Medical Welfare," 270–74.

70. N. A. Manakov, *Kol'tse blokady: Khoziaistvo i byt osazhdennogo goroda* (Leningrad: Lenizdat, 1961), 108.

71. Zelenskaia, entry for 25 April 1942, 78. Also see Ostrovskaia, entry for 27 November 1942, 90–90ob.

72. Likhacheva, entry for 20 June 1942, 688. Gel'fer received extra food from this clinic. See Gel'fer, entry for 16 May 1942, 22ob.

73. On the emerging "science of starvation" in wartime Europe, see Myron Winick, ed., *Hunger Disease: Studies by the Jewish Physicians in the Warsaw Ghetto* (New York: Wiley, 1979)*;* René Zimmer, Joseph Weill, and Maurice Dobbs, "The Nutritional Situation in the Camps of the Unoccupied Zone of France in 1941 and 1942 and Its Consequences," *New England Journal of Medicine* 230, no. 11 (1944): 303–14; Dana Simmons, "Starvation Science from Colonies to Metropole," in *Food and Globalization: Consumption, Markets, and Politics in the Modern World,* ed. Alexander Nützenadel and Frank Trentmann (Oxford, UK: Berg, 2008), 173–91.

74. American researchers comment on the blockade's medical importance in Brožek, Wells, and Keys, "Aspects of Semi-starvation," 78–85; Keys, Brožek, Henschel, Mickelsen, and Taylor, *Biology of Human Starvation,* 2: 789–818.

75. Gladkikh, *Zdravookhranenie,* 28.

76. Sigerist and Older, *Medicine and Health,* 282; G. S. Pondoev, *Notes of a Soviet Doctor* (London: Chapman and Hall, 1959), 57, 191, 236. Medical studies from the blockade are summarized in I. V. Danilovskii, "Sbornik trudov Leningradskikh uchenykh v dni blokady, 15/IV/46," OR RNB, f. 240, d. 20.

77. Ostrovskaia, entry for 3 November 1941, 111.

78. Ibid., entry for 13 April 1942, 490b.

79. Mariia Aleksandrovna Sadova, "Biblioteka v osazhdennom gorode (1941–42). Vospominaniia. 1944," OR RNB, f. 666, op. L, d. 90, l. 12; Galina Aleksandrovna Ozerova, "Leningradskie knigi perioda blokady, 20/VI/1947," OR RNB, f. 1000, op. 2, d. 999, ll. 24–25.

80. On lectures and exhibits, see V. Sokolov and P. Krasil'nikov, "V botanicheskom institute," *Leningrad* 7 (1943): 15; *LP*, 31/III/44, no. 78 (8802), 4; 20/III/42, no. 66 (8172), 2; 2/IV/42, no. 77 (8183), 3; 21/VI/42, no. 93 (8199), 3; 5/V/42, no. 105 (8211), 2; 129/V/42, no. 126 (8232), 2.

81. Sedel'nikova, entry for 22–23 December 1941, 57.

82. Vladimir Garshin, "Tam, gde smert pomogaet zhizni," *Arkhiv patalogii* 46, no. 5 (1984): 83–88; Anna Reid, *Leningrad: The Epic Siege of World War II, 1941–1944* (New York: Walker and Company, 2011), 341.

83. Uskova, entry for 13 August 1941, 22.

84. Konopleva, entry for 9 June 1942, 81.

85. Matiushina, undated entry, Diary, 112; Nikol'skii, OR RNB, f. 1037, dd. 900, 902, 907, 911.

86. Zelenskaia, entries for 6 February, 18 January 1942, 610b, 55.

87. Ibid., entry for 6 May 1942, 80.

88. Ibid., entry for 12 May 1942, 800b.

89. Ginzburg, "Zapiski blokadnogo cheloveka," 357; translation from Ginzburg, *Blockade Diary*, 74.

90. Rebecca Manley, "Nutritional Dystrophy: The Science and Semantics of Starvation in World War II," in *Hunger and War: Food Provisioning in the Soviet Union during World War II,* ed. Wendy Z. Goldman and Donald Filtzer (Bloomington: Indiana University Press, 2015), 218. In the 1940s and 1950s, researchers from many national contexts classified hunger as a disease. See Robert Dirks, "Social Reponses during Severe Food Shortages and Famine," *Current Anthropology* 21, no. 1 (1980): 23–24; Simmons, "Starvation Science," 173–87.

91. On the adoption of *distrofiia* in the gulag, see Manley, "Nutritional Dystrophy," 252n176. For references to *distrofiia* as a "Leningrad disease," see Kozlovskii, entry for 18 January 1942, 574–75; M. M. Gubergritz, "Ob alimentarnoi toksicheskoi distrofii," *Vrachebnoe delo* 11–12 (1945): 547; Sobolev, *Uchenye Leningrada,* 68; Varlam Shalamov, "Shakhmaty Doktora Kuzmenko," in *Kolymskie rasskazy,* vol. 2 (Moscow: Russkaia kniga, 1992), 368.

92. Jacques Rossi, *The Gulag Handbook: An Encyclopedia Dictionary of Soviet Penitentiary Institutions and Terms Related to the Forced Labor Camps,* trans. William A. Burhans (New York: Paragon House, 1989), 103. Rebecca Manley argues this view in "Nutritional Dystrophy," 206–64.

93. On *distrofiia* as a euphemism, see Cherepenina, "Assessing the Scale of Famine," 39–40; Lisa A. Kirschenbaum, "'The Alienated Body': Gender, Identity and the Memory of the Siege of Leningrad," in *Gender and War in Twentieth-Century Eastern Europe,* ed. Nancy M. Wingfield and Maria Bucur (Bloomington: Indiana University Press, 2006), 225; Conroy, *Medicines for the Soviet Masses,* 117. On the use of medical discourse

to depoliticize hunger, see Jenny Edkins, *Whose Hunger? Concepts of Famine, Practices of Aid* (Minneapolis: University of Minnesota Press, 2000); Nancy Scheper-Hughes, *Death without Weeping: The Violence of Everyday Life in Brazil* (Berkeley: University of California Press, 1992); Diana Wylie, *Starving on a Full Stomach: Hunger and the Triumph of Cultural Racism in Modern South Africa* (Charlottesville: University of Virginia Press, 2001).

94. M. V. Chernorutskii, "Problemy alimentarnoi distrofii," *Raboty leningradskikh vrachei za god otechestvennoi voiny* 3 (1943): 3–13.

95. Cherepenina, "Assessing the Scale of Famine," 40.

96. Chernovskii, entry for 8 April 1942, 133.

97. Gladkikh, *Zdravookhranenie,* 37–38; Cherepenina, "Assessing the Scale of Famine," 40.

98. "Iz otcheta komiteta po izucheniiu alimentarnoi distrofii i avitaminozov o rabote v pervoi polovine 1944 (9/VIII/1944)," in *Ot voiny k miru, Leningrad 1944–1945: Sbornik dokumentov,* ed. N. B. Lebedeva, G. I. Lisovskaia, N. Iu. Cherepenina (St. Petersburg: Liki Rossii, 2013), 77. Landmark publications include I. D. Strashun and V. L. Venderovich, eds., *Alimentarnaia distrofiia i avitaminozy* (Leningrad: Gosizdatel'stvo Meditsinskoi Literatury, 1944); A. L. Miasnikov, ed., *Alimentarnaia distrofiia: Sbornik rabot* (Leningrad: Upravlenie voenno-morskogo izdatel'stva, 1944); Miasnikov, *Klinika alimentarnoi distrofii* (Leningrad: Voenno-morskaia meditsinskaia akademiia, 1945); F.I. Mashanskii, ed., *Raboty leningradskikh vrachei za gody Otechestvennoi Voiny,* vols. 1–7 (Leningrad: Izdatel'stvo meditsinskoi literatury, 1943–5); M. V. Chernorutskii, ed., *Alimentarnaia distrofiia v blokirovannom Leningrade* (Leningrad: Medgiz, 1947). In 1945, Leningrad's branch of the Academy of Sciences published a summary of its scholarly achievements; it included studies on *distrofiia* starting in late 1942. Danilovskii, "Sbornik trudov," 230–31.

99. Sedel'nikova, entries for 18, 22–23 December 1941, 52, 58.

100. Stages are detailed in Chernorutskii, "Problemy alimentarnoi distrofiii," 3–13; Miasnikov, *Klinika alimentarnoi distrofii,* 8–42.

101. Levina, entry for 11 February 1942, 8.

102. Likhacheva, entry for 16 May 1942, 684.

103. Archivists at OR RNB gave Peto's account an ambiguous designation, classifying it as: "notes of a diary-like *[dnevnikovskii]* character." In 1944, Peto recopied the text from its original.

104. Ibid., 4–40b.

105. Ibid., 5–50b. Despite Peto's benign descriptions, DPR conditions could be very harsh. See Catriona Kelly, *Children's World: Growing Up in Russia, 1890–1991* (New Haven, CT: Yale University Press, 2007), 242–57.

106. Peto, 70b.

107. Ibid., 10, 130b.

108. Ibid., 5–6, 14, 16.

109. From the vast literature on illness as a construction that delineates social norms from deviance, I draw on Nancy Scheper-Hughes and Margaret M. Lock, "Speaking 'Truth' to Illness: Metaphors, Reification, and a Pedagogy for Patients," *Medical Anthropology*

Quarterly 17, no. 5 (1986): 138–39; Peter Conrad, *The Medicalization of Society: On the Transformation of Human Conditions into Treatable Diseases* (Baltimore: Johns Hopkins University Press, 2007).

110. Zabolotskaia, entry for 25 October 1942, 6, 19. "Dystrophic" was written in diaries both as *distroficheskii* or *distrofichnyi*, although the former was more common.

111. Vinokurov, 281–82.

112. Kozlovskii, entries for 18 January, 5 April 1942, 575.

113. Ales' Adamovich and Daniil Granin, *Blokadnaia kniga* (St. Petersburg: Pechatnyi dvor, 1994), 326. Ancel Keys and colleagues reported that group identity was strongest in his subjects when starvation was severe. As they recovered, individual identity returned (Keys, Brožek, and Henschel, *Biology of Human Starvation*, 2:838).

114. For examples, see Chernovskii, entry for 2 February 1942, 81–82; Likhacheva, entry for 17 June 1942, 687–88.

115. Ostrovskaia, entry for 4 April 1942, 42–43.

116. Ol'ga Berggol'ts, "Iz dnevnikov," *Zvezda* 5 (1990): 190.

117. Ostrovskaia, entry for 4 July 1942, 70.

118. Zelenskaia, entry for 22 August 1942, 96–96ob. Polina Barskova has convincingly shown how the body of the *distrofik* became a distasteful reminder of one's possible fate. Barskova, "The Corpse, the Corpulent, and the Other: A Study in the Tropology of Siege Body Representation," *Ab Imperio* 1 (2009): 361–86.

119. Boldyrev, entry for 22 September 1942, 164–65; translation from Reid, *Leningrad*, 355.

120. Levina, entry for 3 June 1942, 22.

121. Konopleva, entry for 18 October 1942, 29.

122. Ostrovskaia, entry for 2 July 1942, 65–65ob.

123. Primo Levi, *Survival in Auschwitz* (1947), trans. Stuart Woolf (New York: Collier Books, 1986), 98.

124. Lidiia Ginzburg, "Otsepenenie (priznaniia utselevshego distrofika)," in *Prokhodiashchie kharaktery: Proza voennykh let, Zapiski blokadnogo cheloveka*, ed. Andrei Zorin and Emily Van Buskirk (Moscow: Novoe, 2011), 437.

125. Levina, entry for 26 February 1942, 11–12.

126. Ibid., entry for 21 April 1942, 19.

127. Byl'ev, entry titled "February March 1942," 9.

128. Nikita A. Lomagin, *Neizvestnaia blokada*, 2 vols. (St. Petersburg: Neva, 2002–4), 1:110; drawn from Manley, "Nutritional Dystrophy," 242.

129. Nicholas Ganson, *The Soviet Famine of 1946–47 in Global and Historical Perspectives* (New York: Palgrave Macmillan, 2009), 140; Nicole M. Eaton, "Exclave: Politics, Ideology, and Everyday Life in Königsberg-Kaliningrad, 1928–1948" (Ph.D. diss., University of California, Berkeley, 2013), 228, 301–16. Eaton shows how in Kaliningrad *distrofiia* went from a neutral descriptive applied to Soviet citizens to a pejorative one describing Germans who were physically and mentally contaminated by fascism.

130. Kozlovskii, entry for 18 January 1942, 574.

131. Zelenskaia, entry for 7 December 1941, 38ob–39.

132. Ibid., entry for 11 October 1941, 22ob.

133. Ibid., entry for 1 March 1942, 650b.
134. V. M. Miasishchev explained, "it was those who gave way to the urge to rest who died" (quoted in Dzeniskevich, "Medical Research Institutes," 106).
135. Zelenskaia, entry for 7 December 1941, 380b.
136. Ibid., entry for 24 May 1942, 820b.
137. Ibid., entry for 18 January 1942, 55.
138. B. Chetvernkov, "Iazyk," *Leningrad* 4–5 (1942): 15.
139. Irina Sandomirskaya, "Biopolitics of Besiegement: Writing, Sacrifice and Bare Life in Lidiia Ginzburg's *Notebooks,*" *Baltic Worlds,* August 2010, 15.
140. Adamovich and Granin, *Blokadnaia kniga,* 18.
141. Kirschenbaum, "Alienated Body," 224–26.
142. Dzeniskevich, "Medical Research Institutes," 105–6; Magaeva, "Physiological and Psychosomatic Prerequisites," 129, 131–32; Chernorutskii, "Problemy alimentarnoi distrofii," 30.
143. Amnon Sella, *The Value of Human Life in Soviet Warfare* (New York: Routledge, 1992), 48–50. Sella argues that Soviet doctors conceived of mental illness narrowly as induced by combat, amputations, wounds, or infections.
144. Pavel Vasilyev, "Alimentary and Pellagra Psychoses in Besieged Leningrad," in *Food and War in Twentieth-Century Europe,* ed. Ina Zweiniger-Bargielowska, Rachel Duffett, and Alain Drouard (Farnham, UK: Ashgate, 2011), 113–14; Dzeniskevich, "Medical Research Institutes," 105–6; Brožek, Wells, and Keys, "Aspects of Semi-starvation," 78.
145. Zagorskaia, entry for 28 January 1942, 12. Also see Kniazev, entries for 29 September, 23 October 1941, 199, 251; Gal'ko, entry 27 December 1943, 545.
146. Zelenskaia, entry for 1 May 1943, 122; S. Bardin, "Shkola voiny," *LP,* 4/XII/41, no. 289 (8082), 2; Liubovskaia, entries for 6 November 1941, 2 December 1941, 5, 16 January 1942, 10 July 1942, 21, 41, 53, 165.
147. Konopleva, entry for 14 November 1941, 169.
148. Sedel'nikova, entry for 14 October 1941, 30.
149. Liubovskaia, entry for 6 November 1941, 4.
150. Liubovskaia, entry for 4 March 1942, 112.
151. Ibid., entry for 6 November, 1941, 4.
152. Lidiia Ginzburg, "Otrezki blokadnogo dnia," in *Prokhodiashchie kharaktery,* 441; translation from Ginzburg, *Blockade Diary,* 108.
153. Matiushina, undated entry, Diary, 76.
154. Liubovskaia, entry for 2 December 1941, 21.
155. Summarized in Keys, Brožek, Henschel, Mickelsen, and Taylor, *Biology of Human Starvation,* 2:820–21, 836.
156. Miasishchev was one of the first doctors to publish the term "hunger psychosis." His work is described in Dzeniskevich, "Medical Research Institutes," 105–6. On the term's early usage and analysis, see B. I. Smirnov, "O nervno-psikhicheskikh rasstroistvakh pri alimentarnoi distrofii," in Miasnikov, *Alimentarnaia distrofiia,* 15–21.
157. Chernorutskii, "Problemy alimentarnoi distrofii," 5, 29; M. I. Khvilitskaia, "Clinical Observations on Pellagra in Leningrad in 1942," cited in Keys, Brožek,Henschel, Mick-

elsen, and Taylor, *Biology of Human Starvation,* 2: 793; Dzeniskevich, "Medical Research Institutes," 136. Recently, scholars have found that deficiencies in protein, iron, zinc, iodine, and vitamins A, C, and the B complex can elicit emotive, cognitive, and psychotic disorders. Pellagra and beriberi can cause psychoses, dementia, and depression due to a dearth of vitamins B3 (niacin) and B1 (thiamine), respectively. I mention these discoveries to contextualize, not correct, the diarists' experiences. See World Health Organization, "Neurological Disorders Associated with Malnutrition," in *Neurological Disorders: A Public Health Approach,* 111–18, http://www.who.int /mental_health/neurology/neurodiso/en/; Tessa J. Roseboom, Jan H. P. van der Meulen, Anita C. J. Ravelli, Clive Osmond, David J. P. Barker, and Otto P. Bleker, "Effects of Prenatal Exposure to the Dutch Famine on Adult Disease in Later Life: An Overview," *Molecular and Cellular Endocrinology* 185 (2001): 93–98; Tessa J. Roseboom, Rebecca C. Painter, Annet F. M. van Abeelen, Marjolein V. E. Veenendaal, and Susanne R. de Rooij, "Hungry in the Womb: What Are the Consequences? Lessons from the Dutch Famine," *Maturitas* 70, no. 2 (2011): 141–45.

158. Zimmer, Weill, and Dobbs, "Nutritional Situation in the Camps," 308; M. Nireberski, "Psychological Investigations of a Group of Internees at Belsen Camp," *Mental Science* 92 (1946): 60–74; Keys, Brožek, Henschel, Mickelsen, and Taylor, *Biology of Human Starvation,* 2:110–11, 659, 799.

159. A. Mironova, entries for 27 December 1941, 15 February 1942, 14–14ob, 17ob.

160. Afanas'ev, entries for 29 May, 18 June 1942, 49–50, 59; Levina, entry for 2 April 1942, 16.

161. Sedel'nikova, entry for 23–24 January 1942, 68.

162. Ibid., entry for 24 December 1941, 58.

163. Ibid., entry for 6 January 1942, 63.

164. Mervol'f, entry for 28 May 1942, 78–79.

165. Uskova, entry for 24 March 1942, 53.

166. Zelenskaia, entry for 13 June 1942, 87.

167. Ibid., entry for 17 August 1942, 95–96.

168. Liubovskaia, entry for 5 January 1942, 41.

169. Ibid., entries for 15 May, 10 June 1942, 150, 165–66.

170. N. Grashchenkov and Y. Lisitsyn, *Achievements in Soviet Medicine* (Moscow: Foreign Publishing House, 1960); Edward Podolsky, *Red Miracle: The Story of Soviet Medicine* (New York: Freeport, 1947); K. Sukhin, "V nauchykh poiskakh," *Leningrad* 11–12 (1943): 22; M. K. Kuz'min, *Sovetskaia meditsina v gody Velikoi Otechestvennoi Voiny: Ocherki* (Moscow: Meditsina, 1979), 145–62; Sigerist and Older, *Medicine and Health,* 286–88; Sella, *Value of Human Life,* 51–54, 77. A major exception to the triumphant tone of these histories of Soviet wartime medicine is Dzeniskevich and Barber's *Life and Death in Besieged Leningrad.*

171. See these issues of *LP:* 11/X/1941, no. 243 (8035), 3; 11/I/1942, no. 9 (8115), 2; 11/VII/1943, no. 162 (8577), 4; 13/VII/1943, no. 163 (8578), 2–3; 15/VII/1943, no. 165 (8580), 1; 23/VII/1943, no. 172 (8587), 2; 31/III/1944, no. 78 (8802), 4.

172. S. I. Avvakumov, ed., *Geroicheskii Leningrad, 1917–1942* (Leningrad: Gospolitizdat, 1943), 170–71.

173. S. Ezerskii, *Vrachi Leningrada* (Leningrad: Leningradskoe gazetno-zhurnal'noe i knizhnoe izdatel'stvo, 1943), 10, 19–21.

174. Kirschenbaum, "Alienated Body," 220–34; Cherepenina, "Assessing the Scale of Famine," 51.

175. Sedel'nikova, entries for 19 February, 4 March 1942, 77, 80.

176. Ibid., entry for 12 March 1942, 83.

7. IN THE MIRROR OF HISTORY

1. Aleksei Tolstoi, "Nesokrushimaia krepost'," 30 December 1942, in *Stat'i: 1942–1943* (Moscow: Gosudarstvennaia khudozhestvenaia literatura, 1944), 43. Also see B. Reizov, "Zhivaia sila istorii," *Zvezda* 3 (1943): 96.

2. On the importance of history for the establishment of a war myth that would reinvigorate and stabilize war-torn Soviet society, see Amir Weiner, "The Making of a Dominant Myth: The Second World War and the Construction of Political Identities within the Soviet Polity," *Russian Review* 55, no. 4 (1996): 638–60; David Brandenberger, *National Bolshevism: Stalinist Mass Culture and the Formation of Modern Russian National Identity, 1931–1956* (Cambridge, MA: Harvard University Press, 2002); David Brandenberger and Kevin M. F. Platt, eds., *Epic Revisionism: Russian History and Literature as Stalinist Propaganda* (Madison: University of Wisconsin Press, 2006).

3. Lisa A. Kirschenbaum, *The Legacy of the Siege of Leningrad, 1941–1995: Myths, Memories, and Monuments* (Cambridge: Cambridge University Press, 2006), 29.

4. These were not the only parallels suggested by the regime or by diarists, but they were the most common ones. Others included World War I, the Paris Commune, and various medieval sieges.

5. Kniazev, entry for 14 October 1941, 227.

6. Dymov, entry for 25 November 1942, in Adamovich and Granin, *Blokadnaia kniga*, 303.

7. Skriabina, entry for 5 September 1941, 31.

8. Savinkov, entry for 5 February 1942, 15.

9. Afanas'ev, entry for 20 January 1942, 86.

10. Ginzburg, "Zapiski blokadnogo cheloveka," 325; translation from Ginzburg, *Blockade Diary*, 26.

11. Galina Aleksandrovna Ozerova, "Leningradskie knigi perioda blokady (opyt bibliografii mestnoi pechati), doklad (20/VI/1947)," OR RNB, f. 1000, op. 2, d. 999, ll. 20–21.

12. Kostrovitskaia, "October [1941]," 14. A collapsing sense of time is featured in Holocaust diaries as well. See Amos Goldberg, *Holocaust Diaries as "Life Stories"* (Jerusalem: Yad Vashem, 2004), 16–17.

13. For examples, see Konopleva, entries for 31 October, 6–8, 30 November, 1 December 1941, 26–27 October 1942, 85–86, 154–55, 187–88, 30–31. For an analysis of such a practice, see Irina Paperno, "What Can Be Done with Diaries?," *Russian Review* 63, no. 4 (2004): 562–66.

14. Savinkov, entry for 12 December 1942, 70. For more examples, see ibid., entry for 2 October 1942, 610b; Gal'ko, entry for 27 December 1942, 533.

15. Nikolai Tikhonov, *Leningradskii god, mai 1942–1943* (Leningrad: Voennoe Izdatel'stvo NKO, 1943), 64.

16. Ibid., 81. The diarist Anna Ostroumova-Lebedeva objected that Tikhonov's *Leningradskii god* was "done carelessly. The language is unedited, banal, has the feel of the newspaper, the style of the daily press. Contents are disposable. It has little feeling of the city itself. One can infer that the author understands little of its beauty [. . .] and does not feel his soul." Ostroumova-Lebedeva, entry for 1 March 1944, 11.

17. Nikolai Ivanovich Vasil'ev, entry for 29 January 1942, GMMOBL, f. RDF, op. 1L, d. 329, l. 10. Vasil'ev was eleven when he wrote most of his entries.

18. Ibid., entry for 10 January 1942, 8.

19. Ibid., entry for 2 February 1942, 12.

20. Georgii Efremovich Lebedev, "Iz dnevnik G. E. Lebedeva," entry for 10 January 1943, in *Russkii Muzei-evakuatsiia, blokada, vosstanovlenie: Iz vospominanii muzeinogo rabotnika,* ed. P. K. Baltun (Moscow: Iskusstvo, 1981), 120–21 (hereafter "G. Lebedev").

21. This request of 9 July 1943 appears on an index card in Konopleva's diary.

22. Irina Paperno, *Stories of the Soviet Experience: Memoirs, Diaries, Dreams* (Ithaca, NY: Cornell University Press, 2009), 9–10; Edward C. Thaden, *The Rise of Historicism in Russia* (New York: Peter Lang, 1999); Jochen Hellbeck "Russian Autobiographical Practice," in *Autobiographical Practices in Russia/Autobiographische Praktiken in Russland,* ed. Jochen Hellbeck and Klaus Heller (Göttingen: V and R Unipress, 2004), 279–99.

23. Jochen Hellbeck, "Working, Struggling, Becoming: Stalin-Era Autobiographical Texts," *Russian Review* 60, no. 3 (2001): 341, 349; Hellbeck, *Revolution on My Mind: Writing a Diary under Stalin* (Cambridge, MA: Harvard University Press, 2006), 53–59.

24. Hellbeck, *Revolution on My Mind,* 17–18.

25. Jochen Hellbeck, "The Diary between History and Literature: A Historian's Critical Response," *Russian Review* 63, no. 4 (2004): 622.

26. "Stenograficheskii otchet soveshchaiusia apparata Kirovskogo RK VKP(b) g. Leningrada 26 / XI / 1941, predsedatel' T. Efremov: TsGAIPD, f. 4000, op. 10, d. 776, l. 2.

27. Ibid., 7, 16.

28. Sokolova, entries for 5, 18, 20, 22, 28 August, 16 September, 11 October, and 1, 23 November 1941, 1–130b, 180b, 22, 25.

29. Ilya Ehrenburg, "The Soul of Russia" (November 1943), in *In One Newspaper: A Chronicle of Unforgettable Years,* by Ilya Ehrenburg and Konstantin Simonov, trans. Anatol Kagan (New York: Sphinx, 1983), 355.

30. Nikulin, entry for 1–10 July 1941, 2.

31. Ibid., entry for 14 January 1942, 160b.

32. Nikulin, 210b. This fragment is undated but probably from the entry for 15–18 January 1942.

33. Nikulin, entry for 15–18 January 1942, 20–200b. For more examples, see ibid., undated entry, 10–11; 19–20 January 1942, 20–21.

34. Ibid., undated fragment, 24–60.

35. N. P. Kopaneva, "Pis'ma dal'emu drugu," Kniazev, *Dni velikikh ispytanii,* 7–8; Anatole G. Mazour, *The Writing of History in the Soviet Union* (Stanford, CA: Hoover Institution Press, 1971), 354.

36. Kniazev, entry for 18 January 1941, 409–10.

37. Kopaneva, "Pis'ma dal'emu drugu," 9–11.

38. Kniazev, entry for 25 June 1941, 33.

39. Ibid., entry for 24 October 1941, 256.

40. Ibid., entry for 1 October 1941, 205.

41. Ibid., entry for 19 August 1941, 134.

42. Ibid., entries for 5 July, 24 October 1941, 54, 255–56.

43. Ibid., entry for 17 November, 1941, 311–12. Also see ibid., entries for 1 July, 26 September, 13 October 1941, 45, 191, 224.

44. Ibid., entry for 4 February 1942, 447.

45. Ibid., entry for 22 February 1942, 501.

46. Chernovskii, entries for 19, 21, 25 February 1942, 100–101.

47. "Plan raboty instituta na 1948," TsGAIPD, f. 4000, op. 1, d. 607, l. 31.

48. Chernovskii, entry for 27 February 1942, 109.

49. Ibid., entry for 11 December 1941, 42.

50. Ibid., entry for 9 April 1942, 133–34.

51. Chernovskii, 137.

52. Katharine Hodgson, *Written with the Bayonet: Soviet Russian Poetry of World War II* (Liverpool: Liverpool University Press, 1996); Brandenberger, *National Bolshevism.* On Soviet wartime historiography, see Aileen G. Rambow, "The Siege of Leningrad: Wartime Literature and Ideological Change," in *The People's War: Responses to World War II in the Soviet Union,* ed. Robert W. Thurston and Bernd Bonwetsch (Urbana: University of Illinois Press, 2000), 154–70; Mazour, *The Writing of History*; Robert D. Markwick, *Rewriting History in Soviet Russia: The Politics of Revisionist Historiography, 1956–1974* (New York: Palgrave, 2001); John Barber, *Soviet Historians in Crisis, 1928–1932* (New York: Holmes and Meier, 1981).

53. Hodgson, *Written with the Bayonet,* 58, 108; David Brandenberger and Kevin M. F. Platt, "Introduction: Tsarist-Era Heroes in Stalinist Mass Culture and Propaganda," in Platt and Brandenberger, *Epic Revisionism,* 9–11; Brandenberger, *National Bolshevism,* 115–16.

54. Brandenberger, *National Bolshevism,* 126–32.

55. Kniazev, entry for 4 August 1941, 106.

56. Kirschenbaum, *Legacy,* 77–80, 91–103; *LP,* 30/I/42, no. 24 (8130), 2. Diarists who lectured include Sokolova, Chernovskii, Inber, Boldyrev, and Kniazev.

57. Kirschenbaum, *Legacy,* 47–49, 80–87. See these issues of *LP:* 25/VI/41, no. 149 (7948); 31/VII/41, no. 181 (7974); 6/VIII/41, no. 186 (7979); 25/XI/41, no. 281 (8074); 14/XII/41, no. 298 (8091); 6/I/42, no. 4 (8110); 27/VIII/42, no. 203 (8309); 5/IX/42, no. 209 (8315); 27/IV/43, no. 18 (8513); 28/IX/43, no. 229 (8644); 26/II/44, no. 74 (8798).

58. Leningradskii gorodskoi komitet VKP(b), protokol No. 5, TsGAIPD, f. 25, op. 2, d. 4895, 3.

59. Tikhonov, *Leningradskii god,* 58–61; Aleksandr Fadeev, *Leningrad v dni blokady: Iz dnevnika* (Moscow: Sovetsii Pisatel', 1944), 25–26; *Komosomol'skaia Pravda,* 3/X/41 (No. 235) (5013), 1; *Sankt-Peterburg XX Vek: Chto, gde, kogda?* (St. Petersburg: Paritet, 2000), 310.

60. In 1943, *LP* reported that 500 books and twenty brochures were published in Leningrad in the first twenty-two months of World War II; other wartime publications claim that 756 new books and pamphlets were published in the first year. Post-Soviet figures put it at 1,500 books and brochures during the blockade. *LP,* 5/V/43, no. 104 (8519), 2; S. I. Avvakumov, ed., *Geroicheskii Leningrad, 1917–1942* (Leningrad: Gospolitizdat, 1943), 172–73; A. F. Veksler, ed., *Knigi nepobezhdennogo Leningrada: Katalog knig izdannykh v Leningrade v gody Velikoi Otechestvennoi Voiny,* vol. 1 (St. Petersburg: N. F. Kupriianov, 1999), 9.

61. T. D. Aizenburg, "Leningradskie bukinisty v gody Otechestvennoi Voiny i blokady goroda (1974)," OR RNB, f. 1298, d. 15, ll. 2, 7.

62. Ozerova, "Leningradskie knigi perioda blokady," 13–30.

63. 110,000 copies each of Tarle's *Dve otechestvennye voiny* and his *Otechestvennaia voina 1812 i razgrom imperii Napoleona* were printed during the siege (Veksler, *Knigi nepobezhdennogo Leningrada, 1:* 87).

64. Ozerova, "Leningradskie knigi perioda blokady," 46–55; Maurice Friedberg, *Russian Classics in Soviet Jackets* (New York: Columbia University Press, 1962), 132, 118, 39–40.

65. *LP,* 3/II/42, no. 27 (8133), 2; *LP,* 19/XII/41, no. 293 (8086), 4; *LP,* 29/XII/42, no. 307 (8413), 4.

66. David Brandenberger, "The 'Short Course' to Modernity: Stalinist History Textbooks, Mass Culture, and the Foundation of Popular Russian National Identity, 1934–1956," (Ph.D. diss., Harvard University, 2000), 262. Also see Brandenberger, *National Bolshevism,* 172–77.

67. "The Great Patriotic War of the Soviet People," *LP,* 23/VI/1941, no. 148 (7941), 3. On official efforts to disseminate the 1812–1941 analogy, see Kirschenbaum, *Legacy,* 29; John Barber, "The Image of Stalin in Soviet Propaganda and Public Opinion during World War II," in *World War II and the Soviet People,* ed. John Garrad and Carol Garrad (New York: Palgrave Macmillan, 1993), 41.

68. See V. Trel'kmeier, "Pamiatniki Otechestvennoi Voiny 1812 goda v gorode Lenina," and V. Glinka, 'Kutuzovskie mesta v Leningrade," *Leningrad 3* (1942): 14–16; Viacheslav Shishkov, "Narodnaia Voina 1812 goda," *Zvezda* 1–2 (1942): 141–53; E.V. Tarle, *Dve otechestvennye voiny (*Moscow and Leningrad: Voenmorizdat, 1941).

69. The term is used in Zagorskaia, entries for 31 December 1941, 14 February 1942, 10, 14–14ob.

70. Aleksei Tolstoi, *The Making of Russia* (London: Hutchinson, 1945), 34–37; Il'ia Ehrenburg, "Vtoroi den' Borodina" (24 January 1942), in *Voina: 1941–1945,* ed. V. Ia. Frezinski (Moscow: Astrel', 2004), 187.

71. Ksaverii Naumovich Sel'tser, diary entry for 16 October 1941, quoted in Sergei Glezerov, *Ot nenavisti k primireniiu* (St. Petersburg: Ostrov, 2006), 45, emphasis added.

72. *LP,* 14/XII/41, no. 298 (8091), 2; *LP,* 8/IX/42, no. 213 (8319), 2; *LP,* 28/IX/43, no. 229 (8644), 2.

73. E. V. Tarle, *How Mikhail Kutuzov Beat Napoleon* (London: Soviet War News, 1944), 9, 15. This study characterizes Napoleon's wars as acts of imperialism and emphasizes Kutuzov's heroism and the role of popular resistance in the Russian victory. This is in contrast to Tarle's earlier work, *Napoleon* (Moscow: Zhurnal'no-gazetnoe ob"edinenie, 1936).

74. Liudmila El'iashova, *Moi blokadnyi universitet* (St. Petersburg: Izmailovskii, 2005), 98.

75. Kniazev, entry for 14 August 1941, 122.

76. Sokolova, entry for 16 August 1941, 40b.

77. Konopleva, entry for 31 July 1941, 35–36.

78. Savinkov, entry for 16 April 1942, 310b. More examples of historical comparison in ibid., entries for 7 October 1941, 21 September 1942, 60b, 580b; Zelenskaia, entry for 22 July 1941, 40b–5.

79. Savinkov, entry for 23 October 1941, 80b.

80. Ibid., entry for 9 September 1942, 56.

81. Sokolova, entry for 26 October 1941, 23.

82. Afanas'ev, entry for 22 March 1942, 105–6. Afanas'ev wrote "1912" instead of "1812."

83. Konopleva, entries for 4, 31 July 1941, 11–12, 35. On this exhibit, also see *LP,* 12/VII/41, no. 164 (7957), 4.

84. On the regime's efforts to guide the public's interpretation of the novel, see William Nickell, "Tolstoi in 1928: In the Mirror of Revolution," in Brandenberger and Platt, *Epic Revisionism,* 18, 24, 31; Friedberg, *Russian Classics,* 2, 9.

85. Friedberg, *Russian Classics,* 37–38, 57, 80; Nickell, "Tolstoi in 1928," 22–23.

86. Krakov, entry for 15 December 1942, 44. Notices were printed in the following issues of *LP:* 12/XII/41, no. 294 (8089), 4; 19/XII/41, no. 276 (8069), 4.

87. Ginzburg, "Zapiski blokadnogo cheloveka," 311; translation from Ginzburg, *Blockade Diary,* 3. Uskova referred to her writing space as "Iasnaia Poliana," the name of Tolstoy's estate (entry for 21 July 1942, 57).

88. Levina, entry for 9 October 1942, 30. Identical text is in Levina, "Pis'ma k drugu," entry for 1 October 1942, 213. This is one of three passages that appear in both her published and unpublished accounts.

89. G. Lebedev, entry for 2 May 1942, 124. In the novel, Tushin's battery helped determine the outcome of the battle of Schöngraben.

90. On the failed siege of Petrograd, see W. Bruce Lincoln, *Red Victory: A History of the Russian Civil War* (New York: Simon and Schuster, 1989), 296–97; Evan Mawdsley, *The Russian Civil War* (Boston: Allen and Unwin, 1987), 200–202.

91. Ozerova, "Leningradskie knigi perioda blokady," 20.

92. *LP,* 14/VII/41, no. 157 (7950), 3; *LP,* 16/IX/41, no. 221 (8014), 3; *LP,* 17/IX/42, no. 216 (8322), 2.

93. Ehrenburg, untitled article of 14 January 1943, *In One Newspaper,* 253.

94. Kirschenbaum, *Legacy,* 77.

95. Lincoln, *Red Victory,* 295–98; G. I. Karaev, "Tovarishch Stalin—Rukovoditel' oborony Petrograda v 1919," *Leningrad* 4–5 (November 1942): 5–6.

96. Sokolova, entry for 18 September 1941, 14.

97. Zagorskaia, entry for 14 February 1942, 14–14ob.

98. Bubnova, entry for November 1941, 40b–50b.

99. G. Lebedev, entry for 10 January 1943, 120.

100. Liubovskaia, entry for 25 February 1942, 102.

101. Ostrovskaia, entry for 27 November 1941 122; Zelenskaia, entry for 25 November 1941, 350b.

102. Sadova, "Biblioteka v osazhdennom gorode," 12.

103. This phrase is from Aleksei Tolstoi's *1918,* part of his Stalin Prize–winning trilogy *The Ordeal* (A. N. Tolstoi, *Izbrannye sochineniia v shesti tomakh, 3* [Moscow: Sovetskii Pisatel', 1951], 297, 300).

104. Liubovskaia, entry for 27 January 1942, 69.

105. Mervol'f, entry for 14 January 1942, 20.

106. Ostrovskaia, entry for 27 November 1941, 116–116ob. Torgsin were state stores that only took hard currency and mostly sold to foreigners.

107. Kirschenbaum argues that during the Civil War, Viktor Shlovksii, Osip Mandelstam, and other intellectuals regarded suffering as a cleansing spiritual experience (*Legacy,* 28).

108. Konopleva, entries for, 7, 8, 9, 10 September 1941, 63–69.

109. Ibid., entry for 8 September 1941, 66–67.

110. Ostrovskaia, entry for 24 January 1942, 140.

111. Zelenskaia, entry for 14 April 1942, 760b.

112. Sokolova, entry for 19 August 1941, 7; also see ibid., entry for 18 September 1941, 130b.

113. Osipova, entry for 24 August 1941, 8.

114. Ibid., entry for 2 September 1941, 11.

115. Mervol'f, entry for 9 February 1942, 32.

116. Vasily Grossman, *Life and Fate* (1959), trans. Robert Chandler (New York: New York Review of Books, 1985), 239–40.

117. Leonid Sobolev, "In the Old Fort," in *Sevastopol: November 1941–July 1942: Articles, Stories, and Eye-Witness Accounts by Soviet War-Correspondents* (New York: Hutchinson, 1943), 61; Sobolev, *Morskaia dusha: Rasskazy* (Moscow: Gosudarstvennoe izdatel'stvo literatury, 1942); "Sevastopol'skie rasskazy," *Leningrad* 3 (1945): 2–3. Also see these issues of *LP*: 22/I/42, no. 18 (8124), 2; 23/VI/42, no. 152 (8258), 2; 1/VII/42, no. 154 (8260), 2; 23/VII/42, no. 173 (8279), 2. A film about Nakhimov was released in 1946.

118. F. S. Oktiabr'skii, "Defense of Sevastopol'," in *Sevastopol',* 70; Ehrenburg, "Sevastopol'," in *Voina,* 243–46.

119. Ehrenburg, "Sevastopol'," in *Voina,* 244.

120. Tikhonov, *Leningradskii god,* 23. Boldyrev lectured on the defense of Sevastopol' for extra rations (entry for 19 April 1942, 90).

121. Leonid Sobolev, "Stranitsy iz sevastopol'skogo dnevnika," in *Svet pobedy: Stat'i i ocherki voennykh let* (Moscow: Sovetskaia Rossiia, 1968), 148–58.

122. Leonid Sobolev, "Yard by Yard," in *Sevastopol',* 57–58; Oktiabr'skii, "Defense of Sevastopol'," 66.

123. Harrison E. Salisbury, *The Nine Hundred Days: The Siege of Leningrad* (1969) (Cambridge: Da Capo Press, 1985), 386; Veksler, ed., *Knigi nepobezhdennogo Leningrada, III,* 140. In 1944, 150,000 copies of a collection of Leo Tolstoy's works, *War Stories,* were published in Leningrad.

124. E. V. Tarle, *Krymskaia Voina* (Leningrad: Institut Istorii Akademii Nauka, 1941); Veksler, *Knigi nepobezhdennogo Leningrada,* 87.

125. Quoted in Brandenberger, "Short Course," 251.

126. Buianov, entry for 13 February 1942, 16. Sergeev-Tsenskii's *Sevastopol'skaia strada* was first published in installments in *Oktiabr',* 7–9 (1937); *Oktiabr',* 1–3 (1938) and then as a book in 1942: *Sevastopol'skaia strada* (Moscow: Gosudarstvennoe izdatel'stvo khudozhestvennoi literatury, 1942).

127. Uskova, entry for 7 June 1942, 56.

128. Ostrovskaia, entry for 4 July 1942, 69. Also see Inber, entry for 28 September 1942, 520b.

129. Gel'fer, entry for 9 June 1942, 260b.

130. One example in Eugene Petrov, "Under Fire," in *Sevastopol',* 60.

131. Inber, entry for 18 February 1942, 90b–10. In published editions, this entry is dated 17 February 1942.

132. Savinkov, entry for 23 April 1942, 33.

133. Ibid., entry for 4 July 1942, 45.

134. Zelenskaia, entry for 18 December 1942, 44–450b; Nikulin, undated entry, 200b.

135. "Instruktsii, voprosniki po stenografirovaniiu vystuplenii rukovoditelei, rabochikh, pamiatniki i drugie dokumenty po sboru materialov po Oborone Leningrada," TsGAIPD, f. 4000, op. 1, d. 194, l. 55.

CONCLUSION

1. Zlotnikova, 16–16ob.

2. Ibid., entries between 1 October 1941 and 4 November 1942, 3–70b; entry for 7 November 1942, 80b.

3. Ibid., 70b.

4. Ibid., entry for 7 November 1942, 10–100b.

5. Ibid., 12.

6. Ibid., 12–120b, 9–90b.

7. Elena Zubkova, *Russia after the War: Hopes, Illusions, and Disappointments, 1945–1957,* trans. Hugh Ragsdale (Armonk, NY: M. E. Sharpe, 1998), 18, 14.

8. Rachel Langford and Russell West, *Marginal Voices, Marginal Forms: Diaries in European Literature and History* (Atlanta: Rodopoi, 1999), 9.

9. Lesin, entry for 14 January 1943, 21.

10. Richard Bidlack and Nikita Lomagin, *The Leningrad Blockade, 1941–44: A New Documentary History from the Soviet Archives* (New Haven, CT: Yale University Press, 2012), 63.

11. Examples of *svodki* in Andrei Dzeniskevich, ed., *Leningrad v osade: Sbornik dokumentov o geroicheskoi oborone Leningrada v gody Velikoi Otechestvennoi Voiny, 1941–*

1944 (St. Petersburg: Liki Rossii, 1995), 472–74; Ostroumova-Lebedeva, entry for 19 January 1943, 177. For similar examples, see Anna Stepanovna Umanskaia (née Kechek), entries for 18, 19 January 1943, OR RNB, f. 1273, d. 72, ll. 48–49 (hereafter "Umanskaia"); Savinkov, entry for 18 January 1943, 76; Konopleva, entry for 19 January 1943, 35–36.

12. Krakov, entry for 18 January 1943, 52–53.

13. Ibid., entry for 19 January 1943, 37–38.

14. They are Zelenskaia, Krakov, Savinkov, Inber, Timofeev, Ostroumova-Lebedeva, Lesin, Umanskaia (Kechek), Kostrovitskaia, Volozhenikov, and A. Mironova.

15. Excellent research on the commemoration of the blockade include Lisa A. Kirschenbaum, *The Legacy of the Siege of Leningrad, 1941–1995: Myths, Memories, and Monuments* (Cambridge: Cambridge University Press, 2006); Steven M. Maddox, *Saving Stalin's Imperial City: Historic Preservation in Leningrad, 1930–1950* (Bloomington: Indiana University Press, 2015); Catriona Kelly, *Remembering St. Petersburg* (Triton, 2014), 34–75, http://www.academia.edu/6847211/remembering_st_petersburg.

16. Andrei Dzeniskevich, "O sozdanii obshchegorodskoi komissii po sboru materialov dlia istorii oborony Leningrada," in *Leningradskaia nauka v gody Velikoi Otechestvennoi Voiny,* ed. V. A. Shishkin (St. Petersburg: Nauka, 1995), 129–39.

17. Ibid., 135–36; Nina Borisovna Lebedeva, "Sotrudniki Leningradskogo instituta istorii," in *Zhenshchina i voina: o roli zhenshchin v oborone Leningrada: 1941–44,* ed. Bozhenkova, Margarita Ivanovna, and Andrei Rostislavovich Dzeniskevich (St. Petersburg: Izdatel'stvo Sankt-Peterburgskogo Universiteta, 2006), 255–60; Nina Borisovna Lebedeva, "Kollektsiia dokumentov po istorii Velikoi Otechestvennoi Voiny v fonde Leningradskogo Instituta Istorii Partii," in *Bitva za Leningrad: Problemy sovremennykh issledovanii* (St. Petersburg: Sankt-Peterburgskii Universitet, 2007), 117–24. The Academy's requests are published in Dzeniskevich, *Leningrad v osade,* 520–22.

18. "Instruktsii, voprosniki po stenografirovaniiu vystuplenii rukovoditelei, rabochikh, pamiatniki i drugie dokumenty po sboru materialov po Oborone Leningrada," TsGAIPD, f. 4000, op. 1, d. 194, ll. 3–6, 19–43, 99. Recollections are analyzed in Andrea Zemskov-Züge, "Remembering the War in Soviet and Post-Soviet Russia. Official and Unofficial Practices of Remembering," in *Unsettling History: Archiving and Narrating in Historiography,* ed. Sebastian Jobs and Alf Lüdtke (Frankfurt: Campus, 2010), 199–217.

19. "Instruktsii, voprosniki po stenografirovaniiu," TsGAIPD, f. 4000, op. 1, d. 194, l. 52.

20. Viktor Demidov and Vladislav Kutuzov, "Poslednii udar. Dokumental'naia povest'," L. I. Zakharov, ed., *Leningradskoe delo* (Leningrad: Lenizdat, 1990), 115; Maddox, *Saving Stalin's Imperial City,* 155–63.

21. "Postanovlenie direktsii IMEL pri TsK VKP(b) o plane raboty instituta za 1944," TsGAIPD, f. 4000, op. 1, d. 222, l. 1; "Akty i raspiski o peredache materialov fonda instituta vystavke 'Geroicheskaia oborona Leningrada' i muzeiu oborony Leningrada, 9 / II / 44–17 / X / 45," TsGAIPD, f. 4000, op. 1, d. 234, ll. 1–17.

22. Krakov, entry for 18 January 1943.

23. Krakov, entry for 16–21 February 1943, 12; Bidlack and Lomagin, *Leningrad Blockade,* 63.

24. Inber, entry for 24 January 1943, 40–41.

25. Ibid., entry for 15 February 1943, 500b.

26. Ibid., entries for 9 May, 28 July, 3, 8 August, 8 November 1943, 610b, 220b, 91–920b, 96, 22–220b. Page numbers are listed in order; they span two separate notebooks that are renumbered to start at page 1.

27. Kostrovitskaia, "August, 1943," 59–60.

28. Savinkov, entries for 23, 25, 26, 27 January 1943, 77–770b. Also see Ostroumova-Lebedeva, entries for 24, 27, 31 January 1943, 184–86, 190–91.

29. Lesin, entry for 28 March 1943, 22.

30. Umanskaia, entry for 16 June 1943, 68.

31. Zagorskaia, entry for 26 June 1943, 31–310b. For another example, see Zelenskaia, entry for 13 April 1943, 1170b–18.

32. Lesin, entry for 28 March 1943, 210b–22.

33. Ostroumova-Lebedeva, entry for 27 January 1944, 4–40b.

34. Ibid., 50b.

35. "Reshenie lengorispolkom ob otmene ogranichenii ustanovlennykh v sviazi s vrazhes-kimi artilleriiskimi obstrelami Leningrada, 29/I/44," in *Ot voiny k miru, Leningrad 1944–1945: Sbornik dokumentov,* ed. S. K. Bernev, N. B. Lebedeva, G. I. Lisovskaia, and N. Iu. Cherepenina (St. Petersburg: Liki Rossii, 2013), 17.

36. "Spetsial'noe soobshchenie UNKVD LO P.S. Popkovu ob uvelichenii chisla grazhdan, pytaiushchikhsia nezakonno vernut'sia v Leningrad, 6/V/1944," in Lebedev et al., *Ot voiny k miru,* 56–58.

37. Rebecca Manley, *To the Tashkent Station: Evacuation and Survival in the Soviet Union at War* (Ithaca, NY: Cornell University Press, 2009), 246, 253, 259–60; *LP* article quoted in Elizabeth White, "After the War Was Over: The Civilian Return to Leningrad," *Europe-Asia Studies* 59, no. 7 (2007): 1154.

38. Robert Dale, "Re-adjusting to Life after War: The Demobilization of Red Army Veterans in Leningrad and the Leningrad Region, 1944–1950" (Ph.D. diss., Queen Mary University of London, 2010), 73–74, 275; "Reshenie suzhennogo zasedaniia Lengorispolkoma ob usilenii okhrany domov, 14/VII/1944," in Lebedev et al., *Ot voiny k miru,* 68.

39. On the tumultuous liberation of other Soviet cities, see Karl D. Qualls, *From Ruins to Reconstruction: Urban Identity in Soviet Sevastopol after World War II* (Ithaca, NY: Cornell University Press, 2009); Jeffrey W. Jones, *Everyday Life and the "Reconstruction" of Soviet Russia during and after the Great Patriotic War* (Bloomington, IN: Slavica, 2008); Kees Boterbloem, *Life and Death under Stalin: Kalinin Province, 1945–1953* (Montreal: McGill-Queen's University Press, 1999); Joon-Seo Song, "The Legacy of World War II on the Stalinist Home Front: Magnitogorsk, 1941–1953" (Ph.D. diss., Michigan State University, 2007).

40. Kirschenbaum, *Legacy,* 115; Maddox, *Saving Stalin's Imperial City,* 155–63; "Postanov-lenie direktsii IMEL pri TsK VKP(b) o plane raboty instituta za 1944," TsGAIPD, f. 4000, op. 1, d. 222, ll. 1–50b.

41. "Postanovlenie direktsii IMEL," TsGAIPD, f. 4000, op. 1, d. 222, ll. 3, 10–14.

42. "Instruktsii, voprosniki po stenografirovaniiu," TsGAIPD, f. 4000, op. 1, d. 194, ll. 61–62.

43. E. Korol'chuk, A. Volkova, "Ot sostavitelei," *Leningradtsy v dni blokady: Sbornik,* ed. Ia. I. Klebanov and A. N. Pazi (Leningrad: Leninzdat, 1947), 3.

44. Nikolai Voronov, "Rabota nad istoriei geroicheskogo Leningrada," *Leningrad* 13–14 (1943): 21. Istpart's early publications include S. I. Avvakumov, ed., *Geroicheskii Leningrad, 1917–1942* (Leningrad: Gospolitizdat, 1943); S. I. Avvakumov, ed., *Leningrad v Velikoi Otechestvennoi Voine Sovetskogo Soiuza: Sbornik dokumentov i materialov,* vol. 1 (Leningrad: Ogiz-Gospolitizdat, 1944); K. G. Sharikov, ed., *Leningrad v Velikoi Otechestvennoi Voine Sovetskogo Soiuza: Sbornik dokumentov i materialov,* vol. 2 (Leningrad: Lenizdat, 1947); S. I. Avvakumov, ed., *Bol'sheviki-organizatory oborony Leningrada* (Leningrad: Lenizdat, 1943); A. F. Volkova, ed., *Zhenshchiny goroda Lenina: Rasskazy i ocherki o zhenshchinakh Leningrada v dni blokady* (Leningrad: Lenizdat, 1944); V. A. Kalmykov, ed., *Velikaia pobeda sovetskikh voisk pod Leningradom* (Leningrad: Voennoe Izdatel'stvo, Narodnogo komissariata oborony, 1945); Klebanov and Pazi, *Leningradtsy v dni blokady.*

45. Volkova ed., *Velikaia pobeda sovetskikh voisk,* 23.

46. Compare Bubnova's diary manuscript and Maia Aleksandrovna Bubnova, "Iz dnevnik Maii Bubnovoi," in Klebanov and Pazi, *Leningradtsy v dni blokady,* 221–32.

47. Inber, entry for 29 February 1944, 270b; Vera Inber, "Pochti tri goda (Leningradskii dnevnik). Povest'," RGALI, f. 1072, op. 1, d. 32, l. 90.

48. Inber, entry for 7 April 1942, 210b.

49. D.A. Polikarpov, "K redkollegii zhurnala 'Znamia,' 9/II/45," in *Literaturnyi Front: Istoriia politicheskoi tsenzury, 1932–1946. Sbornik dokumentov,* ed. D.L. Babichenko (Moscow: Entsiklopediia rossiiskikh dereven', 1994), 151–56; "Iz vystupleniia P. Gromova," *Leningrad* 7–8 (1945), 27.

50. Polikarpov, "K redkollegii zhurnala 'Znamia,' 9 / II / 45," *Literaturnyi Front,* 151–52.

51. Arlen Blium, *Kak eto delalos' v Leningrade: Tsenzura v gody ottepeli, zastoia i perestroika 1953–1991* (St. Petersburg: Akademicheskii proekt, 2005), 163–65. For a partial list of banned books on the siege, see "Iz perepiski glavlita s TsK VKP(b) po voprosam tsenzury, 11 / III / 50," Arlen Blium, ed., *Tsenzura v Sovetskom Soiuze 1917–1991: Dokumenty* (Moscow: Rosspen, 2004), 361.

52. Vishnevskii, entry for 24 November 1943 in Vsevolod Vishnevskii, *Leningrad: dnevniki voennykh let 2* (Moscow: Voenizdat, 2002), 235.

53. P. Vershigora, "O 'byvalykh liudiakh' i ikh kritikakh," *Zvezda* 6 (June 1948), 106–7. Also see "On the Writers' Tribunal," *Zvezda* 4 (April 1948): 143–44.

54. On the ambiguities of victory, see Amir Weiner, *Making Sense of War: The Second World War and the Fate of the Bolshevik Revolution* (Princeton, NJ: Princeton University Press, 2001); Mark Edele, *Soviet Veterans of the Second World War: A Popular Movement in an Authoritarian Society, 1941–1991* (Oxford: Oxford University Press, 2008); E. S. Seniavskaia, *1941–1945: Frontovoe pokolenie. Istoriko-psikhologicheskoe issledovanie* (Moscow: Institut istorii RAN, 1995); Zubkova, *Russia after the War.*

55. Yoram Gorlizki and Oleg Vital'evich Khlevniuk, *Cold Peace: Stalin and the Soviet Ruling Circle, 1945–1953* (Oxford: Oxford University Press, 2004), 31–33.

56. Numerous other cities, communities, and groups were persecuted in the postwar Stalin period. The vast literature on this includes Zubkova, *Russia after the War,* 130–38;

Konstantin Azadovskii and Boris Egorov, "From Anti-Westernism to Anti-Semitism: Stalin and the Impact of the 'Anti-Cosmopolitan' Campaigns on Soviet Culture," *Journal of Cold War Studies* 4, no. 1 (2002): 66–80; Terry Martin, "The Origins of Soviet Ethnic Cleansing," *Journal of Modern History* 70, no. 4 (1998): 813–61; Zvi Gitelman, "History, Memory and Politics: The Holocaust in the Soviet Union," *Holocaust and Genocide Studies* 5, no. 1 (1990): 23–37.

57. Richard Bidlack, "Ideological or Political Origins of the Leningrad Affair? A Response to David Brandenberger," *Russian Review* 64, no. 1 (2005): 90–95. David Brandenberger alternatively argued that the Leningrad Affair was a response to efforts to establish a Leningrad-based communist party organization for Russian Soviet Federative Socialist Republic. Brandenberger, "Stalin, the Leningrad Affair and the Limits of Postwar Russocentrism," *Russian Review* 63, no. 2 (2004): 241–55.

58. A. A. Danilov and A. V. Pyzhikov, *Rozhdenie sverkhderzhavy: SSSR v pervye poslevoennye gody* (Moscow: Rosspen, 2001), 8, 44–45; Gorlizki and Khlevniuk, *Cold Peace,* 3–6; Maddox, *Saving Stalin's Imperial City,* 175–76. On the independence of Leningrad's wartime party organization, see Kirill Anatol'evich Boldovskii, "Apparat Leningradskoi gorodskoi partiinoi organizatsii i ego mesto v sisteme vlastnykh otnoshchenii v SSSR, 1945–53," Dissertatsiia na soiskanie uchenoi stepeni kandidata istoricheskikh nauk (St. Petersburg: Institut istorii RAN, 2013).

59. Benjamin Tromly, "The Leningrad Affair and Soviet Patronage Politics, 1949–1950," *Europe-Asia Studies* 56, no. 5 (2004): 707–29; C. N. Boterbloem, "The Death of Andrei Zhdanov," *Slavonic and East European Review* 80, no. 2 (2002): 287; Gorlizki and Khlevniuk, *Cold Peace,* 74.

60. Quoted in Bidlack and Lomagin, *Leningrad Blockade,* 73.

61. Demidov and Kutuzov, "Poslednii udar," in Zakharov, ed. *Leningradskoe delo,* 118.

62. "Prikaz upolnomochennogo soveta ministrov SSSR i nachal'nika Glavlita 'O rabote Lenoblgorlita, 6 / II / 1947;" "O proverke bibliotechnykh fondov, 24 / V / 1947;" "Ob iz'iatii knig iz bibliotek, 2 / XI / 1949;" "Iz perepiski glavlita s TsK VKP (b) po voprosam tsenzury, 11 / III / 1950" in Blium, *Tsenzura v Sovetskom Soiuze,* 341, 345, 357; Blium, *Kak eto delalos',* 160–62; Dzeniskevich, *Blokada i politika,* 11.

63. "Otchet o rabote instituta za 1946 s prolozheniem spiska nauchnykh rabot," TsGAIPD, f. 4000, op. 1, d. 335.

64. 'Proekt postanovleniia biuro Leningradskogo GK VKP(b) o rabote instituta, 1947," TsGAIPD, f. 4000, op. 1, d. 468, ll. 1–4, 9–10; "O privedenie v poriadok arkhivnykh materialov instituta, 1949," TsGAIPD, f. 4000, op. 1, d. 734; "Protokol zasedaniia ekspertno-proverochnoi komissii Partarkhiva, otborochnye spiski na materialy, ne podlezhashchikh khranenii, zakliuchenie Tsentral'nogo Partarkhiva IMEL i akty ob unichtozhenii materialov, 3 / XII / 49–2 / III / 50," TsGAIPD, f. 4000, op. 1, d. 738; "Plan raboty instituta na 1948," TsGAIPD, f. 4000, op. 1, d. 607, ll. 1, 4, 7.

65. Demidov and Kutuzov, "Poslednii udar," in Zakharov, ed. *Leningradskoe delo,* 119–20.

66. Blium, *Kak eto delalos',* 162.

67. Maddox, *Saving Stalin's Imperial City,* 185, 190–91. The diaries that I use from the museum were donated after it was resurrected in the post-Stalin era.

68. This is argued in Demidov and Kutuzov, "Poslednii udar," in Zakharov, ed., *Leningradskoe delo,* 114–20, 130; Maddox, *Saving Stalin's Imperial City,* 171, 187; Dzeniskevich, *Leningradskaia nauka,* 42; Kirschenbaum, *The Legacy,* 115–16, 142–44.

69. Dzeniskevich, *Blokada i politika,* 13–14. I speculate that some diaries may have been destroyed because Istpart reports allude to the destruction of some holdings and list several diaries, which are no longer in its catalogue. See "Plan raboty instituta na nauchnykh sotrudnikov, svedeniia i pamiatki po sobraniiu i obrabotke materialov o geroicheskoi zashchite Leningrada v gody Velikoi Otechestvennoi Voiny, 1944," TsGAIPD, f. 4000, op. 1, d. 226.

70. The encyclopedia entry on Leningrad highlights the city's military and industrial contributions to the war effort "despite the difficult conditions of the blockade"—this is the only reference to the siege (B. A. Vvedenskii, ed., *Bol'shaia sovetskaia entsiklopediia vol. 24* (Moscow: Gosudarstvennoe nauchnoe izdatel'stvo 'Bol'shaia sovetskaia entsiklopediia,' 1952), 524. The blockade is discussed but with scant mention of hunger in: L.S. Shaumian, ed., *Leningrad: entsiklopedicheskii spravochnik* (Moscow: Gosudarstvennoe nauchnoe izdatel'stvo 'Bol'shaia sovetskaia entsiklopediia,' 1957), 123–33.

71. Maddox, *Saving Stalin's Imperial City,* 189.

72. Examples include A. V. Karasev, *Leningradtsy v gody blokady, 1941–1943* (Moscow: Izdatel'stvo Akademii Nauk SSSR, 1959); Nikolai Shumilov, *V dni blokady* (Moscow: Mysl', 1974). Soviet historiography of the blockade, from the 1940s to the 2000s is reviewed in G. L. Sobolev, "Blokada Leningrada: postizhenie pravdy," *Noveishaia istoriia Rossiia* 2 (2012), 72–87.

73. Diaries published soon after Stalin's death include Ksenia Polzikova-Rubets, *Oni uchilis' v Leningrade: Dnevnik uchitel'nitsy* (Leningrad: Gosudarstvennoe izdatel'stvo detskoi literatury, 1954); M. Z. Zakharova, ed., *Leningrada: 1941–1944: Vospominaniiu, dnevniki uchastnikov* (Leningrad: Nauka, 1968); *V dni blokady* (Leningrad: Khudozhnik RSFSR, 1969). Also see the collections: Tokarev, Iu. S., *Deviatsot geroicheskikh dnei: sbornik dokumentov i materialov o geroicheskoi bor'be trudiashchikhsia leningrada v 1941–1944 gg.* (Leningrad: Nauka, 1966); F. I. Sirota, *Leningrad gorod-geroi* (Leningrad: Lenizdat, 1960).

Selected Bibliography

PERIODICALS

The American Review of Soviet Medicine
Komsomol'skaia Pravda
Leningrad
Leningradskaia Pravda
Smena
Znamia
Zvezda

UNPUBLISHED DIARIES

The unpublished diaries that inform this study are organized here by author's last name.
I have included the diary's archival location and, when available, the author's main
occupation during the war.

Afanas'ev, Dmitrii Vladimirovich. Text courtesy of Natal'ia Aleksandrovna Afanas'eva.
    Thirteen- year-old student when World War II began. Excerpts appear in Tamara
    Staleva, *Vechnyi deti blokady: Dokumental'nye ocherki* (Moscow: Author, 1995), 4–14.
Bardovskii, Aleksandr Aleksandrovich. TsGAIPD, f. 4000, op. 11, d. 7. Taught literature
    at School 156 and studied at Leningrad State University.
Basalaev, Innokentii Memnonovich. OR RNB, f. 1076 d. 16.
Belov, Boris Aleksandrovich. TsGAIPD, f. 4000, op. 11, d. 9. Party representative for the
    Stalin factory and fought at the front.

Berngardt, Nikolai Aleksandrovich. TsGAIPD, f. 4000, op. 11, d. 1807. Worked for Lengorkom.

Borichevskii, Ivan Adamovich. OR RNB, f. 1448, d. 9.

Borovikova, Aleksandra Nikiforovna. TsGAIPD, f. 4000, op. 11, d. 15. A mechanical engineer who held management positions at the Volodarskii Sawmill Factory and at Bread Factory 6.

Bubnova, Maia Aleksandrovna. "Dnevnik." TsGAIPD, f. 4000, op. 11, d. 16. An eighth grader at School 221. Excerpts of the diary appear in Klebanov and Pazi, ed., *Leningradtsy v dni blokady*, 221–32.

Budogoskaia, Lidiia Anatol'evna. TsGALI, f. 427, op. 1, d. 112. A wartime nurse, worked for the State Marionette Theater and as a journalist after World War II.

Buianov, Aleksandr Matveevich. "Dnevnik." TsGAIPD, f. 4000, op. 11, d. 19. Political instructor for Vasil'evskii Island District's *raikom* and assisted in the local procurator's office.

Byl'ev (Protopopov), Nikolai Mikhailovich. "Otryvki iz blokadnikh zapisei, 1941–42." TsGALI, f. 109, op. 1, d. 9. Artist who exhibited under the pseudonym Byl'ev. Excerpts of the diary are published in Brodskii, *Khudozhniki goroda-fronta*, 311–44.

Chepurko, Margarita Sergeevna (née Malkova). GMMOBL, f. RDF, op. 1L, d. 10. Schoolgirl during World War II.

Chernovskii, Aleksei Alekseevich. "Dnevnik. V Leningrade, 1941–42." TsGAIPD, f. 4000, op. 11, d. 119. Historian and senior employee at the Museum of the History and Development of Leningrad.

Enman, Natal'ia Aleksandrovna. TsGAIPD, f. 4000, op. 10, d. 1396. Senior scholarly employee at the Kirov Museum.

Erokhana, Nina Nikolaevna (née Klishevich). "Blokadnyi dnevnik Niny Nikolaevny Erokhanoi." GMMOBL, f. RDF, op. 1L, d. 490. Eighteen-year-old student during World War II. The diary initially was cowritten with her uncle, but Erokhana destroyed those pages in 1945.

Evdokilov, Aleksei Fedorovich. GMMOBL, f. RDF, op. 1R, d. 30. Foreman at the Red Banner Factory and an MPVO worker. Excerpts of his diary appear in Levtov and David, *Budni podviga*.

Evlakhov, Orest Aleksandrovich. TsGALI, f. 466, op. 1, d. 73. Composer and professor at the Leningrad Conservatory, was a secretary for the Leningrad Branch of the Union of Soviet Composers.

Freman, Max Aleksandrovich. OR RNB, f. 709, d. 302.

Frumberg, Aleksei Mikhailovich. TsGAIPD, f. 4000, op. 11, d. 114. A secretary in Voskov Factory's party organization.

Gakkel', Iakov Modestovich. OR RNB, f. 1005, d. 26.

Gel'fer, Gesel' Aizikovich. "Dnevnik." TsGAIPD, f. 4000, op. 11, d. 24. Electrician and engineer in Workshop 3 of the Stalin Factory.

Gorbunova, Nina Georgievna. "Dnevnik 22/VI/41–11/V.43. Leningrad." TsGAIPD, f. 4000, op. 11, d. 27. Directed Orphanage 58.

Grishkevich, Aleksandr Pavlovich. TsGAIPD, f. 4000, op. 11, d. 28. Sectional manager in Lengorkom's printing department.

Grizova-Rudykovskaia, Tat'iana Leonidovna (née Rudykovskaia). "Dnevnik." GMMOBL, f. RDF, op. 1R, d. 1, punkt 7. She was nine years old when World War II began.

Ianovich, Tat'iana L'vovna. TsGAIPD, f. 4000, op. 11, d. 122.

Ianushevich, Zoia Vasil'evna. GMMOBL, f. RDF, op. 1R, d. 91. Studied at the Vavilov All-Union Institute of Plant Industry.

Inber, Vera Mikhailovna. "Dnevnik voennykh let." OR RNB, f. 312, dd. 12, 44–50. "Pochti tri goda (Leningradskii dnevnik). Povest'." RGALI, f. 1072, op. 1, dd. 32, 73. Professional poet and writer. Inber reworked her manuscripts before publishing them. Two of the major publications of her diary are *Pochti tri goda: Leningradskii dnevnik* (1947) and *Pochti tri goda* (1968).

Iushekhonov, Aleksei Gavrilovich. TsGAIPD, f. 4000, op. 11, d. 96. Worked at the Russian Diesel Engine Factory.

Ivanov, Vsevolod. OR RNB, f. 1000, op. 2, d. 515.

Ivleva, Valentina Mikhailovna. GMMOBL, f. RDF, op. 1L, d. 431. Taught Russian at School 36 in the Vyborg District. Portions of her diary are reproduced in Levtov and David, *Budni podviga*.

Kalinin, Vladimir Vasil'evch. Diary courtesy of Tamara Vladimirovna Staleva. Worked at the Hermitage. Parts of his story are discussed in P. K. Baltun, *Russkii Muzei: Evakuatsiia, blokada, vosstanovlenie* (Leningrad: Izobrazitel'noe Iskusstvo, 1981).

Kapitonova, Vera Mikhailovna. TsGAIPD, f. 4000, op. 11, d. 41. Worked in the Moscow District's Propaganda and Agitation Department.

Kedrov, Aleksandr Tikhonovich. TsGAIPD, f. 4000, op. 11, d. 44. Acting director of Factory 224, Sverdlovsk District.

Ketov, Aleksandr Dmitrievich. MNM, k.p. 6512, f. 1, d. 655. Text courtesy of the D. D. Shostakovich Middle School 235. Artist and designer at the Theater of Musical Comedy.

Kleveryi, Iulii Iul'evich. TsGALI, f. 154, op. 1, d. 67. Artist and set designer at Leningrad's Pioneer Theater, Marionette Theater, and others. This diary was kept by Oscar Iul'evich from a concentration camp in the Vydogoshch' area and refers to blockaded Leningrad.

Klykov, Vladimir Andreevich. TsGAIPD, f. 4000, op. 11, d. 45. Manager for the October Railway.

Kniazev, Georgii Alekseevich. ARAN SPb, f. 929, op. 2, dd. 95, 98 Historian and archivist at the Naval archive between 1917 and 1926 and in 1929 at the Leningrad Branch of the Academy of Sciences. His diary was published as *Dni velikikh ispytanii, dnevniki 1941–1945*, ed. N. P. Kopaneva (St. Petersburg: Nauka, 2009).

Kogan, Lev Rudol'fovich. OR RNB, f. 1035, d. 1. Dramaturge.

Kok, Georgii Mikhailovich. TsGAIPD, f. 4000, op. 11, d. 48. Head of the planning department at Leningrad's Factory for Radio Technology.

Kolbantseva, Rogneda Viktorovna. GMMOBL, f. RDF, op. 1L, d. 215. Schoolgirl during World War II.

Koltunov, Iosif Grigor'evich. OR RNB, f. 552, d. 39.

Komsomol organization of North Cable Factory (Sevkabel'). TsGAIPD, f. 4000, op. 11, d. 130. This collectively authored diary includes the red pencil comments of the group's superiors.

Kononova, Elena. OR RNB. This diary did not have a catalogue number at the time of consultation.

Konopleva, Mariia Sergeevna. "V blokirovannom Leningrade: Zapiski." OR RNB, f. 368, dd. 1–3. Archivist and librarian specializing in art, who worked at the Russian Museum and the Hermitage. During the war, she did secretarial work in Clinic 22.

Korneeva, Glafira Nikolaevna. TsGAIPD, f. 4000, op. 11, d. 51. Directed School 3 in Sverdlovsk region and did inspections for RONO.

Kostrovitskaia, Vera Sergeevna. TsGALI, f. 157, op. 1, d. 28. Ballerina at the Kirov Theater and a choreographer and dance instructor in the Department of Pedagogy at the Petrograd Choreography School. A redacted version of her diary was published in *Neva* 9 (1973).

Koterli (née Kondakova), Elena Iosifovna. TsGALI, f. 187, op. 1, d. 7. Did many jobs, including factory work, journalism, and novel writing.

Kozlovskii, Aleksei Kornil'evich. TsGAIPD, f. 4000, op. 11, d. 46. Director of high-tension lines at Lenenergo and later director of the Northern Cable Factory

Krakov, M. M. "Dnevnik." TsGAIPD, f. 4000, op. 11, dd. 52, 55. Senior engineer at Electrical Station 10.

Kropacheva, Mariia Viacheslavovna. OR RNB, f. 1000, op. 2, d. 676. Schoolteacher and MPVO volunteer. Excerpts of the diary appear in Simmons and Perlina, *Writing the Siege*, 53–57.

Kruikov, Aleksei Nikolaevich. Text courtesy of the Kriukov family. Musician and composer. Portions of this text appear in Andrei Kriukov, *Muzika v efire voennogo Leningrada* (St. Petersburg: Kompozitor, 2005).

Kurbanov, M. M. OR RNB, f. 406, dd. 237, 239.

Larionov, Leonid Vasil'evich. OR RNB, f. 422, d. 44. Worked at Leningrad's Naval Museum.

Lebedev, G. E. Diary courtesy of Tamara Vladimirovna Staleva. A front-line actor. Part of his story is documented in V. Ia. Merkulova-Mashirova and S. A. Ponomarenko, eds., *Bez antrakta: Akteri goroda Lenina v gody blokady* (Leningrad: Lenizdat, 1970).

Lebedev, Ivan Vladimirovich. TsGALI, f. 231, op. 1, d. 7. Artist, writer, and circus performer who used the stage name "Uncle Vania."

Lebedev, Viktor Vladimirovich. Diary courtesy of Tamara Vladimirovna Staleva. Architect and academic.

Lepkovich, Arkadii A. "Dnevnik Arkadiia Lepkovicha, 1/XII/41–20/IX/1942." TsGAIPD, f. 4000, op. 11, d. 85. Worked at the broadcast center for Leningrad Radio.

Lesin, Boris Apollonovich. "Dnevnik Borisa Apollonovicha Lesina." TsGAIPD, f. 4000, op. 11, d. 61. Writer and editor for the October Railway's newspaper *Stalinets*.

Levina, Esfir' Gustanovna. "Dnevnik. 12/I–24/XI/42." TsGAIPD, f. 4000, op. 11, d. 57. Architect who worked for the architectural-planning division of the Leningrad city soviet. Her other wartime account, which overlaps with the diary, is: Levina, "Pis'ma k drugu," in *Leningradtsy v dni blokady*, ed. Klebanov and Pazi, 195–220.

Liubovskaia, Aleksandra Pavlovna. "Leningrad, 1941–42: Zapiski zhitelia blokadnogo goroda." Text courtesy of Igor' Liubovskii. Technical translator, knowing over twenty languages, and librarian in a milling factory.

Lukin, Vladimir Andreevich, and Tamara Petrovna Nekliudova. "Delo Lukina, V. A. i ego zheny T. P. Nekliuovoi." GMMOBL, f. RDF, op. 1L, d. 238. Actor. File contains his and his wife's diaries.

Makarov, Vladimir Kuz'mich. OR RNB, f. 1135, dd. 54–55. Art and architecture historian as well as preservationist for the Russian Museum.

Malysheva, Vasilisa Petrovna. TsGAIPD, f. 4000, op. 11, d. 65. Editor for the Molotov Factory newspaper and later for Leningrad Radio. She was a delegate for the Sverdlovsk District soviet.

Mantul, Vladimir Grigor'evich. TsGAIPD, f. 4000, op. 11, d. 67. Grinder and polisher at the Stalin Factory.

Mashkova, Mariia Vasil'evna. OR RNB, f. 1407, d. 21. Librarian at the Central Branch of the Leningrad Public Library. Selections of this diary are published in: A. N. Maslova, P. L. Vakhtina; M. K. Svichenskaia, eds., *Publichnaia biblioteka v gody voiny: 1941–1945: dnevniki, vospominaniia, pis'ma, dokumenty* (St. Petersburg: Rossiiskaia natsional'naia biblioteka, 2005).

Matiushina, Ol'ga Konstantinovna. "Dnevnik." TsGAIPD, f. 4000, op. 11, d. 68. Artist and writer.

Matus, Kseniia Markianovna. MNM, k.p. 4153, f. 2, d. 2804. Text courtesy of the D. D. Shostakovich Middle School 235. Musician with the Leningrad Philharmonic, and played oboe in Shostakovich's Seventh Symphony. An interview with her appears in Simmons and Perlina, *Writing the Siege,* 147–55.

Mervol'f, Nina Rudal'fovna. MNM, k.p. 6580, f. 2, d. 5579. Text courtesy of the D. D. Shostakovich Middle School 235. Eighteen-year-old theater student during World War II.

Mikhaileva-Kasotkina, Nadezhda Leonidovna. TsGAIPD, f. 8921 op. 1, d. 196. Pianist. Most of the diary is published in M. I. Bozhenkova, A. I. Burlakov, A. R. Dzeniskevich, A. N. Rubtsov, T. A. Postrelova, I. D. Khodanovich, ed., *Zhenshchina i voina: O roli zhenshchin v oborone Leningrada: 1941–44* (St. Petersburg: Izdatel'stvo Sankt-Peterburgskogo Universiteta, 2006), 299–310.

Miliutina, Vera Vladimirovna. TsGALI, f. 495, op. 1, d. 164. Artist at Leningrad's Artists' Academy and the Repin Institute of Proletarian Graphic Arts.

Mironova, Aleksandra Nikolaevna. TsGAIPD, f. 4000, op. 11, d. 71. History teacher at School 10 and during World War II worked as an inspector for RONO and in additional schools and orphanages. Excerpts of her diary appear in Dagin, *Oborona Leningrada, 1941–1944.*

Mironova, Evgeniia Ivanovna. GMMOBL, f. RDF, op. 1L, d. 449.

Molchanov, Anatolii Vladimirovich. "Ia na voine byl shkol'nikom blokadnym: Vospominaniia." Text courtesy of Evgeniia Alekseevna Molchanova. Schoolboy during World War II.

Molodezhnikov, Viktor Dmitrievich. MNM 6, k.p 2489, f. zhit., d. 186. Text courtesy of the D. D. Shostakovich Middle School 235. Worked in a metallurgical factory.

Mukhina, Elena Vladimirovna. TsGAIPD, f. 4000, op. 11, d. 72. She was a sixteen-year-old student when the siege began. Most of her diary was published in Mukhina, *Sokhrani moiu pechal'nuiu istoriiu.*

Namochilin, Ivan Stepanovich. TsGAIPD, f. 4000, op. 11, d. 79. Director of the Propaganda and Agitation Department of Leningrad Railroad's Baltic branch.

Nikitin, Fedor Mikhailovich. "Dnevnik." MNM, k.p. 6920, f. 1, d. 5580. Text courtesy of the D. D. Shostakovich Middle School 235. Actor at the Kommisarzhevskaia Theater and agitator for the Leningrad House of the Red Army.

Nikol'skii, Aleksandr Sergeevich. OR RNB, f. 1037, dd. 900–901. Artist whose diary is mostly pictorial.

Nikulin, Anisim Prokof'evich. TsGAIPD, f. 4000, op. 11, d. 80. A *raikom* representative for the October District.

Osipova, Lidiia. HIA, Box 1, 80033-10. A writer, she escaped Leningrad and became a German propagandist in the Leningrad suburb of Slutsk (Pavlovsk).

Osipova, Natal'ia Petrovna. TsGAIPD, f. 4000, op. 11, d. 89. Statistician in the planning department of Workshop 4 in the Molotov Factory.

Ostroumova-Lebedeva, Anna Petrovna. OR RNB, f. 1015, dd. 36, 57–61. Painter and artist. She reworked portions of her diary and published them as: Ostroumova-Lebedeva, *Avtobiograficheskii zapiski, vols. 1–3* (Moscow: Tsentrpoligraf, 2003). Excerpts appear in Simmons and Perlina, *Writing the Siege,* 25–32.

Ostrovskaia, Sof'ia Kazimirovna. OR RNB, f. 1448, dd. 9–12. Professional writer and editor, she worked for the Literature Department of *Leningradskaia Pravda* during World War II. Most of the diary is published in *Russkoe proshloe: istoriko-dokumental'nykh al'manakh,* vol. 10 (St. Petersburg, 2006), 191–323.

Ots, Liudmila. TsGAIPD, f. 4000, op. 11, d. 85. Student at School 11, also volunteered in wartime hospitals.

Perel'man, Irma Oznasovna. MNM, k.p. 6517, f. 5, d. 668. Text courtesy of the D. D. Shostakovich Middle School 235.

Peshel', Petr Vasil'evich. TsGAIPD, f. 4000, op. 11, d. 92. Head mechanic at Electrical Station 10.

Peterson, Valia. "Dnevnik." TsGAIPD, f. 4000, op. 11, d. 86. In seventh grade at School 239 when the siege began.

Peto, Ol'ga Richardovna. "Deti blokady: Deti Leningrada, 1942–1943." OR RNB, f. 1273, d. 52. A medical doctor, she searched for abandoned children and worked for the emergency medical services.

Petrova, Tat'iana Andreevna. TsGAIPD, f. 4000, op. 11, d. 91. A Lengorkom instructor.

Polzikova-Rubets, Kseniia Vladimirovna. TsGAIPD, f. 4000, op. 11, d. 94. Teacher at School 239. There are two, very different published editions of her diary: *Oni uchilis' v Leningrade* (1954); *Dnevnik uchitelia blokadnoi shkoly* (2000).

Poshekhonov, Aleksei Gavrilovich. TsGAIPD, f. 4000, op. 11, d. 96. Chief engineer at the Demianskii District Integrated Industrial Plant.

Propaganda and Agitation Department for the Moscow district *raikom.* "Dnevnik otdela propagandy i agitatsii RK VKP(b) Moskovskogo raiona." TsGAIPD, f. 4000, op. 11, d. 124. This collectively authored diary was inspected by the authors' superiors and is marked with red underlining.

Rabinovich, Mikhail Borisovich. GMMOBL, f. RDF, op 1L, d. 51. Teacher at Leningrad State University and MPVO worker.

Rozman, B. Iu. Diary courtesy of Tamara Vladimirovna Staleva. Chemist.

Rudnev, Aleksei Georgievich. TsGALI, f. 223, op. 1, d. 65. Philologist and teacher of library science and Russian at the Herzen State Pedagogical Institute.

Rusakov, Sergei Aleksandrovich. TsGALI, f. 418. Correspondent for TASS and editor at *Molodaia gvardiia.*

Ryvina, Elena Izrail'evna. TsGALI, f. 471, op. 1, d. 180. Wrote for and edited various Leningrad newspapers.

Ryzhikov, Mikhail Ivanovich. GMMOBL, f. RDF, op. 1L, d. 352. Worked on medical train VSP 109 before serving at the front.

Samarin, Petr Mikhailovich. GMMOBL, f. RDF, op. 1L, d. 338. Factory worker.

Savinkov, Ivan Alekseevich. "Dnevnik, 1941–45." TsGAIPD, f. 4000, op. 11, d. 99. Engineer, managed Workshop 9 of the Molotov Factory.

Semenov, Sergei Aleksandrovich. OR RNB, f. 685, dd. 16, 30, 32.

Shaporina, Liubov' Vasil'evna. OR RNB, f. 1086, dd. 7, 9, 10, 11. Artist and nurse. Excerpts of her diary appear in Simmons and Perlina, *Writing the Siege*, 21–24.

Shpak, Aleksandr Illarionovich. TsGAIPD, f. 4000, op. 11, d. 120. Head of Glavneftesnab for the Leningrad region.

Sinakevich, Ol'ga Viktorovna. OR RNB, f. 163, dd. 311, 356–58. Writer and poet.

Sinishchin, Aleksandr Dmitrievich. MNM, k.p. 6513, f. 3 d. 23. Text courtesy of the D. D. Shostakovich Middle School 235.

Sinitsyna, N. I. TsGAIPD, f. 4000, op. 11, d. 107. Political organizer for Housing Committee 124 (Krasnogvardeisk District) and worked in Factory 370.

Sokolova, Elizaveta Aleksandrovna. "Dnevnik." TsGAIPD, f. 4000, op. 11, d. 109. Acting director of Istpart.

Sudakova, N. "Dnevnik." TsGAIPD, f. 4000, op. 10, d. 1387.

Tikhomirova, Marina Aleksandrovna. "Dnevniki (1943–57)." TsGALI, f. 510, op. 1, dd. 38–39. Historian and tour guide, worked at the Museum of the History and Development of Leningrad.

Timofeev, Vasilii Egorovich. TsGAIPD, f. 4000, op. 11, d. 113. Directed the Kolpinskii Bread Factory.

Umanskaia, Anna Stepanovna (née Kechck). OR RNB, f. 1273, d. 72. Schoolgirl during World War II.

Uskova, Natal'ia Borisovna. MNM, k.p. 6518, f. 1, d. 5577. Text courtesy of the D. D. Shostakovich Middle School 235. Philologist.

Uspenskii, Lev Vasil'evich. TsGALI, f. 98, op. 1, d. 148. Art historian and author, wrote for several journals and oversaw a brigade of authors covering the Baltic Fleet.

Vasil'ev, Nikolai Ivanovich. GMMOBL, f. RDF, op. 1L, d. 329. Eleven years old when the siege began, became a professional actor as adult.

Vasiutina, Evgeniia Konstantinovna. TsGALI, f. 522, op. 1, d. 42. Technical engineer, writer and journalist.

Veisberg, Iuliia Lazarovna. OR RNB, f. 639, d. 95.

Vinogradova, Praskovia Fedorovna. TsGAIPD, f. 4000, op. 11, d. 23.

Vladimirov, Vasilii and Boris. GMMOBL, f. RDF, op. 1L, d. 385. Diary was written by both brothers.

Volozheninov, Ivan Klement'evich. TsGALI, f. 393, op. 1, d. 3. Epidemiologist at the
   Leningrad Sanitation-Epidemiological Station, published on the history of St. Peters-
   burg and its environs.
Zabolotskaia, Lidiia Korlovna. "Dnevnik Shkol'nogo inspektora Sverdlovskogo Raion-
   nogo Otdela Obrazovaniia." TsGAIPD, f. 4000, op. 11, d. 30. Inspector for Sverdlovsk
   District's education department (RONO).
Zagorskaia, Aleksandra Pavlovna. TsGAIPD, f. 4000, op. 11, d. 33. Chair of the "Red
   Case-maker" artel in the Fruzensk District.
Zelenskaia, Irina Dmitrievna. TsGAIPD, f. 4000, op. 11, d. 35. Statistician and econo-
   mist, managed the planning department at Electrical Station 7. Portions of her diary
   are published in V. M. Kolval'chuk, ed., *"Ia ne sdamsia do poslednogo": Zapiski iz
   blokadnogo Leningrada* (St. Petersburg: Nestor-Istoriia, 2010).
Zinov'eva, N. B. TsGAIPD, f. 4000, op. 11, d. 37. Secretary in the party organization at
   Factory 756.
Zlotnikova, Berta Abramovna. "Dnevnik." TsGAIPD, f. 4000, op. 11, d. 39. Worked for
   the Northern Press Factory and the Pioneer organization.
Zveinek, Asia. OR RNB, f. 1000, op. 2, d. 504. Student at Leningrad State University.

SELECTED PUBLISHED DIARIES, MEMOIRS, AND DOCUMENTARY SOURCES

Adamovich, Ales', and Daniil Granin. *Blokadnaia kniga.* St. Petersburg: Pechatnyi dvor,
   1994. Translated by Hilda Perham as *A Book of the Blockade* (Moscow: Raduga, 1983).
———. *Leningrad under Siege: First-hand Accounts of the Ordeal.* Translated by Clare
   Burstall and Vladimir Kisselnikov. Barnsley, UK: Military Pen and Sword, 2007.
Baltun, P. K. *Russkii Muzei-evakuatsiia, blokada, vosstanovlenie: Iz vospominanii
   muzeinogo rabotnika.* Moscow: Iskusstvo, 1981.
Baranov, Nikolai Varfolomeevich. *Siluety blokady: Zapiski glavnogo arkhitektura goroda.*
   Leningrad: Lenizdat, 1982.
Berggol'ts, Ol'ga. "Blokadnyi dnevnik." *Aprel'* 4 (1991): 128–44.
———. "Iz dnevnikov." *Zvezda* 5 (1990): 182–91.
———. *Vstrecha.* Moscow: Russkaia Kniga, 2000.
Bernev, Stanislav Konstantinovich, and Sergei Vladimirovich Chernov, eds. *Blokadnye
   dnevniki i dokumenty.* St. Petersburg: Evropeiskii Dom, 2004.
Boldyrev, Aleksandr N. *Osadnaia zapis': Blokadnyi dnevnik.* Edited by V. S. Garbuzova
   and I. M. Steblin-Kamenskii. St. Petersburg: Evropeiskii Dom, 1998.
Bozhenkova, M. I., A. I. Burlakov, A. R. Dzeniskevich, A. N. Rubtsov, T. A. Postrelova,
   and I. D. Khodanovich, ed. *Zhenshchina i voina: O roli zhenshchin v oborone Leningrada:
   1941–44* (St. Petersburg: Izdatel'stvo Sankt-Peterburgskogo Universiteta, 2006).
Brodskii, Iosif Antol'evich, ed. *Khudozhniki goroda-fronta. Vospominaniia i dnevniki
   leningadskikh khudozhnikov.* Leningrad: Khudozhnik RSFSR, 1973.
Cherkrizov, Vasilii F. *Dnevnik blokadnogo vremeni.* St. Petersburg: Trudy gosudarstven-
   nogo muzeia istorii Sankt-Peterburga, 2004.
Chernorutskii, M. V., ed. *Alimentarnaia distrofiia v blokirovannom Leningrade.*
   Leningrad: Medgiz, 1947.

———. "Problema alimintarnoi distrofii." *Raboty leningradskikh vrachei za god Otechest-vennoi Voiny* 3 (1943): 3–13.

Dagin, E. G., ed. *Oborona Leningrada, 1941–1944: Vospominaniia i dnevniki uchastnikov.* Leningrad: Nauka, 1996.

Ehrenburg, Ilya. *Russia at War.* Translated by Gerard Shelley. London: Hamish Hamilton, 1943.

———. *Voina: 1941–1945.* Edited by V. Ia. Frezinski. Moscow: Astrel', 2004.

Ehrenburg, Ilya, and Konstantin Simonov. *In One Newspaper: A Chronicle of Unforget-table Years.* Translated by Anatol Kagan. New York: Sphinx, 1985.

El'iashova, Liudmila. *Moi blokadnnyi universitet.* St. Petersburg: Izmailovskii, 2005.

Ezerskii, S. *Vrachi Leningrada.* Leningrad: Leningradskoe gazetno-zhurnal'noe i knizhnoe izdatel'stvo, 1943.

Fadeev, Aleksandr. *Leningrad v dni blokady: Iz dnevnika.* Moscow: Sovetsii Pisatel', 1944.

Freidenberg, Ol'ga. "Osada cheloveka." *Minuvshee,* vol. 3. Paris: Athenaeum, 1987, 7–44.

Garshin, Vladimir. "Tam, gde smert pomogaet zhizni." *Arkhiv patalogii* 46, no. 5 (1984): 83–88.

Ginzburg, Lidiia. *Blockade Diary.* Translated by Alan Myers. London: Harvill, 1996.

———. *Prokhodiashchie kharaktery: Proza voennykh let, Zapiski blokadnogo cheloveka,* edited by Andrei Zorin and Emily Van Buskirk. Moscow: Novoe, 2011.

———. *Zapisnye knizhki. Vospominaniia. Esse,* edited by A. S. Kushner. St. Petersburg: Iskusstvo, 2002.

Glezerov, Sergei. *Ot nenavisti k primireniiu.* St. Petersburg: Ostrov, 2006.

Glebova, Tat'iana. "Risovat', kak letopisets: stranitsy blokadnogo dnevnika," *Iskusstvo Leningrada,* 1 (1990): 28–40.

———. "Risovat', kak letopisets: stranitsy blokadnogo dnevnika," *Iskusstvo Leningrada,* 2 (1990): 14–28.

Gorkhart, Sof'ia. "Leningrad. Blokada," in *Dve sud'by v velikoi otechestvennoi voine,* ed V. L. Vikhnovicha. St. Petersburg: Gumanitarnaia Akademiia, 2006.

Gorshkov, Nikolai Pavlovich. *Siloiu Sveta v polsvechi: Blokadnyi dnevnik, naidennyi cherez 50 let v sekretnykh arkhivakh KGB.* St. Petersburg: BEL', 1993.

Gradov, Petr. *Chelovek-cheloveku.* Edited by M. M. Zhigalova. Moscow: Pravda, 1989.

Grossman, Vasily. *Life and Fate.* 1959. Translated by Robert Chandler. New York: New York Review of Books, 1985.

Gubergrits, M. M. "Ob alimentarnoi toksicheskoi distrofii," *Vrachebnoe delo* 11–12 (1945), 548–54.

Heroic Leningrad: Documents, Sketches, and Stories of its Siege and Relief. Moscow: Foreign Languages Publishing House, 1945.

Il'f, Il'ia, and Evgenii Petrov. *Kak sozdavalsia Robinzon: Fel'etony i rasskazy.* Moscow: Tekst, 2007.

Inber, Vera. *Dusha Leningrada: Izbrannoe.* Leningrad: Lenizdat, 1979.

———. *Pochti tri goda.* Moscow: Sovetskaia Rossiia, 1968.

———. "Pochti tri goda (Leningradskii dnevnik)." *Znamia* 1 (1945): 65–181.

———. *Pochti tri goda: Leningradskii dnevnik.* Moscow: Sovetskii pisatel', 1947.

———. *Pulkovskii meridian.* Moscow: Ogiz, 1944.

Kalmykov, V. A. *Velikaia pobeda sovetskikh voisk pod Leningradom.* Leningrad: Voennoe izdatel'stvo, Narodnogo komissariata oborony, 1945.

Klebanov, Ia. I., and A. N. Pazi, ed. *Leningradtsy v dni blokady: Sbornik.* Leningrad: Leninzdat, 1947.

Kniazev, Georgii Alekseevich. *Dni velikikh ispytanii, dnevniki 1941–1945.* Edited by N. P. Kopaneva. St. Petersburg: Nauka, 2009.

Kochina, Elena. *Blockade Diary.* Translated and with an introduction by Samuel C. Ramer. Ann Arbor, MI: Ardis, 1990.

———. "Blokadnyi dnevnik." In *Pamiat': Istoricheskii sbornik,* vol. 4. Moscow and Paris: YMCA Press, 1979–81, 153–208.

Komlev, V. P. *Blokada: "Ia v polku pozharnom."* Leningrad: Lenizdat, 1983.

Kozlova, Natalia, ed. *Sovetskie liudi: Stseni iz istorii.* Moscow: Evropa, 2005.

Kriukov, Andrei. *Muzyka v efire voennogo Leningrada.* St. Petersburg: Kompozitor, 2005.

Kulagin, Georgii Andreevich. *Dnevnik i pamiat'.* Leningrad: Lenizdat, 1978.

Lebedev, Georgii Efremovich. "Iz dnevnik G. E. Lebedeva." In *Russkii Muzei-evakuatsiia, blokada, vosstanovlenie: Iz vospominanii muzeinogo rabotnika,* edited by P. K. Baltun. Moscow: Iskusstvo, 1981, 110–28.

Lenin, V. I. *The Emancipation of Women: From the Writings of V. I. Lenin.* New York: International Publishers, 1969.

———. *Essential Works of Lenin: "What Is to Be Done" and Other Writings.* Edited by Henry M. Christman. New York: Dover, 1987.

Levi, Primo. *Survival in Auschwitz.* 1947. Translated by Stuart Woolf. New York: Collier Books, 1986.

Levtov, V. E., and V. M. David, eds. *Budni podviga: Blokadnaia zhizn' leningradstev v dnevnikakh, risunkakh, dokumentakh, 8 sentiabria 1941–27 ianvaria 1944.* St. Petersburg: Informatsionno-izdatel'skoe agentstvo "LIK," 2007.

Mashanskii, F. I., ed. *Raboty leningradskikh vrachei za gody Otechestvennoi Voiny, I–VII.* Leningrad: Izdatel'stvo meditsinskoi literatury, 1943–45.

Maslova, A. N. , P. L. Vakhtina, and M. K. Svichenskaia, eds. *Publichnaia biblioteka v gody voiny: 1941–1945: dnevniki, vospominaniia, pis'ma, dokumenty.* St. Petersburg: Rossiiskaia natsional'naia biblioteka, 2005.

Matiushina, Ol'ga. *Pesn' o zhizni: Avtograficheskaia povest'.* Leningrad: Molodaia Gvardiia, 1946.

———. *Pesn' o zhizni: Povest'.* Leningrad: Lenizdat, 1970.

———. "Zapiski." *Zvezda* 2 (1943): 55–81.

Miasnikov, A. L. *Alimentarnaia distrofiia: Sbornik rabot.* Leningrad: Upravlenie voenno-morskogo izdatel'stvo, 1944.

———. *Klinika alimentarnoi distrofii.* Leningrad: Voenno-morskaia meditsinskaia akademiia, 1945.

Mukhina, Elena Vladimirovna. *Sokhrani moiu pechal'nuiu istoriiu . . . : Blokadnyi dnevnik Eleny Mukhanoi.* Edited by Koval'chuk, V. M., A. I. Rupasov, and A. N. Chistikov. St. Petersburg: Azbuka, 2011.

Nireberski, M. "Psychological Investigations of a Group of Internees at Belsen Camp." *Mental Science* 92 (1946): 60–74.

Ostrovskaia, S. K. "Blokadnye dnevniki." In *Russkoe Proshloe: Istoriko-dokumental'nyx al'manax,* vol. 10, 191–323. St. Petersburg, 2006.

Pavlov, Dmitri V. *Leningrad 1941.* Translated by John Clinton Adams. Chicago: University of Chicago Press, 1965.

Petrov, Vladimir. *Zapiski blokadnika.* Riazan: Poverennyi, 2003.

Polzikova-Rubets, Kseniia. *Dnevnik uchitelia blokadnoi shkoly, 1941–1946.* St. Petersburg: Tema, 2000.

———. *Oni uchilis' v Leningrade: Dnevnik uchitel'nitsy.* Leningrad: Gosudarstvennoe izdatel'stvo detskoi literatury, 1954.

Punin, Nikolai. "Blokadnyi dnevnik." *Zvezda* 1 (1994): 96–104.

———. *The Diaries of Nikolay Punin: 1904–1953.* Edited by Sidney Monas and Jennifer Greene Krupala. Translated by Jennifer Greene Krupala. Austin: University of Texas Press, 1999.

Riabinkin, Iura Ivanovich. In Ales' Adamovich and Daniil Granin, *Leningrad under Siege: First-hand Accounts of the Ordeal,* translated by Clare Burstall and Vladimir Kisselnikov. Barnsely, UK: Military Pen and Sword, 2007, 6–10, 39–42, 47–51, 73–80, 94–115, 128–53.

Saianov, Vissarion. *Leningradskii dnevnik.* Moscow: Voennoe izdatel'stvo ministerstva oboronu SSSR, 1963.

Sedel'nikova, Zinaida Sergeevna. *279 dnei voiny: Blokadnyi dnevnik.* Volgograd: Volgogradskii Komitet Popetchi, 1995.

Sevastopol': November 1941–July 1942: Articles, Stories, and Eye-Witness Accounts by Soviet War-Correspondents. New York: Hutchinson and Co., Ltd., 1943.

Shalamov, Varlam. *Kolymskie rasskazy,* vol. 2. Moscow: Russkaia kniga, 1992.

Shaumian, L. S., ed. *Leningrad: entsiklopedicheskii spravochnik.* Moscow: Gosudarstvennoe nauchnoe izdatel'stvo 'Bol'shaia sovetskaia entsiklopediia,' 1957.

Shnitser, I. S. "Alimentarnaia distrofiia." *Fel'dsher i akusherka* 3 (1943).

Shumilov, Nikolai. *V dni blokady.* Moscow: Mysl', 1974.

Sirota, F. I. *Leningrad: gorod-geroi.* Leningrad: Lenizdat, 1960.

Skomorovsky, Boris, and E. G. Morris. *The Siege of Leningrad.* New York: Dutton, 1944.

Skriabina, Elena. *V blokade: Dnevnik materi.* Iowa City: Herausgeber, 1964.

Sobolev, Leonid. *Morskaia dusha: Rasskazy.* Moscow: Gosudarstvennoe izdatel'stvo literatury, 1942.

Strashun, I. D., and V. L. Venderovich, eds. *Alimentarnaia distrofiia i avitaminozy.* Leningrad: Gosizdat Meditsinskoi Literatury, 1944.

Suborov, N. M. *Sireny zovut na posti: Stranitsy blokadnogo dnevnika.* Leningrad: Lenizdat, 1980.

Tarle, E. V. *Dve otechestvennye voiny.* Moscow and Leningrad: Voenmorizdat, 1941.

———. *How Mikhail Kutuzov Beat Napoleon.* London: Soviet War News, 1944.

———. *Krymskaia Voina.* Leningrad: Institut Istorii Akademii Nauk, 1941.

Tikhonov, Nikolai, ed. *Cherty sovetskogo cheloveka. Leningradskie rasskazy.* Moscow: Pravda, 1942.

———. *The Defence of Leningrad: Eye-witness Accounts of the Siege.* London: Hutchinson, 1943.

————. *Leningradskii god, mai 1942–1943.* Leningrad: Voennoe Izdatel'stvo NKO, 1943.

Tolstoi, Aleksei Nikolaevich. *Izbrannye sochineniia v shesti tomakh*, vol. 3. Moscow: Sovetskii Pisatel', 1951.

————. *The Making of Russia.* London: Hutchinson, 1945.

————. "Nesokrushimaia krepost'." 30 December 1942. In *Stat'i: 1942–1943.* Moscow: Gosudarstvennaia khudozhestvenaia literatura, 1944.

————. *Stat'i: 1942–1943.* Moscow: Gosudarstvennaia khudozhestvenaia literatura, 1944.

Vikhnovicha, V. L., ed. *Dve sud'by v Velikoi Otechestvennoi Voine.* St. Petersburg: Gumanitarnaia Akademiia, 2006.

Vishnevskii, Vsevolod. *Leningrad: dnevniki voennykh let*, vol. 2. Moscow: Voenizdat, 2002.

Vvedenskii, B. A., ed. *Bol'shaia sovetskaia entsiklopediia*, vol. 14. Moscow: Gosudarstvennoe nauchnoe izdatel'stvo 'Bol'shaia sovetskaia entsiklopediia,' 1952.

Werth, Alexander. *Leningrad.* New York: Knopf, 1944.

Wiesel, Eliezer. *Night.* Translated by Stella Rodway. New York: Bantham Books, 1986.

Zimmer, René, Joseph Weill, and Maurice Dobbs. "The Nutritional Situation in the Camps of the Unoccupied Zone of France in 1941 and 1942 and Its Consequences." *New England Journal of Medicine* 230, no. 11 (1944): 303–14.

DOCUMENT COLLECTIONS

Arkharova, Vera, ed. *Pamiat': Pis'ma o voine i blockade.* Lenizdat, 1985.

Avvakumov, S. I., ed. *Bol'sheviki-organizatory oborony Leningrada.* Leningrad: Lenizdat, 1943.

————, ed. *Geroicheskii Leningrad, 1917–1942.* Leningrad: Gospolitizdat, 1943.

————, ed. *Leningrad v Velikoi Otechestvennoi Voine Sovetskogo Soiuza: Sbornik dokumentov i materialov.* Vol. 1. Leningrad: Ogiz-Gospolitizdat, 1944.

Babichenko, D. L., ed. *Literaturnyi front: Istoriiia politicheskoi tsenzury, 1932–1946; Sbornik dokumentov.* Moscow: Entsiklopediia Rossiiskikh dereven', 1994.

Blium, Arlen. *Kak eto delalos' v Leningrade: Tsenzura v gody ottepeli, zastoia i perestroika 1953–1991.* St. Petersburg: Akademicheskii proekt, 2005.

————, ed. *Tsenzura v Sovetskom Soiuze 1917–1991: Dokumenty.* Moscow: Rosspen, 2004.

Dzeniskevich, Andrei, ed. *Leningrad v osade: Sbornik dokumentov o geroicheskoi oborone Leningrada v gody Velikoi Otechestvennoi Voiny, 1941–1944.* St. Petersburg: Liki Rossii, 1995.

Golubeva, T. M., ed. *Deti i blokada: Vospominaniia, fragment dnevnikov, svidetel'stva ochevidtsev, dokumental'nye materialy.* St. Petersburg: IPK Vesti, 2000.

Grin, Ts. I. *V pamiat' ushedshikh i vo slavu zhivushchikh: dnevniki, vospominaniia, pis'ma.* St. Petersburg: Rossiiskaia natsional'naia biblioteka, 1995.

Lebedeva, N. B., G. I. Lisovskaia, N. Iu. Cherepenina, eds. *Ot voiny k miru, Leningrad 1944–1945: Sbornik dokumentov.* St. Petersburg: Liki Rossii, 2013.

Loskutovoi, M. V., ed. *Pamiat' o blokade: Svidetel'stva ochevidtsev i istoricheskoe soznanie obshchestva.* Moscow: Novoe, 2006.

Sharikov, K. G., ed. *Leningrad v Velikoi Otechestvennoi Voine Sovetskogo Soiuza: Sbornik dokumentov i materialov.* Vol. 2. Leningrad: Lenizdat, 1947.

Siegelbaum, Lewis, and Andrei Sokolov. *Stalinism as a Way of Life: A Narrative in Documents.* New Haven, CT: Yale University Press, 2000.

Simmons, Cynthia, and Nina Perlina. *Writing the Siege of Leningrad: Women's Diaries, Memoirs, and Documentary Prose.* Pittsburgh: University of Pittsburgh Press, 2002.

Tokarev, Iu. S. *Deviatsot geroicheskikh dnei: sbornik dokumentov i materialov o geroicheskoi bor'be trudiashchikhsia leningrada v 1941–1944 gg.* Leningrad: Nauka, 1966.

V dni blokady. Leningrad: Khudozhnik RSFSR, 1966.

Volkova, A. F., ed. *Zhenshchiny goroda Lenina: Rasskazy i ocherki o zhenshchinakh Leningrada v dni blokady.* Leningrad: Lenizdat, 1944.

Acknowledgments

In the course of writing this book, I was blessed to have incomparable teachers, colleagues, and friends. I am deeply indebted to my academic advisers at the University of California, Berkeley. Irina Paperno inspired me to study diaries and tirelessly shared her tremendous insight and invaluable feedback. Yuri Slezkine brought a combination of rigorous critique and warmth to every intellectual exchange. From them, I learned countless lessons about teaching and research and about remaining humble and hungry in both undertakings.

I am grateful for many other teachers who discussed this project with me and inspired me through their scholarship: Susanna Barrows, Polina Barskova, Richard Bidlack, Susan Burch, Aleksandr Chistikov, John Connelly, Don Filtzer, Victoria Frede, Wendy Goldman, Rivi Handler-Spitz, Jeffrey Hass, Sergei Iarov, Penny Ismay, Lisa Kirschenbaum, Nikita Lomagin, Rebecca Manley, Ethan Pollock, Hank Reichman, Il'ia Utekhin, Alexandra Vasil'eva, Tatiana Voronina, Ned Walker, Aleksei Yurchak, and Milia Zakirova. My sincere thanks to the working group members who slogged through my rough drafts: Catherine Ashcraft, Nicole Eaton, Christine Evans, Elisa Gollub, Jamie McCallum, Brandon Schechter, Erik Scott, and Max Ward.

This project would have been impossible without the assistance of scholars and friends in the Russian Federation. I owe an immeasurable debt to those who shared their personal papers with me: Igor' and Denis Liubovskii, Natal'ia and

327

Ol'ga Afanas'eva, Aleksei Kriukov and the Kriukov family, Evgeniia Molcha-nova, Timofei Stakhovskii at D. D. Shostakovich School 235, and Tat'iana Mu-sina. I will never forget how Tamara Staleva took me under her wing and shared her insights, documents, and contacts. My warmest thanks to these superb scholars and archivists: Natal'ia Rogova and Mariia Svichenskaia at OR RNB, Zoia Korganova, Ol'ga Prutt, and the incredible staff at MNM, Natal'ia Bykova at TsGAIPD, and Sergei Kurnosov and Natal'ia Semicheva at GMMOBL.

I greatly appreciate Laura Auketayeva, Aglaya Glebova, Lydia Petrovic, Ana-toly Pinsky, and Anna Sukhorukova, who provided outstanding assistance. A special thanks to Prof. Alexandra Baker, who painstakingly reviewed my trans-lations, to Drs. John Swartzberg and Andrea Garber, who shared their exper-tise on hunger and disease, and to Gregory T. Woolston, who did a beautiful job with the maps.

This project was generously funded by Fulbright-IIE; Phi Beta Kappa; the Mabelle McLeod Lewis Memorial Fund; the Abigail Reynolds Hodgen Publi-cation Fund; the University of California, Berkeley (History Department, Graduate Division, Institute of East European and Eurasian Studies, and Berkeley Program in East European and Eurasian Studies); Middlebury Col-lege; and Boston University.

Indiana University Press and *The Soviet and Post-Soviet Review* provided ideal settings for me to develop themes discussed here. Portions of Chapter 5 are reprinted by permission from "Queues, Canteens, and the Politics of Loca-tion in Diaries of the Leningrad Blockade, 1941–42," Donald Filtzer and Wendy Z. Goldman, ed., *Hunger and War: Food Provisioning in the Soviet Union during World War II* (Bloomington: Indiana University Press, 2015), Copyright © 2015 by Indiana University Press. Chapter 7 expands on arguments originally set forth in "Revisiting the Past: History and Historical Memory during the Leningrad Blockade," *The Soviet and Post-Soviet Review* 38, no. 2 (Fall, 2011), 105–29.

Most of all, I am grateful to my family. I could not have completed this project without my parents, who gave me so many opportunities, including the freedom to study whatever I wanted, and who instilled in me a love of reading. Bobby and Amiee Peri unfailingly helped me keep perspective and a sense of humor. No one guided me through the completion of this more than Hanns Hartman. His steadfast encouragement and reassurance kept me striving and smiling. Thank you for lending me your strength and for being the love of my life.

Illustration Credits

Illustrations follow page 126

Dima Afanas'ev. Courtesy of Natal'ia and Ol'ga Afanas'eva.

"Gatchina burns." Courtesy of Natal'ia and Ol'ga Afanas'eva.

"Adolf Hitler." Courtesy of Natal'ia and Ol'ga Afanas'eva.

Aleksandra Liubovskaia. Courtesy of Igor' Liubovskii.

Kseniia Matus. Courtesy of D. D. Shostakovich Middle School 235, St. Petersburg (k.p. 3399, f. 2, d. 1707).

"Manuscripts Department." Courtesy of D. D. Shostakovich Middle School 235, St. Petersburg (k.p. 6513, f. 3, d. 23).

"Destroy the German Monster!" Courtesy of BPK Berlin/German-Russian Museum Berlin-Karlshorst/Art Resource, New York.

Leningraders gathering water. Courtesy of BPK Berlin/German-Russian Museum Berlin-Karlshorst/Art Resource, New York.

A sled carrying a corpse. Courtesy of Russian State Documentary Film and Photo Archive (RGAKFD), Krasnogorsk, Russia. Serial number: C 0-4640. File number: 4640.

Leningrad in winter 1942. Courtesy of D. D. Shostakovich Middle School 235, St. Petersburg (k.p. 5122, f. 1, d. 5088).

Elena Mukhina. Courtesy of Tat'iana Sergeevna Musina.

A healthy man and a *distrofik*. Courtesy of BPK Berlin/German-Russian Museum Berlin-Karlshorst/Art Resource, New York.

First page of the diary of Nina Mervol'f. Courtesy of D. D. Shostakovich Middle School 235, St. Petersburg (k.p. 6580, f. 2, d. 5579).

Pages from the diary of Nina Mervol'f, January 1942. Courtesy of D. D. Shostakovich Middle School 235, St. Petersburg (k.p. 6580, f. 2, d. 5579).

Leningraders queue for bread. Courtesy of Russian State Documentary Film and Photo Archive (RGAKFD), Krasnogorsk, Russia. Serial number: 0-366881. File number: 366881.

Leningrad clinic. Courtesy of BPK Berlin/German-Russian Museum Berlin-Karlshorst/Art Resource, New York.

Page from Chernorutskii and Garshin's *Nutritional Dystrophy in Blockaded Leningrad (Alimentarnaia distrofiia v blokirovannom Leningrade)* (Leningrad: Medgiz, 1947).

"Prophetic Prediction: Napoleon and Others—our past, our future," by V. Gal'ba. *Leningradskaia Pravda,* 28 September 1941, 4.

Truck gathers corpses. Courtesy of BPK Berlin/German-Russian Museum Berlin-Karlshorst/Art Resource, New York.

"Broken Ring." Courtesy of Aleksandr Shchepin/Fotobank Lori.

Index

Adamovich, Ales', 3, 9, 62–63, 104, 191

Afanas'ev, Dmitrii (Dima): analysis of press, 32–33; historical reflections of, 203, 219; on hunger psychosis, 195; responsibilities of, 3, 24, 95, 136; social observations by, 129

Aging. *See* Body

Akhmatova, Anna, 58, 225

Alimentarnaia distrofiia. See Dystrophy, nutritional

American-Soviet Medical Society, 177

Assumptive world, 7–10, 237, 257–258n21

Avvakumov, S. I., 241–242, 250

Bania. *See* Bathhouse

Barber, John, 4, 277–278n12, 285n47, 291nn9–10

Barskova, Polina, 159, 289n127, 297n118

Bathhouse: revealing equality, 155–157; revealing inequality, 157–159; Russian tradition of, 155; wartime conditions of, 155–156

Battle for Leningrad: bombing of city, 5–6, 25–29, 47, 53, 93–94, 143, 192; break in siege, 240–243; casualties of, 4, 25; civilian defense in, 5, 23–24, 42, 227; lifting of siege, 244–245

Bekhterev State Psycho-Neurological Institute, 192, 194

Berggol'ts, Ol'ga, 12, 92, 157–158, 186, 248

Beriia, Lavrentii, 107, 249

Berngardt, Nikolai, 156

Bidlack, Richard, 24, 107, 143, 172, 285n47

Biopower, 164, 290n8

Blockade wife, 131, 145–147, 157–158

Blokadnik (blokadniki): identification as, 74, 158; traits of, 2, 39, 41, 56, 65–68

Body: hands, 59; legs, 59–60, 64; premature aging of, 37, 45–47, 155, 184, 243; stomach, 60–63, 237; transformation of, 37, 39–41, 45, 66. *See also* Sense perception

Boldyrev, Aleksandr, 187

Bolshevik Revolution. *See* October Revolution

Bombardment. *See* Battle for Leningrad

Bomb psychosis. *See* Psychosis

Books: banning of, 250; reading tastes, 178, 203–204, 215, 220, 224; supply of, 216, 303n60; wartime publication of, 203, 216, 220, 229, 306n123

Borovikova, Aleksandra, 15, 30, 37–38

Borrero, Mauricio, 134

Brandenberger, David, 214, 216, 310n57

Brezhnev, Leonid, 252

Bubnova, Maia, 24, 27, 223, 247

Buianov, Aleksandr, 3, 33–34, 38, 230

Burton, Christopher, 165, 172, 174

Byl'ev, Nikolai (Protopopov), 46, 158–159, 188

Cafeterias: decorum in, 140–141, 153–154; for elites, 152–154; observation in, 140–141; strife in, 150–151, 225

Cafeteria wife. *See* Blockade wife

331